MUSLIM AMERICAN
RENAISSANCE PROJECT

MUSLIM AMERICAN
RENAISSANCE PROJECT

Answering The Call Of God And
The Country And Inspiring Change

Dr. Souheil Ghannouchi

To order additional copies of this book, contact:
Xlibris Corporation
1-888-795-4274
www.Xlibris.com
Orders@Xlibris.com
109161

TO GOD, TO WHOM I OWE EVERYTHING AND
AM GRATEFUL FOR EVERYTHING;

To the souls of my parents who made me the person I am;

To my family whose support was vital;

To the core group who believed in the vision and worked tirelessly
to turn that vision into reality and get the book published;

And to everyone who taught me something.

Acknowledgments

I am very grateful to God for enabling me to write this book.

I owe a great debt of gratitude to my wife Ibtissem and my children Ousswa, Zulfa, and Ahilla for their encouragement and sacrifices.

A special note of thanks to the core group of founders of the movement for their support and input.

I thank the reviewers for their insightful and helpful feedback.

I also thank the wonderful copy editors Amina Cisse Muhammad and Claiborne Clark whose enthusiasm and hard work have substantially upgraded the original manuscripts.

TABLE OF CONTENTS

PART I:

INTRODUCTION—OUR NATION, OUR COMMUNITY, AND OUR MOVEMENT PROJECT

Most Americans would agree that our society is in urgent need of fundamental change. Indeed, it was President Obama's advocacy for change that helped him win the 2008 presidential election. Nonetheless, America is still off track and is nowhere close to where it should be or could be. Americans are longing for real change that gives them more control over their own lives and more optimism about their future. The country needs change that will enable America to overcome its multifaceted crisis and maintain its global leadership in this increasingly complex and competitive world.

We may disagree about what changes are needed and why, and about the scope, the depth, and the pace of change. There is, however, a general agreement that neither more of the same nor a patchwork reform will meet the long and growing list of challenges facing our country and the American people.

In this context, we are launching a movement for societal reform. Our platform entails a specific vision for America yet calls on all American citizens and on the communities of all religious and political orientations to become more civically aware and engaged, to keep the country's well-being and the citizens' welfare at heart, and to constantly challenge themselves to contribute more to the greater good. This movement calls for civic interest and compassion from Americans of all religious and political orientations, including not only those who agree with our platform but also those who disagree with us. That's because the key to the change that we need and seek in our society is the awareness and engagement of as many citizens and communities, including Muslims, as possible.

This movement will echo President Kennedy's plea to our nation a half century ago: "My fellow Americans, ask not what your country can do for you. Ask what you can do for your country." It will advocate the rallying of all American people to stand behind our long-held dream of a just, fair, and prosperous America for all. Finally, the movement will challenge us all to work hard at protecting the democracy that America has come to represent and at preserving the institutions that sustain that democracy.

A REVIVAL/RENEWAL, RENAISSANCE, AND REFORM MOVEMENT

This project is an Islam-inspired societal reform movement that was developed in response to the call of God and the call of country. It is designed to seek God's pleasure (our ultimate goal) by striving to fulfill His purpose (our mission), which is essentially to uplift ourselves, our people, our country, and our world. These connections are at the heart of this project. Muslim scholars, past and present, concur that "Islam came to ensure the well-being of all people, in this life and in the hereafter." Therefore, the divine guidance encompasses everything that serves the common good.

God calls upon each and every human being (and, particularly, the followers of Muhammad) to enjoin (strongly and firmly advocate) good and forbid evil. This is a direct injunction to work toward the betterment of our societies—regardless of whether we live in a predominantly Muslim society or not. In order to obey God and gain His pleasure (the ultimate goal of all God-fearing people), we must be engaged in societal efforts to uplift ourselves and those around us. This is the fundamental essence of societal reform.

Somehow, however, many Muslims in America have evidently assumed that it is not necessary for them to be actively involved in their various communities, much less in society at large.

Our movement and our vision are inspired by Islam and bound by the essentials of Islam. However, even though this whole idea is Islam inspired and is therefore actually divine in its source of inspiration and its ultimate goal, this project is civic in nature, objectives, and methods. Therefore, it is directed toward the involvement and benefit of all citizens. Our movement will not only address the interests of the general public but also will be open to participation by all citizens, whether they buy into our platform fully as members or partially as advocates or partners.

America is a ship that carries many different kinds of citizens. To ensure a safe journey, we must all do our best to take good care of the ship. We must all keep a lookout for rocks and shoals and lighthouses. While ours is a large and stable ship, we must be vigilant to ensure that no one rocks the boat too severely. Capsizing would be disastrous for everyone. As citizens, we could also compare ourselves to members of a sports team. It is shortsighted and futile for individual players to focus on their own success at the expense of that of the team. We need to work together.

Muslim Americans, of course, constitute a small percentage of the overall U.S. population.[1] However, in order for any reform movement to be successful, it must draw not only the interest of nearly everyone but also the support and actual involvement of as many people as possible. Therefore, even though we refer to our movement as Islam inspired, it cannot and will not be focused on, or limited to, the Muslim American community. Most Muslim American projects, in contrast to this project, are conducted by Muslims and for Muslims. Indeed, this is not a "Muslim community project" per se; rather, this is a societal project that passionately advocates societal reform through direct involvement and engagement in society. And it is to be implemented at two tiers. On one hand, we are advocating and rallying people behind a specific vision and platform, which we shall use to engage different components of society. On the other hand, we are appealing to all fellow citizens—irrespective of their views—to be more civically aware, concerned, and engaged because that will strengthen our society and our democracy and therefore help to fulfill the purpose of the project.

One might ask, "If this movement is not confined to the Muslim American community, why the great emphasis on Islam and Muslims in this book?" The answer is simply that because this movement project is Islam inspired, it would be only natural to expect Muslims to be at the forefront of it. Indeed, while the focus is on societal reform, we seriously hope to see Muslim Americans play the biggest possible role in ensuring the best possible future for America. In fact, this is the thrust of the project: We advocate and seek the best possible conditions for America and the biggest possible contribution by

---

1   Gallup Institute. (2009). *Muslim Americans: A National Portrait: An in-depth analysis of America's most diverse religious community* [Report].

Muslim Americans.[2] The best possible conditions for America would entail an overall reform to create a more cohesive and morally sound society, a more robust economy, and improved educational and healthcare systems. It would mean an America that stands for greater social and economic justice at home and abroad. This project advocates the biggest possible contribution from Muslim Americans because the successful implementation of the project will be accelerated and ensured by a successful renaissance of our Muslim American community. And while our platform is civic in nature and is addressed to all citizens and communities, our initial focus on Muslim American individuals and communities stems from the fact that this is our base. We enjoy relatively easy access to our fellow Muslim Americans, and we believe Muslim Americans will be among the first to understand the benefits of this project to American Muslims, to our country, and to the world. After all, this civic platform is inspired by Islam, and it is a translation of the mission and the teachings of Islam.

Also, we firmly believe that it is high time for Muslim Americans (both individually and institutionally) to become conscientious and assertive members of our society—rather than a silent, victimized minority. Therefore, we encourage Muslim Americans to open up to their environments and to personally engage directly in societal reform through the system as faithful citizens. They are also invited to try to pull various segments and organizations of the Muslim community and the community at large in this direction. Nothing would earn God's pleasure more than Muslim Americans being at the helm of needed change in our country.

So our project is to be executed not only at two levels but also through parallel tracks: reform of the society and renaissance of the Muslim American community.

Like American society at large, the Muslim American community is experiencing a huge crisis; and before our community can fulfill its mission and effect a significant societal reform, we must confront this current crisis. In our attempt to address our community's challenges, it was essential for us to first conduct an in-depth historical analysis and an honest assessment[3] of our community's current state; both of which are missing in the very limited literature

---

2   All Muslim Americans—irrespective of their race, ethnicity, gender, age, level of education, level of commitment, and/or any other classification.

3   This analysis and assessment are presented in part 3.

currently available on Muslim Americans. This analysis and diagnosis, along with a proposal outlining our vision for the future, constitute the bulk of this book.

Upon completing our analysis, we have concluded that our crisis is a direct result of our community's abandonment of its defining mission in life.[4] This shortcoming is, in turn, largely due to our improper and inadequate understanding and implementation of Islam, as well as the serious deficiency in our commitment to it.

Therefore, while the project is about societal reform and community renaissance, we believe that those aspects cannot be effectively implemented unless we begin a process of rediscovery, revival, and renewal of Islam among Muslim Americans. That effort should result in a fresh, authentic, and indigenous Islamic construct that is relevant and inspiring. That's how Islam may reassert its timeless applicability and its capacity to inspire reform and change things for the better—both in our community and in our country.

So this project aims to make a significant and sustained contribution to three main goals: revival/renewal of Islam, renaissance of the Muslim American community, and reform of the American society. Primarily, it is a revival/renewal of Islam that should engender a societal reform movement, which will operate directly in society, and will—in parallel—stimulate the renaissance of our community, converting us into a mission-driven and country-focused community. That's how we may fuse the Islamic and American components of our identity and the religious and civic components of our mission. This is the surest way, if not the only way, we may transform and rebuild our community into a genuine and relevant American Islamic movement that fulfills the divine mission and effects a significant and sustained positive change.

To effect such a transformation, concern about the state of our country must inevitably become the focus of our conversation and our operations. Our exclusive concern for what benefits us individually and concern about our needs as a religious community must be eclipsed, somewhat, by concern for the greater public good. We must learn to measure and evaluate our efforts based upon their impact on this country, as well as their contribution to the advancement of our cause and the fulfillment of our mission.

This new perspective represents a major departure from our current position as an inwardly focused, socially isolated, and civically disengaged community. This shift can only occur following the engagement of our

---

4   In brief, our defining mission is to "enjoin good and forbid evil" and work toward the betterment of our society. This collective human mission will be discussed in detail in part 2.

community's leaders, organizations, and members in the affairs of our nation at all levels, local, state, and federal. Focusing exclusively on things that directly affect us as Muslims will no longer cut it. This is a real paradigm shift that can only be inspired by a new and proper understanding of Islam. We must embrace Islam as a mission of reform that is centered on serving the greater good and energized by a genuine concern for the well-being of the entire country. Thus, our religious and civic motivations are fused together as one.

Indeed, this revival/renewal, renaissance, and reform project is built on the commitment to Islam as a life mission (of reform) and to America as a homeland. Such commitment will emerge as a natural outcome of the revival/renewal process, which will restore Islam's compelling sense of mission and great sense of compassion, as well as its strong humane and civic dimensions.

Having thus introduced the project's main pillars, the remainder of this chapter will briefly discuss the state of the nation, the state of the Muslim American community, and the predominant Islamic constructs in our community. This discussion will highlight the urgent need for fundamental change in all three areas on which this project will focus. These, again, are revival/renewal of Islam, renaissance of the Muslim American community, and the improvement of American society.

CURRENT STATE OF OUR NATION

Every societal reform project must be based on a clear understanding of society and a solid commitment to societal well-being. One of the primary factors hindering the progress of our Muslim American community has been its lack of understanding of the social composition and historical background of America. As a group, we have also lacked a genuine commitment to the betterment of America as our homeland. There is a lot of confusion (religious, political, psychological) and ambivalence about American society, history, and politics. This book will, hopefully, shed some light on these matters and tackle the underlying causes of those obstacles.

The vast majority of Americans agree that our society urgently needs fundamental change. Many became convinced after witnessing the quagmires of Iraq and Afghanistan. Most remaining doubts about the need for change were removed from the public mind by the 2008 financial meltdown caused by a murky financial system and irresponsible behavior. By the end of the first decade in the twenty-first century, most Americans understood the need for fundamental societal reform.

Broken politics, failed policies, and a string of political and financial blunders produced disastrous results, both at home and abroad.[5] For many Americans, the result has been shattered dreams. There is no shortage of alarming indications that the country is off track. The two catastrophic wars and the acute financial crisis exacerbated our country's chronic problems (healthcare, housing, education, deficit). This has meant society-wide (even global) economic havoc, and it has caused unbearable circumstances for an increasing number of Americans. More and more Americans are struggling to make ends meet, even as they work harder and longer than ever before. More and more of us are facing a declining standard of living. Millions have lost their jobs or businesses, their life's savings and investments, their retirement funds.

Compared to many other developed countries, America has lagged behind when it comes to education, healthcare, and even infrastructure. Washington seems to have plenty of anxiety, but few answers. Education needs improvement, according to recent data from the Programme for International Student Assessment (PISA).[6] The data seems to show that, compared with other countries, U.S. student literacy in reading, math, and science is, in a word, mediocre. Healthcare is in trouble too. While well-funded lobbyists push and pull at Congress over healthcare, the baby-boomers are aging, insurance premiums are rising, services are ebbing, and statisticians are wondering where it will end. A 2011 study[7] by the Urban Land Institute says the U.S. needs to invest $2 trillion to restore or rebuild roads, bridges, water treatment facilities, water lines, sewage systems, levees, and dams that are reaching the end of their designed life expectancy. Meanwhile, with a shrinking economy, we have a growing population. Moreover, we can't turn to the production and manufacturing sector or to exports for economic

---

5   Jeffery D. Sachs. (2011). *The Price of Civilization: Reawakening American Virtue and Prosperity* [Book]. Chapter One: Diagnosing America's Economic Crisis. Page 3–11. Jeffery D. Sachs states: "At the root of America's economic crisis lies a moral crisis: the decline of civic virtue among America's political and economic elite. A society of markets, laws, and elections is not enough if the rich and powerful fail to behave with respect, honesty, and compassion toward the rest of society and toward the world."

6   Brown Center. (2010). *The 2010 Brown Center Report on American Education* [Report].

7   *The Washington Post.* (2011). "Study: $2 trillion needed for U.S. infrastructure." [Article]

relief, because to a greater extent than many other developed countries, the U.S. has seen these sectors diminish as financial speculation and the service sector have become dominant. Finally, as the world has become increasingly competitive, America's image and leverage have rapidly deteriorated. And our problems can no longer be exported abroad or deferred to the future.

A number of factors have combined to create a vicious cycle that has alienated most Americans who have no meaningful participation in the political process, and this has weakened our democracy. These factors include the corruptive role of money in politics and the undue influence of special interest groups and lobbyists.[8] These weaknesses in our political system have resulted in the ever-increasing concentration of wealth and power in the hands of the already privileged few. Thus, the political process has come to resemble a form of legalized bribery (one dollar equals one vote). The repeated personal and financial scandals involving public officials have not helped matters. Moreover, the tacit disregard/removal of some fundamental issues from the political debate, the fading differences between Democrats and Republicans, and the shallowness and shortsightedness of both parties are all among the issues that have discouraged meaningful political participation. Our democracy has been downgraded by the largely commercial, costly, and primarily ceremonial election campaigns. The political process has also been plagued with cynicism and partisan politics, both during and in between elections.[9]

In such circumstances, healthy social life and civic participation have seemingly become luxuries that are beyond the reach of most people who

8   Jeffery D. Sachs. (2011). *The Price of Civilization: Reawakening American Virtue and Prosperity* [Book]. Page 47. In Chapter 4, "Washington's Retreat from Public Purpose," Jeffery D. Sachs asks, "How did we get into the dreadful situation in which the federal government is in the lap of the corporate lobby? Why has the federal government stopped providing the public goods that Americans need to remain globally competitive in a fair and sustainable society?" –– Page 11. In Chapter 2, "Prosperity Lost," Sachs states, "There can be no doubt that something has gone terribly wrong in the U.S. economy, politics, and society in general . . . Americans are deeply estranged from Washington. A large majority, 71 percent to 15 percent, describes the federal government as 'a special interest group that looks out primarily for its own interests,' a startling commentary on the miserable state of American democracy."

9   President Bill Clinton. (2011). *Back to Work* [Book]. Page 11: President Clinton states, "I believe the challenges we face, which are tough enough on their own, are made even more difficult by the highly polarized, deeply ideological political climate in Washington."

are constrained by time and resources. The family itself has been cracking under the economic pressure combined with the assaults of some social ills. Many Americans don't have much real incentive, or access or opportunity for meaningful political participation. As a result, many, many Americans have basically lost faith in both politics and politicians and also in the utility of civic engagement.

WHERE DID WE GO ASTRAY?

There are many intertwined factors and chain reactions that have brought us to this sad point. Ironically, however, the thing that now poses the greatest threat to the survival of America as we know it is the abuse of some of the very elements that have made America great. Indeed, America could not have become the envy of the world without individualism, self-reliance, capitalism, and limited government. These ingredients acted to spark the creativity that led to the healthy competition of American citizens, communities, and corporations; and it is that competition that is responsible for the prosperity that America has enjoyed in its short history.

Today, America's factors of success have been so abused that they are beginning to backfire and turn into mechanisms for failure. Individualism has become selfishness, self-centeredness, and social disintegration. Excessive deregulation and government "hands off" policies have allowed greed and recklessness to permeate our financial and business institutions.

The once-healthy motivation to make a profit has become an obsession to maximize profit by any means, at any cost. This has created a constant need to produce more goods and increase the public's desire to consume them. It has also resulted in alarming levels of environmental pollution and contamination of the food chain, which, respectively, have disrupted the climate and exacerbated the nation's health problems.

A culture of consumption has become the driving force of our economy, replacing the long-held values of frugality and thriftiness. This has increased economic pressure on most families. This vicious cycle is directly responsible for our nation's out-of-control public and private deficit and debt. Ben Franklin's picture is still on the $100 bill, if you haven't seen one lately. However, we have twisted one of his quotations to the point that, today, "a penny saved" is already owed on our credit card!

We now see a shallow and cynical political process, which is largely inaccessible to the masses, combining with a shaky financial system (runaway deficit, widening wealth gap, and unprecedented corporate greed), to create a system that is unsustainable. Moreover, excessive materialism and individualism are threatening personal and family wellness and social cohesion. Unless these processes are reversed, the ongoing vicious cycle will continue to hurt America's well-being and standing in the world, weaken our democracy, and compromise our society's future. Americans had clearly decided, when they took to heart and endorsed President Obama's campaign promises for change, that they were not willing to tolerate more irresponsible behavior and that a mere patchwork of reform could not sufficiently restore our nation's economy and health.

The above description of the current state of our nation is definitely not the picture that America's founding fathers envisioned less than 250 years ago. However, our drift toward where we presently stand did start a long time ago—despite the warning of some of our nation's greatest leaders, such as George Washington and Dwight Eisenhower in their respective farewell addresses.[10]

One of the causes for our deviation is the fact that the vast majority of our leaders (particularly in recent times) have lacked the wisdom and courage to confront the brutal facts, tell the truth about where we stand, and tackle our problems at their roots. Rather, they have been obsessed with attaining short-term political gains and opting for patchwork solutions. They isolate themselves while attempting to appear accessible, and they employ deceptive discourse when they are forced to address the public. With the people disconnected from the decision-making process and misinformed by their leaders via the media, the powers-that-be are free to cater to special interest groups in exchange for votes and campaign funds. It has been said that we have the best government money can buy. Many of our government officials

---

10 "In the councils of government, we must guard against the acquisition of unwarranted influence, whether sought or unsought, by the military-industrial complex. The potential for the disastrous rise of misplaced power exists and will persist . . . Another factor in maintaining balance involves the element of time. As we peer into society's future, we—you and I, and our government—must avoid the impulse to live only for today, plundering for, for our own ease and convenience, the precious resources of tomorrow. We cannot mortgage the material assets of our grandchildren without asking the loss also of their political and spiritual heritage. We want democracy to survive for all generations to come, not to become the insolvent phantom of tomorrow." President Dwight D. Eisenhower, Farewell Address to the Nation, January 17, 1961.

have become rather daring—doing as they see fit *and* with considerable impunity, even as people maintain the right to protest. Didn't Vice President Dick Cheney say "So?" when he was told about the opposition of the majority of Americans to the war on Iraq![11]

The very same money that corrupted our political system had already turned our media into corporate-run commercial entities. Over the years, more of our major media outlets have come under the ownership of fewer corporations. In many cases, the corporations that own the networks are tied to special interests. Pun intended or not, the fox is in the chicken house! This explains the sparse coverage of campaign political debates, the shallow nature of the media-organized debates, and the dismissal of fundamental matters from both debates and news coverage—either because the topics are too controversial or because there is consensus between the two parties. The assumed role of the media has been to keep public attention away from certain issues whenever possible and to sell the public on a particular position whenever needed. This is particularly true when it comes to major foreign policies, such as the decision to go to war. Indeed, the media's very limited and contrived role over the last couple of decades has reinforced the public's alienation and its ignorance about America's politics.

We did not reach this point of acute crisis suddenly or mysteriously. Rather, our situation has been compounded over time because of what we have done and what we have failed to do. As might be expected, problems that were not tackled adequately have weakened our society, our democracy, and our economy.

REFORM IS STILL POSSIBLE, BUT WHAT WILL IT TAKE?

The good news is that in such a dynamic society, the systems, the norms, and the policies are amenable to reform by committed and well-organized people (no matter how limited they may be in numbers and resources). Indeed, in spite of some serious recent regression and straying, America continues to be unique and great—largely because of its Constitution and its founding values, such as those in the Declaration of Independence, which guarantee fundamental rights and liberties for all citizens. In our country, to

---

11   Vice President Dick Cheney, responding to an ABC News correspondent who cited a poll showing that most Americans do not believe the Iraq War was worth fighting, March 19, 2008.

a degree, a level playing field and fair rules for civic engagement are enshrined in the legal code. America's deeply entrenched pluralism uniquely affords all citizens the opportunity to realize their dreams and provides communities the opportunity to organize and make a difference.

The Obama phenomenon quite obviously generated hope and excitement, inspiring scores of inactive people to become civically engaged. From the outset of his campaign, he and his administration did take steps that reflected a genuine and serious desire to effect change. However, his wavering on some issues has certainly raised doubts about his ability (and possibly willingness) to effect the needed change and transform his exceptional and popular presidential campaign into a sustained movement for change.

To be fair, President Obama was busy cleaning up the huge mess he inherited. Plus, his failed pursuit of bipartisanship through compromise disheartened his base and derailed his agenda. As a result, an increasing number of people were forced to lower their expectations regarding the pace, the scope, and the depth of the change that President Obama could possibly effect—even if he succeeded in winning a second term. Make no mistake, the American people still wanted change and still felt frustrated, as evidenced by the "Occupy Wall Street" movement in the latter part of 2011. The one thing the political polls were showing with the greatest reliability was widespread frustration with politicians in general and with the government and the economy.[12]

Given the fact that the crisis we face is large and complicated and took several decades to develop, it may not be realistic to expect that one president—no matter how articulate and popular he is—can significantly tackle our problems at their roots and effect fundamental change. The opportunity for dramatic one-term change is also delimited by the convoluted dynamics of our political system. For many years, our presidents and their administrations have chosen to largely maintain the status quo, patching the symptoms of our problems. And the George W. Bush administration, which preceded President Obama's, actually worsened our situation across the board.

Only by implementing structural reforms to the system itself and tackling the root causes of the problem will we save America. Whether this will be done, however, depends ultimately on the awareness, commitment,

---

12   Polling Report. (2011). American Public Opinion regarding *"Congress," "Direction of the Country,"* and *"National Priorities."*

and engagement of America's citizens—not on the occupant of the White House. Indeed, the ultimate root causes and the keys to any solutions have more to do with citizens' awareness and engagement than with anything else. Only an aware and engaged citizenry may effect and sustain significant change. Therefore, the bulk of any reform efforts should focus on inspiring and empowering citizens to become more civically aware and engaged in working for the common good.

Indeed, one of the main reasons behind our prevailing conditions and one of the main obstacles to reform is the epidemic of self-centeredness that has swept through our society. Most people possess a mind-set that confines their thinking to what serves them and them alone. They are simply unaware of, or indifferent to, what is going on in their immediate environments, let alone in the country or the world at large. Additionally, most people appear to be largely complacent and shallow. They have narrow, self-centered aspirations, typically limited to self-image enhancement and acquisition of material possessions. When individuals and communities don't have the country's well-being at heart, irrespective of how high their aspirations are, their impact on the country's well-being and future is severely limited. In fact, the impact can be very negative, as egocentric aspirations are often achieved through the exploitation and/or neglect of fellow citizens and the public welfare. This is indeed a recipe for disaster. Daniel Webster once wrote,

> I apprehend no danger to our country from a foreign foe . . . Our destruction, should it come at all, will be from another quarter. From the inattention of the people to the concerns of their government, from their carelessness and negligence, I must confess that I do apprehend some danger. I fear that they may place too implicit a confidence in their public servants, and fail properly to scrutinize their conduct; that in this way they may be made the dupes of designing men, and become the instruments of their own undoing. Make them intelligent, and they will be vigilant; give them the means of detecting the wrong, and they will apply the remedy.[13]

America is caught in a severe vicious cycle that consists of a system

---

13   Daniel Webster, June 1, 1837.

and a culture that spiral into one another, leading to further alienation, disengagement, and even general public despair.

In order for this vicious cycle of alienation to be broken, our political system needs to become much more accessible to the general public and much less vulnerable to big money and special interests. American capitalism has to be practiced in a far more humane and responsible manner. The public must be both inspired and empowered to reach for the sky while maintaining a primary focus on the country's well-being and future.

A genuine and total commitment to our country and to a higher purpose than self would unleash the creative energies of citizens and communities, transforming and mobilizing them to generate sustained societal reform. People and communities who are driven by a cause and commitment to their country naturally find themselves striving to be exemplary and engaged citizens, making the overall society stronger and more cohesive.

Having said all of that and irrespective of any objectionable aspects of American history, politics, or culture, this new movement is built on—and driven by—our commitment to America as a homeland and our yearning for the best conditions for this homeland and for our fellow citizens. Our movement is also built with a somewhat unique perspective—at least within the Muslim community—on America's history, society, culture, and political system.

As is true of the history of every great nation or civilization (including the Muslim civilization and all empires), American history is a mixed bag and certainly contains some dark moments. However, it has many bright moments too. The Qur'an teaches us that we should learn from history, not remain hostage to it.

When it comes to history, our approach is as follows: If there is anything that could realistically be remedied, we certainly want to see it fixed. Otherwise, history is good only for the lessons it teaches us and to help us understand the context of the present time. Also, like most fellow citizens, we certainly object to some domestic and foreign policies and some social norms and aspects of the American culture. Otherwise, there would be no need for reform. However, this is not a reason to become ambivalent toward America and attempt to justify our civic and social disengagement, as some Muslims do. Rather than dampening our commitment to America, the negative aspects should serve to fuel our motivation for social interaction and civic engagement. Islamic values and American values are very compatible.

We should aim at reforming undesirable and unhealthy qualities about our society, whereas the positive aspects should be preserved and reinforced.

In our assessment of American history, society, and politics, we must be as objective and fair as possible—carefully avoiding a biased approach that only perceives the glass as half empty (or for that matter, half full). It is for good reasons that the United States achieved world prominence and became the envy of the world. If historical or societal blemishes were to bar a nation from the loyalty of its citizenship, no nation would have loyal citizens simply because no nation in the world is flawless. In fact, a fair comparison would show that Americans have many more reasons to be loyal citizens than do the citizens of most of the countries in the world. In America, citizens at least have mechanisms through which to voice their concerns and attempt to reform policies and social norms.

Finally, even though this project is Islam inspired and advocates comprehensive reform, it will be executed within the guidelines of the U.S. Constitution and in compatibility with the secular nature of the state and the pluralistic nature of the society. Moreover, this position is genuine and strategic, not tactical; and it is based on solid Islamic and pragmatic arguments.

AN HONEST APPRAISAL OF OUR MUSLIM AMERICAN COMMUNITY

The renaissance of the community requires a thorough diagnosis of its current situation and an in-depth analysis of our history. Conducting a thorough assessment of our community's past and present performance is problematic because our institutions never set clear missions, goals, or objectives that could have been used as measuring sticks to evaluate ourselves. Our negligence in this critical first step in community building largely explains our erratic operation and expansion.

Virtually the only clear goals we have had since coming to America have been the fulfillment of our immediate religious and social needs and the preservation of our identities as Muslims. These goals have been largely achieved through the establishment of Islamic centers and schools. These have constituted the only clear community projects. Since then, it seems we've only been able to either set up more facilities or expand the existing ones. It is no wonder that, following the euphoria that accompanied the incredibly successful campaign of establishing Islamic centers, we have been largely stagnant and/or spinning our wheels.

The Muslim American community (particularly the immigrant segment) was built not only for a limited purpose (which was quickly achieved) but also with a limited planned timeframe. Most of our immigrant leaders and members were planning to go back home after they accomplished what they came here to do. Because most of us never did return to our former homelands, we refer to this misconception as the "myth of return." Additionally, the immigrants' children who have been born in America have never known any other home, but many were taught to expect that they would move back to their parents' homeland. Thus, an immigrant and minority mind-set, and sometimes a victim mind-set, has remained deeply entrenched within our psyche. As well, knowingly or unknowingly, many Muslim American leaders and organizations (both local and national) have reinforced that mind-set. So the so-called myth of return has remained in the minds of many who will never choose to make that move, even if/when it becomes possible.

The pioneers of the community have certainly been sincere and have worked very hard, but they had limited goals and have been using an inefficient and nonscalable model to build the community. What is needed now is a model that is scalable, meaning one which can be modified and adapted to match current circumstances and current needs. We need a new design that fits current community membership, inspires progress, and keeps up with change. The pioneers have also lacked much-needed vision and skills to lead the community beyond the first phase. It is no wonder that the community has been mushrooming haphazardly without translating that proliferation into relevance or impact.

On the surface, our numerous buildings, activities, Web sites, e-mail blasts, and literature may appear impressive. However, a true and honest look at our community reveals alarming signs: civic disengagement, social isolation, fragmentation, widespread apathy and alienation, complacency, stagnation, and a leadership void and mess. At the roots of this severe crisis, we suffer from the lack of a sense of mission and direction, an acute identity crisis, and serious deficiencies in our understanding and implementation of Islam. Our commitment to it is, for most of us, sporadic and shallow.

Just as our nation's crisis didn't manifest overnight, neither did our community's. The seeds of our community crisis date back to the difficult backgrounds of the two major segments of the Muslim American community—African Americans and immigrants. The crisis has continued to grow because of our founding limitations and has snowballed because of our premature relaxation and our inadequate response to major challenges and changes. As a result, our community has become "stuck" and is in dire need of a fundamental paradigm shift and a new beginning.

Indeed, it is incumbent on our generation to sort out our experience so that we might pass on to future generations only lessons learned and a sound vision for the future. We must spare them our baggage and our multitude of problems, so they may have a head start and focus on their own problems and challenges. Otherwise, it is likely that future generations of Muslim Americans will inherit only physical buildings and lots of shackling baggage and liabilities.

Muslims rise and fall on their understanding and implementation of Islam and their commitment to it. Even though it doesn't entail major and explicit deviations in matters of belief, the prevailing version of Islam in our community leaves a lot to be desired; and that largely explains our unenviable situation.

In fact, we have a substantially mutilated version of Islam that has been stripped of a sense of mission. Frankly, it is spiritually dull, unduly rigid, and ethically weak. Some major aspects have been neglected, while others have been overemphasized. In particular, the prevalent version has very weak humane and civic dimensions, which explains the social isolation and civic disengagement of the majority of our community, particularly the devout ones. It is also too ritualistic, too legalistic, and too formalistic.

In our assessment, our current situation is largely due to our inadequate understanding and implementation of Islam and our consequent neglect of our defining mission.

Islam is usually defined as submission to God (implicitly carrying a passive connotation), or as a way of life, making it a private or personal matter. It is rarely defined as a life mission. This explains why most Muslims are basically passive worshippers who are neither civically engaged nor socially connected outside their small circle. Plus, there is neither a compelling mission nor an inspiring leadership to mobilize and rally the community.

Moreover, the prevalent version of Islam is a foreign religion that precludes integration and compatibility with American culture. It is also mixed with unhealthy heritage and culture and with a strong dose of anti-American political views.

From our perspective, Islam means constantly striving to fulfill the purpose of God in pursuit of His pleasure. This lifelong mission, which constitutes the purpose of creation and of God's revelation, entails a constant quest—both as individuals and collectively—to become better embodiments and instruments of His will.

Muslims must strive—individually and collectively—to become mindful of God as is His due and to strive in His way as is His due. That's how Islam inspires, uplifts, and unifies its followers and transforms them into agents of change and a movement of change. Indeed, Islam is a great message/mission of renaissance and reform; and when it stops being that, people must question their understanding and implementation of Islam and their commitment to it.

However, the embodiment and execution of the divine guidance must be relevant. That's why God regularly sent a new and customized revelation to every nation in language that resonated with them and through messengers who were from among them.

We sent not an apostle except (to teach) in the language of his (own) people, in order to make (things) clear to them [Qur'an 14:4].

The Qur'an calls each messenger the brother of his people, and messengers engaged their people and addressed them with very compassionate discourse, repeatedly calling upon them with the affectionate expression, "O my people!"

This pattern continued up to the seal of prophets, Muhammad, who was sent "as a mercy to humanity" with a universal and timeless message, the Qur'an, which God promised to preserve. This was a turning point in the history of humanity, with tremendous implications. First, it means that Islam is valid for all times and contexts and compatible with all cultures. However, it is Muslims—through their understanding and implementation—that make Islam relevant or irrelevant. Second, it means that Muhammad's mission and the duty to preserve and convey his message were passed on to all his followers until the end of time. And, third, it means that Muslims at all times and places are required to understand and implement the original texts of Islam in their own contemporary context, and to produce an original and viable indigenous experience, and to use the prophetic model to build a vibrant movement for societal reform. This revival/renewal of Islam is crucial if we are to ensure the continuous relevance and freshness of Islam.

When this process stalls for too long (as is the current situation) or when the divine guidance is taken to a new country or territory, a fresh construct is due. This is generated by applying the original texts in the new context to produce a relevant and inspiring Islamic construct and build a relevant, indigenous, and impactful movement. All previous constructs may still be useful, but they should neither be seen as binding nor limiting.

This exercise was performed with reasonable success by the contemporary Islamic movement, but has not been well sustained, and it was never performed in our community. Thus, the need for our project in general and for its revival/renewal component in particular is obvious. The revival/renewal component requires the understanding and implementation of the original sources of Islam in the American context in order to produce an original and indigenous Muslim American experience. It also involves the translation of divine guidance and the divine mission into a universal message, a civic platform, and a reform project.

Our revival and renewal exercise shall help to restore the relevance of Islam and its compelling sense of mission. That will spark the renaissance of the community and pave the way for Islam and Muslims to make a significant and sustained contribution to societal reform. The good news is that while we are proposing a formidable project to a community that already faces daunting internal and external challenges, our great faith and source of inspiration, our great country that offers boundless opportunities, and our great and largely untapped potential—all constitute strong bases for hope. In fact, if we proceed appropriately, as explained herein, and with God's help, we cannot fail.

PART II:

THE IDEOLOGICAL AND INTELLECTUAL FOUNDATIONS OF OUR ISLAM-INSPIRED REFORM MOVEMENT

In part 1 of this book, the concept of an Islam-inspired societal reform movement was set forth, the need for such a movement was explained, and the context in which this project is to be executed was described. Part 2 will establish the ideological and intellectual underpinnings for such a movement and introduce a number of key concepts that are used throughout the book. It is against this philosophical backdrop that we have diagnosed the history and present reality of the Muslim American community and constructed the vision and platform for the future. That vision is presented in detail later in the book. Therefore, an understanding of the ideas laid forth in this section is a prerequisite to understanding the rationale behind our proposed movement.

The movement we are launching is far different from the many charter organizations that have been established thus far in the Muslim American community. Our focus far exceeds the mere incorporation of an organization, the development of bylaws and/or the construction of a facility for programs and services. Rather, we are developing a comprehensive religious and societal reform movement based on a unique perspective on fundamental Islamic concepts regarding God, creation, life, revelation, prophethood, and the hereafter. Also particularly important to our movement are our perspectives regarding Muhammad's prophethood and divine mission, his prophetic model and legacy, Islamic history, and the legacy of the contemporary Islamic movement. These are the main issues that will be discussed in this chapter, and these constitute the ideological foundations of our project.

Although the great majority of Muslims would not disagree significantly with most of these concepts, we consider our perspective to be original on several counts. In fact, this project may be viewed as a launch, not a simple course correction. This is because our new perspectives do stand in profound contrast with those that have been prevalent in our community. Consider the ways in which this is a departure from the past:

1. ***Our ideological/intellectual basis is crystal clear.*** Most Islamic organizations are service providing and activity oriented, and they neither have nor need a clear ideological/intellectual foundation. When a foundation does exist, it is typically vague, either because of the nature of the organization or because of inherent limitations. Their primary focus usually tends to be on the maintenance of the organizations and ongoing activities; therefore fundraising becomes a top priority. Organizations that are membership based are usually consumed with bureaucracy and conflict resolution, trying to preserve their existence and maintain the unity of their assorted membership. They have no rallying cause, no clear vision, and no inspiring leadership. Having witnessed the shortsightedness of this approach in the Islamic movement and in the Muslim American community, we are committed to ensuring perpetual and permanent clarity in our ideological foundation and our guiding principles. In fact, the nature and scope of this project will not permit vagueness.

2. ***Our construct/perspective is coherent.*** We are not suggesting that Muslim organizations and groups are totally ineffective. Not only do they offer needed programs and services, but also each has correctly interpreted some of the tenets of the Islamic paradigm. However, some of their constructs lack coherence and a sense of wholeness because they disproportionately emphasize certain aspects of Islam at the expense of others. Most current constructs were imported from Muslim groups abroad with only minor customization. They represent a mere patchwork of ideas that do not provide a sound vision for the future, nor do they allow effective assessment of our community's reality or effective engagement of our American environment. In this project, we are taking the correct steps to implement a reform movement. We are developing

an authentic, coherent, and relevant framework, which will enable us to better understand our religion and our society and effectively assess our community. This will make it possible to leverage Islam's great capacity to guide and elevate personal and public lives and to develop sound vision and strategy for the future.

3. *We will walk the talk*. Another limitation of prevalent Islamic constructs is that some of their positive tenets are never implemented, so there is a disparity between what is said and what is actually done. It is not uncommon to find Muslim organizations with lofty visions and mission statements and strategic plans that have very little to do with their actual operations. Often, this is because their founders "acted first" before they posed the necessary questions. They rushed to incorporate as an organization in order to meet immediate but short-term objectives; and when they found themselves needing to market their organizations to attract necessary human and financial resources, they developed impressive brochures and Web sites. Actions and inactions speak louder than words however. Our operations will match our ideology, vision, and strategy.

4. *We will be accountable.* Again, not only are we striving to take the right steps in the correct order in our movement, but we also plan to ensure consistency between what we lay down on paper and our day-to-day operations. Additionally, we want to ensure that our movement's work is guided and gauged by our intellectual framework, our vision, and our strategy, not by haphazard or convenient indicators. We also plan to establish a steady flow of ideas through brainstorming, planning, and execution. This will be energized and nourished through a synergetic feedback process between our intellectual framework, vision, and strategy on the one hand, and our plans and action on the other. All of this vision, revision, and refinement will be transparent, and we will hold ourselves accountable for results.

Established in Response to God's Call

Again, as mentioned in part 1, this movement has been established to seek God's pleasure by carrying out His will and fulfilling the purpose of His creation. This is the essence of Islam: a life mission of revival, renewal, renaissance, and reform. In fulfilling this mission, people should strive—individually and collectively—to become the best possible embodiments and instruments of God's will.

This life mission is emphasized in a number of different places in the Qur'an, but it is nicely encapsulated in these three consecutive verses:

> You who believe, be mindful of Allah as is His due, and make sure you devote yourselves to Him, to your dying moment.

> Hold fast to God's rope all together; do not split into factions. Remember God's favor to you: you were enemies and then He brought your hearts together and you became brothers by His grace; you were about to fall into a pit of Fire and He saved you from it—in this way God makes His revelations clear to you so that you may be rightly guided.

> Be a community that calls for what is good, urges what is right, and forbids what is wrong: those who do this are the successful ones [Qur'an 3:102–104].

These verses clearly call on believers to be mindful of God as is His due and to unite to fulfill the divine purpose. The divine purpose consists of calling for what is good, urging what is right and forbidding what is wrong. In today's language, this is a call for civic engagement and service of the greater good. This is an order, or a command from God, and it represents the essence of all revelation and the mission of all prophets and is the very same message and mission that we are championing in this movement.

Islam is not a new religion, but rather it is the religion of all God's prophets. Likewise, our movement is a call for the revival of the message that God sent to humanity by way of His prophets throughout history: the message of *Tawheed* (the doctrine of the "Oneness of God"), which essentially guides us to God (who is our Creator) and to what is best for us in this life and in the hereafter. Indeed, all the prophets preached about the Oneness of God and about our individual accountability on the Day of Reckoning.

> Every soul is pledged for what it has earned [Qur'an 74:39].

> Whoso does right, does it for his own soul; and whoso does

wrong, does so to its detriment. Then to your Lord will you all be brought back [Qur'an 45:16].

The prophets invited people to seek salvation through worshiping one God only and through performing good deeds. Additionally, every prophet's mission included an essential component of reform that addressed the pertinent issues of their time.

The beliefs in the Oneness of God, in the Day of Judgment, and in individual accountability serve as the ideological pillars of this movement, and all have far-reaching implications. Our belief in only One True and Universal God who is the Creator and Sustainer of everything and the Disposer of all affairs implies that everything else, including the prophets and angels, is a part of creation. We also believe that there is no intermediary between God and His creation and that the revelations and the miracles with which God empowered his prophets (such as Moses's direct communication with God or the miraculous births of Adam, Eve, and Jesus) do not make them more than humans.

Our belief in God's Supremeness over creation includes the belief that God is free from any imperfection. His knowledge, wisdom, and mercy are transcendent. Not only does He know what is best for His creation, but also as "The Beneficent" and "The Merciful," He wants the best for them and His bounty is infinite. Consequently, we—as humans—should gladly worship God. As His grateful servants, we should have no doubt that whatever He commands is best for us and whatever He forbids is harmful for us (in this life and in the hereafter) even when the benefits or detriments of those acts are not obvious.

Our belief in individual responsibility and in reckoning implies that God created humanity for a specific purpose—to worship Him and to act as His vicegerents (stewards) on earth. God declared this to the angels before He even created Adam:

> [Prophet], when your Lord told the angels, "I am creating a successor on earth" [Qur'an 2:30].

Upon Adam's descent to earth, God informed Adam of this purpose and promised him His divine guidance in fulfilling it. He also equipped Adam with the power of reasoning and the will to choose (particularly in response to divine guidance). Additionally, God explained to Adam the potential consequences of exercising that will.

Our fate as human beings depends on our performance in fulfilling the divine purpose, which calls on members of the human family to strive to be exemplary and engaged members of their society, to aspire highly, to realize their full potential, and to cooperate for the common good. We are, therefore, instructed to support and advocate freedom, justice, peace, and prosperity for all human beings. To reap its fruits in this life, the alignment with the divine guidance and the fulfillment of the divine purpose need not be intentional, and therefore those fruits are not limited to believers.

The tools of reasoning and choice are intended to help us better understand and manage our personal lives, as well as the physical world we live in. In addition, God has established laws or rules (*sunan*) that govern both the human and physical aspects of the universe. He has embedded those laws inside of creation and in His revelation, which He sent to humanity not only to liberate us but also to stimulate our minds. His divine guidance and our God-given intellect make it possible for us to discover and leverage these laws to our benefit.

In addition to the specific purpose for which we are created, everything that God gives us in this life is a trust as well as a test. How we handle these trusts and tests also determines our fate—in this world and in the hereafter:

> We test you all through the bad and the good, and to Us you will all return [Qur'an 21:32].

> Be aware that your possessions and your children are only a test, and that there is a tremendous reward with God [Qur'an 8:127].

> On that day, you will be asked about your pleasures [Qur'an 102:8].

Life is not only a mission, an act of worship, a trust, and a testing ground, but it is also a race for perfection. All of this is to take place in the context of an eternal struggle (*jihad*) between good and evil, truth and falsehood. Humankind's struggle began the moment Satan refused to prostrate himself before Adam and vowed to attempt to mislead the children of Adam until the Day of Judgment. Upon the descent of Adam, Eve, and Satan to earth, God said,

> Get ye down, both of you,—all together, from the Garden
> with enmity between yourselves [Qur'an 20:123].

This eternal struggle continually forces us to choose between the call of God and the call of Satan. The call of God invites us to that which is beneficial (although sometimes inconvenient) for us in this life and in the hereafter. The call of Satan invites us to that which is harmful (although sometimes easier and alluring) both in this life and in the hereafter. God calls us by His messengers and servants; Satan whispers to us directly or through his recruits.

> Satan threatens you with poverty and enjoins upon you what
> is foul, whereas Allah promises you forgiveness from Himself
> and bounty. And Allah is Bountiful, All- Knowing [Qur'an
> 2:269].

We face this struggle at all levels of our existence: internally, interpersonally, in our societies, and even globally. The dynamics and the outcome of this struggle determine our individual and collective condition—in this life and in the hereafter. As followers of God's prophets, we *must* take an active role in this struggle. This is particularly so of Muslims who follow Muhammad, the seal of the prophets, because after Muhammad, the responsibility of the divine mission was handed over to the community of believers. As God's stewards (representatives) on earth and as the heirs to the prophets, we are responsible not only for ourselves but also for all of humanity.

Those who do not willfully participate in the struggle may believe that they are exempt from its negative consequences, but they are not. In fact, they are often the subject matter of the struggle. Unfortunately, the vast majority of Muslims and Islamic groups fall into this category because they have largely abandoned their defining mission, the mission that automatically compels them to be engaged.

Looking at our history from this perspective, it can be said that our human experience has been one of repeated divine calling and eternal struggle.

People's experience is affected and defined by their response to the divine call and by their participation in the eternal struggle. Moreover, there are consequences based upon their response and their participation.

Although God has promised to support those who convey His message and champion His cause, this promise is for those who do everything they possibly can do—and in accordance with the divine laws of the universe. Those who discover and leverage these laws are bound to prevail and to reap the fruits of their efforts *in this life*—irrespective of their intention and whether or not they have purposely aligned themselves with divine guidance. On the other hand, no matter how devout the believers are, they cannot count on God's decisive help if they don't learn and follow these divine rules. If they don't do the right thing and/or they don't do things right, they have only themselves to blame for the consequences. Muhammad's community learned this reality the hard way after their defeat in the Battle of Uhud, when God told them, "It is from yourselves" [Qur'an 3:165]. This reality has been confirmed in several places in the Qur'an (4:79, 42:30).

Both the divine call and the struggle are eternal. However, they were meant to be delivered and conducted in two different ways and in two very different contexts. The first was before Muhammad's prophethood when a number of prophets, beginning with Adam and ending with Jesus, brought the divine message to their communities. The second was after Muhammad's death, when humanity had been weaned of prophethood. His followers were thenceforth assigned full responsibility for delivering the divine message and carrying out the divine mission till the end of time.

A History of Deviation in Understanding the Prophetic Model

Again, because it came from our Creator who knows and wants what is best for us, we know that revelation is designed to liberate us, unlock our potential, and ensure our happiness and harmony in this life and our salvation in the hereafter. It guides people to that which is best for them in both worlds. Yet there are always those who reject or even fight God's call. There are also those who misinterpret the divine guidance and, as a result, harm themselves and/or others in the name of religion.

Throughout history, there has been a repeated tendency for humanity to deviate in their conception of God and in their understanding and implementation of His guidance. Before the seal of prophethood, whenever these deviations occurred, religion became irrelevant and obsolete, necessitating that God send a new messenger with a renewed revelation. After Muhammad, this same pattern periodically resulted in the emergence of revivalists and reformers with a renewed Islamic construct.

Some of these deviations were conceptual, relating to matters of belief or to the contextualization of religion. Others were practical, relating to matters of worship or conduct. Typically, the deviations crept in, starting small but then proliferating. Most of the deviations have resulted from negligence or from excesses that diminished the coherence of religion. Other times, deviation has been the result of dogmatic rigidity that precluded the ability of the religion to remain relevant to its adherents and the never-ending challenges and changes they faced. Consequently, some people found themselves unnecessarily confined (conceptually or practically). Others fell into extremism. Additional pitfalls made some Muslims hostages of artificial dichotomies, such as divine revelation versus human reason, this life versus the hereafter, spiritual versus mundane, salvation through faith versus salvation through good deeds, etc.

Unsurprisingly, these deviations ultimately caused people to hurt themselves and/or one another. Religion is meant to free people from confusion, to uplift and integrate/streamline their lives, and to grant them focus in their thinking. Religion properly practiced should then help people in their efforts to be engaged in their environment and to be positive members of society:

> He releases them from their heavy burdens and from the yokes that are upon them. So it is those who believe in him, help him, and follow the light which is sent down with him,—it is they who will prosper [Qur'an 7:157].

> Whoever works righteousness, man or woman, and has Faith, verily, to him will We give a new Life, a life that is good and pure and We will bestow on such their reward according to the best of their actions [Qur'an 16:97].

Before Muhammad, all of the messengers were sent to a specific people during a specific era. God did not preserve these earlier scriptures, which were society specific and situation specific. Instead, He renewed them by sending another messenger with a new situation-specific, relevant revelation. That process of succession was ended and sealed with the advent of Muhammad and the final, universal, and timeless message of the Qur'an, which God promised to preserve. This represented a major turning point in history, and it had tremendous implications.

The Qur'an constitutes the only certain revelation from God, yet it does not deliver a new message. Rather, it is a reaffirmation and a perfection of all the previous messages brought by all the previous prophets. Because it is universal and timeless, God made it valid and relevant for all times, all circumstances, and all people. This is the reason that the Qur'an consists primarily of inspirational verses and of general guidelines to be observed in conducting our individual and collective lives. To be sure, the Qur'an is more specific on some matters (e.g., fundamental issues related to creed and worship, etiquette, and family) than on others.

Muhammad's life and traditions were also meticulously documented apart from the Qur'an. This information is also essential and fulfills two functions:

1. It delineates (in words and in deeds) matters of creed, worship, and character.
2. It provides a model for the individual and collective understanding, implementation, and advocacy of Qur'anic teachings so that believers might fulfill their divine mission of fully embodying and executing the will of God.

The thrust of Islam is to provide people with a higher meaning of life. Islam does this by granting believers a life mission that challenges them to realize their full potential and impact positively on society, as they strive to be the best embodiments and instruments of God's will.

The thrust of the prophetic model is to galvanize and unify people through a compelling mission and unified leadership (unity of purpose and leadership) and to sustain that state of mobilization and unity through an expansive vision and sound strategy. In this way, the community can move smoothly from one phase to the next.

Utilizing this model, Muhammad built a community that changed the face of earth and the course of history in the span of one generation. Because it was meant to be a replicable model that was not exclusive to the Prophet and his community, it did not rely on miracles that cannot be replicated. Rather, it is a model based on human effort, which has required considerable sweat and pain and has sometimes involved ineffective decisions and setbacks. Apart from conveying and exemplifying the revelation of the Qur'an, Muhammad conducted himself and implemented his model mostly as the leader of the community, not as an infallible messenger.

The ability to replicate the prophetic model was initially demonstrated by the model's incredible success in an environment that was as unfavorable as it could be. It succeeded in the face of the hostile, idol-worshipping Meccans and in the desert among poor, illiterate Bedouin tribes who were constantly fighting each other, sometimes over petty issues. Despite drastically scarce human and financial resources, Islam succeeded from the start, and it continued to work perfectly for about a half of a century—a period that was almost evenly divided by the death of the Prophet.

The second half of this period, the twenty-five years after Muhammad's death, is called the era of the rightly guided Caliphs (al-Khulafā'u r-Rāshidūn). Then, for a number of reasons to be discussed later in depth, the model began to crumble following the assassination of Uthman (the third rightly guided Caliph ... or in current transliteration, *Khalifa*).[14] His death triggered two bloody civil wars that claimed the lives of eighty thousand Muslims in little more than a year. Under the leadership of Ali (the fourth and last rightly guided *Khalifa*), this era continued for just six more years. Then came the era of dynasties for about twelve centuries until the collapse of the Ottoman Empire in the 1920s.

From the Islamic perspective, this 1,200-year period was a time of overall decline—albeit slow and inconsistent. Muslims championed a great civilization and rebounded many times from numerous troubles and assaults,

---

14 Caliph is an English word for *khalifa*, the Arabic word literally meaning "one who replaces someone else who left or died." In the context of the history of Islam, though, the Khalifa (capitalized) was the successor (in a line of successors) to Prophet Muhammad as the political and religious leader of all Muslims. Note that Muhammad was the last of the prophets according to Islam, so the rightly guided Caliphs (or Khalifas) were certainly not prophets. The word Khalifa (or Caliph, capitalized) has also been used historically as the title of the head of an Islamic government (similar to the title President). As we will see later in this book, in the context of Islam today, *khalifa* (lower cased) takes on a different but related and most important meaning for Muslims (individually and collectively): God, through His last prophet Muhammad, has called upon each and every Muslim to serve as God's *khalifa* (representative or steward) on Earth. This is the duty of all Muslims until the end of time.

including the devastating blows of the Crusades and the Mongols. Indeed, Muslims made impressive strides and contributions and led the world in the advancement of science and the arts. The overall Islamic paradigm was generally working. Muslims continued to pioneer in several fields, and Islam continued to spread by example. Moreover, during those twelve centuries, there were several exceptional periods during which substantial reforms were enacted and the Islamic paradigm was more or less restored.

The robustness of the prophetic model can be seen in the fact that, despite its inadequate implementation, it survived so long after the Prophet's death and produced some great results in all kinds of circumstances. However, because its adherents failed to ensure its evolution, they were eventually unable to keep up with life's challenges and changes. Islam became a marginalized religion, and many Muslims became detached from their environments and largely irrelevant.

The fall of the Ottoman Empire, which marked the end of this mixed-record era, opened a can of worms, triggering a chain reaction of events that resulted in the disintegration of the Muslim world, colonialism, forced westernization, successful independence movements (mostly inspired by Islam), and inept or disastrous state/nation-building by both liberal and dictatorial regimes.

The sequence, timing, and pace of those phenomena varied from one country to another. Oftentimes, the sequence of events overlapped and made it difficult to discern cause and effect. However, two things are certain: (1) taken as a whole, the process has constituted a vicious, self-destructive cycle that has brought Muslims to their current unenviable position and (2) the collapse of the Ottoman Empire in 1924 prompted, in Egypt in 1928, the emergence of the Islamic movement, which then spread throughout the Muslim world either via franchising (as in Jordan and Syria) or through indirectly influencing local initiatives (in North Africa and the subcontinent).

Although their emergence and their specific circumstances and trajectories may have differed, there was a similar pattern in most, if not all, of these movements:

1. They experienced a remarkable takeoff and great success in reconciling their Islamic identities with life in general and in reviving Islam so that it greatly enhanced the religiosity of many people and made them proud to be Muslims.

2. This success, however, was followed by a miserable failure of the movement to sustain its relevance and to effect the renaissance and reform of society. A chronic stalemate between those movements and the local regimes developed, especially in the Arab world. It was only recently that such a stalemate was broken, at least in some countries. That change was effected through the sweeping popular revolutions that were launched spontaneously by the young generations that were caught in the deadlock and tired of stalemate.

A mixture of both internal and external factors (to be discussed later) conspired to prevent the Islamic movements from effectively engaging their environments. This made it impossible for the movements to sustain their growth and relevance and precluded their smooth transition from one phase to another. Strategic blunders on the part of their leadership also reduced their impact. As one might guess, these failures and shortcomings worked together to yield secret and rigid organizations, which served merely to provide limited services to their members and supporters but generated fairly inconsequential noise for ruling governments.

It was this type of Islamic activism that was brought to the U.S. by some movement activists who were also the pioneers/founders of the Muslim American community. Its proponents were mainly individuals who migrated here to pursue higher education and/or better opportunities and freedom. They used a limited model of community building, a model that was nonscalable, meaning it was poorly designed to meet community needs when the circumstances, the community, and the needs changed. For the most part, the product of their efforts has been the all too familiar two-stage pattern: (1) tremendous success in the founding phase characterized by establishing Islamic centers and providing basic programs and services aimed at preserving the community's Islamic identity, followed by (2) stagnation and failure in leading the community toward integration, relevance, and impact. The exception was that, this time, the process was complicated by their new minority status in a foreign land and the mythological "promise of return" they held on to, both of which fed their already-present feelings of victimization.

In reality, they built communities in America in the image of their movements at home: with a private organization for the members and facades (Islamic centers) to educate, serve, indoctrinate, and recruit.

Belief in the impermanency of their American residence (the "myth of return") and the minority mind-set they developed acted to lower the ceiling of their aspirations. That helped community leaders and members to rationalize their isolation from society in general. The focus of the leaders' work was on organizational control and routine activism with no clear driving mission. There was no sense of direction, no competent and inspiring leadership, no expansive vision, and no sound strategy. Importantly, there were no clear performance indicators.

Overall, movement activists were a mixed blessing for the community. On one hand, their background was instrumental in building the community and reasonably protecting the community from extremism. On the other hand, their intellectual, strategic, and leadership weaknesses caught up with them and inadvertently limited the community's growth, integration, relevance, and impact. As with their mother movements, these groups have ended up in a situation in which they are unable to lead, but they are also unwilling to follow or simply step out of the way. Consequently, not only did the Muslim community become a microcosm of the Muslim world, but also it stagnated in a strikingly similar manner, as did movements in most Muslim countries, and for very similar reasons. Moreover, our stalemate here is being justified by the same excuses offered elsewhere in most other Islamic movements.

All of these unfavorable elements were exacerbated by the tacit but disastrous exchange between the immigrant community and the indigenous African American Muslim community. Immigrant leaders preached a version of Islam that made many African American Muslims feel like foreigners in their own country. Furthermore, the immigrants' own victim mentality and that of African Americans due to their harsh experiences only reinforced one another. Accordingly, victimization constitutes an essential element of the Muslim American community's discourse—despite the fact that there is no room for it in a free, competitive society or in Islam, which teaches us to take full responsibility for our mistakes and failures:

> What! When a single disaster smites you, although ye smote (your enemies) with one twice as great, do ye say?—"Whence is this?" Say (to them): "It is from yourselves: For Allah hath power over all things" [Qur'an 3:165].

> Whatever good, (O man!) happens to thee, is from Allah.

But whatever evil happens to thee, is from thy (own) soul [Qur'an 4:79].

Whatever misfortune befalls you [people], it is because of what your own hands have done, and for many (of them) God grants forgiveness [Qur'an 42:30].

Corruption has appeared on land and sea as a result of people's actions and He will make them taste the consequences of some of their own actions so that they may turn back [Qur'an 30:41].

Rather than perceiving and conducting themselves as citizens, the vast majority of our community leaders and members think and behave like a foreign, victimized minority. This tends to not only preclude our successful integration within American society but also perpetuate our identity crisis, our disengagement, and our negative image.

Our Movement's Objectives

It is in this context that we are proposing to launch a movement of societal reform inspired by our unique and empowering interpretation of our divine mission: We are Muslims seeking to earn God's pleasure. This project is an ambitious but humble attempt to understand and implement the original texts of Islam within the American context. Our first objective is to produce an original and viable Muslim American experience. By applying the prophetic model, we can rebuild our community into a vibrant and relevant societal reform movement. It is our understanding that this is the duty of Muslims at all times and in all places.

As followers of Muhammad, the seal of the prophets and the universal messenger, it is our duty to preserve his legacy, which consisted of the divine guidance, his divinely inspired model, and his movement. In order to fulfill this duty, it is necessary that we constantly ensure the relevance of the divine guidance, the prophetic model, and the movement. Because this process has stalled for too long, a new beginning and a new Islamic construct are due in order to inspire a revived, relevant, and indigenous Islamic movement. That is the mission of this project.

Indeed, this exercise was performed with reasonable success by the contemporary Islamic movement, but it was not sustained and was never performed within the Muslim American community—a community that was built with a transplanted and stagnant model and designed largely as a temporary shelter for temporary immigrants. The African American Muslim community was built with an equally alien paradigm and inefficient model. And both segments have difficult heritages.

The limited paradigm that was the basis for the development of our community expired a long time ago, and we have wasted precious time and energy performing patchwork and spinning our wheels ever since. In the absence of visionary leadership and a compelling mission, not only did the community relax prematurely and get stuck in transition, but it also failed to keep up with and respond in a proper and timely manner to the changes it encountered. Deeply entrenched in their comfort zones, Muslim American organizations and activities are doing little beyond maintaining themselves and preserving the status quo.

The renaissance of our community requires us to chart a new course that runs in parallel with necessary ongoing work. The movement we are proposing is not intended to interrupt current activities. Rather, we are praying and planning for as smooth a transition as possible. We invite the participation of all members and leaders of the community, including those who are sustaining existing operations as well as those who will now champion this renaissance project. We will function as members of a relay team; and at the end of the day, the only thing that matters is that the entire team wins the race. This win-win approach calls on each of us to do our best and successfully pass the torch to the next generations for whom this project is ultimately designed.

Our American Legacy

So far, we have only touched upon our Islamic roots. However, since this project is intended to involve the overall American society as well, one might ask, "What about our American legacy?"

Indeed, because this is a societal reform movement designed to be championed by Americans and for Americans and for America, our intellectual framework must address both American history and the present American reality. Moreover, to be relevant, our understanding and implementation of Islam require an in-depth understanding of both the texts and the context. Realizing that the scope and methodology of our proposed reform are significantly dependent upon an accurate assessment of American society and that our effectiveness ultimately depends on the engagement of the wider society, we sought to develop a thorough and comprehensive knowledge of how our society and our community were shaped and how it all works. This was discussed briefly in part 1, and it will be discussed in extensive detail later. As the reader progresses through these pages, we will provide more emphasis on the Muslim American community, since that is the primary target audience of this book and the *initial* focus of our movement.

Although our movement advocates a civic platform for the well-being of all Americans, its ultimate aim is still the fulfillment of God's divine purpose and the seeking of His pleasure. The concept of God (specifically, the Oneness of God) is paramount to the proper understanding and execution of the movement. This is because the foundation of our ideology is constituted by our belief in the Oneness of God (and in the authority of the Qur'an and authentic Islamic texts). Therefore, the remainder of part 2 will present a brief explanation of the following fundamental Islamic concepts as they constitute an essential backdrop for our movement:

1. the concept of God in Islam; specifically, per the doctrine of the "Oneness of God" (*Tawheed*);
2. the purpose of creation; this life and the hereafter (the origin of the divine mission);
3. revelation and prophethood;
4. Muhammad's prophethood;
5. the prophetic model, life, and legacy;
6. the divine mission;
7. Islamic history; and
8. the contemporary Islamic movement.

We might add, however, that our religious beliefs and sources of inspiration are not meant to, nor do they have to, preclude those of other faiths from championing our platform—either fully or partially. Religion will not prevent us from working with fellow citizens on issues of common concern.

THE ONE TRUE AND UNIVERSAL GOD
(called Allah in Arabic)

By definition, God can only be one. In the beginning, there was nothing save God who has no beginning. And at the end of time, everything will have vanished except God who has no end. He is the Creator of everything, the Disposer of all affairs, the Cherisher and Sustainer of the worlds, the Supreme and the Irresistible. To Him belongs every perfection, and He is free of any imperfection. He is free of all needs. There is no limit to His power, knowledge, wisdom, and mercy, which are all transcendent and absolute. Even though these beliefs are obvious and compelling, humanity has eternally struggled with the concept of God and His oneness and with the concepts of the resurrection, the reckoning, and personal accountability.

> Say He is God the One, God the eternal. He fathered no one nor was He fathered. No one is comparable to Him [Qur'an 112:1–4].

Everyone and everything on the earth and in the heavens is a part of His creation, and there are neither intermediaries nor any intermediate status between the Creator and the creation. He is the source and center of all power and all goodness.

For all these reasons, worship is due to Him alone. Our success in this life depends upon aligning ourselves with His will, knowingly and unknowingly. Our salvation in the hereafter depends on bearing witness that He alone is worthy of worship and on abiding by His guidance and on striving to fulfill His purpose to the best of our abilities.

God demanded and received this covenant from all the children of Adam:

> [Prophet] When your Lord drew forth from the Children of Adam—from their loins—their descendants, and made them testify concerning themselves, (saying): "Am I not your Lord (who cherishes and sustains you)?"—They said: "Yea! We do testify!" (This), lest ye should say on the Day of Judgment: "Of this we were never mindful" [Qur'an 7:172].

The purpose of all creation is to worship God:

> I created jinn and mankind only to worship Me [Qur'an 52:56].

The Qur'an tells us that all of the messengers called their people to worship none but God:

> For We assuredly sent amongst every People an apostle, (with the Command), "Serve God, and eschew Evil" [Qur'an 16:36].

> Behold, the apostles came to them, from before them and behind them, (preaching): "Serve none but God" [Qur'an 41:14].

Worshiping God exclusively involves full submission to Him, together with complete love for Him. God also created mankind to be His vicegerent (*khalifa*), meaning His representative, steward, and deputy. This responsibility and obligation requires us to conduct all aspects of our lives and to develop and manage the universe according to His will (expressed through the *sunan*, or laws that govern the universe). An integral part of our life mission involves discovering these laws so that we can follow them and leverage them for our benefit.

THE CREATION AND ITS PURPOSE— LIFE AND THE HEREAFTER

These concepts were lumped together because they are intertwined. Indeed, life is meant to fulfill the purpose of creation, and the hereafter is when people's performance of that task will be judged. The hereafter and belief in Allah constitute the paramount incentives for believers to strive for perfection and for the realization of their full potential and impact.

The Creation and its Purpose

Mankind is God's greatest creation. Indeed, God created everything for man, and He created man for a very special purpose—to worship Him and to serve as His vicegerent. Man was also created in a very special way—God molded Adam from clay with His own hands, and blew into him His Spirit. The distinction and honor that God conferred upon Adam and upon mankind, as Adam's descendants, are proportional to our designated duties and responsibilities as His vicegerents (*khalifa*).

The extent to which we fulfill our life purpose will be judged in the hereafter. Therefore, if we truly believe in God, we should strive toward perfecting our worship and acting as His *khalifa* (which involves the realization of our full potential and impact in life). Our success or failure in these endeavors will be of paramount importance to us.

The power of reasoning and the ability to distinguish and to choose right from wrong are the most precious gifts that God gave to Adam and to us. Properly using these tools and following God's guidance will not only save us from going astray and from misery and despair but also allow us to reach the high and noble destiny that He intends for us. On the other hand, if we rebel against God and follow evil instead, we will suffer in this life and in the hereafter, and we will be abased to the lowest possible position:

> We create man in the finest state then reduce him to the lowest of the low, except those who believe and do good deeds [Qur'an 95:4–6].

After creating Adam, God ordered the angels to bow down before him. Sin originated with Satan (who was with the angels) when he arrogantly refused to do so, claiming that he was better than Adam who was made of clay. He then vowed to misguide and deceive Adam and his descendants (except the devoted servants of God). Rebellion against Allah is the original sin and the origin of all sins. This rebellion is what caused Satan to be cursed by God. Likewise, anyone who rebels against God will be cursed—except those who repent. In attempting to justify his rebellion, Satan committed four cardinal sins: jealousy, arrogance, lying, and injustice. These four sins account for most of the harm that has affected and will affect humanity.

God placed Adam and Eve in the Garden for a trial period, and He forewarned them that Satan was their enemy. However, Satan used his powerful tool of deception to capitalize on their weaknesses, and he caused them to forget God's warning and to disobey His instructions. They were about to be lost when God's grace came to their aid. Unlike Satan, they were not arrogant after committing their sin. They repented to God who mercifully accepted their repentance. Islam does not accept the idea of Adam and Eve's original sin and believes instead in individual responsibility for both sinning and repentance.

Adam and Eve were then sent down to earth from the Garden of Eden where, according to God's decree, they and their offspring would dwell until the Day of Judgment. Equipped with knowledge, determination, experience in dealing with his enemy, and the assurance of divine guidance, Adam took on his appointed role as God's vicegerent or steward. God informed them that their fate in this life and in the hereafter would depend on their acceptance or rejection of His guidance. The stage was then set for mankind's fulfillment of the divine purpose in the context of an everlasting struggle between righteousness on one hand and evil on the other:

> But when guidance comes from Me, as it certainly will, there will no fear for those who follow My guidance nor will they grieve. Those who disbelieve and deny Our messages shall be the inhabitants of the Fire, and there they will remain [Qur'an 2:38–39].

> Whoever follows My guidance, when it comes to you [people], will not go astray nor fall into misery, but whoever turns away from it will have a life of hardship. We shall bring him blind to the Assembly on the Day of Resurrection [Qur'an 20:123–124].

Our success in fulfilling the role of stewardship depends on understanding this universe and discovering and leveraging the rules (*sunan*) and the resources that Allah has embedded in it. This is an essential part of our task of worshipping God and our mission of stewardship. This exercise starts with the understanding of the nature of life and its different aspects, including its relationship to the hereafter (to be discussed below). It also depends on our compliance with divine guidance and our ability to properly balance faith and reason, revelation and intellect (to be discussed in the next section).

The Different Aspects of Life:

1. Life is a mission.

Islam is a life mission to fulfill God's purpose; and it calls on people to know Him, to exclusively worship Him, to aim high, and to realize their potential. Muslims are also directed to establish and maintain justice and to cooperate for the common good. This is true despite the reality that ambitions, differences, greed, and arrogance can sometimes drive individuals and nations to compete with, exploit, and oppress one another.

The thrust of this life mission is to conduct our lives, deal with one another, and develop and manage the earth in compliance with God's divine guidance and in pursuit of His pleasure and of the greater good. Just as an honest and loyal yet ambitious manager can pursue his/her own success while still ensuring the satisfaction of their employer, we can have high aspirations that are geared toward earning God's pleasure and the greater good. Our aspirations should be realized through legitimate means and should not be to the detriment of other individuals, or nations, or future generations.

This divine mission—specified, at least in general terms, even before man was created—not only gives our lives a sense of meaning and purpose but also serves as a great motivator.

2. Life is an act of worship.

God says, "I created jinn and mankind only to worship Me" [Qur'an 52:56].

This means that we should strive to make our entire lives an act of worship. This does not require being in a particular place, like in a mosque, or engaging in a specific form of worship, like praying or reading the Qur'an. Rather, it entails striving

- to be constantly mindful of God as is His due [Qur'an 2:102].
- at all times and in all circumstances to fulfill His purpose by doing that which is most pleasing to Him and brings you closer to Him. The deeds that are most loved by God are those that are most beneficial to us—individually and collectively—in this life and in the hereafter. Muhammad taught Muslims that the most beloved to God are those who are the most beneficial to people. The scholars agree that

Islam came to serve the well-being of people—in this life and in the hereafter, and whatever serves the well-being of people is part of the divine guidance.
- to dedicate everything we do or say to God: "Say: 'Truly, my prayer and my service of sacrifice, my life and my death, are (all) for God, the Cherisher of the Worlds'" [Qur'an 6:162].

This is the beauty of Islam: We dedicate all of our acts to God (who is free of all needs), yet we reap the fruits of those acts. "It is not their meat or their blood that reaches God; it is your piety that reaches Him" [22:37]. Indeed, Islam establishes a strong, organic connection between God's pleasure and the happiness, harmony, and salvation of His servants.

Throughout our history, this simple but profound fact has eluded many people. While they concentrated on the reality of God having no need for our good deeds, or the fact that our good deeds are never good enough for God, they missed the essential point that God does ask us to constantly push ourselves to the best of our abilities ("So be mindful of Allah as much as you can" [Qur'an 64:16].) We are supposed to do that while hoping and praying for, and trusting in, His mercy and forgiveness of our shortcomings.

If our lives are to be a mission and an act of worship, we must strive to be the best embodiments and instruments of God's will and to live for God and with God.

3. Life is a trust.

Everything in the universe belongs to God, the Owner of the earth, the heavens, and everything in between. We owe Him all our faculties, our possessions, and life itself. We are just trustees of everything He has given us (including life), and He will hold us accountable for the way we handle that trust and for our performance in fulfilling the roles He has assigned to us:

And pursue not that of which thou hast no knowledge; for every act of hearing or of seeing or of (feeling in) the heart will be enquired into (on the Day of Reckoning) [Qur'an 17:36].

Believe in Allah and His apostle, and spend (in charity) out

of the (substance) whereof He has made you heirs/trustees.
For, those of you who believe and spend (in charity), for them
is a great Reward [Qur'an 57:7].

Muhammad indicated that, on the Day of Judgment, every person will be asked how he or she spent their lifetime (particularly the years of youth) and how he or she earned and spent money. This belief in the reckoning represents a line of demarcation between believers and nonbelievers, and it strongly reinforces our self-restraint. The manner in which we handle a trust that is given to us is typically different from the way we handle our own possessions, particularly if that trust belongs to God and its management carries grave consequences.

The belief that life is a trust from God implies that we should use all of the tools He gave us in order to carry out His plan. This principle of honoring a trust and taking appropriate action is one that is readily accepted by most people when it is applied to their employment and their relationship with their bosses, yet many find it difficult to apply to their relationship with their Creator.

4. Life is a testing ground.

This aspect of life is related to its being a trust from God. Indeed, God not only tests our utilization of our entrusted faculties and resources, but He also tests us in our handling of different circumstances. As long as we live, we will move from one test to another. Some tests may be easy, whereas others will be hard. Our handling of some tests carries major consequences, while other tests have only minor consequences. Whether we consider a life episode as good or bad, the important factor is how we deal with it. The good, the bad, the easy, and the difficult—all tests are intended to make us better people.

We test you all through the bad and the good, and to Us you
will all return [Qur'an 21:32].

He Who created Death and Life, that He may try which of
you is best in deed [Qur'an 67:2].

Our proper handling of life's tests complements our own self-development efforts to become better people. In a remarkably concise way, the Qur'an tells us how to regard and handle all our life tests:

> Whatever good, (O man!) happens to thee, is from God. but whatever evil happens to thee, is from thy (own) soul [Qur'an 4:79].

Fortunate incidents should be attributed to God and should make us ever-more grateful in both words and deeds. On the other hand, we have only ourselves to blame for unfortunate incidents. Still, we should meet such incidents with patience, perseverance, and humility; and we should pray for God's help and forgiveness as these occasions may well be the result of a mistake or a sin we have committed. When properly handled, these situations can remind us of our limitations and our dire need for God. They also help cleanse our hearts and improve our record with God. Thereby, they can improve our chances of being admitted to heaven. Describing this win-win situation, Muhammad indicated that all matters in life are good for the believer as long as he/she meets bounty with gratitude and calamity with patience.

Without such a perspective, we might become confused or distraught by the trials of life and mishandle them. As a result, we might become desperate or even arrogant and plunge further into sin and error. Then, we would not learn any lessons from such experiences; and most likely, we wouldn't accept responsibility for our mistakes and wouldn't work to resolve and avoid them.

In summary, all of life's tests should bring us closer to God and make us better people—both due to our proper handling of them and because of the lessons we draw from them.

5. Life is a race for perfection.

One of the fundamental but overlooked aspects of life is that humans are created with tremendous potential that needs to be cultivated and realized. Indeed, our lives should be a journey of continuous improvement and empowerment. We should always push ourselves to be stronger and better people, and we should strive to perfect everything we do. Muhammad indicated that God loves for His servants to perfect what they do and that a strong believer is better and more beloved to God than a weak believer. Muhammad also indicated that a person is considered to be unfortunate if any two consecutive days of his or hers are equal in contribution (if he or she does not improve from one day to another).

6. Life is a struggle.

Each of the above aspects of life should be considered within the context of the eternal struggle that mankind must undergo—between good/truth and evil/falsehood. This struggle is constantly taking place at all levels of existence, from our own individual lives all the way up to the global level. However, the primary level of struggle for each of us is our experience in the society in which we live.

In this struggle, Satan has been true to his vow to enlist as many people in evil as possible (or at least sideline them). His first "success" on earth was the recruitment of Cain to kill his brother Abel.

God has told us that the struggle against Satan and his soldiers protects humanity from the spread of mischief and oppression:

> And did not God check one set of people by means of another, the earth would indeed be full of mischief [Qur'an 2:251].

> (They are) those who have been expelled from their homes in defiance of right, (for no cause) except that they say, "Our Lord is God." Did not God check one set of people by means of another, there would surely have been pulled down monasteries, churches, synagogues, and mosques, in which the name of God is commemorated in abundant measure. God will certainly aid those who aid his (cause); for verily God is full of Strength, Exalted in Might, (able to enforce His Will) [Qur'an 22:40].

God tells us that the transgressors are not the only ones who are affected by evil:

> Beware of discord that harms not only the wrongdoers among

you, and know that God is strict in punishment [Qur'an 8:25].

Those that do not actively participate in the struggle against evil due to lack of awareness or denial of their responsibility toward society are not exempt from its consequences. In fact, they often become its subject matter. Therefore, the only positive option for us is to be aware, vigilant, and actively engaged on the side of righteousness.

In an eloquent analogy, Muhammad illustrates that if wrongdoing (even with the best of intentions) is not prevented, it will affect everyone. He used a parable of people in the lower deck of a ship who wanted to dig a hole in the ship in order to get water so they could avoid disturbing those on the upper deck. If that were allowed, everyone would sink.[15]

More importantly, Muhammad made it clear that God does not accept retreating from the struggle against evil—even by His most pious servants. When an angel was instructed to punish a certain town, he was at a loss for what he should do with a very pious man who was dedicated to worship. God told the angel to start with that man because he had been indifferent to the mischief around him.

The struggle for good and truth involves winning the hearts and minds of people and directing them toward happiness and harmony in this life and toward their salvation in the hereafter. It is a struggle to enlist them in resisting and defeating Satan and his soldiers who attempt to direct people toward mischief and suffering in this life and toward punishment in the hereafter. An essential part of our mission on earth is to not only know and worship God ourselves but also guide others and make it easy for them to do the same (ta'beed). We not only need to be virtuous people ourselves, but also we need to see to it that goodness and virtue become societal norms and easier choices for our fellow human beings.

The struggle for good and truth is like a soccer game. A good offense is always the best defense. Defense and retreat are losing strategies, as Satan and his players will always be pressing forward, trying to gain more yards and to push the righteous people back.

---

15   Hadith narrated by Al-Numan bin Basheer and reported in Sahih Al-Bukhari. The Hadith books are collections of Hadiths, traditional narratives about Muhammad's sayings, rulings, opinions and actions as assembled and published by a number of famous scholars. The Sunna, the way of life prescribed in Islam, is based on the Hadith and on the Qur'an.

7. Life is a short probation and therefore a race for goodness.

Another obvious and fundamental aspect of life that we tend to forget is that it is temporary and short. What makes this all the riskier is the fact that we do not know when our lives will end. However, the clock is always ticking, and we are constantly getting closer to that end. No matter what we try, we cannot stop the clock, nor can we recover time that is gone. Muhammad indicated that each and every new day calls on people to take advantage of it because it will never return. Thus, we should strive to live our lives at our peak performance right now, as "today" may always be the day we leave this life and return to God.

The sense of urgency that comes from remembering our inevitable mortality causes people to race in different directions, or to race in the same direction but for different purposes. The concept of "hereafter" causes people to race toward good and to live for a higher cause. It also prompts people to exercise self-restraint in pursuing their dreams and ambitions, which guards against rampant selfishness, greed, and abuse in society. When we find those in authority capitalizing on legal loopholes and/or bending the law to their own favor, we can be pretty sure that they are living with disregard for the hereafter. As is said, "Impunity corrupts."

By informing us that most people will end up in the hellfire because of procrastination, Muhammad was aiming to heighten our sense of urgency. Often, people plan a lot of good, but they don't act fast enough.[16] Muhammad said that if one of us sees the signs of the Day of Judgment while he has a seedling in his hand, he should rush to plant it (even as life is ending and apparently there is no use).[17] In other words, when we have the opportunity to do good, we should neither procrastinate nor spend time contemplating the difference our action might make. Rather, we should rush to do all the good we can do and in the most effective and impactful way we can do it.

In another Hadith, Muhammad also emphasized the importance of having a sense of urgency: "Take advantage of five matters before five other

---

16   John P. Kotter. (1996). *Leading Change* [Book]. Page 36: Kotter states, "Establishing a sense of urgency is crucial to gaining needed cooperation. With complacency high, transformations usually go nowhere because few people are even interested in working on the change problem . . . if many others don't feel the same sense of urgency, the momentum for change will probably die far short of the finish line."

17   Hadith narrated by Anas and reported in the books of Imam Ahmad and Al-Bukhari.

matters: (1) your youth before you become old; (2) your health before you fall sick; (3) your richness before you become poor; (4) your free time before you become busy; and (5) your life before your death."[18] This reminds us that what we can do today, we may not be able to do tomorrow and that there may be no tomorrow.

Muhammad summed up this fundamental life aspect by saying, "Be in this life as a stranger or a wayfarer."[19] He also instructed us to remember death frequently, using such remembrance on a person's part as an indicator of their piety. The companions were praising someone who had passed away when Muhammad asked, "How was his remembrance of death?" Upon their negative response, he simply said, "He may not have been as good as you think."

The instruction to remember death is not meant to spoil our lives. Rather, it is meant to intensify our consciousness of the temporary nature of life and to prompt our preparation for the afterlife—the real and eternal life. As sad as death may be, it is not a full-stop end of our existence. Rather, it is a transition to a different stage of life—the true beginning of reaping the fruits of this life. While it is the end of being tested, it is also the end of opportunities to improve our record with God. Muhammad indicated that our worldly life is like a farm, while the hereafter is the harvest. Those who worked hard at doing right to pass life's tests and seized opportunities to please God will move on to a much better life. All of us will wish we had done a better job, and most will ask to be sent back to life in order to do so.

The Hereafter

During our lifespan, we should do our best to strive to fulfill the purpose of our creation and to be successful in all of life's aspects. In the hereafter (which begins at the time of death), our performance will be evaluated, and our fate will be determined.

Believing in individual accountability and in the hereafter has a colossal effect on the way we perceive and conduct our lives. These beliefs substantially boost our humility, our incentive to do good, and our ability to restrain ourselves. This has the effect of making all of us our very own monitors

18   Hadith narrated by ibn Abbas and reported in Musnad Imam Ahmad, and others, with an authentic chain of narration.

19   Hadith narrated by Ibn Umar and reported in Sahih Bukhari, Volume 8, Book 76, Number 425.

or police. When the majority of a society possesses these beliefs, there is a greater collective incentive to contribute to the common good, as well as a substantial reduction in behaviors that are harmful to the overall society and to its individual members.

It is no wonder that the doctrines about the reckoning and the hereafter along with *Tawheed* (the doctrine of the "Oneness of God") constitute the essence of the message brought by all prophets and the basis for inspiring people to do good and shun evil. Doing as God commanded is in our best interest in this life and improves our record in the hereafter. It is also the way to express our gratitude, trust, and love for God. The opposite goes for engaging in destructive and sinful behavior.

The belief in God instills God-consciousness in our hearts. Let us be mindful that God is with us wherever we go and at all times. It is God on whom we are completely dependent and to whom we owe everything. Our love, reverence, gratitude, dependence, fear, and shame before God drive us to live righteously and to shun evil. Knowing that we will all stand before God for our reckoning and knowing that our action determines our fate, we have reason for hope. This knowledge instills in our hearts a longing for the rewards and for heaven that God has promised for doing good. However, we also have reason to fear the unfathomable torment of His punishment and hellfire for committing evil. The contrast is huge. The stakes are very high, and no remedy will be possible if we lose.

These two beliefs, in God and in the hereafter, are very powerful engines for goodness and very strong shields against evil. They also engender another important but perhaps ironic benefit—that of solace. No matter how hard we may work in this life to realize our potential and to stand firm against injustice and no matter how just our laws may be, many injustices go unchecked, and many of our desires are not fulfilled. This fact can be depressing. However, when we firmly believe that a day will come when absolute justice will be rendered and all of our good deeds will be generously rewarded, we are protected from despair and feelings of helplessness.

Through the belief in Allah, in the hereafter, and in the divine destiny, Islam miraculously engenders this consolation. However, it also assigns humans a humongous mission. We are called upon to work hard, to constantly challenge ourselves to realize our full potential, and to stand out firmly against injustice. Genuinely undertaking this mission will preclude any tendency toward complacency.

O ye who believe! Stand out firmly for justice, as witnesses to God [Qur'an 4:135].

Both concepts, *Tawheed* and the hereafter, are very straightforward and rational beliefs that are very similar to undisputable life principles. For example, most of us accept the accountability of employees of any business to their supervisors, and we agree that they should aim to please them by performing the duties they were hired to fulfill according to certain standards and expectations regarding the job. Similarly, we expect alleged criminals to appear in court and, if convicted, to pay for their crimes.

Likewise, we should have no problem accepting that we are all created for a specific purpose, that we will be held accountable for our performance in fulfilling this purpose, and that our fate in the hereafter will depend on our performance and on how well pleased God is with us.

Yet throughout history, humanity has deviated from the pure concept of *Tawheed* and struggled with the self-evident concept of individual accountability and the reckoning. Mankind has used all kinds of excuses and arguments to justify circumvention or rejection of these truths. Moreover, it is only when these tenets of faith have been seriously misunderstood that some Muslims have fallen into such complacency and illogicality that, in trying to justify their own failure and deny responsibility, they have actually tried to use concepts like divine destiny and self-sacrifice of life on earth in favor of the hereafter! Earth is not simply the "abode of suffering," and it is not a place for poor excuses. It is our opportunity for achievement.

Generally, deviations start small and then proliferate. Most are products of Satan's deception. They are also the work of Satan's soldiers who capitalize on people's ignorance, desires, and weaknesses (sometimes, even their misdirected goodwill). Satan's soldiers mislead people onto an "exit" from the straight path. The Prophet used an analogy to illustrate how Satan works. While sitting with his companions, Muhammad once drew both a straight line and a crooked line. He told them that at every crooked line, there is a Satan who tries to lead people astray, and he read the following Qur'anic verse:

Verily, this is My way, leading straight. Follow it; follow not (other) paths. They will scatter you about from His (great) path [Qur'an 6:135].

One of the arguments against the reality of the hereafter is the question of resurrection. People ask how they could be sent back to life after death. This argument is very weak and absurd, given the power of God to create all of us and everything in existence in the first place.

> "(Yet shall ye be raised up)!" then will they say: "Who will cause us to return?" Say: "He who created you first!" [Qur'an 17:51].

Imagine the Omnipotent, all-Knowing, and all-Wise Creator being unable to resurrect what He Himself created. To say that there is something that God cannot do, or something that is difficult for Him, is an oxymoron. By definition, God's knowledge, power, and wisdom are infinite.

A plausible explanation for Satan's "success" in misleading so many in regard to these obvious beliefs is that truly abiding by these beliefs involves self-accountability and calls for great self-restraint. Many people want to do as they please, and so they do their best to avoid accountability—in this life, not to mention the hereafter. Satan capitalizes on these human tendencies by causing people to reject or confuse two concepts: God and the hereafter. Satan wants us to reject, ignore, or confuse those concepts so that they lose their impact in our lives and in this world.

Most people, however, do not absolutely reject the concept of the hereafter. Instead, they attempt to avoid its implications. Some do so by arguing that God's mercy and forgiveness will encompass everyone on the Day of Reckoning. Others say God has no need for our good deeds, which could never be good enough for Him anyway. It is true that God does not need our good deeds and that there is nothing we can do to thank God enough for His countless favors. However, our good deeds are for our own benefit—not for God who is free of all needs. Despite the fact that our good deeds are not sufficient for salvation, they *are* required by Him. Through them, we can hope to remedy our mistakes and sins so that we qualify for God's mercy, which is what can admit us to heaven.

Often (as is the case with many Muslims), the doctrine of hereafter is neither rejected nor distorted, but instead, it has been significantly watered down. However, no matter whether it has been rejected, twisted, or diluted, the outcome is the same. Its intended effect of motivating people to do good and to refrain from wrongdoing is severely weakened. As a result, many people live their lives as if they have been guaranteed admission to heaven.

The recurring deviation in human understanding of these doctrines warranted God sending messengers periodically to remind people in their communities of the basic truths. The prophets invited people to act accordingly by worshiping none but God, the Creator, and by striving to seek His pleasure through fulfilling His purpose (the mission of all humans). Those who answered the call of the messengers were promised a pleasant, fulfilled life on earth and eternal bliss in heaven.

REVELATION AND PROPHETHOOD

God placed Adam on earth after forgiving his sin and "inoculating" him against Satan. Therefore, as Islam teaches us, Adam began his life and mission on earth as a faithful servant of God. Moreover, all of Adam's descendants have been born pure and faithful; and all have been equipped with the power of reasoning and the ability to choose. Humanity is God's greatest creation. Even though the nature of man is good, however, God also created us as weak and forgetful beings. Because of this and because of the vicious threat posed by Satan as our enemy, God promised Adam and Eve (and all of us) His guidance. However, He also warned of the enormous consequences—in this life and in the hereafter—of accepting or rejecting that guidance.

> We said: "Get ye down all from here; and if, as is sure, there comes to you guidance from me, whosoever follows my guidance, on them shall be no fear, nor shall they grieve. But those who reject faith and belie our signs, they shall be companions of the Fire; they shall abide therein" [Qur'an 2:38–39].

> O ye Children of Adam! Whenever there come to you apostles from amongst you, rehearsing My signs unto you, those who are righteous and mend (their lives), on them shall be no fear nor shall they grieve. But those who reject Our signs and treat them with arrogance,- they are companions of the Fire, to dwell therein (for ever) [Qur'an 7:35–36].

He said: "Get ye down, both of you,- all together, from the Garden, with enmity one to another: but if, as is sure, there comes to you guidance from Me, whosoever follows my guidance, will not lose his way, nor fall into misery. But whosoever turns away from my message, verily for him is a life narrowed down, and We shall raise him up blind on the Day of Judgment" [Qur'an 20:123].

In a way, these verses indicate that those who fail in this life should question their compliance with the divine guidance and expectations.

That good and bad consequences for our choices exist in the hereafter is certain. Some of the consequences in this life may, however, be deferred. God may avert bad consequences out of His mercy or due to our repentance. Sometimes, bad consequences are averted because a person unknowingly complies with divine guidance and with the laws that govern the universe.

Our weak and forgetful nature results in our often getting caught up in a web of customs, superstitions, selfish desires, and/or false teaching. These shortcomings make it easier for Satan to fulfill his vow to assault us, as Adam's descendants, from all angles. Satan does this in order to mislead us from God's path. When we succumb to Satan's misguidance, we become unclean and contentious, and we long after what is forbidden. Our pure worship of the one true God is deflected, along with our love for our fellow human beings.

Under these circumstances, our only hope for salvation (individually or collectively as a society) rests on our avoidance of this misguidance and on the restoration of our natural inclination to submit to God's will. Our belief in spiritual truths has to be renewed, and the latent ability to distinguish between good and evil has to be reawakened. Because God is truly merciful, He does not merely abandon us when we stray, nor does He punish us without due warning through an accredited messenger:

Your Lord will never destroy towns without first raising a messenger in their capital to recite Our messages to them [Qur'an 28:59].

It is due to God's mercy that He sent a messenger to every nation to confirm the message of *Tawheed* and of the hereafter and to warn their people of the consequences of their rejection of God's guidance. Some three hundred messengers came with new revelations or scriptures. These served as the expression of God's will and the true standard of right and wrong. Some one hundred twenty-four thousand prophets (from Adam to Muhammad) came to remind their people of their duty to worship and serve God. Through Muhammad, the last to receive and deliver revelation from God, God completed that message to humanity with the Qur'an (the divine guidance) and terminated prophethood.

Many of these messengers are mentioned in the Qur'an, but most of them are not.

> Of some apostles We have already told thee the story; of others We have not;- and to Moses Allah spoke direct [Qur'an 4:164].

Those that came with scriptures include Moses with the Torah, Jesus with the Gospel, David with the Psalms, and Muhammad with the Qur'an.

> We have sent thee inspiration, as We sent it to Noah and the Messengers after him: we sent inspiration to Abraham, Isma'il, Isaac, Jacob and the Tribes, to Jesus, Job, Jonah, Aaron, and Solomon, and to David We gave the Psalms [Qur'an 4:163].

The Qur'an is the only authentic scripture from God that remains. The others are now either extinct or have been altered over the centuries by the hand of man.

In addition to embodying and preaching the message of *Tawheed*, all of these prophets and messengers led efforts of reform. They addressed people's deviations in faith and in conduct, particularly those that involved idolatry and the sin of rebellion against God. They all worked to establish justice and defeat evil. They taught that faith and obedience to God result in happiness, well-being, and salvation. As God's agents, they represented a powerful antidote to the satanic diseases that had permeated their societies. These prophets worked, never for their own benefit, but because they had been chosen by God to help people reconnect with Him as their Creator. The prophets were guided to live righteous, peaceful lives with one another and with the universe.

Because there is only one true and universal God, it follows that there can be only one true and universal faith. Islam, which literally means submission to God, is simply the name of that faith. All God's messengers since Adam delivered the same message. Therefore, all the messengers and prophets were messengers of Islam, and their true followers were Muslims (which simply means devoted servants).

From Adam to Muhammad, not only did the main tenets of belief remain the same but so did the tenets of worship and of morality. However, because all the books of revelation before the Qur'an (and all the messengers before Muhammad) were intended for a specific people during a specific time period, these earlier teachings focused on contemporary issues that were pertinent in their time. They were not meant to be universal or timeless. That is why they were not comprehensive, and it is also why God did not choose to preserve them in their original form.

Revelation Is a Gift

Given their impact on our lives now and in the hereafter, revelation and the messengers who brought it were God's greatest gifts to humanity. It would be disastrous for humanity to live without divine guidance. Imagine trying to operate a complex machine without access to a manual. Life is far more complex and has far higher stakes. Plus, salvation in the hereafter hinges on our performance in embodying and propagating the divine guidance. Declining the chance for salvation means voluntarily choosing eternal perpetuation in hellfire.

Unfortunately, though, all of us must contend with all the tricks and traps that our staunch enemy, Satan, has vowed to use to deceive and mislead us. Sadly, many will follow him in this life and end up ashamed and regretful on the Day of Judgment.

> Did I not enjoin on you, O ye Children of Adam, that ye should not worship (follow) Satan; for that he was to you an enemy avowed? [Qur'an 36:60].

Divine guidance is the best protection we have against Satan, so our compliance or our rejection of it has enormous consequences, not only in the hereafter but also in this life as well. Satan is seeking our demise in this life too. We can compare his work to the work of human viruses. Viruses are substantially more dangerous if our immune systems are weakened. Indeed, divine guidance is our spiritual immune system. It is the light that enables us to see truth as truth and falsehood as falsehood. Satan's work is made easier when we are either unaware or neglectful of divine guidance. This does not suggest, however, that when we follow divine guidance, we are completely immune. Satan never gives up on anyone. However, if we follow divine guidance, we will be more resistant to Satan's deception; and like a healthy body, we will be able to fight back.

The fact that our *purposeful* alignment with (or rejection of) divine guidance will exclusively determine our fate in the hereafter is sufficient reason for us to strive to understand it and live by it. Revelation is also our sole source of information about the unseen, with which our intellect is neither designed nor equipped to deal. The reality of God, many aspects of creation (and its purpose), life after death, and the resurrection and judgment are just a few of the unseen elements that we learn about only through revelation.

The glimpse that revelation gives us into the unseen is very important in at least two ways. First, without it, we could see only part of the total picture of life and creation, so our judgment could only be further compromised. Second, through granting us knowledge (albeit limited) of the unseen, revelation frees our intellect so that it can work to discover and leverage the laws that govern the universe and put them to use. That is what our intellect was designed to do, and that is how we can realize our full potential and fulfill our mission as God's stewards.

To be sure, throughout history, humanity has squandered tremendous time and effort and experienced considerable confusion in attempting to decode the unseen. This is true despite the fact that revelation provides incredibly simple and self-evident, yet compelling, truths regarding issues that have perplexed humanity for ages. Nonetheless, due to either an improper understanding of revelation or its total rejection, humanity has repeatedly failed to strike the necessary balance between faith and reason. Our straying from this balance, in either direction, has always been detrimental.

The multiple benefits of revelation may be difficult to perceive by those whose experience of religion is one of wars and/or the zealot's stifling of science and human progress. However, revelation itself had nothing to do with these horrible acts. Such human-made tragedies are mainly the result of mankind twisting the tenets of religion, an abuse typically driven by greed and a lust for power.

Revelation (divine guidance) is God's greatest gift to humanity. Following divine guidance determines our fate in the hereafter, helps us to maintain balance between faith and reason, informs us about the unseen, and ensures our proper use of faculties and resources. Clearly, compliance with revelation is crucial for our success, both in the hereafter and in this life. Remember, revelation is provided not only so that we can have salvation in the hereafter but also so that we may enjoy greater happiness and harmony in this life.

How Does Revelation Ensure Our Happiness?

The answer is very simple: Revelation from God ensures our happiness, as well as harmony among humans and with the universe, because of two facts: God is the Creator of all, and He intends for us to be happy and harmonious. Who knows better than God how to fulfill that intention? The Qur'an says:

> How could He who created not know His own creation? [Qur'an 67:14].

Because He is the Creator of everything, God knows best how we should conduct our lives and how we should interact with one another and with the universe so that we can experience inner peace and accord. Through revelation, God provides us with a robust and definite scale for determining right (therefore, beneficial) from wrong (therefore, harmful). Without such a scale, right and wrong would become subject to people's wishes and desires and to the prevailing balance of power (i.e., "might makes right" and the "law of the jungle"). Revelation helps to temper greed and arrogance by instilling humility and self-restraint. When properly applied, it helps to prevent man's misuse of knowledge and resources and our abuse of nature and of one another.

When people have entirely rejected the balance offered through revelation, or have misinterpreted or misapplied it, the result has been great mischief, abuse, and suffering. When (and if) we finally got it right, it was usually after considerable unnecessary suffering and wasting of time, resources, and human life.

Whereas our salvation in the hereafter hinges on our purposeful compliance with divine guidance, we do not have to intentionally align with divine guidance to enjoy individual and/or collective success and progress in this life. While God reserved His forgiveness, blessings, and rewards in the hereafter for those who consciously seek to earn them by doing the right things and doing things right, He made success in this life attainable to those who effectively leverage the laws He has embedded in the universe: the scientific laws. To get the best of both worlds, we must purposefully comply with divine guidance; *and* we must also do our utmost to discover and apply scientific laws—those governing the universe's physical aspects and those governing its social aspects. To illustrate this important concept, Ibn Khaldoun, a legendary Muslim sociologist, pointed to the vital importance of justice. He said justice is the foundation of civilization and prosperity regardless of the source of inspiration for such justice, while injustice ushers in destruction and the decline of civilization even when those involved are believers. And Ibn Taymiyyah, renowned Muslim scholar, said, "God makes the just nation of disbelievers prevail over the unjust nation of believers."

What makes people comply with divine guidance and reap the fruits of such compliance in this life and in the hereafter? Knowledge about divine guidance and belief in the hereafter do significantly increase the prospects. However, even that and knowledge about the benefits of compliance and the risks of rebellion do not guarantee compliance. On the other hand, people may accidentally comply with the divine guidance and may do the right thing because of instinct, mundane knowledge, previous experience, ambition, or because it is the norm and/or the law of society. However, there is nothing more effective than divine guidance in pointing out the shortest and surest path to righteousness and success and in boosting our self-restraint and our motivation to be righteous and successful.

The ability to discern right from wrong and the ability to choose are invaluable gifts from God, and they distinguish us from other creatures. Still, we have to defeat Satan's (direct and indirect) relentless attempts to blur the line between right and wrong and to weaken our resolve to do right and shun wrong. We must remember that he will capitalize on our ignorance, our weakness, and our desires. However, we can win out against him and save ourselves from misery and despair by faithfully following God's guidance and properly using our mental faculties. Doing so allows us to realize the noble destiny that God intended for us.

In summary, all revelation from God through His messengers was, and is, intended to instill a consciousness in humans of the one true and universal God. If we comply with the guidance provided in revelation, our lives will have a higher purpose. Revelation cultivates an incentive to do good and exercise self-restraint—critical elements for man's salvation in the hereafter and his happiness and harmony in this life too.

When we drive a car, the steering wheel, gas pedal, brakes, and road signs are necessary to instruct, steer, and restrain motorists. These are the necessary elements to enable us to drive safely from one location to another. Similarly, revelation instructs, steers, and restrains those who follow it. Revelation, when followed as intended, helps to ensure that we reach our destination safely, without hurting ourselves or others in the process and without suppressing lawful desires or stifling legitimate aspirations.

Clearly, for all the reasons we have stated and for others as well, the role of the divine guidance as a fixed and objective reference/criterion (*furqan*) and as an inspiration is crucial. Moreover, the proper understanding, embodiment, dissemination, and advocacy of the divine guidance are the main individual and collective duties of believers at all times and in all circumstances.

THE PROPHETHOOD OF MUHAMMAD (PBUH) AND THE PROPHETIC MODEL, LIFE, AND LEGACY

The Prophethood of Muhammad

Even though Muhammad reaffirmed the message of all the previous messengers, his prophethood is the most impactful event that has occurred or will ever occur—from the creation of Adam up until the Day of Judgment. Serving as the line of demarcation between two stages of the human journey, the divine guidance given to humanity through Muhammad marked the seal of prophethood and revelation as well as the maturity of humanity. After Muhammad's death, humanity was weaned of prophethood. His followers have, ever since, been entrusted with his complete and universal message and with his highly effective model for understanding, implementing, and promoting the timeless divine guidance within all earthly contexts until the end of time.

The messages that had been brought by others—beginning with Adam (the first prophet) up through Jesus—were all customized for the societies to which they came. The prophets' miracles involved physical and tangible (*hissiyah*) elements, many of which were witnessed by the respective prophet's own people. They also were able to view the remnants left after the destruction of disbelievers that had preceded them. Up to Abraham's prophethood, the consequences for people's accepting or rejecting divine guidance were immediate and also physical and tangible: The rejecters were annihilated, and the prophets and their followers were saved. Eventually, however, deviation would creep in among their progeny, a new messenger was sent as a reminder, and the cycle repeated itself.

A turning point in the history of prophethood was the life and leadership of Abraham, who is referred to as the father of the prophets:

> And We gave (Abraham) Isaac and Jacob, and ordained among his progeny Prophethood and Revelation [Qur'an 29:27].

With the advent of Abraham (and more precisely, with the appearance of his grandson Jacob who is also known as Israel), the divine mission—which had been entrusted to individual prophets since the time of Adam—was entrusted to an entire nation of people: the children of Israel. God empowered them in many ways, particularly by appointing prophets and kings among them:

> Remember Moses said to his people: "O my people! Call in remembrance the favor of God unto you, when He produced prophets among you, made you kings, and gave you what He had not given to any other among the peoples" [Qur'an 5:20].

From Abraham up through Jesus (the last prophet before Muhammad), messengers continued to be sent to a specific people at a specific time. These messengers performed concrete miracles and delivered divine guidance in order to uplift their people and teach them about the consequences of their choices. People also learned about the consequences of good or bad performance in fulfilling their life mission. However, nations/communities were no longer destroyed when they failed to carry out their mission or rejected the message of divine guidance.

As was true in Adam's experience in heaven, this approach (utilized through all the prophets before Muhammad) aimed to spiritually awaken and enlighten people and to stimulate the human faculties of reasoning and the will to choose. It taught people about the consequences of their choices, and it prepared humanity to take full responsibility for the divine mission after being weaned of prophethood.

With Muhammad's message, God perfected and promised to preserve His universal and eternal guidance—a guidance that contained all the elements that people would need in all contexts until the end of time. The guidance spelled out what needed to be spelled out, but it was flexible enough to stand the test of time. Muhammad's mission involved inviting, directly and indirectly (through his followers), all of humanity to comply with the divine guidance and to individually and collectively fulfill the purpose of creation by taking on the mission of the prophets.

In this regard, Muhammad's prophethood initiated a different approach to ensuring the relevance of God's message to society. Whereas before Muhammad, a new messenger was sent to his own people with a customized message in their own language; afterward, all of humanity was charged with the responsibility of developing and constantly evolving a relevant Islamic construct:

> We sent not an apostle except (to teach) in the language of his (own) people, in order to make (things) clear to them [Qur'an 14:4].

The message that had been presented to selected messengers and given to particular nations through those messengers would now be provided to all humanity. God's assignments, carried in that divine guidance, would also now go to all humanity.

In order to be truly universal, Muhammad's message had (and has) to be "contagious." It is the duty of each and every one of his followers to act as Muhammad's emissary. That means we are to convey his message to everyone around us in the best possible way, and we should encourage all those who accept it to do the same. Hence, we are to become witnesses for all people, just as Muhammad was a witness for his companions:

> Thus, have We made of you an umma justly balanced, that ye might be witnesses over the nations, and the Messenger a witness over yourselves [Qur'an 2:143].

And strive in His cause as ye ought to strive, (with sincerity and under discipline). He has chosen you, and has imposed no difficulties on you in religion; it is the cult of your father Abraham. It is He who has named you Muslims, both before and in this (Revelation); that the Messenger may be a witness for you, and ye be witnesses for mankind [Qur'an 22:78].

The Sunna (the divinely inspired, scrutinized, and preserved words and deeds) of Muhammad serves to further detail and/or explain God's guidance. Both the Qur'an and Sunna are tremendously flexible. Outside of matters of belief, worship, and morality, they provide only general guidelines and leave considerable room for human ingenuity and creativity. Their main focus is the purification of the human soul through instilling God-consciousness and connecting people to God, thus committing people to their divine mission. This gives people a higher life meaning and purpose, and it provides them with a consistent frame of reference. The Sunna also presents the necessary model for our successful understanding, implementation, and promotion of God's message (individually and collectively) and for our building and leading a mission-driven community of believers (a movement).

Equipped with the perfect, universal, and timeless guidance of the Qur'an and the versatile prophetic model, humanity (in general, but particularly the followers of Muhammad) was assigned the duty of ensuring the relevance/ freshness and the spread of the divine guidance in all contexts at all times. Individually and collectively, humanity became not only the custodian of the earth but also the custodian of the divine guidance. Our mission is to properly and efficiently develop and manage the earth and to embody, disseminate, and advocate the divine guidance in a relevant way. It goes without saying that this huge responsibility requires that we strive to become the best possible embodiments of the divine guidance. We must strive to be mindful of God and to completely surrender to Him as is His due. It is also our responsibility to ensure appropriate and constant evolution of that guidance and, when necessary, to undertake a periodic revival/renewal of its understanding and application. Importantly, when divine guidance is being introduced to a new culture, a fresh Islamic construct is needed; and it should be produced by projecting Islam's original texts within the new cultural context. All other constructs may well be useful, but they should neither be binding nor limiting.

In conclusion, Muhammad's prophethood reaffirmed and superseded previous revelations. It also delineated the divine mission, making that mission the explicit individual and collective responsibility of all humanity until the end of time. People no longer had an excuse, and there was no additional prophet for whom we should wait. An essential part of our mission is to properly replicate the prophetic model.

The Prophetic Model

Muhammad's model and legacy constitute essential elements of our proposed movement because they are critical to understanding Islamic history and confronting the reality that Muslims face today. Indeed, the prophetic model is the key to developing a vision and strategy for communal and societal reform. To be sure, the main reason behind the decline of the great Islamic civilizations was their neglect and/or twisting of the divine guidance, the divine mission, and the prophetic model. That led to the civilizations' subsequent practice of Islam in a superficial, rigid, out-of-context manner. People neglected certain essential elements while overemphasizing other minor elements.

The prophetic model was designed to be a replicable model of individual and collective fulfillment of the divine purpose within different contexts. However, in attempting to replicate it, our strategy is to determine, based on what Muhammad actually did during his life, what he *would* do here and now within *our* society during our time. This requires an in-depth analysis and understanding of the model. This project is essentially an attempt to answer that fundamental question: What would Muhammad do in twenty-first century America?

By all accounts, the prophetic model was (and is) an incredibly successful model for building a very effective community—a community that championed a great civilization under very unfavorable conditions. Its greatness is actually due to its replicability, which is essential in ensuring the timeless and universal relevance of the divine guidance that the prophetic model propagated. In essence, Muhammad was successful in giving his followers a life mission and a way of life. He inspired and empowered them to fulfill the divine mission in their respective environments. He also built a movement that fulfilled this divine mission within the larger society. His model transformed and groomed the members of his community, both individually and collectively, so that they were inspired and driven by this mission. The resulting unity of purpose and leadership that was grounded in faith cemented the community and generated an unstoppable force that changed the face of earth and the course of history within one generation.

All of this was made possible simply through Muhammad's advocacy of the same message that had been delivered by all of God's previous messengers: that man was created to fulfill the divine purpose—worshiping God and striving to be the best embodiments and instruments of His will. The commitment to such a mission places believers on a lifelong journey. Three constant aspects of that journey are self-development (*tazkiya*), reaching out to others and cooperating for the common good as we deliver the message of Islam (*dawa*), and civic engagement (*islah*). These three endeavors serve to purify the believers' souls and help them to realize their full potential while effecting positive change within their environments.

Also key to the transformation of Muhammad's companions and followers was the incredibly effective leadership component of his model. A brief mention of its main tenets will suffice here, as the details of his leadership will be discussed later.

Like other tenets of Islam, the prophetic leadership model is unbelievably simple. It is firmly grounded in faith and based on the consent of the people. In this model, leaders and their advisors and followers all execute their various roles as an act of worship performed to earn the pleasure of God and the well-being of their community or nation. That is how this model was effective in combining elements that are usually perceived as incompatible. The result was the achievement of desired outcomes that other leadership models have been struggling to achieve up until this very day. Some of those elements include consultation, decisiveness, discipline, individual and collective leadership, reverence of leadership, and empowerment of members.

Best described as a "leader-of-leaders" model, Muhammad's model reveres leadership but mandates both consultation and compliance on the part of everyone (leaders and members). Compliance is required in the following areas: with tenets of Islam, with any binding agreements or laws, and with any properly made decision. Fostering in each believer a sense of ownership of their community's mission and also a sense of responsibility for advancing the well-being of humanity, the model encourages everyone to lead. Within every context and at every level, however, a leader is appointed or selected to lead all these leaders (with their consent). This leader of leaders fully understands the magnitude (both in this life and, most importantly, in the hereafter) of his or her responsibility to make the best final decisions on behalf of the community. This realization pushes each leader to strive to be the best possible example of seeking God's pleasure and to render the decisions that are most pleasing to God. The leader of leaders is consequently propelled to not only exercise due caution but also seek the advice and expertise of his or her constituents. Consultation, therefore, is viewed as neither a formality nor an act of flattery, but rather as an obligation, a Sunna of Muhammad, and a fundamental characteristic of the community of believers:

> . . . and consult them in affairs (of moment) [Qur'an 3:159].

> Those who hearken to their Lord, and establish regular prayer; who (conduct) their affairs by mutual consultation [Qur'an 42:38].

When this leadership model is functioning properly, individuals don't abandon their responsibility and role in ensuring that the best decision is made. They don't hesitate to advise their leader—both as a right and as a duty.

In other words, the appointed leader's heightened sense of responsibility does not diminish the constituents' sense of responsibility; nor does the extensive consultation process act to paralyze the community or shrink the leader's authority. So while the roles may differ, the goal is to reach the best decision; and everyone should contribute toward that goal.

Additionally, the leader cannot make a decision that violates either God's commandments or any agreed-upon covenant without being confronted by the community's efforts to correct him or her. If necessary, the community may override or refuse to comply with a bad decision and/or impeach a wayward leader.

Magically, the model makes everyone responsible without undermining the authority of the leader, which is commensurate with his/her greater responsibility. It combines the best of individual and collective leadership models.

Once a decision is properly made, the focus shifts to its successful and disciplined implementation, irrespective of anyone's prior positions. This approach adds to the unity of purpose and direction created by the movement's compelling mission. That's what will sustain the mobilization and cohesion of the community without compromising decisiveness and discipline. Finally, because all the tenets of the model are grounded in faith, they are executed devoutly, spontaneously, and effectively. This is all done with a great sense of discipline and responsibility.

One of the key ingredients in the success of the prophetic model was its strategy, as this has made the model a timeless blueprint for building and leading a movement to fulfill its mission and effect change. Not only did Muhammad have a clear vision, but he also had a roadmap that delineated very clear stages and milestones for achievement. His course of action was based on the relentless engagement of an ever-widening circle, with each stage of reform overlapping the next to ensure a smooth transition from one phase to another. The process is comparable to a relay race wherein the overlap and transition are crucial to winning the race.

The compelling mission engendered high aspirations and motivations, which one companion expressed by saying, "God sent us to save humanity." Meanwhile, the leadership model ensured decisiveness and discipline and precluded power struggle and paralysis. The mission and the leadership model worked together to ensure the sustained cohesion and mobilization of the community, while the overall strategy ensured continued motivation and growth. Everything worked together to prevent stagnation and preclude power struggles and paralysis. The rest is history.

The Prophet used his model to build an incredibly effective movement. That movement effected momentous and lasting global change and gave birth to a leading world civilization within the three decades following Muhammad's death. The movement was an essential part of the prophetic legacy, which included a mission/message and a model, as well as the movement.

Muhammad's Legacy

Even though Muhammad's followers were mostly illiterate people in a fairly primitive society, they thoroughly understood the implications of his final and universal prophethood and their role as his heirs. His companions wholeheartedly accepted their individual and collective duties to fulfill the divine purpose of creation and the mission of all of the prophets. They fully comprehended the gravity of their obligation to convey and preserve God's final and universal message to all people until the end of time.

It is apparent from the way the companions handled matters after Muhammad's death that they assumed, without the slightest reservation or doubt, total responsibility for fulfilling the divine purpose and for expanding and sustaining the movement Muhammad had led for almost a quarter of a century. It can be easily concluded from their behavior that the companions completely grasped the grave necessity of ensuring the timeless and universal relevance of the divine message that the Prophet had brought to humanity. The companions understood that which we must understand: the divine message calls for and requires the constant and successful transfer and adaptation of the whole paradigm across all cultures and generations.

The unequivocal adoption of the prophetic mission during the era of the rightly guided Caliphs may have been due to Muhammad's followers' matchless devotion, the Prophet's superior leadership and mentorship, and possibly their mastery of the Arabic language. As a result, they developed an in-depth and coherent understanding of the letter and spirit of both the Qur'an and Islam in general. Probably of additional importance was the fact that they recognized Muhammad's dual role as

- the infallible human being that God had elected to receive, embody, and convey His final and universal message to humanity; and as
- their leader whose life, leadership, and movement were to serve as a model for humanity during, not only Muhammad's earthly life but also until the end of time.

Understanding Muhammad's dual role seems to be one of the main factors that helped the companions comprehend the prophetic paradigm. Certain Qur'anic verses indicate that the companions well understood that Muhammad's role as God's messenger would only continue for a limited timeframe. They well knew that after the revelation had been perfected and completed, Muhammad would eventually leave this world:

> This day have I perfected your religion for you, completed my favor upon you, and have chosen for you Islam as your religion [Qur'an 5:3].

> Truly thou wilt die (one day), and truly they (too) will die (one day) [Qur'an 39:30].

They knew that after Muhammad, there would be no revelations and no messengers. God promised to protect His final and universal message from corruption. "We have, without doubt, sent down the Message; and We will assuredly guard it (from corruption)" [Qur'an 15:9]. However, it would be the believers' individual and collective duty to ensure the continuous relevance of the divine guidance through constant revival/renewal and fresh constructs.

All these conclusions could be easily deduced from the way the companions dealt with the Prophet and handled the transition after his death and from their individual and collective behavior during the subsequent era of the rightly guided Caliphs. Indeed, a number of incidents that took place during the Prophet's life testify to the companions' understanding of Muhammad's dual role. For example, following the Prophet's decision regarding where they were to camp before the battle of Badr, Al-Hubab ibn al-Mundhir asked him whether his choice was the result of divine inspiration or whether it was merely his decision as their leader. Indeed, with respect to Muhammad's second role as a leader, a number of decisions made during the critical period after his death illustrate the realization by his companions that, in addition to swift and smooth transition of leadership, continuous application of the prophetic model was vital. That was the only way to continuously implement the divine guidance and fulfill the divine mission in different contexts. Cases in point include three decisions made by Muhammad's successor: Abu Bakr's decided to fight against the mutiny that erupted, he decided to assemble the Qur'an, and he decided to appoint Omar as his successor. Another example is Omar's decision to suspend the penalty for theft during the year of famine.

A number of decisions like these, made after the Prophet died, prove that the companions understood that the Prophet's life was a model of how to comprehend and implement divine guidance and fulfill the divine mission in different contexts. The companions understood not only the letter but also the spirit of the divine guidance and the prophetic model.

Their actions were based on their in-depth understanding of the Prophet's decisions. That understanding led them to ask and correctly answer the questions: "What would the Prophet have done under these circumstances?" – and "What course of action will be most pleasing to God?" Some of the decisions made by Muhammad's successors were opposed by some of the companions on the basis of a literal understanding of the Qur'an and Sunna and/or because the decisions involved doing things that Muhammad hadn't actually done himself (e.g., the collection and assembly of the Qur'an).

The model worked well for about three decades after the death of the

Prophet. It was not until the assassination of Uthman (Omar's successor) that the prophetic model started to crumble. Still, its foundations were so strong that it didn't entirely collapse until twelve centuries later with the demise of the Ottoman Empire. Despite a gradual weakening of the model's main tenets over the 1,200-year period, like a healthy body, the Muslim world kept rebounding from internal diseases and external assaults—and it kept sustaining the great world civilization that had emerged from the prophetic model and legacy.

Unfortunately, however, Muslims (even, often, devout Muslims) either neglected, or committed a compounded injustice against, the prophetic model. First, they overlooked the most important elements of Muhammad's legacy: his mission, his leadership model, and his movement. In particular, they disregarded the essential reality that his life was intended to serve as a model for building and sustaining a movement to fulfill the divine mission assigned to all humans. Instead, they focused exclusively on the personal aspects of his life and his worship—often still neglecting his most important character and personality traits, such as his vibrant spirituality, his robust character, and his unmatched compassion.

Their whole approach to understanding and implementing Muhammad's model became flawed because their focus was on his actions—without ever attempting to understand the "why" behind them, much less to figure out what he probably would have done within their own contemporary context. The result was a superficial, literal and rigid, incoherent, and imbalanced interpretation that largely accounts for our inability and/or our unwillingness to try to replicate his model so that we might produce similar results. In a nutshell, the consequence is our current and unenviable situation.

The project outlined in this book is an attempt to restore the prophetic model in our current American context and to apply it in transforming our stagnant and fragmented community into a vibrant, relevant, and impactful movement.

THE DIVINE MISSION

Typically, Islam is defined as submission to God or as a way of life. However, both of these definitions focus on Islam's religious and/or personal aspects and fail to take into account its social and civic aspects. The concept of submission to God could carry a passive connotation, and most Muslims view Islam as a way of life in the context of personal and family life. One of the most obvious but overlooked characteristics of Islam is that it is a life mission, with very entrenched humane, civic, and social dimensions.

Here, when we speak of Islam, we are referring to an individual and collective life mission. Islam is a mission that is divine because it constitutes the purpose for our creation: to worship God and to serve as His vicegerent or representative on earth. It is also a mission upon which our reckoning will be based. It is a mission that was assigned by God to all human beings, both individually and collectively, making it eternal and universal. We must all strive and cooperate to fulfill the divine purpose. Therefore, Islam is neither a religion, in the traditional sense of the word, nor simply a way of life as many devout Muslims believe.

From the outset, fulfilling the divine mission and, therefore, the divine purpose has always been both an individual and a social duty. The individual component of this duty consists of worship (*ibaadah*) and self-development (*tazkiya*). The social component consists of conveying the message of Islam and inviting others to it (*dawa /ta'beed*), as well as reform (*islah*). Although the methodology, the discourse, and the ordering of priorities of the divine mission may differ from one context to another, the purpose and goal are always the same: the uplifting of society toward excellence in this life (freedom, justice, harmony/peace, social cohesion, and prosperity) and salvation in the hereafter. We must somehow manage to cooperate with each other to fulfill this mission, even as we strive to compete to meet our needs, serve our interests, and fulfill our ambitions. Circumstances may well find us in conflict with each other, particularly as the world becomes smaller and more complex, but we must still work together to fulfill the divine purpose.

Even though the divine mission is eternal and universal, before Muhammad's prophethood, it was primarily entrusted to individual messengers and their disciples. Their societies were fairly simple at that point, and God's message to them was a customized message, brought by a messenger from their own people. That message called people to God and addressed the pertinent issues of their time. The seal of God's messengers, Muhammad, was sent with a universal and timeless message that, unlike previous messages, spelled out the divine mission and humanity's responsibility toward fulfilling it. Moreover, the divine mission (particularly its reform component) became more structured and elaborate, involving a movement based on Muhammad's model for understanding and implementing the fixed divine guidance within changing contexts.

Muhammad passed on to his followers—until the end of time—not only the divine guidance and the divine mission but also a movement and a model. Our main—individual and collective—duty is to preserve this legacy: to properly use the model to rebuild and/or expand the movement and fulfill the mission, which should be "translated" into a relevant and inspiring rallying cause and a platform. This is, of course, easier said than done, and this individual and collective duty entails the following crucial tasks:

- Ensuring the freshness and relevance of the divine guidance, which God promised to preserve and guard against corruption. Because the divine guidance is constant, but life is always changing (from one place to another and from one era to another), there is a constant need to revitalize society's understanding, implementation, and promotion of Islam and to develop a new construct whenever necessary, particularly when the process of renewal has stalled or Islam is being introduced to a new society. It also requires Muslims to be engaged in their environments and abreast of life's challenges and changes. Before Muhammad, the continuous relevance of the divine guidance was ensured by repeatedly sending a new messenger, with a fresh and customized revelation, to every nation and every historical era.

- Striving to worship and to be mindful of God as is His due. This involves striving to make all of life an act of worship, challenging and pushing ourselves to improve everything we do and increasing our efforts to get closer to God. Together with the process of constant renewal and revival, our worship and self-development will help us to become the best embodiments of God's will (the divine guidance) and the best models for society. This will pave the way for the promotion and advocacy of the divine guidance.

- Conveying God's final and universal message to all of humanity, starting with the people in our immediate environments. This is done most effectively through our exemplary conduct, viable models, relevant discourse, active outreach, and our significant and sustained contribution to the common good. Our goal should not be converting others to Islam, but simply informing them of God's final message (sent to them just as it was sent to us) in a compassionate and natural manner that makes it easy for them to accept that which is best for all of us—both in this life and in the hereafter. When someone shows an interest in learning about Islam, we must be careful to inform them in the correct manner and time and in the correct dosage. *Dawa* is not about preaching or converting; rather, it is about guiding and connecting people to God through our example and advice.

Call unto the way of thy Lord with wisdom and goodly exhortation, and argue with them in a way that is best. Surely, thy Lord knows best who has strayed from His way; and He knows those who are rightly guided [Qur'an 16:126].

Conveying the message in the proper way is both an individual and a collective duty that should be fulfilled until all people have received His final and universal message (i.e., until the end of time). Whether or not our message is received positively should not affect our kindness and fairness toward others, nor should it affect our mutual respect and our cooperation with fellow citizens and other members of the human family. This component of the divine mission should propel the believers to reach out to the people around them and to establish and nurture an ever-growing social network.

– Striving to make the world a better place, starting with our respective environments and those around us. This involves striving to positively impact on society by contributing to the common good and constantly expanding our social circles. It is necessary, in today's world, that believers be constantly aware and engaged civically and that they constantly strive to uplift their society and their fellow human beings.

– "Translating" the divine guidance and the divine mission into a viable way of life, a compelling cause, and a platform for reform.

– Cooperating with other believers in fulfilling the divine mission. All these tasks are not only individual but also collective responsibilities. That's why the Prophet built a movement, which his followers must maintain, expand whenever possible, and rebuild whenever necessary. The movement should be built and run according to the prophetic model, which, like the divine guidance, was meant to be universal and timeless. Believers must ensure its renewed freshness and relevance.

Throughout much of Islam's history, Muslims have more or less fulfilled these components of the divine mission and preserved the prophetic legacy. As a result, the divine guidance remained more or less relevant, and Muslims remained more or less mobilized and united. However, gradually (and for some time now), the divine mission was abandoned. Muslims largely lost their unity and their relevance, and the prevailing construct(s) of Islam became too rigid to keep up with the world's changes and too localized and culturally biased to be effectively established in a new context. Although their failure to significantly renew and revive Islam has been partly out of an attempt to protect it from heresy, Muslims' understanding and implementation of Islam has become more and more formalistic, legalistic, and ritualistic. In other words, Islam (or specifically Muslims' understanding of it) has become confined in both time and in space, losing its relevance, coherence, and ability to inspire.

Moreover, the neglect of the divine mission and also neglect of essential elements of the prophetic model have resulted in Islam being perceived more as a personal and private religion and way of life. Thus, Islam has been effectively stripped of its power to mobilize and unify believers. Consequently, Muslim communities have become largely stagnant, fragmented, and disengaged.

Communities and nations can't generally thrive without a driving cause. This is particularly true of our Muslim community because we are dependent on our divine mission to define who we are and to motivate and unify us. Our mission is our raison d'être. Only a divine mission can engender and sustain a true and impactful community of believers.

Historically, there has hardly been a better indicator of the state of our Muslim community than our commitment to—and our proper translation of—the mission of Islam and our sincerity, generosity, and efficiency in carrying it out. That's what has always determined our relevance and impact and our contribution to the advancement of humanity at large.

It was indeed in order to fulfill the divine mission (which necessitated effecting change) that Muhammad built his movement. That's what caused the Quraish (the leading tribe in Mecca) to fight them so relentlessly, and that has always been people's main source of objection to their messengers. Before his prophethood, the Quraish weren't bothered by the fact that Muhammad (as well as a few others in Mecca) did not worship idols, because his individual position regarding idolatry did not seriously challenge the status quo. They also would not have cared if, after the advent of his prophethood, he and his followers had simply wanted to build a community of Muslims (or in today's terms, a community of "activists"), as long as they stuck to managing their own affairs without attempting to effect societal change. The Quraish attacks against Muhammad and the Muslims were not waged in order to defend their idols; rather, they merely wanted to maintain the status quo.

The divine mission is a pivotal component of this movement, which shall be championed by mission-driven, patriotic, and compassionate Muslim Americans who are committed to Islam as a life mission and to America as a homeland. Let us take a more detailed look at this mission in the following section.

The Divine Mission Explained

As stated before, the divine mission is eternal and universal. It constitutes the purpose of the creation and the basis for our reckoning, and it is assigned to all human beings. Essentially, fulfilling the divine purpose requires that we strive to the best of our ability (and to the bitter end) to fulfill God's purpose in pursuit of His pleasure. It means that we completely surrender our lives to God and conduct all of our affairs according to His guidance. Indeed, God created us but to worship Him and appointed us to be His stewards (*khalifa*) on earth. This implies that we must constantly strive and challenge ourselves, individually and collectively, to be the best embodiments and instruments of His will.

Before Muhammad's prophethood, this mission was entrusted to God's messengers and their close disciples. Regarding Moses, the Qur'an says,

> We did aforetime give Moses the (Book of) Guidance, and We gave the book in inheritance to the Children of Israel [Qur'an 40:53].

However, after Muhammad, the divine mission was assigned to all of humanity and particularly to Muhammad's followers until the end of time. The Qur'an is explicit about the transfer of the responsibility for the divine mission to the believers:

Thus, have We made of you an umma justly balanced, that ye might be witnesses over the nations, and the Messenger a witness over yourselves [Qur'an 2:143].

And strive in His cause as ye ought to strive, (with sincerity and under discipline). He has chosen you, and has imposed no difficulties on you in religion; it is the cult of your father Abraham. It is He who has named you Muslims, both before and in this (Revelation); that the Messenger may be a witness for you, and ye be witnesses for mankind [Qur'an 22:178].

In his farewell sermon, Muhammad instructed those who were present to convey the message to those who were absent. Because his was the final and universal message, by "those who were absent," he meant all people until the end of time.

The Qur'an not only reaffirmed the divine mission but also delineated a number of roles that humanity in general and particularly believers must play:

1. Vicegerent/steward (khalifa) on earth

In announcing the creation of man, God told the angels that He was appointing him as a vicegerent on earth:

... when your Lord told the angels, "I am creating a successor on earth" [Qur'an 2:30].

Put another way, if managing the earth is viewed as a business, man is the manager (as opposed to being simply an employee) responsible for running and overseeing the entire business according to the specifications of the owner, who is God.

As God's vicegerents, it is up to us to discover His laws for the governance of both the physical and human aspects of the universe. The Qur'an reveals some of these laws, but it repeatedly urges us to contemplate the way the universe functions so that we might discover other laws. Understanding and properly leveraging the laws of the universe is a must if we are to succeed in managing and developing the earth. Indeed, the Qur'an is full of verses that explicitly and implicitly invite people to ponder creation and to contemplate the rise and fall of societies/nations. The Qur'an praises those who do contemplate these events and phenomena. One verse praises the men of understanding— those who engage in spiritual and intellectual development.

> Behold! in the creation of the heavens and the earth, and the alternation of night and day,- there are indeed signs for men of understanding,- Men who celebrate the praises of Allah, standing, sitting, and lying down on their sides, and contemplate the (wonders of) creation in the heavens and the earth, (With the thought) [Qur'an 3:190–191].

And in another verse, God says that the role of the messenger is to explain the message so that others may reflect.

> And We have sent down unto thee (also) the Message; that thou mayest explain clearly to men what is sent for them, and that they may ponder [Qur'an 16:44].

2. Worshiping God (Ibadah)

In indicating the purpose of creation, God says, "I did not create jinn and humans except to worship me" [Qur'an 52:56]. Therefore, if worshiping God is the sole purpose of creation, we must strive to make our entire lives a continuous act of worship so that we are ever conscious of Him and ever drawing closer to Him. We must work at cultivating an increasingly intimate relationship with Him. Muhammad informed us that God says, "My servant keeps coming closer to me with extra deeds until I love him."[20] The Qur'an sets the bar very high when it commands us to be mindful of God, as is His due [Qur'an 3:102].

Along with our role as *khalifa*, this aspect of the divine mission indicates that we are to strive to live with God and for God and to be the best embodiments and instruments of His will:

> Say: "Truly, my prayer and my service of sacrifice, my life

---

20   Hadith narrated by Abu Hurayrah and reported in Sahih Al-Bukhari.

and my death, are (all) for God, the Cherisher of the Worlds"
[Qur'an 6:162].

3. God's helpers (Ansar)

God says, "O ye who believe! Be ye helpers of Allah. As said Jesus the son of Mary to the Disciples, 'Who will be my helpers to (the work of) Allah.' Said the disciples, 'We are Allah's helpers!'" [Qur'an 61:14].

This verse commands all believers, until the end of time, to champion God's cause—like the disciples who responded to Jesus's call to support him in his mission.

Championing the cause of God is synonymous with fulfilling His purpose and doing His will. Thus, believers should constantly strive to become the best embodiments and instruments of God's will. This is the thrust of the message of Islam, and it is a condition for God's help, which makes it possible for believers to prevail. Without God's help, we would be on our own:

God is sure to help those who help His cause [Qur'an 22:40].

You who believe, if you help God, He will help you and make you stand firm [Qur'an 47:7].

If God helps you, none can overcome you: If He forsakes you, who is there, after that, that can help you? In God, then, let believers put their trust [Qur'an 3:160].

4. Standing for God (kawwamina lillah)

O ye who believe! Stand out firmly for God, as witnesses to fair dealing [Qur'an 5:8].

This aspect is very similar to the previous aspect of helping God. It reinforces the mandate of believers to serve as soldiers and advocates of God.

5. Witnesses for God (over nations) and heirs to prophets:

This aspect refers to guiding people to God and to the truth through our actions and our interaction with others. Consider a witness in a courtroom.

His or her testimony helps the judge and/or jury come to an informed decision. Believers should help the people around them make informed decisions that serve their best interests—in this life and in the hereafter. This is exactly the role played by the prophets and messengers with their people and should be carried out with passion and compassion.

6. Inviting others to the way of God

Invite (all) to the Way of thy Lord with wisdom and beautiful preaching [Qur'an 16:125].

Who is better in speech than one who calls (men) to God, works righteousness, and says, "I am of those who bow in Islam"? [Qur'an 41:33].

Inviting others to Islam means guiding them to God and to what is best for them in this life and the hereafter. Fulfilling this role reaffirms the transfer of the message from the prophets to the believers, following the seal of prophethood. These verses also emphasize the importance of exercising wisdom and appropriateness in calling people to the way of God.

7. Commanding that which is good and forbidding that which is evil

Ye are the best of peoples, evolved for mankind, enjoining what is right, forbidding what is wrong, and believing in God [Qur'an 3:110].

Let there arise out of you a band of people inviting to all that is good, enjoining what is right, and forbidding what is wrong. They are the ones to attain felicity [Qur'an 3:104].

The believers, men and women, are protectors one of another: they enjoin what is just and forbid what is evil; they observe regular prayers, practice regular charity, and obey God and His Messenger. On them will God pour His mercy, for God is exalted in power, wise [Qur'an 9:71].

(They are) those who, if We establish them in the land, establish regular prayer and give regular charity, enjoin the right and forbid wrong; with God rests the end (and decision) of (all) affairs [Qur'an 22:41].

In the above verses, enjoining good and forbidding evil is linked to faith, prayer, and *zakat* (regular charity)—indicating that it is as important and that it is an individual and collective obligation. It is a loaded concept as it assigns the role of effecting positive change to the believers—wherever they might live. It is the fulfillment of this duty that confers a special status upon the community of believers.

Muhammad repeatedly emphasized the importance of taking a stand for righteousness. In one Hadith (saying of the Prophet), he said, "Whoever sees a wrongdoing, let him correct it."[21] In another Hadith, he made it clear that passiveness in the face of mischief is not an (accepted) option and does not protect even the most devout person from God's wrath. And in a third, the Prophet warned about the grave consequences of passiveness in the face of wrongdoing, even if the wrongdoers have the best of intentions. The same Hadith also indicates that wrongdoing affects everyone, including those who allow it to happen. Believers are not expected to simply avoid mischief and wrongdoing, or to just curse and/or complain about it as many do nowadays. They must seek to correct it through any legitimate and effective means that are available to them, provided that this does not result in greater mischief.

"Commanding that which is good and forbidding that which is evil" is closely related to another Qur'anic concept called engagement (*tadaafu'*). Indeed, as we become more and more positive and take a stand when needed, we will automatically engage other societal groups and forces. The Qur'an tells us that if it were not for this engagement, mischief and destruction would spread on earth, and freedom (of religion) would be abolished.

By Allah's will they routed them; and David slew Goliath; and Allah gave him power and wisdom and taught him whatever (else) He willed. And did not Allah Check one set of people by means of another, the earth would indeed be

---

21 Hadith narrated by Abu Saeed Al-Khudary and reported in the Hadith book of Imam Ahmad.

full of mischief: But Allah is full of bounty to all the worlds [Qur'an 2:251].

(They are) those who have been expelled from their homes in defiance of right,- (for no cause) except that they say, "our Lord is Allah. Did not Allah check one set of people by means of another, there would surely have been pulled down monasteries, churches, synagogues, and mosques, in which the name of Allah is commemorated in abundant measure. Allah will certainly aid those who aid his (cause);- for verily Allah is full of Strength, Exalted in Might, (able to enforce His will)" [Qur'an 22:40].

8. Reform/Betterment (Islah)

In speaking of prophet Shuaib, the Qur'an summarized the mission of all the prophets and, therefore, of all their followers in one word: *islah*, which means reform, betterment, or simply serving the greater good.

He (Shuaib) said: "O my people! see ye whether I have a Clear (Sign) from my Lord, and He hath given me sustenance (pure and) good as from Himself? I wish not, in opposition to you, to do that which I forbid you to do. I only desire (your) betterment to the best of my power; and my success (in my task) can only come from Allah. In Him I trust, and unto Him I look" [Qur'an 11:88].

Indeed, the Qur'an makes it clear that the prophets were both messengers and reformers. The indications that we are to effect reform are very similar to those suggesting that we are to encourage that which is good and forbid that which is evil. Both suggest that, wherever they are, believers should seek to attain the best possible conditions for their people and their nation.

9. Inviting to that which is good

Be a community that calls for what is good. [Qur'an 3:104].

This aspect of the divine mission reaffirms the fact that God invites all humans to do and to experience that which is good for them and in their best interests, both in this life and in the hereafter. The invitation (*dawa*) concept also entails believers inviting others to act in their own best interests. We are to try to positively influence other people's choices and lives—both through our examples and our interaction with them. The invitation to experience that which is good also implies that we should seek that which is good from all sources. Muhammad indicated that believers should always be on the lookout for wisdom, wherever it may be.

10. Standing for Justice

O you who believe stand out firmly for justice [Qur'an 4:135].

Among all the good that we should seek and support, justice comes first. God commands justice, and justice is the purpose for His sending messengers and revelations to humanity:

> Allah commands justice, the doing of good, and liberality to kith and kin, and He forbids all shameful deeds, and injustice and rebellion: He instructs you, that ye may receive admonition [Qur'an 16:90].

> We sent aforetime our apostles with Clear Signs and sent down with them the Book and the Balance (of Right and Wrong), that men may stand forth in justice [Qur'an 57:25].

Indeed, when a person rejects faith, he/she hurts only him/herself, according to the Qur'an; but when a person commits injustice, he/she hurts others as well as him/herself—in this life and/or in the hereafter.

Ibn Khaldoun, the great Muslim sociologist, calls justice the foundation of civilization and says injustice causes the demise of nations. Indeed, history has confirmed that communities and nations only thrive in an environment of justice. Unlike most people (including many Muslims) who are concerned about attaining justice only for themselves, believers must stand for justice for all in all circumstances. They should not employ double standards in their treatment of others.

O ye who believe! Stand out firmly for Allah, as witnesses to fair dealing, and let not the hatred of others to you make you swerve to wrong and depart from justice. Be just: that is next to piety: and fear Allah. For Allah is well-acquainted with all that ye do [Qur'an 5:8].

O ye who believe! Stand out firmly for justice, as witnesses to Allah, even as against yourselves, or your parents, or your kin, and whether it be (against) rich or poor: for Allah can best protect both. Follow not the lusts (of your hearts), lest ye swerve, and if ye distort (justice) or decline to do justice, verily Allah is well- acquainted with all that ye do [Qur'an 4:135].

11. Striving for God as is His due

And strive in His cause as ye ought to strive, (with sincerity and under discipline) [Qur'an 22:78].

This verse commands us to strive for the cause of God, and it encompasses all the aspects of the divine mission that are mentioned above. However, it also adds a new and critical element—"*as ye ought to strive.*" In striking contrast to what many Muslim activists think and do, this implies that not only should we work for God's cause, but we should also work for Him with intensity and efficiency, as is His due.

The prevailing attitude toward Islamic activism is that we just need to be active, for example by getting involved in some activities and/or with some organizations—or by giving some of our time and/or financial resources for God. Additionally, activists usually disavow responsibility for the results and impact of their work. However, the Qur'an is telling us here that our duty is not just to be active (or even to increase and improve our efforts) but also to constantly push ourselves to seek the best ways to implement the will of God and fulfill His purpose. Along with the verse admonishing us to "be mindful of God as is His due," this verse commands us to constantly strive to realize our full potential and impact, and to perpetually raise the bar of performance.

Finally, in three verses that illustrate our mission, Allah (*swt*) describes the community of believers as the selected community (22/78), as the best community (3/110), and as a balanced and leading community (2/143). This is a clear indication that an integral part of our mission is to develop ourselves into individual and collective role models.

ISLAMIC HISTORY (IN PART)

By no means is this discussion a detailed narration of Islamic history. Rather, it is only an attempt to track the evolving condition of Muslims over time and to examine how that condition correlates with Muslims' practice of Islam—their adherence to the divine guidance and the prophetic model and their commitment to the divine mission.

As indicated previously, the prophetic model worked incredibly well for more than two decades after the death of Muhammad. During these decades, there was continuity, and there were three smooth transitions in leadership. However, the model (particularly its leadership aspect) was not institutionalized, so it was unable to adapt to change and keep up with the explosive growth of the small community into a vast empire. This shortcoming prevented a smooth transition from one generation of Muslims to another. The model became affixed, and remained so, to the personality (devotion, discipline, and character) of the Muslims who implemented it and of their leaders. The repercussions of the model's lack of evolution and institutionalization were masked by the exceptional leadership of Omar, the second Caliph whose tenure witnessed most the community's growth. However, as Muhammad had prophesized, the crumbling of the Islamic paradigm began with malfunction of the leadership/governance aspect. That actually started with the rebellion against Uthman and his eventual assassination. And as Omar stated, "There can be no effective community of believers without the prophetic leadership model being fully implemented."

The undermining of the leadership of Uthman (the third successor of Muhammad) ended with his assassination. Within little more than a year, two devastating civil wars claimed the lives of eighty thousand Muslims—a huge number, especially when compared to the number of casualties in the two greatest battles of the Muslims against prevailing superpowers of the day: eight thousand died in Al-Qadisiyya, which ended the Persian Empire; and three thousand five hundred died in Al-Yarmuk, which terminated the Roman Empire's presence in the Middle East. Incidentally, those two battles, which happened simultaneously, are considered among the world's major history-changing battles. However, again, the civil wars after Uthman's assassination claimed tens of thousands more lives.

The tenure of Ali, the fourth successor of Muhammad, was very unstable and constituted a rocky transition from the era of the rightly guided Caliphs to the era of Islamic dynasties. Ali was once asked about the instability during his leadership compared to the stability under his predecessors. His response was "That is because they were ruling people like me, and I am ruling people like you." Indeed, the tremendous growth that the community had experienced (which by far exceeded its mentorship capacity and organizational structure) was accompanied by a transition from the generation of the companions to the next generation of Muslims.

Uthman's assassination dealt a major blow to the prophetic model, simply because the leadership model is an essential pillar of the prophetic model. Omar was also assassinated, but it was an isolated incident—unlike the undermining of Uthman's authority and the mutiny that preceded his assassination.

The unity of the Muslim community is another pillar of the prophetic model, and unity is very dependent on the soundness of the leadership model. Uthman's assassination also undermined unity. The subsequent civil wars and numerous rebellions were the precursors of what has turned into lasting divisions between groups of Muslims, particularly between the Sunni and Shia. The wars and rebellions also set the stage for many of the chronic troubles that have characterized some phases of Islamic history.

These unfortunate occurrences inadvertently paved the way for the era of dynasties. Muslims (and scholars in particular) became more receptive to the idea of rule by dynasties, as long as the dynasties could restore order and stability. This is why the majority of the population—willingly or unwillingly—acquiesced when Muawiya, the founder of the Umawi dynasty that succeeded the rightly guided Caliphs, appointed his son as a "crown prince" (heir). Any opposition that occurred at all was merely suppressed.

Under the rule of dynasties, Muslims may have regained order and stability (at least temporarily), but they permanently lost a fundamental element of the prophetic model. To be specific, the most important functional loss was the leadership model: leadership by the consent and appointment of the people along with their right to correct and, if necessary, remove their leaders. Even though many components of the prophetic model were more or less upheld during most of the dynasty era (outside of the periods of rocky transition from one ruler to the next), this enormous loss had disastrous and cumulative effects over the centuries.

Without the consent of the people and without solid governing institutions, the situation of the community during this twelve-century period was determined largely by the character and strength of their leader at any particular point in time. Consequently, overall, the era of dynasties, which lasted for twelve centuries, was a mixed bag and had frequent ups and downs. How it is regarded as a phase in our history depends on whether one is comparing it with the far-better phase that preceded it or with the far worse phase that followed.

On one hand, although there were some deviations in the interpretation and implementation of both the divine guidance and the prophetic model, no one ever seriously questioned their upholding nor was it significantly affected by the private indulgence of many of the leaders. Also, even though their intentions may not have been pure, most of the leaders continued to expand their empires; and many were great patrons of scholarship, art, and science. As a result, Muslims continued to be pioneers in several scientific and civic fields.

On the other hand, the sense of the divine mission among Muslims was fading, and they failed to maintain the relevance of the divine guidance through its continuous renewal and revival. As a result, the divine guidance slowly lost its appeal, relevance, and its capacity to guide and inspire people. There was also a gradual but steady detachment between religion and life. The entire prophetic paradigm is built on a compelling mission, revered but accountable leadership, and relevant constructs of the divine guidance and the prophetic model. With all of these things fading, it is no wonder that, during those twelve centuries, the entire prophetic paradigm was falling apart.

The dynasty model that would follow would engender an overall weakness in the masses in Muslim society that would eventually pave the way for the advent of colonialism and totalitarian regimes. Two main factors, however, sustained the dynasty model for centuries and delayed its ultimate implications. First, there was an unspoken contract between the rulers and the people, particularly the scholars: As long as the people didn't challenge the legitimacy of the dynasty, the rulers would, in turn, uphold the tenets of Islam and also allow substantial autonomy for individuals, scholars, and society at large. This explains the vibrant civil society and array of autonomous institutions (in particular, endowments) that flourished during the era.

Second, even though the people's consent was no longer a source of legitimacy, the heirs to the throne were typically well prepared, having been trained for their job since early childhood. They had studied not only the process of governance (which is important) but also an extensive body of knowledge that included Islam, which still served as the source of legitimacy and legislation.

However, the ultimate fate of the Muslim world was overdependent on the ruling dynasty's strength. Much depended on the character and competence of the leader. This accounted for the frequent ebb and flow during the reign of each dynasty and for the bloody and messy transition from one to another. The repeated mutinies that characterized periods of weakness during a dynasty did not settle until another stronger dynasty took over and reestablished order. Plus, there were recurrent hostilities between the dynasties that controlled different regions.

This dark side of Islamic history does not take away from the greatness of Islamic civilization. When we consider the magnificent contributions to the advancement of justice and morality and the many achievements in the arts and sciences, indeed, there is a lot in Islamic history that should make Muslims proud. That testifies to the greatness and resilience of Islam. The dynasty phase (usually overlooked by Muslims) is emphasized here so that we can demonstrate that the status of Muslims depends on their success in fulfilling the divine mission, ensuring the continued relevance of the divine guidance, and upholding the prophetic model. Performance of these duties is crucial to our well-being and continued relevance—both individually and collectively.

Moreover, if Muslims were able to champion a great civilization and prolong the era of the largely benevolent dynasties for twelve centuries after the prophetic paradigm began to crumble, it was due to the fact that some of its elements were still at work—among the elite and, particularly, among the masses. As indicated earlier, there were factors that kept the rulers' corruption in check and limited their negative impact on the well-being of the state and society. Moreover, many individuals continued to be highly devoted and continued to have a great sense of mission. Plus, many people continued to be inspired by Islam to excel in what they do and to embark on scientific and research endeavors, as God instructed.

However, as Islam became further and further detached from life and as the prevailing Islamic constructs froze and became increasingly rigid and out of touch, the Muslim body lost its ability to fight the chronic diseases that had been threatening it for centuries and had steadily become more entrenched and more widespread. Muslims' vulnerability was exposed by the emergence of other civilizations on the world stage. In addition, the world had become far more competitive. All of these factors added up to accelerate the inevitable collapse of the Ottoman Empire, the last Muslim dynasty.

While some Muslim countries were able to maintain their independence, most of the Muslim world was divided and ruled by colonial powers. Capitalizing on the weaknesses engendered over the centuries-long era of dynasties, colonialism (which lasted from the mid-nineteenth century to the mid-twentieth) caused untold and across-the-board devastation to the Muslim identity and self-esteem, as well as to the Muslim world's unity and its economic well-being. It resembled a potent virus—attacking cell after cell while self-duplicating to further destroy the entire Muslim body. Indeed, in most cases, the colonial powers were not interested in merely usurping their colonies' resources. Rather, their intention also included the permanent annexation and subjugation of the colonies themselves. The plan was to transform the colonies into vassal states. Immediately suppressing any opposition, the colonial powers made every effort to weaken and fragment the societies they occupied by destroying the people's sense of identity and by imposing their own cultures.

With colonialism, a new phase of Islamic history began, and it has continued up to this point. It has involved four major and interrelated phenomena: independence movements against the colonialists, the totalitarian regimes that followed and failed in nation building, Islamic movements that rose against those regimes, and finally the very recent spontaneous and popular revolutions sweeping across the Arab world.

Inspired by Islam and driven by the compelling cause of independence (which was espoused by many as a divine mission), the Muslim populations put up a brave resistance to foreign occupation. This led to the independence of most Muslim countries by the mid-twentieth century. However, as passionate and remarkable as their mobilization may have been, it did not address the root cause of the Muslim world's problems: its vulnerability and complacency (on both the individual and collective levels) as products of its slanted and fading Islamic paradigm. The leaders of the emancipated Muslim states were unable, and/or unwilling, to tackle (much less fix) the real problem that had taken hold of the Muslim world's mind and psyche over the centuries of rule by dynasty and rule by colonialism.

The triumph of the movements for independence was followed by the premature retreat of the masses and the miserable failure of the elite at building liberated states. The new leaders only bolstered existing problems by imposing excessive and superficial westernization on their societies. Their incompetence, their power-induced greed, and their corruption created a "perfect storm" for bad governance. This led them to become notorious dictators who presided over totalitarian regimes. Faces changed, mostly as a result of death or coups; but the situation went from bad to worse—to the point that most Muslim countries fell to the bottom of the list of countries worldwide in terms of freedom, justice, good governance, and development.

Whether these rulers were traitors or simply inept is irrelevant and does not deserve all the attention it is given. Even though, as leaders, they bear the lion's share of responsibility for what happened, this fact does not exonerate the other two main players during the period following independence: first, the elite among the government and the opposition (both secular and Islamic); and second, the masses. The opposition always focused on overthrowing the prevailing regime (rather than on comprehensive societal reform and state-building); and the masses became complacent, choosing to be apathetic and disengaged in the face of their rulers' corruption and oppression.

During the century-long era of colonialism, a number of Muslim reformers and reform movements emerged in response to the deteriorating Muslim world. Their goal (as is ours) was to tackle the root causes of their community's decadence by first seeking to understand what went wrong and why and then developing a new and relevant construct of Islam in order to spearhead needed renaissance and reform in their societies.

Because it focused on the revival and renewal of Islam, in which it had a great success, the Islamic movement did a much better job than the independence movement in tackling the root causes of the decadence. Thus, the Islamic movement had a much bigger and more lasting effect, especially on individuals. However, not unlike the independence movement, the Islamic movement experienced success followed by failure, as the great success in reviving Islam and inspiring people was followed by miserable failure in reforming societies.

Once again, Muslims had failed to capitalize on a transition, and the resulting stalemate caused substantial harm to the Muslim world. Another great opportunity for much-needed renaissance and reform was missed. One way or another, intentionally or unintentionally, the three main players, the regimes, the elites/opposition, and the masses, all contributed to the stalemate.

THE ISLAMIC MOVEMENT

Together with the movement for independence, the Islamic movement constitutes the most important phenomenon to take place in the Muslim world since the collapse of the Ottoman Empire and the advent of colonialism. In many cases, the two movements overlapped and/or were intertwined—Islam inspired the masses to liberate their countries and inspired both movements—albeit to different extents.

Capitalizing on the work of great reformers, such as Sayyid Jamal al-Din al-Afghani, Shaykh Muhammad Abduh, and Rashid Rida,[22] the contemporary Islamic movement (under the name of the Muslim Brotherhood) was founded in 1928 in Egypt by Hassan al-Banna. Over a few decades, it spread across the Muslim world with various local movements being affiliated with the mother organization to varying degrees. Some movements started primarily as local initiatives. They were all, however, very dependent on the Brotherhood's literature, particularly during their start-up phases. Although some movements were more selective than others in adopting the literature and although some even localized it, few went so far as to produce original materials. With the exception of the Jamaat Islami in the Indian subcontinent, which emerged somewhat independently in 1947 and had its own literature (mainly the writings of the founder, Al-Mawdudi), hardly any non-Egyptian movement literature was produced during the first four decades after the establishment of the Brotherhood. Furthermore, hardly any original movement literature or innovative strategies were produced before the 1970s and 1980s. A notable exception to this was the work of Malik bin Nabi of Algeria. Though, technically, it is not considered movement literature (at least from the Brotherhood perspective), when it comes to intellectual depth and originality, there was barely a match to his writings. Then, during the 1970s and 1980s, the world saw the writings of al-Turabi and al-Ghannouchi, two men who led the Brotherhood-inspired movements in Sudan and in Tunisia, respectively.

---

22   John J. Donohue and John Esposito. (1982). *Islam in Transition: Muslim Perspectives* [Book].

While there were some Islamic groups (such as the Salafi, Sufi, and Tableegh groups) that were largely apolitical, the Brotherhood and its branches either began as both religious and political movements or were quickly politicized. However, in most cases, the combination of religion and politics was not effective. That was one of the main reasons that the movement eventually stalled and ended in the chronic stalemate that plagued the Muslim world.

Three essential elements characterized the intellectual foundation of the Brotherhood:

1. A strong belief that Islam is the solution to the Muslim world's problems. The Brotherhood confronted a situation in which there was an increasing tendency to blame society's problems on the practice of Islam among the elite (in government as well as the opposition). There were also increasing calls for forceful secularization of society and marginalization of Islam (Ataturk style). The Islamic movement held that the problem was not Islam, but rather Muslims' understanding, implementation, and commitment to it. The movement argued that what had transpired in the Muslim world was in spite of Islam, not because of it.
2. A belief in the comprehensiveness of Islam as a way of life that regulates and guides all aspects of life.
3. A belief that people should go directly to the sources of Islam in order to properly understand and implement that teaching within a contemporary context.

Led by these three convictions and appalled by the rampant deviation and deterioration within the Muslim world, the Brotherhood and its affiliates worked on three major fronts:

1. The revival and renewal of Islam to reconcile it with life and modernity as well as to revamp and reinforce the Islamic identity;
2. Societal reform and the renaissance of the Muslim world;
3. The establishment of an Islamic state and the restoration of the Islamic *khilafa*, the last version of it having been the Ottoman Empire, which collapsed in 1924.

By all accounts, on the first front, the Islamic movement achieved a colossal success. A strong Islamic identity became a given for many people who rediscovered and committed to their faith. The impact was especially powerful on the young and the educated, most of whom had largely abandoned Islam. The majority of students and professionals (particularly those in the sciences and technical fields) became devout Muslim activists or movement sympathizers and largely dominated student unions, professional organizations, and, to some extent, labor unions.

In the original Brotherhood reform approach, the next step, after the revival of faith and the reform of the individual/family, would be the reform of the overall society. That should, then, eventually pave the way for the restoration of the Islamic state and *khilafa*. Most Brotherhood affiliates more or less followed this bottom-up approach, at least for some time. However, a combination of internal, domestic, and international developments resulted in the switching of the order of steps. This pushed the Islamic movement in many countries toward taking the "shortcut" of attempting to overthrow the government. The idea was that, once the government was overthrown, the apparatus of the state could be used to reform the society from the top down. That was a major blunder as it precipitated the movement's clash with the regimes that were in place and served as a principal reason for the massive failure of the movement's reform efforts despite their great beginning. The movement failed to rally the masses; and its members and sympathizers bore the cost of those clashes. The whole society suffered as well. The movement was unable to change the regime, and the regime could not eradicate the movement. The resulting stalemate caused the marginalization of the movement and the disengagement of the masses, which led to weaker societies and increasingly corrupt and oppressive regimes that became ever-more dependent on outside forces to remain in power.

The following factors were instrumental in this fateful progression in Egypt: (1) a secret organization, which had initially been established by Al-Banna to support resistance efforts in Palestine, spun out of control and began using violence toward political ends; (2) Al-Banna was assassinated; and (3) the emergence of Sayyid Qutb as the movement's most prominent and influential thinker, whose top-down approach largely replaced Al-Banna's bottom-up methodology.

Rather than focusing on the reform of society and the government, Qutb called for isolation and replacing the society with an "alternative community" that would continue to expand until it fully replaced the existing Jahiliyya (a word used to denote the pre-Islamic era) society and government. The void in the Brotherhood following Al-Banna's assassination in 1949 and the ruthless oppression the Brotherhood suffered at the hands of Nasser's regime fostered a fertile ground for Qutb's vision and for the most radical interpretation of his writings.

The situation led to a sequence of events that usually resulted in disaster. An initial change of strategy was followed by the establishment of secret organizations to carry out the movement's improvised and naïve engagement in politics. Next came various attempts to overthrow the ruling regimes. Typically, this resulted in violent clashes. Sooner or later, this sequence reverberated throughout the different branches of the movement in various Muslim countries. In only a very few cases (such as Turkey and Morocco) was the movement able to recalibrate and avoid a chronic stalemate between the movement and the tyrannical rulers before it was too late.

Did the movement's change in strategy precipitate its clash with the ruling regimes, or did the regimes' harassment and efforts to squash the movement lead to the movement's change in strategy? Or were the two processes parallel, with the two parties meeting somewhat in the middle, sparking a vicious cycle? Whatever the case, these events may have fulfilled both parties' prophecies, but they also resulted in a decades-long deadlock that caused untold damage to the movement and to the people.

In all of these circumstances, the underlying factors leading to failure were the movement's intellectual vagueness and its strategic weakness. While Al-Banna was a visionary and an inspiring leader and a brilliant organizer, the movement as a whole was always running short on thinkers and strategists. The shift in the movement's methodology away from Al-Banna's ideas and toward those of Qutb was profound. Instead of focusing first on societal reform, the movement would focus first on building a parallel/alternative community to replace the existing regime. Only after the regime changed would there be a focus on societal reform. The shift toward Qutb's ideas was inadvertently facilitated by two key elements of Al-Banna's vision: (1) The concept of the comprehensiveness of Islam—for many, this equated to the comprehensiveness of the movement. That meant being everything for everybody, which practically necessitated that the movement remains intellectually vague and that it has a central leadership to oversee all its various operations in their different domains. (2) The strong emphasis on establishing an Islamic state—Al-Banna had seen this as a natural but eventual outcome of comprehensive societal reform. Qutb, on the other hand, thought it would be futile to attempt to reform a Jahiliyya society that was ruled by a Jahiliyya government.

The movement's rhetoric around Islam's comprehensiveness, together with its vagueness, formed the perfect combination to attract a hodgepodge of members who joined the movement for a number of different reasons. However, such a diverse membership with no clear vision or strategy became very "high maintenance" and was next to impossible to steer in any definitive direction. Thus, the movement entrapped itself. It was ultimately forced to choose between intellectual clarity and integrity on the one hand, and the unity and retention of its varied membership on the other. In other words, at the same time that the movement's large membership base was its greatest asset (due to its sheer size and organizational discipline), it was also its greatest liability (due to its lack of clarity, cohesion, and sophistication).

The large and well-organized membership base that resulted from the successful revival phase and the general Islamic rhetoric that focused on comprehensiveness made the "takeover" option a plausible shortcut. The attraction of that approach was reinforced by the various governments' harassment of and crackdown on the movement. That's why, in several countries, the movement tried—in vain—to topple the regimes through elections, coups, and, at times, through armed confrontation (as was the case with the Brotherhood in Syria in 1982 and the non-Brotherhood FIS/GIA in Algeria in1992). Many Islamic groups never gave up on that goal, except when the circumstances made it very difficult to persist in such efforts. In some countries, the regimes were finally toppled by spontaneous mass movements.

The movement's strategic weakness was badly exposed in its improvised and fateful transition from religious revival/renewal to political/societal reform. Not realizing that these were two completely different ball games involving different players in different fields governed by different rules, its leaders wrongly assumed that they could automatically leverage their success in reviving Islam into effecting societal reform. Most importantly, they failed to understand that the acquisition and exercise of power is in no way, shape, or form, a game. This error in judgment turned their focus away from societal reform and toward challenging the government, which proved to be a draining task with very limited return.

Throughout its history (and particularly after its marginalization), the movement tried in vain to make up for its intellectual vagueness and strategic weakness through developing an indoctrination process and a rigorous organizational structure (*tarbiya* and *tanzeem*) and also through relentless activism. These components were responsible for the movement's survival as mainly a service provider and protest organization. These activities lasted long after power-struggle entanglements brought the movement's reform efforts to a halt.

Overall, despite the Islamic movement's significant positive impact on the religiosity of more than four generations of people, it had little effect on societal and political reform. In fact, in several cases, its reform efforts (which required tremendous sacrifices—willful and unwitting—by a large number of people) actually backfired as the governments they targeted became even more oppressive and corrupt. Some of the societies activists attempted to reform also became weaker and more complacent.

Indeed, even though they use different tactics, and many of them have the best of intentions, most political Islam groups aim first at gaining control of their field of operations in their country or community. That's why almost every Islamic center is controlled by a particular group. This shortsighted approach does eliminate competition, but it also takes a heavy toll on the group's members and image and on the community at large. As in business, monopoly compromises quality and results in complacency, abuse, and frustration. Likewise, members of the controlling group are neither challenged to perform nor accountable for their performance, and they don't feel the need to involve others in the decision making. On the other hand, the masses become—willingly or unwillingly—alienated and disengaged.

Seeking control or prominence is not a problem in and of itself because, at the end of the day, all political parties aim at acquiring power. It becomes problematic when the power is not earned, when a group's true agenda is unclear, when there is an unsuccessful attempt to blend religion with politics, when there is no sound strategy and roadmap in place, when the means/tactics are not appropriate, and when the actual context in which a movement is being implemented is not taken into full consideration. Under such circumstances, reform efforts are bound to fail or backfire, causing more harm than good.

This approach partly explains the pattern of achieving great initial success, followed by a miserable failure to move to the next level, followed by a stalemate. This has become a typical and reoccurring phenomenon in the recent history of Muslims. That's what happened with the independence movement, with the Islamic movement, and with the Muslim American community, as will be discussed in the next part of the book.

In most cases, things that halted movement projects involved a failed transition from religious revival to political reform and the shift of strategy toward control first. This approach turned the movement's focus inward and on the government (away from society). It also pushed the movement toward secrecy, rigidity, and a confrontational attitude. Conflicts may have started as verbal ones, but they degenerated in some countries—one way or another—into violence.

For the purpose of this book and our movement project, what matters is not only the numerous lessons that could be learned from the Islamic movement's long and rich history but also the fact that several pioneers of the Muslim American community were the product of the Islamic movement.

While most of the Muslim world's many different groups—with their varying ideologies, methodologies, and priorities—are represented to some degree among Muslim Americans, several of the pioneers of our community are products of the Brotherhood-inspired Islamic movements (hence, the focus in this book on those movements' disproportionate influence on the Muslim American community). More specifically, those pioneers were the product of the ineffective model that was characterized by intellectual vagueness, strategic weakness, the existence of secret organizations, rigidity, obsession with bureaucracy, and focus on activism irrespective of its relevance or impact. And even though they have been operating here in America within a completely different context that calls for a new construct, a number of reasons combined to cause those sincere and dedicated pioneers to build a Muslim American community (or more specifically the nucleus of the community) in the very image of their original movements.

In the half century since its inception, the Muslim American community has grown tremendously (but mostly haphazardly) in terms of its actual size. The community has also grown in terms of the number of Islamic centers and organizations that have been established to serve it. Although several momentous developments have taken place, most of these institutions largely mirror—in thought and in action—the original movements of their founders. In most cases, we find only minimal and mostly superficial modifications. In fact, in several instances, the "duplicate" institutions are more rigid and are progressing at a slower pace than their models did.

SUMMARY

The ideological and historical backgrounds for our movement have been presented in this section, part 2 of this book, in order to enable our readers to understand and appreciate why and how both the book and movement came to be, particularly our assessment of the situation facing Muslim Americans today and our vision for the future of both our community and American society at large.

The ideological discussion was intended to elucidate Islam's role in defining the Muslim American community as well as this movement. Throughout our history, our circumstances and conditions have always hinged on our success in understanding, implementing, and presenting Islam in a relevant way—and translating its teachings into viable models, rallying causes and plausible solutions for the issues confronting society. Therefore, every serious reform movement led by Muslims must begin with a solid religious revival component.

The historical discussion was necessary because it is not possible to shape the future without first understanding our current situation, which in turn requires a thorough analysis of history. Both the ideological and historical dimensions are critical in

- translating our ideology (which indicates what should happen in general terms) into a compelling mission and an inspiring and expansive vision for the future (what should happen within our contemporary context?). This involves translating and customizing the divine mission and the transformation of broad dreams into specific and attainable goals.
- coming to an understanding of what went wrong in the past, and why and how we came to this point.
- developing a viable frame of reference for assessing our current situation, learning our lessons, and developing both solutions and the strategies to implement them.

In summary, we began part 2 with an account of the Islamic beliefs regarding God's oneness as the Creator and Owner of everything that exists. We looked at the nature of the divine purpose of our creation, which is to worship God and to serve as His vicegerents on earth. We examined our individual and collective responsibilities toward fulfilling the divine mission (which is both eternal and universal). We established that humanity was not created just to passively worship God but to actively strive to become effective embodiments and instruments of His will. This entails advocating and helping God's cause and ensuring that His divine guidance (delivered through messengers whom He sent to each nation) is constantly renewed, followed, and disseminated. All of God's messengers came with essentially the same message. They spoke of the Oneness of God and our individual responsibility. They also spoke about the fact that happiness and harmony in this life and salvation in the hereafter hinge on our alignment with the divine guidance and our fulfillment of the divine mission. They also taught that our mission is centered on uplifting people, upholding justice, and serving the greater good.

The responsibility for divine guidance and the divine mission was initially assigned to prophets and their disciples. With Muhammad's prophethood (which sealed the succession of messengers), the divine mission was spelled out and clearly assigned to all believers until the end of time. This mission involves a struggle between good/truth and evil/falsehood, which is essentially a struggle against Satan and his soldiers. However, God equipped us for this mission with the power of reasoning (the intellect), the divine guidance, and the will to choose. That's how we are able to come to know God and to understand life as well as our role in it (which requires that we discover and leverage the divine rules and laws that govern both the physical and human aspects of the universe).

That's also how we may properly use the various faculties and resources that God has given us as a trust and successfully handle the never-ending tests of this life. Indeed, life itself is not only a divine mission but also a trust and a testing ground. As we fulfill the divine mission and successfully manage our trust and pass our tests, we will continually grow and realize our full potential and uplift ourselves and our fellow humans. We will improve our world.

Our success in this life depends on our alignment (whether it be intentional or unintentional) with the divine guidance, our fulfillment of the divine mission, our discovery and leverage of the divine rules, and our effective engagement with society. However, in the hereafter, our success and salvation depend on our belief in the one and only true God, as well as our purposefully striving to obey Him and do His work.

As God's stewards and representatives, we must willfully take part in the eternal struggle against evil as its outcome affects all of us, including those who disengage themselves from society. When believers purposely devote their efforts to God, and they do everything within their power correctly, they can count on God's decisive help in the earthly struggle against evil, injustice, and falsehood.

God delivered His guidance through accredited messengers who confirmed one another and were sent to their people with a renewed revelation. The messengers were not only preachers but also reformers. In addition to the standard teachings, their messages included customized reforms to tackle the pertinent issues of their respective times. After they delivered their compelling message, they and their followers were saved, and the rest were destroyed. Eventually, however, deviation crept in among the progeny of the faithful, and a new messenger was sent as a reminder of God's truths and of the fate of those who rejected the message before them. Thus, the cycle repeated itself. Oftentimes, people saw not only the miracles of their messengers but also the remnants from the destruction of the rebellious/disbelievers before them.

Muhammad's completion of the prophethood was a turning point in human history. He was God's final and universal messenger who brought God's final and universal message, the Qur'an, for all times. With the Qur'an, God perfected His religion. He promised to preserve it. Therefore, the Qur'an is the only certain message from God. Muhammad's life was meant to serve as a model for understanding and implementing the divine guidance and fulfilling the divine mission within different contexts.

The mission, which has remained constant since the creation, consists of worship and stewardship and was spelled out in two components: *dawa* (conveying God's message and inviting people to worship none but Him) and *islah* (performing and advocating that which is good, and shunning that which is evil). Again, because there will be no other prophet after Muhammad, this mission has become the individual and collective responsibility of all believers until the Day of Judgment.

Muhammad also used a divinely inspired model to build a movement whose members constantly strive (individually and collectively) to embody the divine guidance and fulfill the divine mission. His prophetic legacy includes the sources of divine guidance, the Qur'an and his Sunna (words and deeds), the divine mission, his model, and his movement. Our responsibility in preserving his legacy consists of

- *dawa* (delivering the message to all people in the most suitable way);
- ensuring the enduring relevance of the sources of guidance by properly understanding and implementing them within different contexts, including developing a new construct whenever the renewal process stalls or the message is being introduced in a new society;
- fulfilling the divine mission to the best of our ability in our respective environments (which entails a lifelong effort to be the best embodiments and instruments of God's will); and
- uniting in a movement centered around the divine mission and under unified leadership.

This is what this project aims to achieve. It is especially important because—for many reasons—our community did not attempt to translate/contextualize the divine guidance and the divine mission and was not built as a movement to fulfill the divine mission.

Throughout history, the condition of Muslims, or more precisely their progress, relevance, and impact, has been a reflection of (1) their success in contextualizing the divine guidance and ensuring its relevance in their lives and (2) their commitment to fulfilling the divine mission. Fulfilling the divine mission depends, as it always has, on Muslims' ability to translate Islam into a relevant platform, their ability to generate meaningful discourse, and their ability to generate viable models and solutions – inspiring an expansive vision and a compelling cause. These elements are all intertwined, and they either form synergy or a vicious cycle.

We as Muslims have thrived whenever we remained passionate about our mission and were engaged in our environment. Passion about mission and engagement in environment motivate us to constantly dig out the treasures of divine guidance to maintain its freshness and relevance. Thus, we are encouraged to engage in wider circles and take on bigger challenges.

On the other hand, when our sense of mission has faded, we have tended to retreat from society; and our understanding and implementation of Islam have lagged behind life's challenges and changes. When this has happened, a leader (scholar, intellectual, or political head) has emerged with a renewed Islamic construct to translate Islam's teachings into a rallying cause of renaissance and reform that galvanized and united large segments of Muslim society. Indeed, Muslims have perpetuated the relevance of the divine guidance, and therefore preserved their own relevance, through consistent renewal efforts and periodic revival movements.

The last such attempt was made by the contemporary Islamic movement(s) founded by Al-Banna, as mentioned earlier, in Egypt in 1928. Over the following decades, movements emerged in every Arab country as a result of local initiatives and because of the influence, literature, and franchising efforts of the Muslim Brotherhood. A similar phenomenon took place in the Indian subcontinent with Imam Mawdudi and his Jamaat. Those movements were the product of efforts by a string of thinkers and reformers who addressed tough questions about the causes of the decline and tried to establish the conditions for the renaissance of Muslims. These thinkers include al-Afghani, Abduh, Rida, Muhammad Iqbal, and al-Kawakibi, and also those who followed them, such as Qutb and bin Nabi.

The contemporary Islamic movement achieved an astonishing degree of success in the revival of Islam, and Islam became relevant and inspirational for a large number of Muslims. However, for the reasons we have discussed (and will expand upon later), the movements did not have similar success in the renaissance and reform of their respective countries or societies. With very few exceptions, these activists fell into chronic clashes with their governments—stalling reform and halting even their revival efforts. The result was an intellectual freeze that caused the movement to become stuck and largely irrelevant, which in turn triggered the emergence of extremism.

Even though they came from largely moderate and nonviolent movements, many of the pioneers of the Muslim community in America were products of this stalemate, and they built a community here based on the model of their original movements. This approach has proven to be vague, rigid, and inadequate. It was ineffective in sustaining the mobilization and unity of the community and ensuring its engagement, integration, relevance, and impact. The fact that the model was being applied in a non-Muslim society by Muslim leaders who neither understood America nor intended to remain here added to the ineffectiveness of the model. Moreover, these pioneers lacked the motivation and the ability to develop a new Islamic construct in order to produce an original Muslim American experience. We needed an indigenous, relevant, and inspiring Islam; and we needed an impactful Islamic movement. We are still waiting.

It is no wonder that the Muslim American community, which was built in the image of the contemporary movement and constitutes a microcosm of the Muslim world, got stuck in transition, even though it enjoyed a successful first phase of development. There are striking similarities between the "system failure" here and the problems with both the independence movement and the Islamic movement in the Muslim world. The reasons may have differed slightly, but the outcome has been the same. And while the Islamic movement(s) did not succeed in preserving the relevance of their Islamic construct and moving on to effectively reform their societies, our Muslim community has not even attempted such an endeavor. Indeed, our community was built on a shaky and vague intellectual foundation and with a limited and ineffective organizational model. It has been guided by a foreign, rigid, and largely irrelevant Islamic construct; and it has lacked a rallying/compelling cause and competent leadership. This largely explains our inability and/or unwillingness to keep up with the tremendous internal and external challenges we have witnessed since our founding.

Several decades after the inception of our community, this movement is calling for a new beginning and for a fresh and right start that builds on previous accomplishments but liberates us from all that has held us back. We need to spark the dawning of a relevant and original Islamic American movement that will positively affect not only us Muslims but also everyone around us. The starting point for such efforts must be in the intellectual and strategic realms and must entail a fierce commitment to acquiring a new and empowering understanding of our faith and an accurate assessment of our reality and history. This is precisely the mission of this book and movement.

PART III:

THE MUSLIM AMERICAN CRISIS OF IDENTITY, PURPOSE, AND LEADERSHIP: ITS MANIFESTATIONS, HISTORICAL PROGRESSION, AND ROOT CAUSES

INTRODUCTION

The term "community" requires definition at this point as different people mean different things when they speak of "our community." Some may even doubt whether we constitute, in fact, one actual community. In the context of this book, "our community" refers to all Muslim Americans—irrespective of their race, ethnicity, gender, age, level of education, level of commitment, or any other classification. And the change we are seeking requires us to redefine "community" to include and involve all Muslim Americans and to refocus their attention and their efforts on society as the real field of operations. Making our community inclusive and mainstream will represent a major shift from the present focus on the mosque's (masjid's) community as both the base and the field of operations. This shift carries tremendous implications for our priorities, our goals, our discourse, our actions, and our performance indicators.

Whether or not they acknowledge it, are concerned about it, or are able to articulate it, the vast majority of Muslim Americans feel that our community is in a state of crisis. Anyone who possesses even a minimal level of awareness about our circumstances is worried about our future. Only those

Muslim Americans who are invested in the status quo, and/or consumed in maintaining it, tend to ignore, deny, or attempt to justify this present reality. The reasons why many members of the community don't seem to be concerned will be discussed later in this section.

The need for change in our community is all too obvious. Unless we are prepared to compromise our future, both in this life and in the hereafter, and remain a marginal entity in society, we must work together toward fundamental change in our community. However, developing an effective vision and strategy for change requires, first, a thorough analysis of our history and, second, an honest assessment of our current situation.

Indeed, this analysis and assessment are long overdue. Without them, we are unable to confront our present reality with the courage it will take for us to forge ahead and become a positive, impactful presence in America. In conducting an accurate appraisal, we must adopt an objective approach to identifying our problems so we can tackle them at their roots and develop practical solutions for overcoming them. Without such an undertaking, a renaissance of our community is impossible; and we will remain stuck in transition—trapped within our prevailing futile approaches to community building and our shallow discourses (be they depressing or deceiving or simply irrelevant). We can be sure that if we do the right things in the right way, with God's help, change is not just possible but is actually within reach. By accepting responsibility for our history and present reality, we can begin to take charge of our future.

History is important. About a third of the Qur'an tells the stories of previous nations, and a significant portion of it explains what happened to those nations and to the prophetic community and why. Remedy begins with assessment. Physicians get a medical history of patients and their family members and perform any necessary diagnostic procedures before prescribing treatment. Our approach is similar.

Crises don't just happen, and complicated crises like ours have deep roots. Unless they are addressed in a timely and appropriate manner, they only worsen with time. Likewise, conditions don't change by themselves, and problems don't just disappear because we choose to deny or justify them or because of wishful thinking. Our future is at stake, as is the future of forthcoming generations, because of our denial and patching of our baggage and our problems. Unless we are willing to repeat our mistakes, continue spinning our wheels, and continue doing the same thing while expecting different results, we must confront the brutal facts of our situation.

This section confronts those brutal facts. From the outset, we realized that this would be an unpleasant and unpopular but inevitable undertaking. We also saw the need to adopt the relentless and undaunted spirit of Muhammad's companions whose resolve simply increased when they were faced with increased challenge:

When the Believers saw the Confederate forces, they said: "This is what God and His Messenger had promised us, and God and His Messenger told us what was true." And it only added to their faith and their zeal in obedience [Qur'an 33:22].

Men said to them: "A great army is gathering against you," and frightened them: But it (only) increased their Faith. They said: "For us God sufficeth, and He is the best disposer of affairs" [Qur'an 3:173].

Our main objective in taking on this tremendous challenge is to sort through our experience and take care of as much of our baggage as possible, so we can pass on to future generations all the best lessons learned and as little liability as possible. Hopefully, this will give them a head start. In order to successfully chart a path toward renaissance and relevance and toward a brighter future for all of us, it is imperative that we understand what brought about our current situation, as the present is merely an extension of the past. As has been said, "Those who cannot remember the past are condemned to repeat it."

We start our discussion with an examination of the manifestations of our community's crisis from the perspective of the larger American community and then from that of our own community. An in-depth look at our community reveals that it is exclusive and self-centered. The ultimate goal of our movement is to transform the Muslim American community into an inclusive, society-focused community that is rooted in and relevant to American society.

We will then trace the historical progression of our crisis through four phases: our unfavorable background; community foundation with built-in limitations; a period of premature relaxation and complacency; and then stagnation due to our failure to transition to the next phase of development. The failure to transition includes our mishandling of fundamental issues and our inadequate response to major external challenges. In assessing our history, we will pay special attention to our response to the catastrophe of 9/11 and to our subsequent situation.

During our examination of the manifestations and historical progression of our crisis, we identified four primary root causes: our neglect of our defining mission as Muslims; an identity dilemma; a leadership void/mess; and our prevailing and troublesome Islamic constructs.

1. Manifestations of Our Community's Crisis

An external and internal examination of our crisis reveals the following manifestations: social isolation, civic disengagement, fragmentation, lack of leadership, no sense of direction, widespread apathy, stagnation, confusing discourse, shallow activism, absence of a rallying cause, intellectual and strategic shallowness, complacency, and resistance to change. These symptoms are sufficiently alarming to make a compelling case for urgent and fundamental change and a new beginning in the Muslim American community. Our crisis can no longer be denied or justified. It is jeopardizing our future and making our current situation both unsustainable and unpromising.

We begin our discussion with a closer look at some of the manifestations of our crisis:

1. Social Isolation and Civic Disengagement (individual and institutional)

These are among the most apparent symptoms of our crisis, particularly when examining our community from the vantage point of our larger society. Indeed, for a number of both typical and unique reasons, the vast majority of practicing and nonpracticing Muslim Americans interact very infrequently with people in their natural environments. Very few are involved in mainstream activities and institutions. Additionally, it is difficult to think of any Muslim organization that has been designed to be a mainstream organization operating within the larger society.

It is not uncommon for minorities to be somewhat isolated from the general society in order to preserve their religious and cultural identities. This tendency may have been initially benign when Muslims (especially immigrant Muslims) were a relatively new and transient group of people that was largely unnoticed. However, this phenomenon was more problematic for Muslim Americans because isolation has been more severe, has had a religious motive, and has been prolonged till it has created a crisis of identity and an image problem. This has hindered our development and our integration into American society.

In addition to the common tendency for minorities to preserve religious and cultural identity, Muslim Americans were driven toward isolation and disengagement by a number of potent forces. These have included the immigrants' "myth of return" (the false notion that they would return to their countries of origin), society's overall misconceptions regarding Islam,[23] and Muslim Americans' own misconceptions regarding American society,[24] as well as the community's grievances toward both past[25] and current American policies.[26]

Today, long after most of the immigrant Muslims have decided to settle here and long after the Civil Rights Act of the 1960s decade, sizeable segments of our community (both African American and immigrant) continue to be largely isolated. Sadly, many have passed this tendency on to their children.

Our lack of participation and involvement in society still may have seemed inconsequential until the 1993 New York City bombing at the World Trade Center (WTC). That event focused American public attention on Islam and Muslims in a negative way, and it worsened already unfavorable sentiments toward our community. Prior to the bombing, the American public image of Islam and Muslims had already suffered, partly because of the dismal situation of the Muslim world and partly because of a number of incidents that took place abroad. Hollywood stereotyping of Muslims did not help. As a result of the first WTC bombing, though, we became a suspect community and the focus of many government and nongovernment agencies, primarily as a security threat. This is a reality that we have been slow in acknowledging and tackling.

---

23 Gallup Institute. (2009). *Religious Perceptions in America: With an In-depth Analysis of U.S. Attitudes Towards Muslim s and Islam* [Report].

24 Gallup Institute. (2010). *Measuring the state of Muslim-West Relations: Assessing the New Beginning* [Report].

25 Explained in more details under "Historical Considerations" on page 189.

26 Explained in more details under "Political Considerations" on page 191.

Consequently, for the most part, our community has been sitting on the sidelines—separated from the mainstream by an invisible wall. This isolation has been constantly reinforced by the wrong perceptions, actions, and reactions that have existed on both sides of the wall.

We need to tear down the wall between the Muslim American community and society at large. By virtue of our divine mission, as Muslims, we are obligated to reach out and must be civically engaged. Unfortunately, there is no easy or quick way to break the vicious cycle of isolation and disengagement. Nonetheless, if we are to fulfill our divine mission and secure our future, we have no other choice. And our first and foremost battle is internal. We must weed out the religious, psychological, and intellectual roots of our isolation and disengagement before we can become a positive, impactful presence in society. Otherwise, our efforts at outreach and civic engagement will remain—as they have been for the last twenty years—largely ceremonial, erratic, reactionary, and inconsequential. Indeed, a lot of the outreach efforts on both sides of the wall lack sincerity, consistency, purpose, and substance.

Some recent individual experiences do, though, reveal the potential positive impact of casting aside our community's isolation. Consider the following cases in point: Two exceptional Muslim American community leaders each decided to get serious about involvement in society at large. After several years of activism as a leader within the Muslim American community, a chief of surgery in a major hospital who also holds a bachelor's degree in political science decided to run for public office. The other case involved a leading figure in Islamic scouting who joined the Boy Scouts of America. Once they shifted the focus of their activism beyond our community, these men both described feeling as if they had just awakened from a deep sleep inside of a cave and as if they were reaching out and interacting with society for the first time. They observed that tearing down the wall of isolation may well be demanding, but that it is not as hard as one might think. Other smaller minority communities with less potential impact are already at America's "civic table."

So even before going inside the community, the examination of our community from outside within the larger American society reveals some serious dilemmas that call for major and urgent change. As long as we remain an isolated and disengaged community, one that is perceived as a "suspect" community, our destiny is not in our hands. Rather, we continue to be at the mercy of incidents outside of our control, and one such incident could be disastrous. In fact, several such incidents have happened, beginning on September 11, 2001. Ever since that terrible day, we have been spotlighted and viewed harshly. We obviously cannot afford to remain in such a precarious and unenviable position. The wall between us and society at large is bad for everyone on both sides of the wall.

2. Stagnation

As we focus on our community, we detect two additional striking features that typically go hand in hand: fragmentation and stagnation. These traits have been standard in recent Islamic history. First, let us consider stagnation.

Not much has been accomplished in the Muslim community in the last two decades except the expansion and remodeling of existing Islamic centers and schools and the establishment of new ones. Most of the buildings that are being expanded are underutilized. In fact, their expansions have been prompted primarily by the need to accommodate worshipers at the Jumaah (Friday) prayers and during Ramadan and to compensate for a lack of competent leadership and vision. The routine activities housed in these centers are largely uninspiring, and they lack creativity and impact.

Of course, some Islamic centers and schools fare better than others. In general, though, most of them are struggling to provide basic services and education to their congregations, and most congregation members only attend the Friday service or show up during Ramadan. Only a small percentage of Muslim children attend an Islamic school. Without a doubt, these services are invaluable to those who patronize them; however they are not adequate given our potential, challenges, and opportunities. Also, given their founding paradigm, these institutions cannot be expected to do much more than what they are doing or to do things differently. Unlike Muhammad's mosque, which was established as a base for his mission-driven community, Islamic centers in America were established as worship places, as shelters to protect an alien community from society, and as service-providing institutions. As things stand, that is about all the Islamic centers and schools can do. Unfortunately, this leaves the community's future and many of its needs and challenges unaddressed.

Most Muslim organizations are also suffering. In the absence of a firm rooting in the community, they are struggling to sustain their operations and prove their relevance. Typically, they are detached from the masses and from one another.[27] In Islamic centers and Muslim organizations, the governance model is usually deficient and is either dictatorial or bureaucratic. Their operations are inefficient and are not integrated, and the workers lack proper training and skills. Most of their efforts go toward maintaining the status quo, and little time or energy is devoted to future planning (outside of that needed to guarantee the delivery of their basic services and education programs). Issues and conflicts are ducked, and decisions take too long to be made, come out late, and are vague and rarely implemented.

In reality, most Islamic institutions are barely surviving, having reached a plateau in their development. The few activists left to sustain them are burned out. As a community, we are basically spinning our wheels (although some people, particularly activists, mistake all our "busyness" for growth). In the absence of high aspirations, challenging goals, and clear performance indicators, buildings and activities are the only criteria by which we measure our community's growth and relevance. Moreover, many activists and organizations have shielded themselves—conceptually and/or structurally—from accountability for specific measurable results. They have not held themselves accountable, nor have they allowed the community to do so. They are using shielding approaches here that do not differ significantly from those that have been used by governments in the Muslim world.

Uninspired and disappointed by the "Muslim establishment's" resistance to evolution and reform, some Muslim Americans, particularly young people, are bypassing the so-called establishment. They are engaging directly in society or are creatively forming their own mainstream organizations. This phenomenon is promising, especially if these individuals and/or organizations come together to form a network to provide an alternative path for civic empowerment and engagement.

3. Fragmentation

Even though the concept of unity is highly cherished in Islam, the level of fragmentation of our community is so flagrant that some people question whether we actually constitute a community. There is hardly any other group in America that is more fragmented.

Historians point to the time preceding the fall of Spain as Islam's worst moment in terms of group fragmentation. There was a different prince

---

27   Gallup Institute. (2011). *Faith, Freedom and the Future* [Report].

ruling over every Spanish province (e.g., Cordoba, Seville, and Granada). In our community today, every ethnic group, every Islamic center, and every organization behaves as if it were an isolated kingdom. And it is not unusual to find more than one faction within the same group—often at odds with one another. Our community is very much divided along ethnic, ideological, organizational, and geographic lines, with no effective mechanisms or strategies in place to coordinate or integrate community efforts on a local, regional, or national level. This fragmentation is compounded by an acute gender and generation gap and by a strict separation between practicing and nonpracticing Muslims.

In attempting to work together with our community, government agencies and civic groups find it difficult to identify the best partners with whom to engage because each of our organizations claims to be the largest or the best at representing Muslims. Many outsiders who have dealt with our community have been shocked by some of the leaders who put their organization's interests before those of our community at large. Some leaders even promote their organization by putting others down. In this regard, as in many other aspects, the Muslim American community is a true microcosm of the Muslim world and has been very faithful to its legacy of fragmentation. However, in the Muslim world, division and fragmentation have been blamed on colonialism, external powers, and oppressive and corrupt regimes. In our case, we don't have those scapegoats; rather, we have only ourselves to blame.

The way we could resolve our fragmentation, though, is no mystery. People are united by visionary leadership around a rallying cause or by some robust structure/system. That's how the German states were unified by Bismarck. It is also how the United States was established, and its unity has been maintained. Even the forever-at-war European countries were finally consolidated as the European Union. Unity also requires a winning and ambitious mind-set that inspires people to prefer to be members of a strong and winning team, rather than being leaders of a weak and losing team.

Unfortunately, none of these requirements apply to our community, and little is being done to reduce our disabling fragmentation. Most of our local and national coordinating councils are minimally functional, and their member organizations have settled for the lowest common denominator and are struggling to maintain the councils themselves. The result is merely a patchwork treatment for the much-deeper problem of fragmentation. The councils' establishment, in the first place, illustrates our typical approach for tackling our problems once denial and/or dodging them has become impossible. Plus, not only were these councils formed with half-hearted intentions, but they also possess the same problems as their constituent organizations: no visionary leadership, absence of a rallying cause, and lack of a sound system/structure.

There was a time when Muslims were fighting for the control of Islamic centers and organizations. However, most of the battles were settled one way or another. Either a faction of their membership (or even a single individual) managed to secure full control, or the infighting resulted in a split. While tight control or partition sometimes made things seem quieter on the surface, both scenarios acted to further weaken our community, alienating the majority of Muslim Americans who typically opted for silent resistance to whatever was occurring on the front lines.

4. Alienation and Apathy of the Masses; Detached Organizations

It is an indisputable fact that the vast majority of Muslim Americans are not associated with any local or national organization. Most of them do not even attend Jumaah (the Friday sermon). Moreover, the vast majority of those who are mosque-goers or are connected with Muslim organizations tend to have little involvement beyond praying in the masjid (mosque), signing up on e-mail lists, or passively participating in basic services and programs. This picture is far worse among our youth.

These individuals are good people with tremendous potential, and their energy and skills should be harnessed for the well-being of the community and the country. They should be part of our plans and participants in our efforts, and we should engage them in a compassionate, respectful, and inclusive way. And while preaching (dawa) remains very important (especially at a time when these people are rapidly losing their religion), our outreach efforts should focus more on services, development, mobilization, and on organizing inclusive forums of belonging, empowerment, and contribution to the common good.

On the contrary, most Muslim organizations are not open to new members, are not inclusive, and are neither transparent nor democratic. They tend to be managed and sustained by a small number of activists who concentrate on maintaining the status quo, which entails maintaining the organization and maintaining their control over it. These organizations tend to cater to a small segment of the community around them. In the absence of a clear guiding vision and without any sound organizational structure and culture, most organizations end up as either a one-man show, or they become too bureaucratic and high maintenance.

It is bad enough that these organizations are isolated from the overall society and disengaged from the Muslim masses, but their leaders are also so detached that they are unable to inspire even their "captive" audiences (their members or congregations). Consequently, most Muslims rarely have a strong sense of belonging to these organizations—never mind seeing themselves as stakeholders. There is hardly an organization within our community that is truly expressing and addressing our concerns and aspirations. The few organizations that attempt to be exceptions to the rule and try to replace complacency with action inevitably find themselves overstretched in terms of human and financial resources. The result is that there are a small number of overwhelmed activists and an alienated majority. Both sides seem sufficiently comfortable with this stalemate to remain inert; although occasionally, both sides complain and exchange blame. Muslim organizations that do hold elections and general assemblies can barely form a quorum, so they repeatedly extend deadlines.

The alienation of a significant segment of our community and the low rate of membership and involvement in Muslim organizations should be worrisome. Many of these Muslims have skills and other resources that our community needs. Many were previously involved or attempted to become involved; but because they didn't fit a particular profile or they were overtalented, or because they were too outspoken and possibly challenged the status quo, they eventually gave up or walked away. The main message most Muslim Americans receive is that their involvement is typically wanted only when their attendance at events or their financial support is needed. It is no wonder that only a small number of people respond to the fainthearted calls for members to participate and that only a small fraction of the community revolves around these organizations.

As mentioned previously, there was a time when people were vying for control of our institutions, but it seems that an unspoken agreement was eventually reached between the victors and the rest. Those who triumphed won all the control (and all the burdens). At best, the majority of Muslim Americans are simply treated by the institutions' leaders as guests or customers. What is most disheartening is that, in the absence of a compelling mission and aspirations, both parties seem to be satisfied with the status quo.

The elitist nature of our organizations, the organizations' detachment from our community, and the apathy of the masses—all combine to deprive the community of needed talent and support, and this mixture hinders the community's growth. Even though more and bigger mosques are being filled, especially during Ramadan and on Fridays, this overcrowdedness does not translate into any true growth or meaningful impact.

This phenomenon of alienation and complacency of the masses is also widespread in the Muslim world and for the same reasons. The following essential elements are missing: a rallying cause, an inspiring vision, a competent leadership, and a sound structure. Without these elements, neither the masses of people in the Muslim world nor the community of Muslim Americans can hope to create a healthy culture that promotes concern and societal involvement. The only difference between the situation overseas and our situation in the United States appears to be that, unlike the typically corrupt and oppressive leaders of the greater Muslim world, our community leaders are largely sincere and dedicated. However, effective leadership demands more than just goodwill and hard work.

The combination of the alienation of the majority of Muslim Americans, together with the fragmentation of the minority who are practicing and active, is hurting our community and curbing its development and evolution. This situation, therefore, calls for serious and immediate action.

5. Confusing Discourse and Shallow Activism

Before addressing more subtle aspects, another obvious manifestation of our crisis must be discussed—the absence of inspiring and empowering discourse in our community.

When was the last time you left a community event with a clear, lasting message to take home? For the most part, the prevailing discourse in our community is shallow and irrelevant—sometimes even confusing, depressing, and/or deceiving. It is not guided by an inspiring vision and often lacks coherence. One could easily spot flagrant inconsistencies or even contradictions between what organizations and activists say and what they do—and discrepancies between statements made in different circumstances. Sometimes speakers have spoken from both sides of their mouths in the same address and used a lot of "yes-but" constructs that leave audiences wondering what the message is and where the speaker stands. Such discourse further isolates attendees and worsens their identity crisis. On the rare occasions when speakers do succeed at inspiring the audience, they usually fail to provide any clear sense of direction for follow-through.

Speakers often seem to be more interested in impressing the audience than in inspiring people, and they are often more intent on promoting their own organization rather than offering a vision for our community. This should come as no surprise, though, since most nonroutine events are usually designed to raise funds (which accounts for the bulk of organizations' efforts). Consequently, rather than being the tools by which a worthy cause is advanced and the community is empowered, Muslim organizations and their activities have become the end objective, in and of themselves. And the maintenance of those organizations (meetings, bylaws, elections, conflict resolution, etc.) consumes a lot of energy and time.

Again, we are not questioning the sincerity and dedication of event organizers and speakers. On the contrary, we are suggesting that their failures are simply the result of their human inability to give that which they don't themselves have. They have no vision to inspire people, and oftentimes their knowledge lacks depth, coherence, and relevance. It is no surprise that this is reflected in the speeches and activities.

6. Lack of a Rallying Cause, a Guiding Vision, and High Aspirations

These are all both the manifestations and the causes of the crisis. They explain not only why our community is isolated, disengaged, stagnant, and fragmented but also why most of us don't seem to be bothered by our situation. Indeed, many of us are conducting our lives as if we have achieved all of our goals, both in this life and in the hereafter. Even Muhammad and his companions, including those who had been promised heaven, were more anxious about their destiny in the hereafter—despite the fact that they were constantly striving to increase and perfect their efforts. They spared no opportunity to serve God's cause. The Qur'an beautifully describes their spirit in several verses. For example:

> And those dispense their charity with their hearts full of fear,
> because they will return to their Lord; it is these who hasten
> in every good work, and these who are foremost in them
> [Qur'an 23:60–61].

Willful change in human behavior (both individual and collective) is usually driven by a compelling cause and high aspirations. These ingredients drive people to constantly push themselves and challenge the status quo, and they preclude people from retreating into a comfort zone (which would inevitably result in stagnation). Sadly, for the most part, as Muslims, we have long abandoned our defining mission; and our background has made us complacent. Most of us live largely aimless and self-centered lives with little or no concern for our community, let alone our country. Our focus rarely goes beyond our families and just getting by and/or the acquisition of materialistic possessions. In fact, after studying a Muslim population for some time, a sociologist concluded that a striking characteristic of these people is that they were living without a dream. And most Muslim leaders and activists have the same problem, except that instead of their aspirations being limited to their family, their hopes are limited to their community (usually their mosque community) or their organization. Indeed, most Muslims have largely abandoned high aspirations ever since they largely abandoned their defining mission.

As a result, we have fallen into the trap of sponsoring irrelevant and inconsequential events and activities that merely maintain the status quo. Our community has (willingly or unwillingly) resigned itself to lateral expansion, so it simply holds more activities in more and larger facilities to accommodate increasing numbers of people. In actuality, all of this increase in activity is not accompanied by genuine community growth and empowerment. With few exceptions, individual and organizational achievements and successes don't really "trickle down" to the community.

Compared to other groups, for example the Jewish community, it is strikingly apparent that our lack of a sense of mission and absence of vision have become defining characteristics of our community.

The reasons Muslim Americans and Muslims in general live without a mission/cause and without high aspirations will be discussed in greater detail later. It should be clear, however, that the version of Islam we are practicing and/or espousing inspires neither a movement nor a change. It is no secret that our community was established for a limited purpose, which was largely achieved with the establishment of Islamic centers and schools as "safe havens" that served the community's basic and immediate needs. The Muslim American community has never been driven by a compelling mission or an expansive vision.

It is, then, no wonder that the level of mobilization that characterized the campaign to establish Islamic centers and schools was not sustained and was followed by a chronic "mission-accomplished" attitude. Unfortunately, in spite of many appearances that may suggest otherwise, our community remains stuck in that paradigm and in that state of complacency.

7. Lack of Leadership, Mentorship, and Trained Cadres

How many members of our community have an accessible leader or a mentor they can relate to? And how many (including activists) are actually trained and/or skilled in any aspect of community organizing and development or civic engagement? Unfortunately, the answer to both questions is "Not many."

Indeed, there is a serious leadership void in our community. While they are dedicated individuals, most of our leaders lack intellectual depth, strategic insight, coherent vision, and other vital leadership skills.

The pathway to becoming a leader in our community has typically paralleled being a member of a particular "clan," or it has involved maneuvering skills. It is a sad irony that possession of the above-listed skills (intellectual depth, strategic insight, coherent vision, etc.) is often a liability—making potential candidates overqualified for the organizations as they exist. Unfortunately, the culture of our community is such that it does not cherish expertise, excellence, and ambition. Few Muslims today truly have either the motivation or the humility to learn. As a result, strong leadership and mentorship in our community are not valued, and in fact, they are even resisted.

The renaissance of any community requires that it be galvanized by a rallying cause and high aspirations. Moreover, the strength of any community is measured by the competence of its leadership, and the discipline and skill set of its cadre of activists. Additionally, continuous progress in any community requires a strong tradition of mentorship.

8. Intellectual and Strategic Shallowness

As indicated in the previous section, our community is in desperate need of intellectual depth and coherence and of strategic, creative, and critical thinking. This is partly because many Muslims, including leaders and activists, are not keen on reading, reflection, and debate. Those who do read often limit their reading to materials that lack depth, diversity, and relevance to our needs as a community. For a number of reasons discussed above, the focus of our community has been on short-term and immediate needs. As a people, we have failed to acquire a tradition of reading and learning beyond what is compulsory in formal schooling. An intellectual foundation and concept development are needed to support a mission, and strategies are required to fulfill that mission and turn a vision into reality.

Another reason for our intellectual and strategic shallowness is that we are relying too much on the work done in other parts of the world and/or in other eras. We have tended to adopt those approaches and ideas, with or without customization, even though their relevance for our community may be questionable. Our "consumer mentality" bars us from intellectual endeavors, and this is seriously hindering our progress. One of the goals of our movement and one of the changes that we are seeking to instill in our community is to cultivate a culture of reading, creative and critical thinking, and substantive discussion and debate. The debate must include discussion about our faith and our mission and about the issues facing our community and country, both now and in the future.

9. The Community's Inadequate Response and Resistance to Change

Despite an acute and multifaceted crisis with many obvious manifestations and many implications for our future, our community has merely imported a number of critically inadequate methods of dealing with the situation. To make matters even worse, the community has then resisted change. This section will briefly discuss some of the approaches we have taken in the prevention of progress.

Denial and/or Justifications: The extent to which our community is inclined toward denial (and sticking our heads in the sand) is simply amazing. It has been our first line of defense against any change, and it has continued to be the "magic solution" that we throw at every problem. We avoid thinking about or discussing a plethora of grave internal and external challenges, partly because of a false sense of pride and partly to avoid the pain of acknowledging and confronting them. Denial, though, has always been a futile approach. Problems that are not addressed in a timely and adequate fashion only get worse, and the costs of fixing them increase, if we even wake up soon enough to fix them at all.

Our second line of defense, when denial proves impossible, has been to justify the situation and to engage in wishful thinking about the future—often misapplying the concepts of qadr (divine destiny), ibtilaa (trial and tribulation), and tawakkul (trust in God) in this context.

In Muslim countries, when their favorite soccer team loses, people tend to blame the weather, the referee, the pitch, even the food—everything except the losing team itself—which is precisely why the teams don't get any better.

"I'm very busy," "We're doing what we can," "Something is better than nothing," "We're better off than we were before," and "We're not responsible for the results" are some of the typical excuses used in our community to justify every situation and rationalize failure. A prime example: A number of activists blame their poor results on a shortage of resources. When they are confronted with the fact that the bulk of our community's human and financial resources are untapped, many activist leaders blame other people for failing to get involved or failing to make contributions. At the same time, the latter blame the leaders and activists for excluding them. The bottom line is that everyone is complaining and finding someone else or something else to blame—never running out of excuses or scapegoats, so they continue to justify the status quo and disavow their responsibility.

Victimization and Conspiracy Theories: The two main segments of our community (African Americans and immigrants) both have a history of traumatic experience, which has ingrained in them a chronic sense of victimization and a tendency to blame their failures on conspiracies. Again, the Islamic concepts of ibtilaa, tawakkul, sabr (patience), and thabat (perseverance and steadfastness)—along with verses of the Qur'an, stories of the prophets, and incidents from the Seera (life of Muhammad)—are invoked to justify a passive attitude in the face of challenge. This prevents us from holding ourselves accountable for our situation and from challenging ourselves to change, and it encourages us to endure our irrelevance as if it were our divine destiny.

Neither the world nor human history is devoid of conspiracy, but at the same time, they are not governed by it either. If we are victims of conspiracy, it is because we are weak and therefore predisposed to being abused by others.

In a competitive society and world such as ours, there is a little room for weak individuals, communities, or nations. Rather than complaining and blaming others for conspiring against us, we need to ask ourselves, "How did we become weak in the first place, and how can we rebound?" We need to inoculate ourselves against excuses as well as conspiracies. Indeed, respect and rights are earned.

Complacency and Frustration: Because the prevailing discourse in our community is typically shallow and irrelevant—even depressing and sometimes deceiving—it is only natural that there is a widespread attitude of complacency and/or frustration within the community. Indeed, we have developed an unprecedented tendency to not only justify practically any situation but also to acquiesce and adapt to it. Despite occasional surface anger and outrage, we are actually a very passive and submissive community that usually vents its frustration in an inconsequential manner.

Although we may spend a lot of time and energy superficially discussing the world's events, we rarely ask the tough questions regarding their causes and what can and should be done about them. This complacency is dangerous because it often paves the way for despair. In fact, there is little difference between complacency and despair, because in both cases, the result is inaction or inconsequential action.

In general, in order for anything meaningful to happen, two essential requirements must be met. First, we must have the will to overcome our internal and external stumbling blocks. Second, we must have the ability to do so. Of the two essentials, the will to effect change is the more critical. As is often said, where there is a will, there is a way. Those with a strong will are driven to acquire the means for reaching their goals regardless of the challenges they may meet along the way; whereas in the absence of willpower, any availability of means would be irrelevant and may actually reinforce an attitude of complacency. If a community of people is not even trying to effect change, the first thing to check out is the strength of their willpower—particularly if they possess the means and the opportunity, which is the general case in our community.

Firefighting and Patchwork: Due to all the above defense mechanisms, more often than not, our community waits for problems to escalate into crises that blow up in our face before we act. Subsequently, we don't have time to trace the roots and resolve things at that level. So as a rule, we end up just putting out the fire and patching up the problem. We then rush back into our comfort zones to wait for the next problem (or even the same problem) to brew and then blow up in our face. And the cycle repeats itself.

On the few occasions that we might manage to overcome all the above-mentioned obstacles and act properly, we rarely sustain our efforts long enough to generate the momentum needed for a breakthrough. Instead, we tend to let up before we make it to the next level and before we completely resolve the issue at hand. As a result, we tend to move in circles; and our problems continue to pile up on us because we either do not address them at all or we do so ineffectively.

In summary, our community (both individuals and institutions) is self-centered, isolated, fragmented, and underdeveloped. There are hardly any substantial, ongoing activities and programs beyond the provision of basic services and education, nominal outreach, and expansion/remodeling of buildings. Our tremendous resources are either untapped or underutilized. Consequently, we are in desperate need of talented, dedicated workers, viable institutions, and adequate facilities. More importantly, our community lacks a rallying cause and a sound, integrated vision. In such a context, our increase in numbers, proliferation of organizations, and our expanded, enhanced facilities and operations do not translate into relevant and genuine progress and growth.

Drastic changes have occurred since the conception of our community. Our founding paradigm has proved more or less inadequate, having been based on the myth that most of us would return to our ancestral homelands. The United States is our homeland. The current state of affairs in the Muslim American community is unsustainable. We cannot continue to merely patch over our problems. A thorough revision and a major paradigm shift are desperately needed and long overdue.

2. HISTORICAL PROGRESSION OF OUR COMMUNITY'S CRISIS

Our snapshot view of the Muslim American community reveals significantly problematic symptoms. It is clear that we are stuck in transition and that change is needed, but the first step in developing a "treatment plan" starts with an accurate diagnosis of the underlying illnesses behind the community's symptoms.

A comprehensive knowledge and analysis of a community's history is crucial if we hope to understand and develop the community. This may be compared to a doctor taking a patient's medical history before prescribing treatment. Events don't just happen, and current conditions are usually the manifestations of an historical progression that must be studied before our problems can be adequately addressed.

The history of a community starts at its birth with its founding nucleus, which constitutes the subject of the next section. However, prior to analyzing that nucleus, let us take note of its roots in the Muslim world and, specifically, in the contemporary Islamic movement. First of all, the conditions of the Muslim world have taken a heavy toll on Muslims who migrated to the United States. Second, Islamic movement activists (primarily those inspired by the Muslim Brotherhood and the Jamaa'a Islami) were disproportionately present among our Muslim American pioneers. They had a disproportionate influence on the founding and evolution of the whole community (not just the immigrants).

As mentioned previously, our community started as a temporary outpost, and it soon became a microcosm of the Muslim world. However, while it largely mirrors the Muslim world, we have had a considerably greater opportunity to thrive and make a difference and fewer reasons for failure and irrelevance than most Muslims elsewhere.

At this point, it is desirable to shed some light on the background of this community and on the vision of its founders.

1- THE COMMUNITY'S UNFAVORABLE HERITAGE

a. The Impact of Recent Islamic History

While this analysis is not complete without taking into account the roots and development of the African American Muslim community, our limited firsthand knowledge of the history and dynamics of that important segment of the Muslim community would necessarily limit our knowledge about pertinent details, which should, otherwise, be provided here. Additionally, our respect for African Americans in general and African American Muslims in particular precludes us from making a less than adequate attempt, one which would surely fall short in outlining their important history. However, it is not necessary to be an expert to observe that, when it comes to the challenge of positively and relevantly applying Islam within the American context, although the African American Muslim community has significant advantages over the immigrant Muslim community, its legacy is also fraught with many limiting factors. Although the focus of this book's analysis is on the immigrant Muslim community, for the most part, its findings are still applicable to our entire community—not only because of similarities between the two groups but also because of the major impact that immigrant Muslims have had on indigenous Muslims.

The root causes of many aspects of our founding, evolution, and current situation are to be found in the effects of recent Muslim history on all of us and also in the effects that the contemporary Islamic movement had on the pioneers of our community.

Indeed, the steady decline of the Muslim world over the last few centuries has taken a very heavy toll on the psyche, personality, thought processes, self-confidence, and aspirations of its inhabitants. Due to a number of intertwined internal and external factors, there was an across-the-board devastation of Muslims around the globe, which culminated in colonialism and has continued up until now, or at least until the recent revolutions that are sweeping across many parts of the Muslim world.

The causes of the decline are numerous. They include the deterioration in our understanding of and commitment to Islam and our failure to foresee (or at least keep up with) the world's changes. Part of the blame goes to Muslim leaders' betrayal and/or ineptitude, and much goes to the corruption and oppressive practices of the governments in Muslim countries. The resulting weakness/vulnerability invited (and combined with) external conspiracies to afflict Muslims with chronic decadence, fragmentation, alienation, irrelevance, despair, complacency, and stagnation. Muslims' lack of a common and empowering rallying cause and the subsequent failure to evolve have been all too costly.

On both an individual and a collective level, we lost our guiding compass, our frame of reference, our sense of purpose and direction, and our motivation and aspirations. A serious lack of understanding of our sociopolitical environment, together with our denial of and/or indifference to the challenges that have been confronting us, acted to create severe passiveness and even despair in our ranks. We lost hope and, with it, the willpower and confidence to act. Even those who were most aware and rebellious lacked the vision, as well as the opportunity and the means, to reverse or halt the situation. For a long time, the Muslim world was caught between the great faith of Islam with its glorious past on one hand and a steadily worsening and out-of-control situation on the other.

To be sure, it was faith in Islam and patriotism that drove the people in occupied Muslim countries to rally behind the cause of liberation and the movement for independence. It was their bravery, resolve, and their generous sacrifices that led to remarkable victories that brought about tremendous momentum and excitement. Unfortunately, the thrust behind these movements was short-lived. As has been typical in recent Islamic history, the people lacked the leadership, the vision, the will, and/or the ability to sustain their mobilization and build on their successes. They got stuck in transition, and the success of the movement for independence was followed by a miserable failure in nation/state-building and development. So it goes when there is a failure to develop an expansive vision, evolve and keep up with the world's changes.

Several decades later and thousands of miles away, the founders of the immigrant Muslim American community would do the exact same thing—getting stuck in transition following their initial mobilization and success here in America. Consequently, they became consumed in managing the status quo in the absence of the rallying cause. Such a cause should have replaced the earlier goal of preserving the identity of the first generation immigrants, a goal which had been largely achieved by the establishment of mosques and institutions to provide basic education and services.

Sustained by some chain reactions and vicious cycles and by some deception, the situation in the Muslim world continued and often worsened, in spite of the tremendous natural resources of many Muslim countries. There were both spontaneous and organized efforts to resist (both actively and passively), but the repeated unsuccessful attempts at reform only fueled the people's disappointment and their complacency.

The Qur'an extensively discusses the devastating effects that living under oppression has on people's personality, thinking, behavior, and aspirations. Unfortunately, most of that discussion is quite applicable to recent Muslim history. Muslims have been and continue to be oppressed by external and internal forces, and the majority of them remain acquiescent most of the time. In the absence of freedom and any channels for participation in public affairs, people have survived by exercising a strict self-censorship and suppressing their views or by expressing their angers in useless talk when they can avoid the omnipresent government's ears and eyes. At the same time, publicly, they have to wear a mask and give no indication of resentment.

Willingly or unwillingly, the majority of people have deserted the public square and minded their own business. Even outside of politics, people's aspirations are not high, both because they lack ambitions and because they lack opportunities in countries that have failed miserably in economic development.

Oppression and complacency have, at least until recently, pervaded the whole Muslim society, including the school and family. Everywhere, people have had to suppress their opinions, feelings, and ambitions. This situation fostered a culture of disconnection between people's hearts and minds and their actions. That resulted in frustration and ambivalence or cynicism toward almost everything, and people have therefore been unable to be themselves or express themselves. People put on a lot of masks to get by, and there was hardly anything authentic or genuine.

Consequently, for quite some time, the majority of Muslims were living obsolete, artificial, and irrelevant lives in their countries; and for the most part, they were depressed by repeated defeats and failures. As a result, people got accustomed to chronic irrelevance and being on the sidelines watching silently (or helplessly complaining) while events that affected their lives were unfolding in front of them. Certainly, over the last couple of decades, a good part of these Muslim countries experienced some economic growth and vibrancy that touched a good segment of the society, but there was no true development, and the bulk of the wealth went straight into the pockets of the small ruling circles.

When comparing the backgrounds of the two main branches of the community in this country, immigrants and African Americans, it is hard to tell which one faced the greatest challenges. Both segments arose from very traumatic experiences that caused enormous damage: the cruelty and ruthlessness of slavery and racism for the African Americans and the oppression of colonialism and dictatorship for the immigrants. The result of both unfavorable legacies was a colossal undermining of their faith, personalities, self-confidence, and thought processes. In both groups, this led to chronic alienation, cynicism, and low aspirations among their heirs.

By rallying behind successful causes, both African American and immigrant Muslims have remarkably improved their conditions, but that did not erase the inner scars. African Americans, who were brought to America in a very cruel way and for centuries were treated ruthlessly, fought very hard and made tremendous sacrifices to win their rights. Beginning with the antislavery movement and culminating in the civil rights movement, African Americans advanced in this society in ways seldom seen in history. Unfortunately though, for reasons that will be discussed later, African American Muslims did not take full advantage of and experience the tremendous positive changes and momentum shift associated with African Americans as a larger group.

Immigrants also had sources of inspiration, including and especially the movement for independence and the Islamic movement. Both generated tremendous momentum and excitement, and both had great positive impact on people. In fact, these movements succeeded in undoing some of the prior damage. However, the movement for independence, which achieved a remarkable victory, failed miserably in the next challenge of nation/state-building and metamorphosed into notoriously oppressive and corrupt regimes that caused tremendous damage to their countries and their people. Likewise, the achievements of the Islamic movement are best described as a "catastrophic success." That is because the movement's achievement in inspiring religious revival and awakening drove its leaders and members into complacency or confrontation, and the end result was miserable failure in terms of societal reform. Plus, it was unable and/or unwilling to evolve and eventually became part of the status quo.

To make matters worse, many of our leaders, as well as our general community members, insist on denying and attempting to conceal the traumatic effects of our oppression on our own personalities and thought processes, instead of confronting and flushing them out. As a result, Muslims have blurred the gems of Islam with a very unhealthy and limiting culture and have made Islam and themselves irrelevant in the process. This is why too many Muslims have trouble in the areas of personality, thinking, will, and aspirations. Our communities lack a mission, effective leadership, and cohesion. It is no wonder that many a Muslim scholar remarked that, in the East, he found Islam but no Muslims, and in the West, he found Muslims without Islam. In many ways, American culture, as imperfect as it is, is far more compatible with Islam than the prevailing culture in the Muslim world.

The Muslim world is, of course, where our community originated. However, it is difficult to find anything in that background that tends to facilitate the successful founding and development of a relevant and empowered community. How can change begin when people have little or no tradition of civic engagement and little or no experience organizing themselves, resolving differences, managing their affairs, or even expressing their opinions freely?

The general background of both branches of our community, African American and immigrant, has not been helpful to the development and execution of an expansive blueprint for a genuine and relevant Muslim American community. Among immigrants, additional problems included ambivalence toward America and the "myth of return," which is (again) the idea held by many immigrants that America was only a temporary stop before going back home.

Our community originated in a part of the world that was steadily declining and largely irrelevant, and this took a heavy toll on people's lives, mind-set, character, hopes, and aspirations. People largely lost their sense of purpose and self-confidence, and all they wanted was to get by through adaptation to any and all circumstances. Living with lots of frustrations and low hopes and aspirations, people became largely introverted and indifferent. They were predisposed to submissiveness when necessary and unruliness when possible. Based on recent history, one might conclude that, with very few exceptions, the only two possible scenarios in the Muslim world are dictatorship or chaos. For quite some time, success has been a rare commodity; and ambition, discipline, authenticity, and concern for the public welfare have been in very short supply.

This situation was largely due to serious deficiencies in people's understanding of and commitment to Islam as a mission. Widespread failure to keep up with change made matters worse. The result was severe internal weakness that invited—and combined with—external conspiracy to put the Muslim world on a steep path of decline.

The next section will discuss, in more detail, the progression of the Islamic movement, which, indirectly, had a tremendous impact on the founding and progression of the Muslim American community. It is not only true that many community founders/pioneers were Islamic movement activists, but for quite some time, they also remained attached to those original/mother movements to which they were planning to return.

b. The Impact of the Contemporary Islamic Movement

There were a number of attempts (first, by various secular groups and later by the Islamic movement) to address the steadily deteriorating situation in the Muslim world, both before and after independence from colonial rule. As discussed before, the Islamic movement proved to be far more effective than secular groups because it tackled some of the root causes of the decline.

The Islamic movement was, indeed, a genuine and relevant strategy for Islamic revival and societal reform that crowned a number of reform initiatives. The motivation for reform was prompted by the steady decline of the Muslim world in the latter centuries of the second millennium. The Islamic movement emerged first in Egypt and in the subcontinent, then spread across the Muslim world. The relocation of Muslim activists to different parts of the world gave the movement global relevance.

Starting in Egypt in 1928 (in the case of the Muslim Brotherhood) and in the Indian subcontinent in 1940 (in the case of the Jamaa'a Islami), the Islamic movement began on the right footing: a founder with a simple and coherent message and a relevant cause that was supported by a cohesive core group. The message and the cause were centered on reviving Islam and on the awakening, the liberation, and the renaissance of the *umma* (community of believers). The thrust of the message was to restore the relevance of Islam and

Muslims by going directly to the roots and sources of Islam and by embracing it as a way of life and as a mission.

The simplicity of the message, the relevance of the cause, and the openness of the movement were behind its quick transformation into an indigenous and relevant Islamic mass movement, which quickly became the voice, the hub, and the hope of the masses. It was a true Islamic revival and societal reform movement, and it was deeply rooted in its time and its society. This movement was later exported to different parts of the Arab and Muslim world and beyond. However, there was little or no customization to accommodate cultural or situational variations, and that delimited the movement's success as it spread. Effective movements are the products of contextually cognizant, tailored responses to present realities.

A true Islamic movement is a relevant implementation and simulation of the divine guidance and the prophetic model tailored to the context of the society at hand. Therefore, movements are neither timeless nor universal, and they are not exportable either in time or in space. One size does not fit all. Ironically, the very same things that make a movement successful and relevant in its country of origin prevent the success of its unmodified transplantation abroad.

There is only one way to build a rooted and relevant Muslim community. We have to understand and implement the divine guidance and the prophetic model in a way that is relevant to the reality at hand. Historical experiences may be helpful, but only as sources of lessons and inspiration.

There are two more reasons why transplanting the Islamic movement, particularly to the West, was not a good idea and did not work. First, like any human endeavor, Islamic movements are not infallible; and it would be futile to repeat mistakes. Some of the deficiencies that took a heavy toll on the Muslim American community included the status of women, absolute gender segregation, and the trading of clarity for unity (achieving neither).

The second reason movement transplantation was not successful is that, long before it was imported to America, the Islamic movement had largely stopped evolving and engaging with society at large. This is simply because, in the Muslim world, the movement's fight for survival had necessarily involved secrecy, seclusion, and intellectual and organizational rigidity. It is unfortunate that this out-of-date model guided the founding and evolution of the Muslim American community. The model was not only transplanted without customization but also had already developed serious deficiencies in its countries of origin, where it had been bent and had become frozen. Detached from reality, both abroad and in America, this model became even more obsolete beyond the community's founding phase. As the idea that immigrants to America would return to their countries of origin (the "myth of return") began to fade, the need for a movement that was more appropriate to America should have become clear.

However, rather than going for a paradigm shift, which is long overdue, we continue to avoid confronting our reality; and we continue struggling to patch this noninclusive and nonscalable model that has largely expired and is clearly inadequate. This is not the way to fulfill the divine mission in twenty-first century America. We cling to the old model despite the obvious fact that our community needs have long outgrown it. For quite some time, the antiquated approach has served only to provide a sense of belonging and a forum for community activism for a limited number of activists and to provide some basic education and services for a small segment of the community. Those limited benefits notwithstanding, the old model has failed to inspire and empower even those whose lives revolve around Islamic centers and Muslim organizations. It has also failed to reach out to the disengaged majority of Muslims, not to mention effectively engaging the wider society.

c. The Contemporary Islamic Movement: Beyond Its Founding

As previously discussed, a number of intertwined internal and external factors worked together to downgrade Islamic movements throughout the Muslim world. The movements were reduced from being dynamic forces of change into being organizations that were basically a part of the status quo.

There was a lack of clarity on some fundamental issues. This compromise was made in the name of comprehensiveness and inclusiveness, and it was based on the hope of expanding membership and maintaining unity. Indeed, different people joined the movement for different purposes, and they came with varying expectations and different interpretations. Thus, there may have been more members, but the price was paid in terms of less cohesion, less coherence, and reduced functionality. Moreover, the movement's structure and sophistication did not keep up with its growth and visibility; and those two aspects, growth and visibility, began to threaten national governments in the Muslim world, as well as those governments' powerful sponsors. Given those circumstances, any continuing ties with the overseas

Muslim world complicated matters for the Muslim community here in the United States.

Ensuring clarity, inclusion, and cohesion may be challenging, but it is crucial for the success of any movement. Failure to do so is limiting and very detrimental. Unfortunately, many Islamic movements and communities have, more or less deliberately, set aside one or more of these critical elements. The lack of clarity on fundamental issues and the lack of cohesion of membership have denied the movements and organizations the agility, decisiveness, and the discipline that are critical. Thus, they have been unable to sustain relevance, to effectively engage their sociopolitical environments, to keep up with changes and challenges, or to evolve and transition smoothly from one phase to another. In a way, the movement's growth and visibility have brought it to the big league, but its inherent limitations have forced the movement to play a Little League game by denying it the mind-set and methods required for relevancy in today's world. Unfortunately, but not surprisingly, that's exactly what happened with the Muslim American community ever since its founding phase and particularly after 9/11.

Consequently, in most parts of the Muslim world, the movement was outmaneuvered by the power and sophistication of autocratic governments (and their sponsors), who decided to crackdown on—or at least prune— those Islamic movements. Through a combination of strategies, governments and their sponsors were able to capitalize on the inherent limitations of Islamic movements. Thus, they could and did confine those movements. They reduced them from forces of change into rigid, secret, and stagnant charity-and-protest organizations (*tanzeem*). Struggling for survival and to maintain their operations and their unity became nearly full-time work for organizations that should have been able to do more.

This pattern—of successful buildup, premature leveling off, and failed transition resulting in stalemate—became typical of the Muslim world, Islamic movements, and Muslim communities. It happened repeatedly in most Muslim countries, with most Islamic movements, and with most Muslim communities in the West. The Muslim American community was no exception. There was one difference in America however. Islamic movements in other countries were limited in social responsiveness by heavy-handed government oppression that capitalized on some inherent societal limitations to prevent meaningful change; whereas for Muslim Americans, the movement's own internal limitations got in the way. Our limited social responsiveness occurred despite the religious and political freedoms the Constitution guarantees. So the Muslim American community failed to evolve because it failed to capitalize on unprecedented freedom and opportunities.

In Egypt, the heavy-handed and persistent oppression did not only abort evolution and preclude successful transition but also stripped from the movement some very critical elements of strength, including its brilliant founder, and its openness and flexibility. But the movement's exportation from Egypt to other Arab and Muslim countries, typically with few (if any) adaptations, stripped away another critical element of the movement's initial relevance: its staunch Egyptian identity.

In America, a number of factors made the founding of the movement still more challenging, and that meant that founding the community was also challenging. First, one could say that the groundwork had been laid on the wrong ground. It was the second model—the reactionary phase of survival, rigidity, and secrecy—that was imported to America by movement activists; and that is what was used to build the Muslim American community, at least the immigrant segment of it. Second, from the beginning, there was neither a guiding mission nor a founder; and even the nucleus of the movement lacked cohesion.

Because the initial goal of Muslims in America was also survival and because their mission and challenges were limited and because their intention was to go back home, the model worked reasonably well from their perspective; and people had no incentive to modify it. Eventually, however, reality exposed the deficiencies and limitations inherent in the roots and foundation of the community. The same typical and familiar pattern of stalemate emerged. This prevented the community from sustaining development, moving to the next level, shifting focus toward society, and tackling the challenges of integration and relevance. As a result, the community ended up stuck in transition.

Overall, the contemporary Islamic movements had a tremendous impact on the Muslim American community, which was largely designed in the image of those older movements. Having a model to go by was a considerable blessing in the founding phase of the community, but it became a limiting factor soon afterward because of design problems with the imported model, shortcomings which were only amplified by transplantation, isolation, and intellectual freeze.

The Muslim American community drifted further and was held back— and even substantially damaged—by events and phenomena in the Muslim world. Particularly harmful was the emergence of radical and intimidating

Islamic groups. This phenomenon further derailed the evolution of both the Islamic movement and the Muslim American community.

In conclusion, our snapshot of the community has revealed some disturbing signs. These include rampant fragmentation, stagnation, and alienation of the majority of Muslim Americans. There is a lack of vision, and there is no rallying cause. We have traced those symptoms to the founding nucleus and model of the community and then to the historical roots of the community. Our diagnosis reveals the depth and complexity of the problems that are holding us back. Thus, we can get an idea about the scope and extent of the work needed if we hope to revamp our community in order to make it relevant and rooted in the here and now. If our community today looks more like a fraternity than a movement, this has been caused more by design than by mistake; and if the community is more or less stagnant, it is because fraternity is the best we can do, given the way we were founded and our guiding model. Without a new approach, we have hit the ceiling.

2- OUR COMMUNITY'S FOUNDING LIMITATIONS (and the First Phase of Its Development)

Islam, in one form or another, has been present in America for centuries. Albanian Muslims established the first actual mosque in the United States, in Biddeford, Maine, about a century ago. The seeds of national organization were sown, separately, by the two main segments of the Muslim American community. In the 1930s, African American Muslims laid the groundwork for the Nation of Islam; and in the 1960s, immigrant Muslims founded the Muslim Students Association (MSA).

A thorough analysis of those seeds reveals the roots of our current dilemma and largely explains why our community is stuck in transition—unable to move to the next level and phase. Indeed, both branches of our community did not grow out of a vision for America and for the future. Rather, they were both conceived as reactions to (and extensions of) the past and as reactions to (and protection from) American society.

Granted, African Americans did not voluntarily come to this country. They were brought here in a very cruel, ruthless way, and they were treated in a demeaning manner for centuries. They fought very hard and made tremendous sacrifices in order to seize and secure their basic rights. The pioneers—and even some of the current leaders of their community—lived through some of the resulting trauma. It is logical that much of their outlook stems not from a hopeful vision for the future but from a bitter reaction to the past and to America. It is unreasonable to expect the victims of such cruelty to possess some automatic sense of nostalgic loyalty to America or a sense of unbridled compassion toward the advantaged descendants of former slave masters. It was also natural that African Americans shunned the system that continued to cast them out long after slavery was abolished in 1865. Indeed, African Americans have continued to experience unequal treatment even after the Civil Rights Act of 1964 outlawed racial segregation in schools, in places of employment, and in other public places. Yet many civil rights leaders have taken the moral high ground, showing exceptional tolerance and willingness to forgive.

Neither the unorthodox nature and racial overtones of the Nation of Islam nor the overconservative foreign brand of Islam that immigrants brought into the picture would prove helpful to most African Americans or improve their regard for America. Unfortunately for African American Muslims, these two prevailing experiences of Islam interfered with the processes of reconciliation with the past and development of a coherent American identity. Reconciliation and a coherent identity are vital if anyone wants to "work the system." To be sure, there have been some attempts to mainstream the African American Muslim community; however, it is difficult to gauge the true impact of such attempts on that community, on the larger African American community, and/or on society at large.

The immigrant community came from a different background and took a different route but ended up in the same predicament in terms of being hostage to its past and isolated from society. Naturally, the seeds of this community carried some of the deficiencies and limitations that were discussed in the previous section. Indeed, it is safe to say that the immigrant Muslim community is a microcosm of the Muslim world that was built in the image of the contemporary Islamic movement.

The influence of the contemporary Islamic movement on the founding of America's immigrant Muslim community could hardly be overestimated. This influence was a mixed blessing. The motivation, the organization, and the activism of movement activists gave the community a jump start and largely pushed the community in the direction of religious moderation and nonviolence. However, because of the same factors, the community was built on weak and vague intellectual and strategic foundations. It did not evolve, either intellectually or even organizationally, beyond the first phase, which mainly consisted of securing and managing basic facilities and services. This situation was complicated by the "myth of return" and by the transplantation of a deficient movement model to a radically different context.

Driven by that "myth of return" (discussed previously in detail), the immigrant Muslim community was initially built as a temporary shelter in order to preserve its members' foreign religious and cultural identities, shielding them from the society that is known worldwide as "the melting pot." The campaign to develop Islamic centers and schools, in order to provide needed programs and services, was successful; and it did help to preserve our cultural identity. The success, however, led to a sense of "mission accomplished" and a sense of self-satisfaction. Meanwhile, ongoing activities and efforts essentially aimed to maintain the status quo—while, we might add, keeping a steady overseas focus. Indeed, immigrant Muslim Americans have provided considerable human and financial resources to many parts of the Muslim world. Isolated by design and "living back home," we did not engage our American environment. Thus, we have ended up frozen in time.

Thus, for immigrant Muslims, there was no reaction to America, and the future was "back home," overseas. For the longest time, America did not really figure into Muslim Americans' individual and communal plans. They were not planning to live in America, so they had no incentive to get to know and engage with American society. Most people tend to shun that which they don't know. Plus, their overconcern for protection, combined with some perceptions about American society and some religious misconceptions, drove most immigrant Muslims further toward isolation.

However, because of their overseas attachment, immigrant Muslims were becoming increasingly resentful of America's growing negative entanglement in the Muslim world. Particularly troubling to Muslims were America's unquestioning support for the government of Israel and Washington's patronage of dictatorial regimes in several Muslim countries. The Islamophobia that arose in the United States, with "help" from the media in the early '90s and snowballed after 9/11, did nothing to win Muslim affection or affinity, nor did the wars in Iraq and Afghanistan. However, while the combination of isolation and resentment did produce apathy among most immigrant Muslim Americans, it did not engender outright enmity, except within some fringe groups.

So if the Muslim American community got stuck in transition, it was because it did not start as a societal project that was geared toward the future. It had no rallying cause, no lasting mission, and no expansive vision. It was not built on a sound intellectual foundation. It was not designed for America. For different reasons, both of our community branches, African American and immigrant Muslims, along with most Muslim organizations, focused on the *masjid* (mosque) community locally and on the *umma* (the worldwide Muslim community) overseas. And both African American and immigrant branches of the community—each for its own reasons—chose isolation and largely shunned the greater American society and the system.

Moreover, community "projects" and most of their spin-off organizations started not with a vision for the future but as reactions to the past and in response to immediate and pressing needs. This resulted in a focus on activities and services rather than on mission and change. That is why our community looks much more like a fraternity than a movement. Plus, the community was not only built for a limited and quickly achieved goal but was also based on a limited model that was not scalable to fit contemporary circumstances and needs. This situation precluded streamlined efforts, and it made our integration into society nearly impossible. It is no wonder that national and local organizational spin-offs have been mostly arbitrary and did not add to the community's relevance and impact.

Overall, there have been very few intellectual efforts to indigenize Islam and root it in America. Early on, as a newly emerged minority, Muslims had more reasons to justify isolation, intellectual stagnation, and low aspirations. Moreover, despite the fact that these limitations were hardwired in the foundations of our community, things worked reasonably well—*as long as* the community did not achieve its limited goal and was comfortable as a foreign minority and was not under the spotlight. However, the dilemma our community faces today resulted from (1) achieving our limited goals and reaching a plateau prematurely and (2) clinging to a deficient and limited paradigm even after it was no longer useful and even after our internal and external circumstances had changed dramatically.

The next section will examine more closely the effects of these two phenomena, which arose from our unfavorable background and our foundational limitations.

3- OUR PREMATURE RELAXATION

To review the situation outlined in the previous section: limited initial goals, an inadequate intellectual foundation, and a deficient and nonscalable organizational model have worked together to guarantee the disengagement, isolation, and stagnation of our Muslim American community.

In most American cities, the immigrant Muslim American community started with the establishment of a chapter of the Muslim Student Association (MSA) on a major university campus. There, the MSA made arrangements for the performance of *Jumaah* (Friday) prayers. Some nonstudent communities, without formal MSA connections, initiated Islamic center projects. The MSA national organization was established in 1963 as an umbrella organization for MSA chapters across the country.

It soon became clear that, while most people still planned to return home, they were extending their stay in America past their original anticipation. Many were staying past graduation. As a result, two things occurred. On the local level, there was a move to acquire facilities in order to establish a more permanent location (a mosque or Islamic center) for Friday prayers and other programs and services. Nationally, there were efforts to establish an organization to serve as an umbrella for local and other national organizations (including Islamic centers).

That's how the local MSA chapters evolved into the Islamic centers, and it's how "MSA National" evolved in 1983 into ISNA (the Islamic Society of North America). A number of other national educational and charitable organizations were also founded. Locally, particularly in college towns, the MSA became part of the Islamic centers; and nationally, the MSA became part of the ISNA.

Regardless of when, where, and how the local community emerged, the establishment of an Islamic center was probably the most exciting and successful phase in its history. The campaign was a clear, challenging, and worthwhile rallying cause that galvanized and more or less unified the community for several years. As expected, the transition from a homogenous student and MSA-driven community to a more diverse, Islamic-center–driven community was not without some bumps in the road; but those bumps were natural and manageable.

A major outgrowth of the Islamic centers was the opening of full-time Islamic schools to address the educational needs of the rising number of children whose parents were not yet ready to return home. Islamic schools were established to do for children what Islamic centers were doing for the older generation of immigrants: preserve their Islamic and cultural identities and protect them from American society until they would go home. At first, this need was satisfied by Sunday and/or weekend schools, but eventually, parents wanted more. However, these initiatives, which were launched by mosque communities, did not marshal the same level of mobilization and enthusiasm as did the campaigns to establish the centers. They were championed primarily by the parents of the students who were enrolled in the schools. Moreover, unlike Islamic centers, Islamic schools served only a subsection of the congregation—children. Plus, only a very small percentage of Muslim children attended Islamic schools.

In the absence of reliable statistics, the success of the Islamic schools is difficult to gauge or judge. The functionality of the Islamic schools' mission has changed as large numbers of parents have continued to indefinitely delay going back home. Instead of preserving the identity of children expected to go home, the Islamic schools find themselves "protecting" and isolating these young people from the very society in which they will have to integrate during both high school and college.

Up to the 1990s (and in many cases up to our present point in time), local communities didn't do much beyond establishing the Islamic center and school and managing and serving their congregation. This was largely a dormant phase, except for the improvised expansion of existing centers and schools and the establishment of new ones. These centers could have become bases from which the communities could engage local society; and their establishment might have been just a phase of development (the means to an end). However, because they were established and used instead as temporary "refuges" for "temporary residents," the centers became the goal in and of themselves.

Our isolation from society and our sense of "mission accomplished" led to a premature demobilization in the late '80s. While the sprouting up of mosques, organizations, and Islamic schools all across America suggested that we were experiencing genuine growth, in truth, they were just indicators of lateral expansion. Essentially, the community relaxed too early—thinking that it was already "there"—which led to a gridlock and the surfacing of all kinds of community divisions and deficiencies. The momentum was then lost, and the tremendous success in the establishment of the Islamic center was followed by a miserable failure in community building, development, organization, and integration.

Having been based on a deficient and limiting paradigm and on a model that lacked a tradition of effective community organizing, most Muslim institutions suffered badly from poor systems of governance. This led to disavowed responsibility, disputed leadership, and chronic power struggles. Organizational weaknesses denied the leaders the mandate they required to effectively lead and deprived the community of the swiftness, stability, and continuity it needed. This sapped organizations' strength, broke their momentum, and prevented breakthroughs and smooth transitions from one phase to another. Consequently, these organizations became bogged down with bureaucracy. They were slow to make decisions; and when they did so, the decisions (designed to please everyone) turned out to be so vague and ineffective that they were rarely implemented. Thus, the absence of a rallying cause, the unavailability of capable leaders, the horrible system of governance, and the lack of skills and experience resulted in community chaos and/or paralysis. All of this was tolerated and sustained by a culture that encourages the denial and ducking of issues and conflicts.

The community fell into the "activity trap" and concentrated on the management of the status quo, limiting itself to lateral expansion. We saw more activities and facilities filled with more people, but with no real growth or empowerment and no real progress or integration.

The stagnation brought to the surface a very serious challenge that, with few exceptions, the community failed miserably in handling: the compounded diversity in the community along racial, ethnic, ideological, gender, and even generational and socioeconomic lines. The setup was too inadequate to manage (let alone to lead) a highly diverse community. Even though the community was usually prepared to trade progress for unity, it seldom achieved either. Sadly, the great diversity of our community translated into rampant fragmentation and exclusivity along all lines, a trend that was exacerbated by all kinds of judgmental attitudes. Even the establishment of ethnic and/or ideologically homogenous mosques and organizations failed to halt cynicism and fragmentation.

The scene was ripe for two phenomena that would create additional setbacks for the community:

– There was a haphazard mushrooming of Islamic centers and organizations, mostly along ethnic lines, resulting in the alienation of the masses. This took place not only partly in response to geographic and/or demographic needs but also due to chronic internal strife about who would be in control. In the absence of a rallying cause and a real mechanism of integration or even coordination, despite the proliferation of Islamic centers, the community missed an opportunity to grow systematically and increase its leverage.

– Community energy and resources that might have been applied in America were channeled abroad instead. Scores of overseas-focused and/or ethno-centered organizations, campaigns, and initiatives were launched, primarily to facilitate "relief."

With missed opportunity and misdirected energy, not only did our community lack vision, insightful, and competent leadership and the incentive to change, but it also lacked the resources to do much more than "more of the same." The focus was almost entirely on maintaining facilities, providing basic services, and managing the status quo.

Consequently, only a small segment of the Muslim population was adequately served and accommodated by the few remaining activists. The activists were busy and struggling just to hold people together and keep things going. The lowest common denominator was the name of the game, and progress was nowhere to be seen. So despite a lot of good efforts by a lot of good people, the result was a strange combination of stagnation and fragmentation, disguised by a lateral expansion and an appearance of growth. The community, which had enjoyed reasonable success in building its basic infrastructure, nonetheless failed miserably to leverage its diversity. Thus, the community was unable to achieve even a minimum meaningful unity and also unable to sustain its momentum and growth.

Part of the blame for this situation also belongs to the "mission accomplished" attitude many people had after mosques and centers were established. Additionally, people lacked the aspirations, the leadership, the vision, the incentive, the experience, and the skills to move forward. Indeed, many of these same people came to America from countries that lacked any democratic tradition and where there was no opportunity for community organizing or civic engagement. Plus, the vast majority, who were planning to go back home anyway, felt no need for anything more than a *masjid* (mosque) and some Islamic schooling for their children.

Whether the chronic crises resulted in chaos and paralysis, or in dictatorship (open or de facto), the result was usually an increased alienation of people and/or further community fragmentation. It was only after people became too tired of community politics or too busy with their own lives that a quiet status quo became the best that an Islamic center or a Muslim organization could hope to achieve.

At the national level, a number of educational and charitable organizations evolved mostly within the same paradigm (community centered, service oriented, and overseas focused) and usually along strict ethnic and/or ideological lines. For one reason or another, most national organizations remained somewhat detached from the local communities that they claimed to represent; and at both the local and national levels, organizations were detached from one another.

It is no wonder that, for the longest time, the community has been stagnant or moving in circles, alternating between power struggle and power vacuum. Most of the time, the community and its organizations are either in—or in between—crises. That is because the leaders don't have either the vision or the mandate to move forward or to swiftly resolve conflict. Therefore, they spend the bulk of their time maintaining or polishing the status quo (activities, bureaucracy, facility, false unity). They struggle to keep things going and keep people together. The system is usually gridlocked, and the only way one gets things done is to work around the system, which is usually an unsustainable process.

By and large, the Islamic activism and work succeeded in educating, serving, preserving, protecting, and defending only small segments of small minorities. Not only did Islamic activism virtually ignore society at large, but it also neglected and alienated the vast majority of its own Muslim people. Additionally, because of the limitations of both the goal and the organizational model and because of isolation and stagnation, there was a rampant and endless fragmentation of all sorts, even within the small activist segment of the community.

Indeed, ever since the founding of the MSA (locally and then nationally), the community evolved and grew tremendously. However, everything took place within the boundaries of the deficient and limited founding paradigm. No significant progress was achieved in moving the community out of the "activity trap" or committing it to the divine mission or shifting its focus from overseas to America. We were self-focused and stuck in isolation, not moving forward toward integration. We were face-frozen into preserving a foreign Islamic identity instead of developing a genuine and coherent American Muslim identity. Instead of taking on the challenges of relevance and developing a vision for our future in America, we have kept ourselves shackled to the past.

In brief, the community has been slow and reluctant in going through a real paradigm shift, even after such a shift became long overdue. Moreover, we relaxed and demobilized too early and continued to manage and polish the status quo and expand laterally, even after everything was calling for change and for a transition to a different level. Unfortunately, failure to foresee coming change and failure to respond appropriately to change that has arrived have both been frequent phenomena in recent Muslim history. Thus, we have stumbled and continued to stumble.

There were actually some serious setbacks involved in our lateral expansion. The proliferation of relief work and ethno-centered organizations and Islamic centers seemed gratifying, but we were kidding ourselves. In reality, the organizations shifted our focus to channel resources overseas, and the haphazard proliferation of Islamic centers actually added to the fragmentation of our community. That is because the focus of many activists was narrowed, from a small—but at least diverse—segment of the community down to one particular ethnicity.

Rather than expanding systematically, our community has been constantly breaking up and producing more disconnected communities. We split into different ethnic communities, different ideological groups, and increasing numbers of Islamic centers. However, there is a way that we could have maintained a sense of collective community if only we had been endowed with a number of essentials. Those necessary elements would have included a rallying cause, a much more sophisticated and effective organizational model, a much more competent leadership, and a much healthier culture. Unfortunately, all those requirements were in short supply.

At the national level, a very similar phenomenon of improvised and ad hoc organizational spin-off took place without a rallying cause to streamline, integrate, and synergize the scattered efforts. A number of organizations emerged, either to meet a specific immediate need or as part of the endless fragmentation of the community on ethnic and ideological grounds.

Both locally and nationally, the arbitrary mushrooming of the community and its organizations, together with the lateral expansion, did not just add up to community fragmentation. This phenomenon also misled people into believing we were experiencing real growth and evolution! Actually, the increase in community members' numbers, organizations, Islamic centers, and activities did not build up to a breakthrough or move the community to a different level. None of this amounted to real growth, nor did it translate into relevance.

To be sure, locally there were a few cases of reasonably effective coordination mechanisms. Nationally, however, ever since its inception, ISNA has failed to live up to its full potential. Many hoped it would be an umbrella for local and national organizations (including Islamic centers); but despite some good efforts, that dream never materialized. And ISNA ended up as another national organization that offers—from a distance—some good programs and services, but remains removed from local communities.

4- FAILED TRANSITIONS, INADEQUATE RESPONSE TO MAJOR CHANGES/CHALLENGES, AND MISHANDLING OF FUNDAMENTAL ISSUES

The 1990s challenged our community in many ways and from several angles. Unfortunately, not only were we ill prepared to confront the issues, but also we were overrelaxed and headed in the wrong direction.

Those intertwined challenges, which confronted the community almost simultaneously, include

- the fading of the "myth of return"—America had become our home,
- the eruption of rigid and/or radical versions of Islam,
- the emergence of new generations, and
- a string of events that negatively exposed Muslims to the very society they had totally neglected, a society from which they thought they were fully isolated and protected.

These circumstances caught Muslim Americans, as a group, completely off guard. This exacerbated existing issues that we had always ducked, issues such as the question of our identity and the role of women. After the events of the 1990s, not to mention the events since then, we have had to ask, "Who exactly are we, as Muslim Americans, and what are we trying to accomplish?" This has had tremendous implications, particularly for our young generations. Another question was "How can we reconcile foreign and archaic ideas about women with life in modern-day America?" This is an issue that has been exacerbated by archconservative beliefs and Islamic misconceptions. Our unwillingness (or inability) to proactively address these concerns weakened us and severely hindered our growth, development, and integration into American society.

Due to our difficult backgrounds and the community's foundational limitations, we not only demobilized prematurely, but also we have operated primarily within a fire-fighting mode. We do our best at crisis management, but we fail to avoid crisis. We fail to anticipate and plan for critical transitions, we mishandle fundamental challenges, and we respond poorly to major changes in our society and the world. In the absence of a rallying cause or high aspirations and lacking any visionary leadership or strategic thinking, we have been virtually asleep. The only thing that has managed to awaken us from our dormancy has been either an internal or external crisis. Then we rally around, put out the fires, and relax again. And the cycle repeats.

We have seldom bothered to trace, never mind tackle, the root causes of our crises. We haven't invested much time or energy in determining how to best repair the damage or how to prevent the crises from recurring in the future. It should, then, come as no surprise that most of these crises have resulted from changes that we neither foresaw nor addressed adequately and from issues that we have denied and/or simply patched up for too long—until they blew up in our faces.

One of the key factors in the incredible and sustained success and growth of Muhammad's movement was that he had a clear vision and a sound strategy with clear phases and milestones. The overlapping of the various phases of the community's development enabled him to prevent a loss of momentum, and this helped the community to transition smoothly. Muhammad was also able to seize opportunities, capitalize on successes, and avoid traps that would have led to failure.

The primary instances in which our Muslim American community has failed to transition to the next stage and examples of issues we have mishandled are presented below.

a- Failed Transition Beyond the Islamic Center

Our community was founded on the premise of the "myth of return," which was, again, the idea that America was temporary for us and that we would one day go home. This prompted a short-term focus and shortsightedness combined with our immigrant (and victimized) mentality to produce severe reactionary tendencies and misdirect our planning and strategic thinking.

Moreover, the community's founding paradigm was very closely linked to the establishment of Islamic centers, the only rallying cause that the community ever had besides responding to crises and attacks.

As long as the community remained engaged in a mosque campaign as a short-term goal and focused on returning home as the ultimate goal and as long as we remained relatively obscure to society, the paradigm worked reasonably well. However, because nothing was envisioned beyond the Islamic center, rather than serving as a springboard to move the community to the next level, the establishment of the Islamic centers ushered in an era of stagnation (and, eventually, fragmentation) from which the community has yet to rebound. Centers became comfortable ghettoes that, down the road, individuals and groups would vie to control and manage.

Muslims fell into an "activity trap": They were consumed by the business (or "busyness") of managing these facilities from which they provided basic programs and services to their congregations. It was as if the construction of a building were the only achievement the community was capable of accomplishing. About the only nonroutine endeavors the congregations undertook, after the establishment of their respective Islamic centers, was to build more centers and/or upgrade existing ones. Even though many of those expansions and acquisitions were warranted, the process was anything but systematic. Those facilities did accommodate more people especially on *Jumaah*, and they helped by deferring some problems. However, they also did amplify and mushroom some serious inherent deficiencies. Plus, many Islamic centers arose out of ethnic or ideological divisions or power struggles, and many expansion projects reflected, not community growth, but rather leaders' lack of vision. It is no wonder that many buildings are underutilized and poorly managed. Certainly, there are a number of Islamic centers that are better managed and more active and which provide better services to their congregations. Even in many of those cases, though, the activities lack creativity and have only limited relevance and impact.

b- Failed Transition Beyond the "Myth of Return"

Although it became clear—beginning in the 1980s—that most of the members of our community would not be going back home to their countries of origin, it took a long time for people to accept this fact; and most have yet to act accordingly, particularly as regards their community life.

Muslims became comfortable with the idea of being residents and indefinitely postponing their intended return. However, becoming American citizens (or otherwise living permanently in America) proved to be a more daunting challenge. For instance, parents struggled between preparing their children to live in America or to live back home. This has all combined to create a real identity crisis for Muslim American immigrants and their children; and it has disrupted the plans of the community and its members, which were mostly based on the premise of the "myth of return."

Because the "myth of return" was a cornerstone in the founding of our community, its fading should have triggered a paradigm shift. The new reality called for the development of a new and genuine Muslim American identity, including a new lifestyle and platform. What was needed, therefore, was deep soul searching and rethinking, and that effort should have been based on a culturally unbiased reexamination of Islamic texts. Instead, however, the community fiercely resisted change—opting for patchwork and superficial adjustments. As a result, Muslim American immigrants of all generations have yet to become comfortable being Americans. We have continued to fail to develop a genuine and coherent Muslim American identity. As a group, we have yet to successfully integrate and root ourselves in society.

Indeed, our community continues to be guided by an immigrant mind-set due to the disproportionate influence of the immigrant generation on Islamic centers and organizations. This immigrant mind-set even applies to those among us who have known no other country or homeland. Moreover, many African American Muslims and many other Americans who have converted to Islam feel like foreigners in their own country—just as do many of the American-born children of immigrant Muslims.

The identity crisis, which has only been getting worse, has combined with subsequent domestic and global events to continually reinforce the alienation of the community and plague it with a severe image problem.

c- Our Confused Identity and Lack of Mission

No community may thrive without resolving an identity issue as serious as ours or without espousing a rallying cause and developing an expansive vision. However, our community has yet to address these deficiencies.

While increasing numbers of us are becoming more comfortable calling ourselves Muslim Americans, we are largely ambivalent about the American dimension of our identity and its relationship with our Islamic values and beliefs. In the '80s, Muslim organizations chose the prefix "North American." In the '90s, an increasing number of new organizations are referring to themselves as Muslim American or American Muslim. However, these self-labels are barely reflected in our lifestyles and/or our organizational approaches and platforms. Both individuals and institutions are still largely disengaged from participation in American society, and both are struggling to reconcile the Islamic and American dimensions of their identity. Exacerbating the issue is the fact that the prevailing version of Islam is infused with foreign cultures and a strong dose of anti-American political views.

Since our community has never been mission driven and since we have yet to develop a real rallying cause beyond the establishment of Islamic centers and the fulfillment of our basic needs, most of us and most of our organizations are not only unclear about who and what we are, but we are also foggy about who and what we want to become. We are not even sure what we want to accomplish, and so we lack a cause to galvanize and streamline our individual and collective efforts. Even when there seems to be a cause, oftentimes, the leaders and members of the same organization don't share the same easily identifiable goals. There may, indeed, be lavish mission statements, and there may even be a vision statement, but the routine activities of most organizations have practically nothing to do with these statements, however elaborately they may have been prepared.

In summary, as a group, we Muslim Americans have yet to unequivocally resolve our identity issues and genuinely commit to America. We have yet to wholeheartedly espouse the divine mission.

d- Interactions between Immigrant and African American Muslims

As indicated earlier, the African American Muslim community has had its own set of problems that have hindered its growth and full integration into American society. Some of these problems stemmed from the past experiences of the general African American community, and some of them were engendered or amplified by the Nation of Islam phenomenon. Nevertheless, Islam (and immigrant Muslims) should have facilitated, rather than disrupted, the integration of African American Muslims into society as American-born citizens who had fought their way into the mainstream.

Unfortunately, though, that's not what happened. As a result of the immigrant community's inadequate ideology and inappropriate strategy for implementing Islam here, many African American Muslims ended up feeling like aliens in their own country and even in the larger African American community. Consequently, many African American Muslims lag behind the broader African American community in terms of social integration.

It may not be clear whether the African American Muslim community was unable and/or unwilling to play host to the immigrants (as the people of Medina did when they hosted the Prophet and his immigrant companions), or whether the immigrants did not give them the chance. Indeed, African American Muslims may have been too consumed with their own issues and challenges to pay much attention to the influx of Muslim immigrants. Moreover, many immigrants were students living in college towns and later in the suburbs, whereas the African American communities tended to be concentrated in inner cities. Additionally, the African American orthodox Muslim community was still in its infancy until the 1960s. That decade witnessed two simultaneous but largely independent developments. These are very important events in the history of Islam in America: (1) We saw the establishment of an immigrant Muslim community, mainly through the founding of the MSA (Muslim Students Association) in 1963. (2) The African American orthodox Muslim community emerged mainly from the growing ranks of the Nation of Islam under the leadership of W. Deen Mohammad.

Each of the two communities went its own way, and there was no serious attempt from either side to establish a meaningful partnership through which they could have assisted and empowered one another. Rather than building on the accomplishments and the advantages of the African American community, immigrant Muslims chose to start from scratch and to go about community building as if they were the first and only Muslims in the United States. When the two groups did interact, it was not beneficial to either group. They passed on problems more than help, and African American Muslims appear to have gotten the "short end of the stick" in the exchange.

Driven by a sense of religious purity and superiority/authority, some immigrant Muslim groups set out to indoctrinate African Americans with foreign ideology and culture. They also tended to transmit their overseas focus and their largely anti-American political views and resentment toward

American foreign policies. As a result, African American Muslims have become even more civically disengaged and ambivalent toward America. This has further alienated them from society at large and even from others in the African American community.

The situation did not improve much after the fading of the "myth of return." Even when immigrants did begin to accept the fact that America had become their new homeland, they were slow to revise their approach to African American Muslims; and by the time they did, the gap between the two groups had seemingly become too wide to be bridged.

If anything, the situation substantially worsened with the upsurge of ultraconservative and radical interpretations of Islam. This approach tended to spread widely in the African American Muslim community, and it had a very negative impact on that community's growth and on its relationship with society. To be sure, there have been some local and national coordination efforts that involved both immigrants and African American leaders and institutions, but they have proved to be mostly ceremonial and superficial.

e- Diversity

As a microcosm of the Muslim world, the Muslim American community is very ethnically, ideologically, and socioeconomically diverse. In the absence of a rallying cause, competent leadership, and sound and inclusive organizational structures, this remarkable diversity has resulted in rampant fragmentation—rather than producing synergy.

With few exceptions, each Islamic center and organization has served as the exclusive enclave of an ethnically or ideologically "pure" group. At best, those who fell outside of this group have been accepted as guests, potential recruits, supporters, or "helping hands." Most community founders and leaders have had limited skill and minimal experience in community organizing; and any coordination efforts, at either the local or national level, have been erratic and inconsequential. Interpersonal conflicts have been routine and have often turned into personal or "tribal" confrontations that metamorphosed into zero-sum power struggles. This has resulted in splits in the community—or in the disenfranchisement of the "losing side." However, as things have played out, the result has been the further weakening of the community overall.

f- The Gender Issue: The Status and Role of Muslim Women

This is probably the one area where our cultural baggage has most limited us. We have imported and clung to obsolete, "old school" ideas, which have nothing to do with Islam and have no place in America. This has resulted in the marginalization of our women—in both our community and in society. We have not permitted or encouraged the involvement of Muslim women in any meaningful personal development endeavors, community efforts, or opportunities for civic engagement. We have not even prepared them sufficiently for child-rearing in our new American homeland. As a result, the community has been deprived of the unique contributions of half its members. Moreover, the alienation of Muslim women has, in countless ways, hurt our families, our future generations, and the image of Islam.

In most parts of the Muslim world, there is considerable confusion as to the status and role of women. Consequently, their situation is even worse than that of men, which is lamentable. Although much of the oppression and exclusion of women is done in the name of Islam, in reality, it runs against the teachings of Islam. In fact, Islam has no genuine gender issue.

To be sure, the situation of women in the Muslim world has improved considerably over the last few decades, but that has had only a limited impact within the Muslim community, which has remained largely isolated and frozen in time. In some ways, cultural changes in the American Muslim community, in terms of women's roles and rights, were not keeping up with the limited changes that were occurring for women overseas; and in no way were we keeping up with the changes in American society at large. Our regard and treatment of our wives, daughters, and sisters made their lives archaic and obsolete—with little incentive or opportunity for meaningful self-development or community involvement. Our chronic "myth of return" provided further disincentive for women to engage with American society. Clinging to the belief that they would return to their countries of origin, many women have spent a huge chunk of their time chasing "sale prices" on items they wanted to take back home. Some women learned to drive to the shopping mall before they learned the language of the land!

As indicated previously, the American Muslim community was designed in the image of contemporary Islamic movements. Those movements have been largely male dominated and gender separated, with a separate organizational structure and only a limited role for women. Indeed, in reaction to the rampant moral laxity in society, for quite some time, the Islamic movement has adopted an excessively conservative stand regarding women and has focused on the hijab (woman's Islamic dress) and duties of women and has paid only lip service to women's emancipation and rights.

As is the case with most other issues, there has been no real shift in our handling of this issue despite the fading of the "myth of return." Instead, this situation, which stems from religious and social conservatism, got much worse in the 1990s. Much of the reason, or blame, can be attributed to the upsurge of the archconservative brand of Islam, a throwback to the past, which is distinguished not only by its puritanical rigidity but also by its Bedouin culture.

As has been true with some of the other cultural baggage we have mixed with Islam, this practice has been passed on to young generations who now find themselves torn between two extreme lifestyles: strict gender segregation in the community on the one hand and totally unrestricted gender interaction at school on the other. Additionally, although there were some successful attempts at organizational integration of our first-generation and second-generation Muslim women, most of those attempts were met with fierce resistance. As a result, there are few exceptions to the rule of parallel structures and activities within most Muslim organizations and Islamic centers. This is generally true even though the rules of gender segregation have relaxed a bit and even though some institutions have modified their organization and practices to facilitate more participation by women. Interestingly, among the youth, sisters seem to be far more active and committed than brothers.

Unsurprisingly, the disenfranchisement of our women has had devastating ripple effects on our growth and advancement as a community, both directly and indirectly. First, the community's planning and operations have been deprived of an indispensable perspective and of substantial resources. This has been particularly wasteful, even foolish, because many women have not been otherwise employed outside the home. These women could have made important contributions to our efforts, given the free time on their hands; but we ignored or squandered that resource. Second, the fact that many Islamic centers and Muslim organizations have not been "women friendly" has resulted in the exclusion of a large number of families who either did not "meet their profile" and did not feel welcome or who found dealing with the situation unfathomable. Moreover, if mothers didn't come out, their children were automatically excluded. This factor has probably excluded more people than any other single aspect of community noninclusiveness. That is because people excluded or marginalized for reasons of ethnicity, ideology, or social status generally have other alternatives. Our treatment of women may well be one of the important reasons that many of our youth have deserted our Islamic centers and organizations.

Moreover, husbands (especially activists) and wives lived in two different worlds. That took a heavy toll on family cohesion and harmony. Also, the disenfranchisement of women has severely limited their ability to teach and mentor their children beyond early childhood. This has widened our generation gap, which was already extreme. We have had parents born and raised overseas on the one side, still planning to return, and American-born and raised children on the other, a new generation with no expectations of leaving America. Finally, the situation contributed significantly to the continued social isolation of our families and community. Our family and communal models have been too obsolete to be acceptable to mainstream America, and they have belied all the talk about the "liberated" status and role of women in Islam.

Fortunately, over the last decade, there have been some courageous voices which have challenged the status quo and effected some notable change. However, as with most other issues, before this one was adequately resolved, the effort and progress seem to have leveled off. The essential changes we still need include

- normalizing the situation of Muslim American women and treating them as full members of the community,
- fully integrating women into the community and eliminating artificial segregation,
- making the facilities and the operations of our centers and organizations more family friendly and women friendly, and
- empowering Muslim women to be stakeholders in the community and to be civically aware and engaged.

As with all needed change, clear-cut Islamic guidelines must be observed. Aside from those requirements, all other considerations are on the table and open for reassessment, adjustment, and if necessary, reversal.

g- Converts

In spite of our limited and largely inefficient *dawa* efforts over the last few decades, thousands of Americans have converted to Islam. Had these individuals been properly welcomed and assimilated, they could have greatly facilitated the demystifying and rooting of Islam and Muslims in America. However, once again, we have never seemed to "miss an opportunity to miss an opportunity."

We should have aimed at giving these newcomers the essence of Islam from original sources, not our foreign and culturally biased version. We should have empowered them to (1) act as role models for the people around them, (2) effectively engage their environments, and (3) serve as liaisons between us and the larger society thus facilitating our integration. What actually happened, though, was almost the opposite.

Socially, many converts were left out in the cold after having been practically snatched out of their immediate environments. Yet they were never properly integrated into our community. The version of Islam that they were taught included elements of an unhealthy heritage and culture mixed with anti-American political views. The outcome was that they became foreigners in their own country and strangers to their own people. This has reinforced American perception of Islam as a foreign and strange religion. Like their fellow immigrant Muslims, the converts became isolated, civically disengaged, and ambivalent toward America.

Islamic groups in America have been more interested in recruiting and indoctrinating converts than in accommodating and empowering them. Also, many converts have become very disappointed with the flagrant contrast between the ideals of Islam and the individual and collective behavior of Muslims. Some, especially women, have had bad personal experiences with Muslims.

Consequently, converts have inherited some of our immigrant baggage, and they have been adversely affected by it. While some have joined existing groups, others have deserted Islam or have at least given up on participation in the community. A third group fell prey to radicalism. Most converts wrestle with the identity crisis that afflicts immigrant Muslims—struggling to reconcile being Muslim and being American, as if Islam were an ethnic entity rather than a universal faith.

h- Muslim American Youth: A Phenomenon That Completely Caught the Community Off Guard

In addition to respecting and enhancing the vital role of women, another of the key factors in the advancement of communities and nations has to do with the youth. Successful transition from one generation to another is essential. In order for communities and nations to thrive, each generation must plan for and prepare future generations—successfully passing the torch on to them. The emerging generations, in turn, must build on the accomplishments of previous ones. In our Muslim American community, these conditions have not been adequately met.

As we have discussed previously, our community was designed as a temporary shelter to protect temporary immigrants from the negative elements of American society until they were ready to go back home. It was established with a focus on meeting immediate needs—not the long-term needs of a community that would end up raising its children here. Consequently, beyond occasional educational programs and Islamic schooling, very little attention was paid to the needs of future generations. The Islamic schools have consisted, for the most part, of either largely inefficient weekend schools or full-time schools that have only catered to a tiny segment of the population. Like our Islamic centers, our schools were not designed to prepare our children for engaging in American society. Rather, they were meant to protect them and prepare them to return to their parents' homeland.

During our community's founding phase, our population consisted primarily of first generation immigrants and their young children. These people were reasonably accommodated by existing organizations, programs, and facilities. However, as immigration to the U.S. became more difficult and the Muslim baby-boom generation came of age, a substantial demographic shift started to take place. Young people who were born and raised here as both Muslims and as Americans were beginning to comprise an increasingly large segment of our community. In our state of "mission-accomplished" dormancy, with all of our internal strife, we did not foresee this change. We were even slow to recognize it. Hence, we were unprepared and slow to acknowledge and respond to this vital issue.

Additionally, with the older generation of immigrants still functioning under the delusional influence of the "myth of return," the entire second generation (particularly teenagers and young adults) outgrew what their Islamic centers and schools had to offer. They were left out in the cold—confused and unprepared for the very society from which they had been protected, but with which they now had to deal. This situation, combined with the disenfranchisement of their mothers and the lack of preparedness of the overall community, again, widened the severe generation gap and accelerated the family breakdown. There was no real precedent for the situation, and we have lacked both resources and support to adequately address the needs of our youth.

For the most part, our community's organizations, programs, and facilities were not designed to accommodate this new segment of Muslim Americans who were caught between two different worlds. The whole setup was not inspiring, appealing, or relevant to them. The community had no way to understand, let alone address, their issues and concerns—either at home or elsewhere. Even though, earlier on, we had begun to speak of our youth as a priority, our actions never really reflected our rhetoric, and neither did the allocation of our resources.

After securing the basic needs of the immigrant generation, the community lost most of its momentum. Its subsequent growth primarily involved mushrooming haphazardly in all directions. Both locally and nationally, the community had managed to start some youth programs, but they were mostly improvised and lacked needed expertise and resources. Most youth programs were initiated without any clear vision and were still being designed to meet the increasingly obsolete goals of isolation and protection. The youth programs were also negatively affected by the baggage and problems of the older Muslim American community. Those inherited problems included ambivalence toward America and failure to abandon the "myth of return"; but more generally, they included a lack of vision, long-term planning, continuity, or stability. It is no wonder that—in spite of the sincerity and hard work of many activists—the programs were not consistent, catered to a small segment of the youth, and had limited impact.

Like so many well-intentioned efforts, our youth programs suffered from marginalization and inadequate management. They lacked any clear vision or long-term plans. Nonetheless, some facilities were built, and some programs were offered; but it was too little and too late to attract the attention of young people. This was a generation that had been left behind by a community that was not designed for the realities of their world. The impact was manifest in the lack of participation at the mosques and organizations even by the sons and daughters of the activists. Although reliable statistics are not available, one can easily observe that a much larger number of youth are detached from the mosques and from our community than was the case with their first-generation immigrant parents. This would apply to the children of first-generation converts as well. When it comes to Islamic activism, our community has largely lost its age continuum.

To be sure, there have always been some serious individual and organizational attempts and initiatives to adequately tackle the youth issue. However, such attempts and initiatives have been consistently halted by the prevailing culture, structure, and bureaucracy.

Only recently have local communities become more serious about our youth and started to commit substantial resources toward their programs. Now, there is a proliferation of youth centers, and youth coordinators and staff are being hired. As a result, many centers are offering more consistent and systematic educational and recreational programs, especially for younger children. However, as young Muslims graduate from high school (or even from middle school), they also "graduate" from those programs; and some of their needs outgrow whatever the community currently has to offer.

In spite of all the good will and all the hard work by many community activists, we have yet to make significant inroads in remedying the "generation breakdown" that is jeopardizing our future as a community. Our young people are our future, and they should be the future of Islam in America. The challenges our young people face regarding their future are far more alarming than we are ready to admit; and it is futile to remain in denial about them or to continue "patching up" our situation.

i- Rigid, Radical, and Extreme Islam Drives the Community in the Wrong Direction at the Wrong Time

From its inception and under the influence of mainstream Islamic movements, for the most part, the Muslim American community has been culturally and socially conservative—but religiously moderate. However, by the early 1990s, this situation was being challenged by newly active and radically religious groups. Their rigid and confrontational interpretations of Islam and their intimidating approaches to fellow Muslims reinforced some of our most severe limitations: our isolation from society, the alienation of our people, the marginalization of Muslim women, and our internal strife. Worse still, some of these groups advocated violence.

Ironically, these new groups emerged just at the moment that the "myth of return" had begun to fade, and people were just beginning to discuss the likelihood of permanently staying in America. We were beginning to debate some fundamental issues, such as our identity and mission and our integration within society (*tawteen*). The contentious discussions led to confusion and chaos in the community over the course of several years, and the situation was only aggravated and prolonged by the forceful push back of the new archconservative groups. Extremism eventually metamorphosed into acts of terrorism such as the 1993 New York World Trade Center (WTC) bombing. That event claimed the lives of six people and injured more than one thousand. Terrorism allegedly "in the name of Islam," of course, introduced Islam and Muslims to the American public in a very negative way, and that greatly reduced the odds of our successful transition toward openness and integration into American society.

The community succeeded reasonably in limiting the spread and immediate damage of radical Islam, but it did not confront its intellectual underpinnings. This was a mistake. As a result, this intimidating phenomenon has had lasting negative effects on some community members' mind-set, lifestyle, and perspective on America. It has also negatively impacted Muslim Americans' overall understanding of Islam and of their role in the community and in society. Both African American and immigrant Muslims have suffered, directly and indirectly, from the consequences of the emergence of radical Islam. As a community, we have only begun to slowly and painfully recover from this devastating blow, which derailed any efforts to indigenize Islam, squandered many opportunities over the years, and pushed some members of the community toward cultural and religious stiffness. The entire community was pushed or drawn further away from mainstream society. In the end, however, it has been this very same trend that has inadvertently forced us to deal with society and with the system, although we were still unprepared and were starting from a weak vantage point—both conceptually and practically.

j- Our Sudden, Forced, and Negative Exposure to the American Society

Prior to the first Persian Gulf War in 1991 and the WTC (World Trade Center) bombing in 1993, most of the previous changes and challenges for our community were largely internal. Our failure to proactively handle them had delayed our inevitable paradigm shift and transition. As a result of the delay and sociopolitical stagnation, we lost our sense of direction. However, following the 1993 bombing, our community problems multiplied. Integration into the mainstream would now be challenged by an increasingly negative domestic and international image. However, yet again, we were way too late in tackling our urgent, new, and deep problems, and our eventual effort was also too superficial.

As the first, direct, armed confrontation between America and a Muslim country was about to begin, our community was forced, for the first time, to really deal with American society. Many Muslim Americans had voiced opposition to the war, and the community braced itself for any subsequent backlash. With the WTC bombings, the foiled plot to bomb other New York City landmarks the same year, and the PBS airing of the infamous "Jihad in America" documentary the following year, the seeds of Islamophobia were irrevocably sown in America. All of the bad exposure posed serious problems for Muslim Americans as individuals, as families, and as a wider group.

Whatever doubt remained about the gravity of our new sociopolitical reality vanished in 1995, when Muslims were automatically and immediately blamed for the bombing of a federal building in Oklahoma City. The blast killed 168 people, including nineteen small children, and it was the deadliest act of terrorism on U.S. soil prior to the 9/11 attacks. Until the real (non-Muslim) perpetrators were identified a couple of days later, media and official fingers-of-blame were pointing toward Muslims. The allegations were false, but damage was done. It was very clear that our image problem was not a small one.

In response to all of these incidents, the 1990s witnessed the slow beginning of Muslim efforts at outreach and political participation. Yet again, Muslims embarked on these efforts without a real vision, trying to do just enough to put out the fire. We were moving along—slowly and reluctantly—when the 9/11 terrorist attacks of 2001 changed everything, both in America and in the whole world. For the Muslim American community, humongous challenges instantly and dramatically raised the bar and widened the gap between where the community was and where it needed to be. The sudden new reality confronted Muslim Americans with the fundamental questions that we had avoided for too long: "Who are we? What is our mission in life? And what is our role in America?"

5- MUSLIM AMERICANS IN POST-9/11 REALITY

While focusing on the post-9/11 phase, this section includes a succinct analysis of the history of Muslim American outreach and civic engagement efforts. This process began toward the end of the founding phase of our community, as the "myth of return" started to fade. At that time, Muslim American immigrants were just beginning to wake up to the fact that we would be living in America permanently, not going back to our former homelands.

To be sure, not all Muslims who came to America arrived with plans to eventually go back home. Those who planned to stay from the beginning were never under the illusion that they would return to their nations of origin. They tended to manage their lives differently from other Muslim Americans, and probably more successfully, on average. Some of them showed an early interest in public affairs, moving in that direction by the mid-'80s, with a timing that coincided beautifully with the end of our community's founding phase. As our previous focus on preserving our identities and building infrastructure became less compelling, a new focus was needed. For these individuals, as was true for Muhammad, the mosque served as a base, not as an enclave. Establishing a mosque was a phase and not the ultimate goal. Indeed, one of the earliest Muslim public affairs institutions (the Muslim Public Affairs Council or MPAC) started as a spin-off of the Islamic Center of Southern California.

Some of those courageous pioneers in public affairs had no hang-ups or inhibitions, and did not yield to the intimidation of radicals and isolationists. They ventured boldly into the public square early on and against all odds. However, for one reason or another, they were not able to bring the community along with them, and the community was moving rapidly in a totally different direction, if indeed it was moving in any direction at all. In fact, in the late 1980s and early 1990s, our community was still focused overseas and inward, consumed by infighting for the control of its institutions, and struggling to transition beyond our "myth of return." Simultaneously, we were trying to contain the damage caused by the blitz of radical Islam. Although the community never fell under the control of radical and isolationist groups, the groups did manage to push the whole community in the wrong direction and to inflict serious and lasting damage on both immigrant and African American Muslims. The damage radical Islam caused to the community included the intellectual intimidation of prominent and moderate groups, which stifled their evolution and integration into society.

Muslims' early engagement in public affairs was largely elitist and did not really take root in the community. It was also limited in scope and was not truly mainstream. Its focus was not on local and domestic mainstream issues. Rather, it was primarily concerned with global issues that were affecting Muslims here or abroad. Still, however, the startup was promising; and from the outset, there were some public affairs activists who did introduce some mainstream flavor. Overall, that was a pioneer effort by visionary leaders, and it did have some impact and made some inroads into the political system. Some aspects of that work continue up to today, while other aspects became bogged down by internal politics and a lack of discipline.

By the mid-'90s, a new breed of Muslim civic and political activism emerged. This breed, which adopted a civil rights strategy and preached victimhood, had the opposite problem when compared to the problems that had limited the early civic pioneers. The Muslim American self-advocacy for civil rights had a much better success in rallying the community and in fundraising, but much less success in the society at large. A number of factors contributed to the visibility and popularity of this effort in the community, but some of the same factors, plus shortsighted vision, limited its evolution and its ability to make inroads in society. Overall, it is debatable whether this wave of activism helped us with integration into society or instead actually contributed to our further alienation.

In Muslim American communities nationwide, at the local level, there were very few efforts at outreach and civic engagement. Those that did take place were basically timid, on-campus *dawa* activities—or occasional, largely symbolic interactions with churches or schools. These sporadic events were initiated by committed individuals who had the best of intentions, but the available educational materials were not appropriate for the American public audience. So people were often forced to "make do" with whatever they had, which included mostly imported and translated books and videos of questionable suitability. There were, however, at least a few exceptions in the form of reasonably tailored and relevant publications by organizations such as the Institute of Islamic Information and Education.

Prior to 9/11, outreach and civic engagement efforts were given very low priority, and those that existed were very limited in scope. With few exceptions, any efforts undertaken lacked sufficient purpose and substance, were not guided by an expansive vision, were slow in growth and evolution, and were inappropriately designed for the mainstream.

As usual, in the absence of a crisis or a threat, the American Muslim community missed about a decade of opportunity between the first wake-up call in early 1993 and the "tsunami" of September 2001. The chance to capitalize calmly on the initiatives of the early outreach pioneers had passed. After 9/11, a large part of the agenda had to be emergency damage control.

Indeed, the terrorist attacks of 9/11 and their aftermath and ramifications had very devastating effects on America and on Islam. This harmed Muslims and Muslim causes everywhere. The attacks killed three thousand innocent people, collapsed the twin towers of the World Trade Center (WTC) in New York, and damaged the Pentagon and several other buildings. Four civilian jetliners were also destroyed, along with their crews and passengers. The attacks constituted a major blow to American national security, as well as to American pride and the economy.

Additionally, 9/11 gave Islamophobes and neoconservatives lots of ammunition to push their destructive agendas at home and abroad; and those people worked effectively to create a hostile environment for Muslim Americans. Moreover, the Bush Administration's all-out war on terrorism, directly and indirectly, pitted America against Muslims in many parts of the world; and Muslim Americans were caught in the middle. On our home front, in an attempt to prevent more attacks, law enforcement agencies cast a wide net. As a result, the Muslim American community was the target of some draconian laws and measures that placed it under siege. Our leaders, activists, and institutions were viewed with suspicion. To be sure, laws and measures targeting the community had started earlier on in response to the first WTC attack, but there was no precedent in Muslim American experience to the societal changes that occurred following 9/11.

On the surface, the whole situation seemed to bolster the barrier between the community and society. The odds against Muslim Americans' success at outreach and integration into society had increased, as society might now be less likely to welcome us or even treat us fairly. For many Muslim Americans who had escaped persecution in their original countries to come to America, this horrible situation was anything but promising. In fact, it was a "déjà vu" experience.

However, the unprecedented scrutiny of our community produced mixed results. On one hand, it caused tremendous and protracted suffering in the community. Everyone felt it at every level, including community leaders, institutions, and average community members. The situation instilled widespread and substantial fear among our people, which only added to the already-long list of excuses for disengagement. On the other hand, however, the adverse climate acted to put the community on its toes. It also strengthened the argument for our integration into society, even if only out of necessity. Looking closely at American Muslims also helped to demystify Islam and Muslims to people outside of our community, in both governmental and nongovernmental circles. Suddenly, we had a need to be known, and everyone had a need to know more about us.

In its response to the post-9/11 realities, the Muslim American community was inspired by an emerging leadership that made a swift and accurate assessment of the situation. These people had both the vision and the "boots on the ground" to lead and mobilize the newly motivated community. They launched an impressive outreach campaign that made up, in weeks and months, for many blunders we had made and opportunities we had missed over the years.

Even though we were shunned and avoided by public officials and demonized by biased media, the response of the Muslim American community to the 9/11 shock was remarkable and impressive in its swiftness, intensity, duration, and extent. It is ironic that our community opened up most during a time that apparently discouraged its members and antagonized American society. Our handling of this crisis was probably the community's most significant accomplishment since our successful campaign to establish Islamic centers and schools nationwide.

For several years before 9/11, there were a lot of low-key, conceptual, and practical efforts to rebuild and transform the community. Many recognized the need to address the protracted recession and stagnation that had started in the late '80s and continued till the mid-'90s. Those transformative efforts brought the community a long way and put it in a much better position to deal with the far-reaching and dangerously threatening 9/11 repercussions. While there was no way for anyone to be prepared for 9/11 and the aftermath, the community's impressive performance proved that it has tremendous latent potential that needs only a cause and leadership to be awakened. The job of leadership is to see to it that the community remains awake, and energy remains kinetic, without need for a cause in the form of a crisis or impending threat. Let's be clear: the job of Muslim American leadership is to inspire and guide community passion for a cause that is centered on our divine mission and blended with a genuine commitment to America. Thus, our leaders must produce, motivate, and maintain a mission-driven and society-focused community.

The second great lesson we learned from 9/11 is that it is the timely, swift, and effective engagement of the environment by visionary leaders that will engender and sustain a relevant movement—not the unduly meticulous plans and procedures prepared and clung to by bureaucrats and perfectionists.

While the repercussions of the attacks constituted a grave external challenge to the community, they inadvertently liberated us from serious internal blocks that had held us back for far too long. Indeed, the tragedy ironically freed our community from chronic reluctance to integrate into American society and from the intimidation of radical and isolationist Muslim groups. We began to get out of our own way.

As a result of our years of mobilization, "outreach" and "civic engagement" became more than just controversial theoretical concepts and low-priority activities. The focus shifted to execution, and our concerns relating to outreach and civic engagement jumped from the bottom of our list of priorities to the top. The evidence can be seen in the increased number of actively engaged individuals and in the increased number of people who at least believe in outreach and engagement. It is also clear that there has been a substantial increase in the resources allocated toward these activities. The numbers of various political, legal, advocacy, and charity activities also speak volumes.

We could have turned our impressive post-9/11 crisis management campaign into a major paradigm shift. The momentum we had as a community could have fostered a widespread culture of outreach and civic engagement. We could have moved American Islam out of the shadowy fringes and begun rooting Islam and Muslim Americans in the center of our society. That is what we needed, but it has not happened. In fact, even a few years post-9/11, we have yet to make that true paradigm shift that we have needed for decades. The community went, yet again, into "mission-accomplished" mode. We demobilized prematurely. So we missed yet another great opportunity to sustain momentum and transition to the next level. Moreover, our outreach and civic engagement really arose from the need to protect ourselves from the anti-Islam atmosphere after 9/11, when isolation became neither possible nor sufficient. Therefore, those efforts were only new mechanisms to serve and preserve our old founding paradigm that was designed to protect us from society. There is nothing wrong with defending the image of Islam and protecting the rights of Muslims; but unless our goals extend beyond that, outreach and civic engagement will continue to be shallow and sporadic activities with questionable relevance and impact.

Although our community landed in a much better position after the post-9/11 crisis calmed somewhat, we still have a long way to go if we want to root civic engagement in Islam and root Muslim Americans in a genuine citizenship—a citizenship that includes commitment to the well-being of America. When our community begins to embody a genuine and coherent American Muslim identity, driven by a mission that fuses the religious and civic dimensions, our civic engagement will become genuine, meaningful, sustained, effective, and efficient.[28] Without that, we will take one step forward and two steps back. Our residual gains from our post-9/11 aggressive outreach will remain scattered and crude. Many newly created opportunities, now waiting to be seized, will wait indefinitely. Much of our vast potential will remain untapped. Finally, many of our chronic issues and deficiencies will not be resolved or even confronted. By and large, statistics indicate that our community is still regarded as "mysterious" and "suspect." From our perspective, that means we are very vulnerable. We have yet to really be invited to "sit at the table." As things stand, our destiny is not in our own hands; rather, it depends on factors that are beyond our control. All of this together leads to one conclusion: complacency is not something we can afford.

In response to this situation, one of the unpublicized outcomes of the post-9/11 societal changes and pressures was the accelerated birth of this project, which had been in the making for several years. After patient cultivation, growing pains, and generous sacrifices and input from scores of people over that period, the plans for this project matured. Herein is offered a solid intellectual foundation and a clear and integrated blueprint for the reconstruction of our community as a genuine and relevant Islamic American movement, a movement that will fulfill the divine mission and effect significant and sustained positive change in our society.

With this, we conclude the depiction of our crisis and the analysis of its historical progression. We now move to trace the root causes of the crisis, as it is through understanding our crisis and its causes that we will become better able to pave the way for the optimal development of our vision and strategy.

---

28   Dr. Maher Hathout. (2006). *In Pursuit of Justice: The Jurisprudence of Human Rights in Islam* [Book].

3. THE ROOT CAUSES OF OUR COMMUNITY'S CRISIS

Contrary to the prevalent Muslim American focus on activities, facilities, and administrative concerns, we strongly believe that resolving our crisis requires something different. Only after thoroughly identifying and understanding the root causes of our crisis will our community be able to develop sound and effective strategies for crisis resolution. We also strongly believe that the key to the renaissance of our community lies in the intellectual and strategic realms, beginning with reexamining our understanding and implementation of Islam. Indeed, our renaissance requires that we rediscover our religion and that we experience a major intellectual and psychological paradigm shift. We must then reset our priorities and revise our methodologies.

In developing a thorough understanding and explanation of our current crisis, we began with an examination of the symptoms as well as the historical progression that led to this situation. The next step in analyzing the crisis will be the enumeration and examination of its root causes. Clarification of those underlying issues should pave the way for a discussion about the tenets of our movement—and also about how we can effectively chart a bright and promising future.

1—A DEFINING MISSION THAT WAS ABANDONED

As indicated in part 2, Islam is a divine life mission that defines Muslims both individually and collectively and constitutes their raison d'être. In general, communities and nations don't thrive without a driving cause. This is particularly so of Muslims, because it is the divine mission that has always defined, inspired, energized, and unified us. That has been true ever since the time of Muhammad, and it is true today. Therefore, the cornerstone of our project is nothing less than the fostering of a genuine and wholehearted commitment to the divine mission of Islam. We aim to promote this not only with Muslim Americans as individuals but also with Muslim American institutions.

Throughout the history of Islam, there has been a vitally strong connection between our commitment to efficient fulfillment of divine mission on the one hand and our condition, relevance, impact, and overall contribution to the advancement of humanity on the other. When Islam is stripped of its sense of divine mission, it becomes a passive and obsolete religion. When Muslims abandon their defining mission, they become complacent, fragmented, and stagnant. Unfortunately, this is exactly what has happened for Muslim Americans, and it is why we are stuck in a crisis from which we cannot emerge without a recommitment to our defining mission. We need to resume our role as God's *khalifa* (steward).

It was in order to fulfill the divine mission and effect needed change that Muhammad built his community. His commitment to the divine mission comprised most of his life, work, and legacy. Indeed, history would have proceeded quite differently had he preached Islam merely as a personal and private faith or a way of life and had he built a community of practicing Muslims (or even Muslim activists) who were consumed with managing their own affairs, as is the case with the majority of the Muslim American community. The work and lives of Muhammad and his companions would have required far less discipline and sacrifice and would have encountered far less resistance had they not been committed to the divine mission and to effecting change. Islam would not have endured, let alone spread across the globe giving birth to a great civilization.

Honest self-analysis reveals that, although our shared beliefs and rituals, and even our activism, do provide us with some sense of community, there are serious questions about how long and in what way this community will survive. In some ways, we resemble a loosely structured fraternity, with limited common goals and recurrent crises, which may galvanize our group, but for only a limited time. Only a genuine commitment to the divine mission can engender and sustain a true community of believers—keeping them continuously motivated and united to realize their full potential and impact. It was their proper and in-depth understanding of Islam as a life mission that led to the wholehearted commitment by Muhammad and the companions. This enabled their continuous vigilance for almost half a century before the

Muslims began their slow descent. Islam then experienced several successful and unsuccessful rebounds before the final collapse and disintegration in the beginning of the twentieth century. Make no mistake: it was the fading of the Muslims' sense of the divine mission and the crumbling of the prophetic model that triggered their descent.

As discussed in part 2, the main reason behind our crisis in America (and throughout the world) is that, individually and collectively, we are no longer mission driven. We don't have a common rallying cause. This is why we lack high aspirations, our motivation is erratic, our resolve is shaky, and our bonds are weak. It is no wonder that we have no voice or impact and that our contributions to America are insignificant. The divine mission is so intertwined with all of the various aspects of our lives that it should come as no surprise at all that our abandoning it has had devastating effects on us, limiting us both personally and communally.

Today, a good number of the millions of Muslim Americans and hundreds of millions of other Muslims worldwide are—more or less—religiously observant. Of this number, a further delineation can be made between those who are active and those who are not. Some activists are "freelancers," volunteering or donating occasionally. Others are dedicated members of some Islamic group or organization. The numbers of participants drop drastically as we move upward along the dimensions of commitment and dedication, from one category to another, starting with the nonpracticing Muslims and ending with the organized activists. Only a tiny percentage of Muslims are as active or involved as they could be. Moreover, there is a category that is largely missing: the mission-driven Muslim individual, group, organization, and community.

An essential tenet of our movement will be to invite all Muslims, however active or observant or committed they may now be, to make a true and genuine commitment to Islam as a life mission. Moreover, we will invite them to make that move directly, without having to go through the different stages, which, throughout history, have trapped so many Muslims who have mistaken one of those stages for the ultimate destination. We believe this form of inclusion will best emulate Muhammad's model of community building. Indeed, during his time, Islam was presented as a mission to everyone, and it was espoused as such by all of those who joined the community of believers—irrespective of the extent of their personal devotion and knowledge.

When individuals converted to Islam, they committed to the cause and to the leadership and joined the community of believers all in one move—as a package deal. They immediately began to fulfill the mission in their environment, which at that time was the tribe. They assumed positions and roles in the community that matched their skills and their dedication to the cause. Because the divine mission represents an incredibly noble, demanding, and lifelong endeavor, commitment to it launched the early Muslim individuals and communities on a path of continuous improvement and empowerment toward the realization of their full potential and full impact.

Their commitment, in turn, led them to become closer and closer to God—the source of all power and guidance—and to seek His help and also His forgiveness for falling short of His expectations. The mission-driven life automatically results in compassion, spiritual vibrancy, and genuine brotherhood. Muhammad described the believers as a solid, cemented structure and as one body. It is no surprise that the night prayer became a mandate for the first core group of Muslims and that they were described as "monks by night, and knights by day."

On the other hand, an Islam that is stripped of any compelling sense of mission is so limited that, even if it involves Islamic activism, it cannot sufficiently inspire and challenge individuals and communities. Without that compelling sense of mission, Islam is unable to sustain people's motivation and unity. Therefore, it is not unusual for Muslim groups that are "practicing" or "observing" that sort of Islam to become stagnant and stuck. In such groups, we find a great deal of apathy and complacency. To be sure, there is a considerable difference between being mission driven versus having the sense of "mission accomplished." It is like the difference between owning an exciting start-up business and simply having a secure job. We need to think about the difference between doing something that just qualifies as good and doing what needs to be done to meet God's expectations of a great people. Jim Collins, the expert on company sustainability and growth, was right on target when he said, "Good is the enemy of great."

Like all human beings, Muslims don't have to be religious people in order to have great personal ambition. With few exceptions, however, the driving cause for dynamic Muslim communities can only stem from Islam. To sustain mobilization and constantly raise the aspirations of individuals and the community, Islam has to be espoused as a life mission. It is no wonder that even nonreligious (secular) Muslim leaders have resorted to Islam to inspire and mobilize their people for various causes, such as the struggle for liberation and independence.

a- Significance of Committing to the Divine Mission

As indicated in part 2, the divine mission is eternal and universal. It was assigned to all human beings with the creation of Adam. It was to be carried out by all of God's prophets and messengers and their followers throughout the history of humanity. The Qur'an and Muhammad's tradition make it clear that God created mankind for a purpose. After Muhammad, as the seal of prophethood, delivered the last direct guidance, God assigned to all believers the mission of relaying divine guidance to the world. This is our mission, individually and collectively, as God has entrusted us with His final and universal revelation. Therefore, our most important obligation is to see to it that the divine purpose is fulfilled and that the divine guidance is constantly renewed so that it remains relevant.

In general terms, fulfillment of the divine mission involves duties that are constant from one era to another and in all cultural environments. These duties include, primarily, the uplifting of ourselves and our people and the betterment of our society. However, in any given context, this generic mission must be "translated" into a platform that is particular to that context—with relevant priorities and discourse. Indeed, even though they delivered essentially the same message (in terms of creed), the reform aspects of the prophets' missions focused on the most pertinent issue(s) of their time; therefore, they differed in their emphasis. The divine mission is similar to a liquid. It has a definitive mass and volume, but it assumes the shape of its container. It is also like a river that takes on the color of the rock layer over which it flows.

Also discussed in part 2 is the fact that the mission of Islam is laid forth in several different ways in the Qur'an and the Hadith, reflecting its flexibility when it comes to platforms and priorities within different contexts. However, in all these contexts, it still essentially teaches us to constantly strive and challenge ourselves (individually and collectively) to be the best possible embodiments and instruments of the will of God. We are called upon to rise to each and every occasion by doing all and everything that needs to be done—come what may.

Much hinges on upholding this paradigm, a paradigm that rests on the fulfillment of the divine mission. Some of the essentials for our community include

- being able to rely on God's help and support ("If you will aid the cause of God, He will aid you, and plant your feet firmly" [Qur'an 47:7]);

- securing our special status as Muslims ("You are the best of peoples, evolved for mankind, enjoining what is right, forbidding what is wrong, and believing in God" [Qur'an 3:110]); and
- preserving religious freedom ("Did not God check one set of people by means of another, there would surely have been pulled down monasteries, churches, synagogues, and mosques in which the name of God is commemorated in abundant measure. God will certainly aid those who aid his (cause)" [Qur'an 22/40]).

All of these things depend on our fulfillment of the divine mission. As discussed above, our espousing of the divine mission puts us (individually and collectively) on a path that leads us to realize our full potential and full impact—a path that is synergetic and knows no limits.

On the other hand, if we Muslims neglect the divine mission, the direct fallout of such neglect (namely, stagnation and fragmentation) always has grave consequences for us, including the suspension of religious freedom and the spreading of mischief.

> And did not God Check one set of people by means of another, the earth would indeed be full of mischief [Qur'an 2:251].

> The Unbelievers are protectors, one of another. Unless ye do this, (protect each other), there would be tumult and oppression on earth, and great mischief [Qur'an 8:73].

Additionally, neglecting the divine mission precipitates the irrelevance and subsequent demise of the Muslim community.

> And fall into no disputes, lest ye lose heart and your power depart [Qur'an 8:46].

Lastly, mission neglect would bring to us God's reprimand and severe punishment.

> O ye who believe! What is the matter with you that when ye are asked to go forth in the cause of God, ye cling heavily to the earth? Do ye prefer the life of this world to the

Hereafter? But little is the comfort of this life as compared with the Hereafter. Unless ye go forth, He will punish you with a grievous penalty and put others in your place [Qur'an 9:38–39].

Besides these Qur'anic warnings about the consequences of neglect, Muhammad also warned us about failure to fulfill the divine mission and about failure to enjoin good and forbid evil. Islam does not permit passiveness or indifference in the face of evil or injustice or wrongdoing: "Whosoever of you sees an evil action, let him change it with his hand; and if he is not able to do so, then with his tongue; and if he is not able to do so, then with his heart; and that is the weakest of faith."[29] This Hadith establishes a strong connection between one's strength of faith and his/her level of engagement in promoting that which is good and forbidding that which is evil.

Muhammad confirmed that those who fail to forbid evil will be subjected to a severe and eminent punishment from God. Another Hadith indicates that a devout person was punished along with his village, even though he himself had never committed a sin. He was punished simply because he was indifferent toward the wrongdoing occurring around him, and he did not stand for God. No amount of devotion and worship can make up for our failure to fulfill the divine mission. Muhammad also warned us against indifference toward wrongdoing, *even if it is done with the best intentions,* because the implications of wrongdoing affect everybody—those who commit it and those who allow it. In part 2, we referred to his parable of the people in the lower decks of a ship who eventually decided to dig a hole in order to get water without bothering the people above them. Muhammad said, "If they were to leave them with this business of theirs, all of them would perish, but if they seized their hands, all of them would be saved."[30]

This parable refutes one of the main arguments that people use to justify their disengagement: that wrongdoers will pay for their action in this life and in the hereafter, while our righteousness and efforts to protect ourselves (including isolation) will save us in both. It does not take much effort to prove that such a self-centered approach is not only inconsistent with Islamic tenets

---

29 Hadith narrated by Abu Saeed Al-Khudary and reported in the Hadith book of Imam Ahmad.

30 Hadith narrated by Al-Numan bin Basheer and reported in Sahih Al-Bukhari.

but is also futile on a practical level. What barrier is thick enough to protect us, our families, and our communities from the repercussions of the things that take place in our societies? The correct approach, both Islamically and practically, is to work toward the development of sound and just social mores and governmental policies aimed at curing societal ills. It is not sufficient to do just what we believe will protect us against them. In fact, Muhammad made it clear that those who fail to stop the oppressor and forbid evil will be subject to God's severe and eminent punishment.

Neglecting or abandoning the divine mission sets off a chain reaction and puts Muslims on a steep path of decline and irrelevance that knows no limits. Along this path, there are several vicious and destructive cycles that cause the demise even of the greatest of nations and civilizations. That's what happened to Muslims in recent history, and that's what explains their severe and compounded crisis and dismal situation.

Nothing other than the neglect of the divine mission explains our crisis, and nothing will fix it except the commitment of our people and our organizations to the divine mission. That's why we call it our defining mission. And that's why the cornerstone of our project is the commitment of Muslim American individuals, centers, and organizations to Islam as a mission.

The divine mission is about living for God and working for God. This includes advocating good and forbidding evil. Therefore, as mentioned before, a commitment to God's divine mission automatically drives us ever closer toward Him. As we strive for God, as is His due, we find ourselves automatically mindful of Him, as is also His due. His ever-increasing presence in our lives then translates into a spiritual vibrancy and an ever-increasing sensitivity to the contrast between good and evil. This combination of vibrancy and awareness, in turn, boosts our motivation and ability to enjoin that which is good and forbid that which is evil, which constitutes the essence of the divine mission. Thus, we end up coming full circle from where we began.

In order to effectively implement the will of God, we must first embody it. Therefore, when we commit to the divine mission, we automatically embark on a lifelong journey that starts with self-development, which includes self-purification and self-empowerment. Not only should this process be continuous and ambitious, but it should also be comprehensive and balanced—encompassing several distinct areas that can be divided into two main categories: material and nonmaterial. Material empowerment focuses on our physical health, financial development, and time management (human being's primary material assets); whereas nonmaterial empowerment includes our spiritual, character, and intellectual development. The latter comprise our real, individual distinguishing features. The commitment to the divine mission shall automatically set off all these aspects of self-development.

The material aspects are obvious. Because the divine mission is very demanding, it requires us to be physically strong, financially stable, and efficient. Also, since an essential element of the divine mission is to be able to positively impact others, our being healthy, successful, and resourceful increases our ability to accomplish that. On the other hand, when we are struggling in our own lives, our influence on others and our contribution to the cause must necessarily be limited.

Among the nonmaterial aspects, spiritual development is an obvious by-product of our commitment to the divine mission; but the other two may require elaboration. Moral teachings and character development are essential parts of divine guidance and of the prophets' mission, which we inherited. They are so central that Muhammad summarized his mission by saying, "I was sent but to perfect people's manners."[31] Consequently, those who are championing the divine mission must strive to have great character and notably good manners.

In confronting the tremendous opposition that Muhammad faced in Mecca, his main sources of strength were his faith and his character. His manners were so perfect that the Quraish were unable to discredit him in the least despite their intense effort. God praised his character ("And thou (standest) on an exalted standard of character" [Qur'an 68:4]), and his wife Aisha said that his character was simply the Qur'an.

Engaging in constant reflection and substantive intellectual debate are musts for mission-driven Muslims (individuals and communities). These are essential to the continuous process as we work to translate the timeless, universal, and perfect divine guidance into a message, a model, and a platform with relevance to our time and circumstances. Note and remember that, because we don't live in a static world, these activities must be ongoing if we are to keep up with the world's changes and challenges. This is the only way to avoid intellectual stagnation. When people are unable to provide viable answers and solutions for the pressing questions and problems of their time, their experience of life becomes irrelevant, and they find themselves socially marginalized.

---

31   Hadith narrated by Abu Hurayrah and reported in Muwatta Maalik and Sahih Al-Bukhari.

Intellectual development is also necessary if we are to understand how the world functions and why events occur. This understanding can enable us to determine the best ways to engage in the world and our environment and to have a positive impact. This is the essence of the divine mission. Because the divine mission is about having a positive impact on our people and our society, espousing it automatically drives us toward social outreach and interaction, including civic engagement (charity, advocacy).

Finally, because the fulfillment of the divine mission, like any movement for change, is taxing and difficult and is usually met with fierce resistance and daunting challenges, it drives us toward God for His supreme guidance and help and toward one another for support in carrying such a momentous load. This has the effect of bolstering our spirituality and our unity. Both of these essential ingredients of life suffer when we neglect the divine mission.

In summary, continuous and comprehensive self-development is an essential aspect of the divine mission. It leads to spiritual vibrancy, unshakable resolve, self-confidence, high aspirations, compassion, meaningful and robust unity, civic engagement, and sustained growth. These are the primary characteristics of mission-driven individuals and communities. On the other hand, abandonment of the divine mission results in the collapse of communities and nations, and that is the cause of the current crisis in the Muslim American community and the Muslim world.

b- Translation of the Divine Mission

Again, although the fulfillment of the divine mission is a constant responsibility, the way in which it must be implemented depends on cultural and temporal contexts. Therefore, the most important individual and collective duty of believers and especially their leadership is to "translate" the divine mission into a suitable and relevant civic reform platform and to rally people behind it—thus creating a reform movement. This requires a proper translation and implementation of both the divine guidance and the prophetic model. That means we need an in-depth understanding of the letter and the spirit of the entire Islamic paradigm, including divine guidance, divine mission, and the prophetic model. It also demands that we have a thorough understanding of the society in which we live, the society where the divine mission is to be implemented. When we fail to properly understand the Islamic paradigm and the nature of society, translation of the divine mission cannot be effective. So by being out of touch with our time and place or misinformed about the Islamic paradigm, we necessarily become ineffective; and so we essentially abandon the divine mission, thereby falling short of divine expectations. This is not acceptable.

There are only two possible scenarios that we might face when it comes to our duty regarding the translation of the divine mission:

1. If we are living in a place and during a time when this translation has been properly performed and has resulted in an efficient and effective paradigm, we must join the movement and contribute our utmost toward advancing God's cause and toward the natural evolution of the paradigm and the continuous betterment of society.

2. If we are living in a place and during a period of time in which the translation of the divine mission has not been properly performed, and/or the prevailing paradigm is outdated and is not producing the desired results, we have no choice but to initiate the translation process. We must develop a fresh Islamic construct by translating the divine guidance, the prophetic model, and the divine mission; and we must rebuild the community accordingly.

In both cases, ensuring the relevance of the divine guidance is an ongoing process of reflection, study, and debate because things are always changing.

Fortunately or unfortunately, we find ourselves in the second case scenario, and this places far greater responsibility on our shoulders. However, we are thereby blessed with increased opportunities for honor and reward. Actually, the context in which we live is very similar to the context that triggered and warranted the emergence of the contemporary Islamic Movement about a century ago. At that time too, Muslims had abandoned the divine mission and were living according to an outdated Islamic construct. The Islamic movement launched what started as a successful attempt to translate the original Islamic texts into a coherent, relevant, and inspiring paradigm that would lead to an indigenous and inclusive mass movement. However, for reasons discussed previously, that paradigm did not evolve beyond a certain point; and so it was a partially translated, stagnant, and defective version that activists brought to the United States. That is what has been used to build our Muslim American community. So here we are.

To be fair though, deficient as it was, the paradigm was good enough to build and manage a transient community whose goal was to preserve members' Islamic identity and keep activists connected till they would return back home. In fact, the Islamic centers, Islamic schools, and some educational programs and service-providing organizations actually did more than simply preserve identity and maintain connectivity. They also enabled many immigrant Muslims to discover their faith, and many people were recruited to the movement.

As was the case in its original countries, that paradigm had tremendous positive effects on the religiosity of individuals but very limited effects on society; and in our case, it has had a limited effect even on the largest segment of our own community, which was largely left behind and did not associate with the Islamic centers or with the Muslim organizations.

Overall, the founding and prevalent paradigm of our community substantially exceeded its original goals, but it has also substantially exceeded its functional timeframe and remained in place, even after it had become exhausted and obsolete. That sums up the dilemma for our community.

For a number of reasons discussed elsewhere in this book, the community, in the beginning, did not feel the need to develop a fresh Islamic construct, nor has it been able or willing to go through a real paradigm shift, even after the need for a new paradigm became obvious and long overdue.

The community's only rallying causes have been partial and temporary translations of the divine mission, a patch-up approach that could not engender sustained mobilization or real unity. The only times our community has functioned as a mission-driven body have been during our campaigns to establish Islamic centers. During those campaigns, which constituted the proper contextual translation of the divine mission, the community dug out a lot of energy, dedication, and creativity, and engendered a remarkable level of brotherhood and unity.

For a number of reasons discussed elsewhere in this book, instead of the new beginnings they could have been, the Islamic centers became the ends in themselves. Each Islamic center became a goal and a refuge from society, rather than becoming a base and a springboard for the fulfillment of the divine mission as the Prophet's masjid did in the prophetic model.

The next phase for our community was neither planned nor foreseen. Stagnation crept in, and the community stumbled and became—ever since—stuck in transition. Activism and management of the status quo were mistaken for the divine mission, and expanding buildings and acquiring new ones were mistaken for real growth.

Not only did we relax prematurely after achieving our initial success, but we were also unwilling and/or unable to properly tackle some fundamental issues and adequately respond to some major changes and challenges within and around our community and in our world. In fact, the only times that we have managed to venture outside of our comfort zone have been in response to crises that have hit the community or other parts of the Muslim world. However, even a major crisis like 9/11 provoked only short-lived campaigns that haven't had a significant, lasting impact.

Other than that, the community has been mostly organizing some routine activities and offering some basic services. Our organizations don't have a compelling cause, an expansive vision, a competent leadership, or inclusive structures to inspire and rally—or even to accommodate—the majority of Muslim Americans.

In conclusion, to drive home the importance of a proper and complete translation of the divine mission, we can actually look at the history of the United States. There have been many campaigns and movements in U.S. history that have truly involved a proper translation of the divine mission, albeit by non-Muslims. Had large numbers of Muslims been present in America at those times and had they been equipped with a proper understanding of Islam, they would have been at the forefront of constructive change. Events that have involved proper translation of the divine mission include the American Revolution; the drafting of the U.S. Constitution; the anti-slavery, anti-segregation, and civil rights movements; the women's rights movement (for suffrage, equal pay, etc.); minimum wage and labor rights activities; antismoking and anti-addiction campaigns; and campaigns related to the various aspects of social, political, economic, or environmental justice—here and/or globally.

Wasn't the Prophet proud of his participation, prior to his commission as a prophet, in the al-Fudul pact[32] to support the oppressed? And didn't he say that he wouldn't hesitate to participate in a similar pact?

This section has demonstrated the relationship between Muslims' abandonment of the divine mission and our current, deplorable condition. Indeed, one of the main root causes of the Muslim American crisis is the

---

32 The Al-Fudul Pact, or Hilf al-Fudul, was a seventh-century alliance created by various Meccans, including the Prophet Muhammad, to establish fair commercial dealing. Because of Muhammad's role in its formation, the alliance plays a significant role in Islamic ethics. Because *fudul* commonly means "virtuous," the alliance is often translated as Alliance of the Virtuous.

fact that we have never been a mission-driven community. We have never attempted to translate the divine mission into a relevant and expansive vision capable of engendering and sustaining our mobilization and unity. We have discussed why this was the case, how it happened, and why this has been severely limiting.

Based on our analysis, we firmly believe that the renaissance of our community must begin with the wholehearted commitment of our people to the divine mission. This requires not only the divine mission's translation into an expansive and inspiring vision and a relevant platform but also the translation of the divine guidance and the prophetic model into a renewed Islamic construct that fulfills the divine purpose. The crucial questions we must ask are these: "What does God ordain?" and "What would the Prophet be doing, here and now, in our twenty-first century America?"

Although the abandonment of our divine mission is of paramount significance, there are other root causes of our crisis that also constitute formidable obstacles to our renaissance. We must resolve these before our community can be pulled out of its unenviable stagnation. Our identity crisis is the topic of the next section. As we did with other aspects of our crisis, we will first trace its roots and then attempt to turn it from a headwind into a tailwind. We undertake this and every other part of this project for the sake of the renaissance of our community, so that we can contribute to the greater good.

2—A CRISIS OF IDENTITY: A COMMUNITY WITHOUT A HOMELAND

History has demonstrated that societies thrive when they have a cause and a country "to fight for." On the contrary, as we have previously discussed, no community or individual can fully thrive without a compelling mission or without a clear sense of identity. Add the effects of those two missing ingredients, and you'll have a crisis of significant proportions.

The confusion we face regarding our sense of identity as Muslim Americans is severely hindering the growth and integration of our community. It sets a low ceiling on our aspirations, confines us to a very limited playing field, guarantees an image problem, and provides the main cause of our alienation from society. It also provides ammunition to those who question our loyalty to America.

We all know that there is substantial religious and political bigotry in America and that bigotry is the culprit behind the demonizing of Islam and Muslims. The fact of the matter is that bigotry thrives on ignorance. Unfortunately, on the topics of Islam and Muslims, widespread ignorance in American society at large has been reinforced by many of the manifestations of our identity crisis. These are two intertwined factors for which we bear full responsibility.

Our movement is not tackling our identity problem as a reaction to Islamophobia, nor are we defensive or apologetic in our approach to addressing our identity issues. Rather, our efforts to fulfill the divine purpose and remove any obstacles in the way of our community's renaissance have led us to a diagnosis of our crisis that points directly to this critical issue: the confluence of our identity crisis with a public bigotry that is fueled by ignorance and misinformation.

There isn't much that any group can accomplish in regard to its mission, or that it can contribute to its country, without first possessing a strong sense of belonging within society. Moreover, no mission can be carried out within a vacuum. This is particularly true when it comes to the divine mission, which is centered on societal reform. Societal reform requires that we engage with and positively impact society's members and institutions. This cannot be accomplished passionately and effectively without two things that also happen to be essential components of patriotism: a strong commitment to the homeland and a strong attachment to fellow citizens. The importance of this kind of commitment and attachment in approaching the divine mission is the main reason why prophets/messengers were selected from—and sent to— their own people. The effect was reflected in the prophets' great compassion in fulfilling their mission.

Our community's situation is highly complicated because, not only do the vast majority of Muslims in America feel that they don't belong here, but also for a number of reasons, many are ambivalent toward America. Most Muslim Americans are struggling to reconcile what seems to them to be two incompatible components of their identity—being Muslim and being American. Ironically, this is true even for those who have known no other country.

However, this need not be the case. These two components of our identity can and should fuse together seamlessly to produce a coherent Muslim American identity and a great synergy between the religious and patriotic engines for inspiration and mobilization. Unfortunately, though, due to our very uninspiring understanding of Islam, most of the members of our community are not motivated—either religiously or civically. They are committed to neither the cause of the divine mission nor to the country. In such a context, any religious motivation that organizations and/or community leaders might manage to inspire may actually push people further into their social isolation and civic disengagement, if not worse.

Instead of looking outward and operating in society (the real field of *tadaafu'* or engagement), our community has been looking inward and operating in an artificially created and conditioned environment of like-minded individuals. We have replaced the thrust of the divine mission (namely, civic engagement) with community activism that has been largely aimless, irrelevant, and nonimpactful; but our alienation didn't stop there. It combined with stagnation to produce several other aspects of our crisis, such as complacency and a lack of sophistication.

Unfortunately, alienation is also a fertile ground for extremism, and extremism can lead to terrorism if the "wrong people" get the motivation and opportunity. In fact, alienation is the main reason behind the recent and alarming phenomenon of youth radicalization to which young Muslims—both devoted and nondevoted—are vulnerable. Youth radicalization may be motivated by religion and/or politics, or even by social conditions as has been the case in some European countries.

The absence of a sense of belonging in America, experienced by most Muslims, has its roots in the backgrounds of each of the two main segments of our Muslim American community—African Americans and immigrants. As we know, African Americans were brought by force to America and cruelly enslaved for generations. Obviously, such trauma does not help to engender a sense of belonging or loyalty, and many members of the African American community have personally experienced severe cruelty on a firsthand basis. Forbearance and struggle against difficult odds are a part of the cultural narrative and legacy for all African Americans. Plus, there is still a widespread perception among many African Americans that the American system continues to treat them unfairly and that American society continues to be plagued with (mostly covert) racial prejudice and discrimination.

As indicated earlier, the ambivalence toward America, among African Americans who are Muslims, has been reinforced by an immigrant version of Islam that is filled with a significant dose of foreign culture. Imported anti-

American political views that stem from resentment toward American foreign policy have also infused the African American Muslim mind-set. As a result, African American Muslims have become even more alienated, not only from the overall society but also from the larger African American community. As other segments of the larger African American community made great strides and inroads in growth and societal integration, disengagement and self-imposed isolation prevented the growth and integration of African American Muslims into society and caused them to lag behind. That seems tragic.

As regards immigrant Muslims, even before migrating to the U.S., most had some sort of identity problem in their countries of origin—for reasons not so different from those of their African American brethren. Indeed, the rampant corruption, oppression, and lack of development in most Muslim countries have gradually but severely eroded most Muslims' sense of belonging and interfered with their development of a real sense of citizenship. In repressive circumstances, civic engagement cannot happen. Prior to their migration to the U.S., most Muslims lived as subjects (of the ruling regime/family/dictator) rather than as citizens of a state. Echoing Louis XIV of France who said, "The state: it's me," the notorious dictators in most Muslim countries have equated themselves and their governments and ruling parties with the state itself. Their Muslim subjects have come to despise the whole package.

With only a tiny segment of the privileged elite possessing all the power and reaping all the benefits, what reason was there for anyone to be concerned about the common good—or even the well-being of the country? The citizenry had neither the incentive nor the means to work toward the betterment of their societies. And it is not uncommon for people, whenever they have the chance, to vent their anger by vandalizing public property. Eventually, lacking any genuine opportunity for happiness in their own countries, the majority more or less acquiesced and adapted to a life in which they had low aspirations, no sense of belonging, no voice, no hope, no freedom, and limited dreams of ever escaping.

With this being the case back home, it was only natural that their migration to another country would further complicate their identity issues. However, the identity problem did not become pressing until the "myth of return" faded. That is when immigrant Muslims came to understand that they would not go back to their countries of origin as they had assumed, and so they found themselves in limbo—belonging nowhere.

There are a number of complications (to be discussed below) that have precluded both the development of a coherent Muslim American identity and the commitment of many Muslim Americans to America as a homeland. These barriers have hindered our integration and our growth, and thus they have obstructed our mission and our renaissance. Some of the factors that held us back are understandable. Yet they were mishandled, and that has led us to the wrong conclusions and unwise courses of action.

This project is built on commitment to Islam as a life mission of reform and on commitment to America as a homeland. Therefore, it requires the unequivocal resolution of the identity issue. Our perspectives on some of the factors that have contributed to the identity crisis are discussed below.

a- Born and Raised Elsewhere

The main reason for our identity problem can be found in the fact that immigrant Muslim Americans were born and raised outside of America. This "first generation" served as the founders of our community, and it continues to have a disproportionate influence on it. They decided to settle in America after they gradually lost any incentive or opportunity to go back home and after they reluctantly ruled out that option. Still, many of them continue to focus their attention and resources overseas—a trend that has been boosted by the Internet and satellite TV channels. This is not to say that these people do not, at all, enjoy being here. They settled in America mainly because it offered them most (if not all) of the things they were missing and yearning for back home.

Though our overseas origins constitute the primary cause of our identity problem, this factor has little direct relevance for our movement. After all, the movement is being designed for those who were born and raised here—our second, third, and future generations. The best role that the founding generation can now play is to serve as a bridge between the past and the future. The way to begin is by sorting through our own experiences so we can pass on the best lessons, but not our problems. Then we need to develop a sound vision for the future. Because our identity issue is one of our community's main hindrances, we must tackle it head on and resolve it once and for all, as it would be unfair to pass it on to future generations.

b- The "Myth of Return"

The vast majority of Muslim immigrants to America did not plan to live here permanently. This reality has been a defining factor in our personal and our communal lives. In particular, it has affected the way we have raised our children. We have essentially isolated them from society to preserve their identity and prepare them to live back home. All of this was more or less normal in the context of a temporary expatriate community. However, even as we prolonged our stay here and eventually settled, we did not foresee the ramifications of this momentous change, and we failed to make the necessary adjustments. Consequently, by the time we started to accept this new reality, an identity crisis was born and was passed on to the next generation.

Unsurprisingly, the crisis was more acute for the younger generations. They were alienated from their country of birth, the United States, but they were no longer going back to their parents' homelands as they had been taught to expect.

The "myth of return" has significantly contributed to our identity crisis in at least two ways:

- It concealed the identity problem, leaving it unaddressed for decades.
- It indirectly contributed to the identity issues among American-born Muslims (who did not have to put up with it) such as African American Muslims, converts to Islam, and the offspring of immigrant Muslims.

The good news is that the "myth of return" has largely faded. The problem remains, however, that its implications are far reaching. It has impacted on the psyche, management, discourse, and priorities of our community—particularly among first-generation immigrants who continue to be the dominant segment of our community. Rather than making a much-needed paradigm shift after the reality of American permanence struck them, these individuals still made only superficial adjustments in their personal and communal lives.

An essential part of our movement is to create this shift among the leaders and activists from the first generation in order to weed out the remnants of the "myth of return" and thereby resolve our identity crisis. At a minimum, we need to make sure it no longer spreads to Muslims who were born and raised in the United States. Undoing the damage of the "myth of return" is a necessary aspect of the first generation's "sorting out" process. It will help them to help future generations to not only start with a clean slate but also have a head start. We must pass to our youth the important lessons learned without the burdensome baggage of problems.

c- America Is a Non-Muslim Society

The majority of Muslim immigrants originated from predominantly Muslim societies, so their faith and their citizenship meshed together seamlessly. Obviously, this was not the case here in America where it has been necessary for us to reconcile our faith with our citizenship in a non-Muslim country. This has puzzled many immigrants who, as indicated earlier, did not have a strong tradition of citizenship in the first place. Plus, most of their Islamic literature and heritage originated in predominantly Muslim societies, and so it sheds little light on the very different circumstances here. In that literature and heritage, for example, the issue of minorities refers to non-Muslims living in an Islamic society.

Because this dilemma has often been framed religiously as an issue of irreconcilable conflicting loyalties—to Islam versus to a non-Muslim country and society—the problem turned into a crippling crisis of identity. According to this flawed logic, the hundreds of millions of Muslims who are native to—or settled into—non-Muslim societies all over the world cannot be faithful citizens. If they want to be loyal to Islam, the misguided thinking asserts, they either have to live as aliens in their own country or possibly relocate to a Muslim country.

In this presentation of Islam, not only is loyal citizenship wrongly associated exclusively with Muslim countries, but also Islam itself was identified with the cultures of those countries so that the two became inseparable and are usually presented as one package deal. Inevitably, many people who were born in non-Muslim societies, or who have converted to Islam, have rejected the culture of their "homeland" and adopted a foreign "Muslim culture."

From the Islamic perspective, this problem is purely artificial and is the result of the severe mutilation to which Islam has been subjected. Certainly, true Islam is universal and, therefore, compatible with all cultures. Restricting the practice of loyal citizenship to Muslim countries, and/or attempting to hard wire Islam to a particular culture (no matter how healthy it might be, let alone if it is a decadent culture), actually strips Islam of its universality and makes it appear more like a national or ethnic affiliation—or even a cult.

Our platform strongly advocates that all Muslim Americans, particularly those who were born and/or raised in the United States, should be loyal citizens and commit to America as a homeland. With the exception of the few sacred mosques, no land is better than any other. All of the land everywhere belongs to God. Islam does not interfere with our patriotism or commitment to our homeland. If anything, by virtue of the divine mission, Muslim Americans have more reasons to be patriotic and more reasons to be loyal and committed to America. After all, this is the land in which God has appointed us to be His stewards, and it is where we are destined to fulfill the divine mission.

We are also advocating that, as much as if not more than any other minority, Muslims should assimilate culturally; and they should do so without compromising the essentials of Islam (*thawabit*). For the first-generation immigrants, this may well be a challenging and inconvenient task that requires special effort. Specifically, the original teachings of Islam must be decoupled from our Islamic heritage and cultures. Also, we must allow those who have been born and raised here the freedom to naturally keep or embrace American culture. Indeed, we should encourage this. This will represent a reversal of the current trend wherein the focus has been on preserving the foreign culture of first-generation immigrants and on fostering the cultural alienation of converts and young generations in their own country.

Needless to say, like every culture, American culture is not flawless. Therefore, it should not be blindly embraced. Rather, those elements that are incompatible with the essentials of Islam, and/or are unsound, should be shunned. However, immigrants should never try to impose their cultures and norms on American-born natives, not under any pretext.

d- The Attitude toward Americans

The issue of one's identity is closely related, not only to commitment to a particular homeland but also to the attitude one has toward the people who live there. Both matters have been wrongly viewed within our religious context. This has created an unnatural and unnecessary conflict between faithfulness to Islam and patriotism toward one's country. It has also led to our categorizing people as either Muslims or non-Muslims. Some Muslims perceive Americans as simply non-Muslims who are to be dealt with only when necessary. This is in striking contrast to the prophetic attitude and to the requirements of the divine mission. These aspects of Islam call on us to be kind and compassionate toward others and to reach out to them irrespective of our differences of faith. Indeed, when it comes to human relationships and interactions, Islam sets fairness as the baseline and puts no limits on kindness.

This misguided religious attitude precludes the development of a coherent Muslim American identity. It also, therefore, hinders our growth and integration. Growth and integration are processes that require not only committing to America as a homeland but also accepting Americans as our people. This is what we believe in and advocate as the mainstay of our project.

The Islamic rationalizations that some Muslims use to justify their ambivalence toward America and Americans do not apply to our situation here—simply because those concepts relate specifically to situations of religious persecution. There is hardly anywhere in the world where Muslims enjoy constitutionally guaranteed freedom of religion and expression. We have all that we need to fulfill our divine mission right here—everything that Muhammad requested of the people of Mecca. If Muslim Americans are stuck in stagnation due to an identity crisis, what can we expect to be the case for Muslim minorities who live in countries that place far more restrictions on their citizens' freedom of religion and of expression?

Even though any negative feelings that some members of the community harbor toward Americans may not be deep seated, these sentiments must really be eradicated if we are to resolve our identity crisis and become connected to and thoroughly engaged in the overall society. The reality is that Americans are our brothers and sisters in humanity and in citizenship. We share tremendous commonalities and concerns, and we also share a common destiny. Just as Islam does not interfere with our commitment to our homeland, nor does it interfere with our connection to our people or our compassion toward them. If anything, Islam reinforces these natural and noble feelings.

By virtue of the divine mission, those Muslims who chose America as their country and those Americans who chose Islam as their faith have ample reasons to commit to America as a homeland and to Americans as their people. Those who are here against their choice are urged to move to wherever they consider home and to commit to fulfilling the mission of Islam and raising their children there.

The underlying religious, historical, and political factors of our identity crisis are intertwined; but after the fading of the "myth of return," the main barriers to resolving the identity crisis now fall in the religious category. Divine guidance needs to be understood in the context of this American place and this present time. Though a sensitive and sticky matter, our religious misconceptions are our own doing. Consequently, we are the ones who must undo them. It is unfair to blame them on Islam or to pass them on to future generations. The historical and political considerations are probably more manageable because they do not hinge on sacred matters; but they are nonetheless problematic because they are related to highly emotional past and present grievances that many Muslim Americans hold.

e- Historical Considerations

The chief historical consideration that directly and indirectly contributes to the Muslim American identity crisis is the cruel and protracted experience of African Americans in slavery. Indeed, the way African Americans were brought to this country and treated for more than three centuries was incredibly inhumane. This trauma is still fresh. Many members of the African American community have heard of it directly from relatives, or from others who experienced it firsthand. It comes as no surprise that some of its victims and their descendants would not be very receptive to the idea of loyal citizenry to the same country that enslaved their people or to the idea of accepting the descendants of their former masters as their "brothers and sisters" or even compatriots.

The attitude of disdain held by some African Americans toward America has indirectly and adversely affected Muslim immigrants because African Americans presumably know this country better, and their tragic stories did not brighten our prospects of integration and indigenization. In different circumstances, African American Muslims could and should have facilitated the integration and indigenization of immigrant Muslims.

Historical considerations may also include the devastatingly bad experiences that some other minorities have had in this country and thus may stretch all the way back to the annihilation of Native Americans.

These undeniable facts of times past have left deep wounds that don't heal easily. Yet we cannot change history, and we cannot afford to remain hostages of the past. We must set our eyes on the future, and we must be willing to do whatever it takes to shape a better one.

History is good only as a source of lessons to be learned to enable us to understand the present and to guide us through it. Our plans and our actions should be inspired by the prospects and the requirements of a brighter future—something we can shape—and not by the horror stories (or even the accomplishments) of the past.

Indeed, ever since they became marginalized and irrelevant and with no major achievements to proclaim, Muslims in general have been living in the past, frozen in time. It is as if life had stopped, and the only thing left for us was to live in the past: to be hostage to past experiences and/or to brag about past accomplishments. We must study history and be aware of it, but not remain hostage to it. If we are to resolve our identity crisis, fulfill our mission, and shape a better future for ourselves and the generations that follow us, we have no other option but to completely turn the page and put our histories behind us. We must ensure that our children and theirs are not held back by history.

While advising us to draw lessons from the stories of those who came before us, the Qur'an also does instruct us to leave history behind us:

> There is, in their stories, instruction for men endued with understanding [Qur'an 12:111].

> That was a people that has passed away. They shall reap the fruit of what they did, and you of what you do! [Qur'an 2:141].

We cannot change history, but we could and should change the present and shape the future. Unfortunately, the communities of both immigrant and African American Muslims were built as extensions of the past and/or angry reactions to it. Neither approach will ever inspire a true renaissance or societal reform movement. Anger may arouse people and erode complacency; but unless our anger is channeled into constructive plans and action, it will be unproductive and may well lead to self-defeat. Only a rejection of the status quo and a yearning for a more-promising future can bring about true reform. Both Malcolm X (after his pilgrimage[33]) and the leaders of the civil rights movement came to realize and advocate this reality. It was that realization that led them to channel their discontent into constructive courses of action.

As is true for all other nations of the world, America has a past that is a mixed bag. No country in the world has a flawless history, nor can any nation claim to be entirely free of some sort of hostility based on race, ethnicity, regionalism, gender, etc. It is both unfair and unhelpful to see only the bleak spots in American history when there are a lot of bright spots as well. While they may be particularly disturbing to the victims and their descendants, problematic events in any country's history are not a valid reason to justify the continued and prolonged ambivalence of segments of the population toward that country or its people as a whole. This flawed logic would preclude the loyal citizenry of almost every person and the cohesiveness of almost every society in the world.

f- Political Considerations

The political underpinnings of our identity crisis have to do with Muslim Americans' resentments toward some American policies, both past and present, domestic and foreign. The U.S. positions on many global affairs, particularly those related to the Muslim world, make it difficult for many members of our community to identify themselves as Americans citizens. And American society's rampant moral decay and other social ills don't help either.

From the vantage point of African Americans, slavery, racism, and discrimination constitute the biggest issues. Slavery, of course, is past history and was discussed in the previous section. Even in the present, though, African Americans can point to a slew of statistics that prove they are still disproportionately affected by a number of governmental policies related to education, healthcare, employment, housing, law enforcement, and the judicial system. These circumstances unequivocally challenge America's highly cherished concepts of equal opportunity and equality before the law.

---

33 Note: Although from the outset, Malcolm X rebelled against the status quo and his discourse aroused many people, it was not until after his pilgrimage to Mecca that he evolved to the point of creating empowering solutions to combat society's injustices.

African Americans may also be resentful of the fact that, unlike most other wealthy countries, America does not guarantee its citizens the basic human needs for a dignified life (such as universal health care, a free college education, living wages, or sustainable unemployment benefits). Plus, in many developed countries, labor laws are more balanced and protective of workers.

On the foreign policy side, immigrants (among others) abhor America's blind support of Israel and Washington's patronage of notorious dictators in the Muslim world. Those Muslim world "leaders" are widely viewed as tyrants, and they are blamed for chronic oppression, corruption, and societal failure in their respective countries. The recent revolutions that swept the Middle East revealed the extent to which the people in those countries hate their regimes. For a long time, that blame and hatred have been transferred to the United States. This anger has worsened during the last two decades as a result of the first Gulf War, the postwar crippling sanctions on Iraq, and then the wars on Afghanistan and Iraq, and the so-called war on terrorism.

To make matters even more abhorrent, America's increased entanglements in the Muslim world and its confrontations with Muslim countries have included disgraceful abuses, blunders, and scandals. Moreover, the way Muslim Americans have been treated, as of late, by law enforcement and immigration agencies has also not helped build an affinity with America.

All of these factors have severely exacerbated the Muslim American identity crisis and hindered the community's integration into society. Again, they are all undeniable facts and valid grievances, but we must ask ourselves if they justify our continued and indefinite identity crisis when it is jeopardizing our future. What are our options? How can we best redirect the energy behind our resentment so that it drives a constructive new course of action to reduce or resolve our identity problems? Isn't that the best way to make sure that future generations will not maintain those negative feelings—or worse, act on them in destructive and self-defeating ways?

Loving one's homeland and country and showing compassion toward one's people is like loving one's family: It must be unconditional. In the words of an Arab poet: "My country is dear to me even if it was not fair to me; and my people are honorable even if they were not kind to me." Sociopolitical difficulties call on us to step up our civic engagement and our outreach so that we can help fix those problems—not to be ambivalent toward our country and our people. If American Muslims cannot undertake civic engagement and outreach in the face of adversity, we cannot expect patriotism and commitment to one's homeland to exist anywhere in the world. After all, no country on the face of this earth is politically or socially flawless. In fact, those who live in most parts of the Muslim world find it even more difficult to be loyal to their corrupt, oppressive, and mediocrity-ridden homelands.

On the other hand, and in spite of some social ills and ill-conceived policies, Muslim Americans have plenty of reasons to be proud of their identity and to be passionately committed to America. They also have plenty of reasons to be connected to and compassionate toward their fellow American citizens.

3—OUR COMMUNITY'S LEADERSHIP VOID AND MESS

One may argue that, in the absence of a compelling cause and without any real challenges that come from societal engagement, there can be no leadership issue. Under those circumstances: "Who needs leadership?" From that perspective, there would be no need even to discuss the leadership issue as a root cause of our crisis. However, the world-class expert on leadership, John Maxwell, said, "Everything rises and falls on leadership"[34] and "Grow a leader, grow the organization."[35] These axioms apply not only to organizations and corporations but also to communities and nations. True leadership may be precisely what our community needs in order to confront its crisis, become relevant and impactful, and chart a better future.

To be sure, one of the most striking features of our community and one of the main causes of our crisis is the scary leadership void and the subsequent organizational mess. This is probably why some people argue whether we even constitute an actual community. One thing is certain, however: if we are a community at all, we are a leaderless community. There are reasons why we have lacked appropriate leadership. True leaders operate in intellectual and strategic domains/realms, but without being detached from their people or from their real world environment.[36] They must possess an in-depth awareness of the history and workings of that world (how it was shaped and how it

---

34 John Maxwell. *The 21 Indispensable Qualities of a Leader* [Book].

35 John Maxwell. *The 5 Levels of Leadership* [Book].

36 Note: By real world environment, we mean the environment in which a leader is functioning and, therefore, needs to engage the constituents. It may be a city, state, nation or the entire world. It should be noted that during this age of globalization, the world has been reduced to somewhat of a global village; therefore, a global perspective is needed, even for leadership at the local level.

functions), and they also need a coherent vision for the future and a sound strategy for getting there.

In this sense, not only do we lack appropriate leadership in our community, but also the void is being filled by people who fall into various categories that are typically mistaken for leaders (just as activism is sometimes mistakenly viewed as fulfilling our mission and organizations are mistakenly seen as movements). These categories include imams, preachers, Islamic scholars, mosque administrators, and managers.

Why we are a leaderless community

Because our movement is about change, our focus is not only on understanding our current situation but also on how and why we got to this point. In the previous sections, we explained that our lack of a defining mission and our neglect of our identity crisis are the reasons we became a community with neither a compelling/rallying cause nor a homeland.

In examining our leadership dilemma, we see that it is one of the oldest aspects of the worldwide and chronic crisis that Muslims face—confirming Muhammad's prophecy that the Islamic governance/leadership model would be the first element of the Islamic paradigm to unravel.

As Omar ibn al-Khattab said, "Islam (which, as understood by Muhammad's companions, means the divine mission) needs a movement, which in turn requires true leadership." It is a short statement that aptly sums up the ups and downs of Islamic history, as well as the current situation of Muslims, including Muslim Americans. However, when Muslims believe that they only need to practice Islam (as a religion and a way of life), manage their personal affairs, and preserve their identities, they probably don't need more than fraternities/organizations run by activists to achieve those "goals." That is the current situation in the minds of most members of our community.

The issue of leadership is of paramount importance in our movement—not only because our crisis has been caused and/or worsened by the lack of qualified leadership, but also because leadership is a critical element in the prophetic model that we are working to emulate and restore. Indeed, a clear and compelling noble cause (clarity of purpose) and unified, respected, and consultative/accountable leadership were at the heart of the incredibly successful blueprint for transformation and community building used by

Muhammad. That is how he was able to unite the fragmented and marginal Arab tribes of his day. Likewise, this is all Muslims need to galvanize and unify people and produce the necessary cohesion, decisiveness, and discipline during any era, including ours.

Exactly how did a pillar of the utmost importance to the prophetic model become one of the main weaknesses of Muslims and one of the main aspects of their chronic crisis after the period of the rightly guided Caliphs? To answer this question, we must trace the history of the Muslim leadership/governance model, starting with a dissection of the prophetic leadership model.

As discussed in detail in part 2, the prophetic model uses a compelling mission and an effective leadership (leader-of-leaders) model to transform individuals, build an effective movement, and mobilize and unify people in a sustained way. The leadership model, in particular, worked perfectly for about a half of a century (with the death of Muhammad as the midpoint of that period). To a large extent, it accounted for the astonishing effectiveness and the results delivered by the entire model.

Following a short summary of how the prophetic leadership model worked and how Muslims deviated from it, we will proceed to discuss our history of leadership. This will enable us to better understand the historical progression and root causes of our leadership mess and void. We will focus on the leadership models of (1) the Muslim countries from which the majority of our community originated, (2) Islamic movements from which most of the pioneers and current leaders of our community originated, and (3) the Muslim American community.

The prophetic leadership model: How did it function and why did it crumble?

Leadership is of paramount importance in Islam. Islam commands Muslims to guide the people around them to God and to that which is beneficial—in this life and in the hereafter. It is about influence, and Islam is a mission that is focused on positively influencing the people and conditions around us. Islam also cherishes two key accompaniments of leadership—self-development and mentorship (*tazkiya*). Self-development is the process by which you develop "the leader within you," while mentorship involves developing "the leaders around you." Thus, *tazkiya* constitutes an essential component of the prophetic mission.

> It is He Who has sent amongst the Unlettered an apostle from among themselves, to rehearse to them His Signs, to sanctify them, and to instruct them in Scripture and Wisdom,- although they had been, before, in manifest error [Qur'an 62:2].

Moreover, leadership and mentorship constitute the key elements of the prophetic model of community building. Indeed, the prophetic model in general and the leadership model in particular are both built on two things: on the compelling divine mission because that transforms individuals into mission-driven leaders, and on the effective leadership and mentorship which cement individuals together into an organized movement. Therefore, when Islam is stripped of its sense of mission and the community abandons the divine mission, it is both impossible and unnecessary to have true leadership; and under those circumstances, it should not be surprising that there is none.

In our humble understanding, the prophetic leadership model works as follows:

Based on contemporary circumstances, a leader develops a relevant construct of the divine guidance, a "translation" of the divine mission into a coherent vision for the future, and a sound strategy for fulfilling the divine mission and effecting necessary reform. Moreover, because the whole thing is about change and involves constructive engagement of the environment, this leader must have some sort of a reasonable worldview. That worldview must include an understanding of how the world functions, awareness and diagnosis of the present reality, and a comprehension of relevant history. In other words, an effective leader knows how we got where we are today and where we should be instead and how the world works.

Often, people start following a leader before they really "buy into" the vision. Based on their belief in the messenger and in the message, a solid core group then joins the leader to form the nucleus of the movement. Individually and collectively, this group starts to engage an ever-wider circle in their environment to effect change and recruit more people to the movement. They then inspire and empower newcomers to replicate the process. And the cycle goes on indefinitely.

Even though the settings, format, and methods may change, this process requires individuals who commit to the divine mission to embark on a lifelong journey of self-development, social outreach, and civic engagement. The personal efforts of all these mission-driven individuals are then streamlined into a movement governed by an effective leadership model, which emulates the prophetic model. That's how people and societies are transformed.

The movement's impact and growth typically depend on the power of the model, at both the individual and collective level. While the movement's success ultimately comes only from God, there are a number of factors that determine success. These include the quality of the message and the effectiveness of delivery, the effectiveness of institutions built by the movement, and the quality of partnerships, alliances, and coalitions that are forged by the movement. Other factors that are associated with successful movements include

- sound, coherent, and relevant vision and strategy;
- honest, competent, and passionate leadership;
- an effective leadership model;
- a cohesive membership comprised of individuals of good character, powerful determination, serious dedication, and strong self-discipline; and
- strong, positive group dynamics and effective performance in the embodiment and delivery of the message and in engaging with the surrounding environment to execute the project and in handling challenges that arise.

In summary, the way the prophetic model could be restored is through a leader with vision and a solid core group of people who systematically and effectively engage an ever-bigger circle of people in the environment. This expanding engagement should be undertaken both individually and collectively. That's how several Islamic movements started, and that's why they produced impressive results in their successful takeoff.

Beyond the founding phase, as the movement grows, the model should be institutionalized as needed. However, care must be taken to ensure that none of the model's three pillars is violated and that their delicate interbalance is not disrupted. If you recall, the prophetic leadership model, which is best described as a leader-of-leaders model, is built upon three pillars that require involvement by all the members of the community as an act of worship. The three often difficult to balance pillars are (1) undisputed and respected leadership by consent (without accepting dictatorship), (2) extensive and substantive consultation that all community members practice as a right and duty in a manner that avoids indecisiveness and paralysis, and (3) the disciplined execution of the final decision by everyone, irrespective of their prior points of view. The effect is exquisite group cooperation, not blind obedience. The people should have a clear mechanism to appoint, approve, and/or remove the leader; and they must make sure that the leader's decisions are in compliance with the tenets of the religion, with the law of the land, and with the community's agreed upon vision, strategy, and policies.

During the first half century of Islam, this model was spontaneously and effectively implemented at all levels and under all circumstances. At every level and in every setting, there was always empowered leadership that, nonetheless, did not take away anything from people's vigilance and sense of responsibility for the cause and for community well-being. Under this extremely efficient leadership model, it is the community's right and duty to counsel the leader and to correct or even replace him/her if he/she violates divine guidance or the community's agreements. The common objective is to make the best decision and execute it successfully.

During Muhammad's time and for the twenty-five or so years that followed his death, countless people were transformed into leaders—despite the humble backgrounds of most of them as feuding idol worshippers, arrogant and spoiled youth, street fighters, or even slaves. Indeed, being surrounded by so many capable and committed people, Muhammad and his successors had no problem selecting someone to fill a leadership position or carry out a given responsibility.

Islam, which transforms its followers into leaders based on their own merit, commands groups of Muslims to always appoint one among them to be the leader, even when as few as three of them are simply traveling. That is the secret of the effectiveness of the prophetic model, which is best described as a leader-of-leaders model. It is a model in which everybody has the sense of responsibility of the leader and the discipline of the soldier.

The individual members of Muhammad's community (the companions) all conducted themselves as leaders in the sense that they all assumed responsibility for the advancement of God's cause and of the community. They took initiative and did not hesitate to propose strategies and solutions, or to take part in the decision-making process. When a decision was properly made, everyone owned the decision and complied as though they were highly disciplined soldiers doing everything they could possibly do to ensure the successful execution of the mission.

This prophetic leadership model, along with the divine guidance and mission, produced the greatest movement and transformation the world has known—turning poor, illiterate Bedouins, who had been constantly fighting one another (sometimes for survival, but sometimes just over silly issues), into champions of a great world civilization, which went on to lead the world for more than twelve centuries. It is this same model that remains capable of producing similar results whenever its three main provisions are upheld and kept in balance.

Obviously, the model must evolve and become institutionalized, but without violating its pillars and without excessive reliance on bureaucracy at the expense of trust and spontaneity. Its failure to do so, and/or its violation in any way, would preclude its proper functioning. That is what happened toward the end of the era of the rightly guided Caliphs. At that time, the model had become almost exclusively dependent on the character of the individuals carrying it out and on the high level of trust between them.

The companions' sincerity, dedication to the cause, and in-depth understanding of the model enabled them to implement it very spontaneously—without even the need for written bylaws.

They also clearly understood Muhammad's dual role as both a messenger of God and as their leader; and that with his death, revelation ended. Then the responsibility for his message was passed on to the whole community, and all his privileges as a leader were passed on to his successor. This facilitated the smooth transition after the death of the Prophet, and it preserved the continuity of the leadership model. The model continued to function with the same level of spontaneity, simplicity, and efficiency. Indeed, during the era of the rightly guided Caliphs (particularly during the tenure of Abu Bakr and Omar), major decisions were made in a strikingly similar manner as was true during Muhammad's life.

However, two phenomena would diminish the total spontaneity and the reliance on individual qualities, as well as the trust among the companions. The first phenomenon was the explosive growth of the small Muslim community and small Islamic state of Medina into a vast empire in the span of just a few years. Since the leadership model had not been institutionalized, explosive growth meant the pillars of the leadership model would be threatened. The rapid expansion also far exceeded the mentorship and organizational capacity of the community. That engendered the second phenomenon—the decline of the average Muslim's devotion to Islam and commitment to the divine mission, the very ingredients that had previously facilitated the spontaneous and effective functioning of the model.

The majority of the growth had taken place during the tenure of Omar. Omar's strong personality and extraordinary decisiveness and the strong support of many key companions delayed the negative repercussions of the noninstitutionalization of the leadership model. It was during the last part of Uthman's tenure, however, that the model started to crumble. Unfounded rumors and acts of defiance were left unchecked and built up into a mutiny, which ultimately resulted in Uthman's assassination.

This turning point dealt a major blow to the two crucial elements of the prophetic model in general and the leadership model in particular—unity of purpose and undisputed leadership. These are the elements that result in sustained unity and mobilization. Uthman's successor and the fourth and final rightly guided Caliph, Ali ibn abu Taleb, had the daunting task of trying to salvage and restore the model; but the unraveling process was clearly irreversible. Within about a year, two civil wars claimed the lives of eighty thousand Muslims. Appalled by the rampant chaos that was triggered by the assassination of Uthman, Muslims in general and scholars in particular longed for order, stability, and unity—at any cost. And that's exactly what dynasty rule offered.

Leadership in Islamic history and the contemporary Muslim world

Although on the surface it resembled the prophetic model, the dynasty model lacked some of the fundamental provisions and was, essentially, more like a monarchy or a benign dictatorship.

Chief among the leadership model tenets that Muslims lost, after the end of the era of the rightly guided Caliphs, was leadership by consent of those being led. In today's terms, this relates to election of the leader by the people. It is true that, during the rightly guided Caliphs' era, the process of selecting a leader was not institutionalized and, therefore, remained rather primitive. However, two things were certain in those days:

- People *freely* approved their leader.
- There was no question about the integrity of the process or about the qualifications of the leader.

These conditions suddenly changed, though, with the advent of the era of the dynasties. Ascension to leadership was now based not on merit but on heredity or loyalty. Any approval by the people was, at best, merely a formality. Sometimes leadership was acquired through force. Ever since that time, many Muslims have been ruled by some sort of dictatorship.

It is true that during the era of dynasties, the dictatorship was generally benign, and the regime was not really totalitarian. However, when it came to leadership, the ideas of public consent and popular sovereignty were lost for most of Islamic history; and those concepts are still nowhere to be seen, in any legitimate sense, across most of the contemporary Muslim world. Even though the dynasty model upheld some elements of the prophetic model and the two appeared similar, the prophetic leadership model was stripped of some vital elements that affected the head and then—over twelve centuries— the whole body of Muslim society.

As indicated in part 2, though, a number of factors helped make the dynasty model palatable and sustainable and enabled it to produce many pious and impressive rulers until it collapsed along with the Ottoman Empire. Then came Western colonialism.

Next, after the struggle for independence, a new era and model emerged in most of the Muslim world. Totalitarian regimes were established, and they ran their countries as though they were a tribe or their own private business. As was true with colonialism, totalitarian regimes caused a rapid and across-the-board decline. They did far more damage to the Muslim psyche and personality in one century than the dynasties had done in twelve.

Muslims abandoned their defining mission and, subsequently, lost their compass. Their faith became dormant and obsolete. Their self-esteem and resolve were shaken badly. Aspirations and optimism were substantially curtailed. Muslims were caught between their great history, a dismal present reality, and an unpromising future. This all plunged Muslims deeper into denial, complacency, and frustration. They lived with no mission, no vision, no aspirations, no true leadership, no sense of direction, and no purpose or hope. As a result, Muslims lost the drive to learn or to venture beyond the confines of their restricted worlds. They even lost the drive to dream.

Could such an environment foster the development of the skills and discipline needed for effective leadership? On the contrary, leadership became synonymous with dictatorship. Therefore, the people rejected it and rebelled against it when they could, or acquiesced when there was no other choice. The concept of leadership by consent became a very distant memory, a seemingly unrealistic idea that never crossed people's minds.

For a very long time, people were trained neither to lead nor to participate in being led by consent. And whatever was happening at the top (generally oppression and corruption) trickled down throughout the entire society. There was very little room for anyone to exercise leadership. However, when there was a chance, those who were interested in a leadership position knew that the only way to get it was by snatching it violently or through corrupt means (by currying favor with those in charge). This contributed to the corruption of the whole society. The vast majority of people, however, were unwilling to be led and unable and unwilling to lead. They acquiesced when they had to, and they rebelled or retreated when they could.

So over the centuries, the leadership culture that the prophetic model had instilled throughout the entire society was replaced by notorious dictators who were constantly struggling for power at the top. The masses at the bottom of society remained acquiescent, apathetic, and occasionally rebellious. Without a rallying cause and true leadership, it is no surprise that these societies became dysfunctional and disintegrated.

Leadership in the Islamic movements

From a governance and leadership perspective, most Islamic movements were launched in a manner that was a reasonable emulation of the prophetic model. A devoted and sincere founder with a clear vision was joined by a devoted and sincere core group. The model, when properly applied, also entailed the following: empowered leadership without dictatorship; collective leadership and responsibility; extensive consultation without a power struggle or paralysis; and unequivocal discipline. The process was simple and spontaneous, and everything was carried out in an atmosphere of trust, cooperation, and serenity. Due to their devotion and common focus on fulfilling the divine mission rather than struggling for power, most movements produced impressive results, as did Muhammad's community.

Like the prophetic community, the Islamic movements also witnessed explosive growth, during which, however, they experienced one of two fatal problems:

- organizational chaos and naivety or
- crippling organizational rigidity.

Indeed, as indicated earlier, the Islamic movements emerged from the launching phase with a large but assorted membership and a vague idea of what to do next. At that critical juncture, a string of undesirable developments occurred. Fierce clashes with governments practically halted the movements' reform projects and did end the movements' ability to function as forces of change. There was also a shift of strategy toward power first and reform later and a move toward secret operations. Some movements lost their founders. Most movements' governance models were not upgraded to keep up with the expansion and major changes in their settings; so they were only useful for the survival of the organizations, or possible lateral expansion, and for the management of the status quo.

We can easily identify the three most important factors that led the movements to adopt a hodgepodge of dysfunctional models that were overrigid and bureaucratic. These factors combined to form a perfect recipe for power struggles and cynicism, with subsequent retreat and isolation.

First, because of the shift in strategy toward regime change and in anticipation of some sort of clash with the regime, the movements turned their focus toward bolstering and protecting their organizational structures (*tanzeems*)—particularly since the police states they were up against never gave up trying (sometimes successfully) to infiltrate them (a tactic that was often reciprocated by the movement). When their goal had been societal reform, the movements had focused on society and on their message, and they had displayed reasonable creativity, flexibility, and openness in their operations and organizations. However, when regime change became the goal, their focus shifted almost totally toward overthrowing the governments (the goal) and toward protecting their own organizational structures (the tool/means). This drove the movements deeper into secrecy and rigidity.

Consequently, the *tanzeems* became military-style shadow governments that were not only constantly clashing with ruling regimes but were also preparing themselves to replace the regimes. A vicious cycle was created that perpetuated the state of confrontation, and the movements became increasingly rigid, secret, isolated, and eventually, self-centered and marginal. Their great societal reform and renaissance projects turned into struggles for power that often degenerated into internal and external struggles for survival.

The second reason for the movements' tendency toward organizational bureaucracy and rigidity was that they needed to fuse together a rank-and-file membership, which was noncohesive and was comprised of people who were not unified intellectually, spiritually, socially, or emotionally. Unification could be viewed as a desperate need, especially given the desire for regime change. The movements relied almost exclusively on strict indoctrination and organization (*tarbiya* and *tanzeem*) to keep the members together and make up for other missing bonds, and on activism to make up for severe intellectual and strategic deficiencies. The whole scenario ultimately became a trap that resulted in a stalemate. Stagnation occurred regardless of the movements' efforts to improve their management and operations and despite efforts to increase their activities and membership.

A third reason for the adoption by movements of a stifling bureaucratic structure was the zero-sum attitude that is prevalent in many Muslim cultures and the tendency to follow and advocate leaders who have not been adequately assessed. That often eventually results in overreaction. In many cases, movement members blindly trusted their leaders whom they considered to be infallible saints and/or supermen who knew everything and could make no mistake. Such an attitude may have been driven by some misconceptions, but it was also a predictable situation, given that the movements were aiming for regime change and had to function in considerable secrecy. When members discovered that their leaders were only human and were, therefore, not infallible in character or judgment, their blind trust evaporated, and many swung to the other extreme. They relied exclusively on the cumbersome and crippling by-products of bureaucracy, such as bylaws. True, insightful leadership was then stifled, and trust was never restored.

In sum, the movement got stuck not only because it entrapped itself in the path of regime change and chronic confrontation with governments and not only because of its intellectual vagueness, strategic weakness, and noncohesive membership, but also because of its cumbersome structure and crippling bureaucracy.

Additional reasons for the movements' excessive and late "institutionalization" include (1) its overreaction to dictatorship (which became like a syndrome) and (2) its misconceptions about democracy. Indeed, as mentioned previously, because many Muslims associated leadership with dictatorship, they shunned both. The movements did very little to resolve this dilemma as many of their members, like most Muslims, had lost touch with the concept of leadership by consent. After all, the closest thing they had experienced to leadership by consent would be more fairly described as forced adulation. Given their outrage toward dictatorship, discovering that movement leaders were not infallible made people even more apprehensive and pushed them in a direction that practically eliminated true leadership. Their reasoning was: "If leaders are always flawed, and will probably become dictators if they get the chance, why take the risk?"

Partly because of this attitude and partly because they were hoping to be states in the making, many of the movements tried to emulate democratic structures and mechanisms with separate legislative, executive, and, oftentimes, judiciary powers. They strived (in vain) to ensure the separation of those powers and to establish checks and balances.

Without a doubt, democracy is the best system to run the affairs of the state that humanity has come up with (or, in Churchill's words, the worst system unless it is compared with all others). And in many cases (especially in America), it meets most of the key provisions of Islamic guidelines and of the prophetic Medina model for governing a state based on a constitution and citizenship. However, taken as a whole, the democratic system is designed for states and not for movements, and the difference between the two is huge.

Within a state or nation, people who believe in all kinds of ideologies are "forced" to live together. Sometimes, the only thing they have in common is citizenship. They may differ on everything else. There is no shared vision or even a shared faith. They very probably do not know—never mind trust—one another. In contrast, people who voluntarily join a movement are generally bound together by their shared faith and vision, a common cause, trust, and brotherhood. A movement still needs to maintain some tenets of democratic governance, but definitely not the entire democratic system with all of its inevitable complications.

Ironically, whereas Muhammad only needed a one-page constitution to govern his very pluralistic and complex state, some movements (or even some chapters of movements) have cumbersome structures and reams of bylaws. Whereas Muhammad only needed to call one meeting to come to a very weighty decision (including whether to go to war or develop a peace treaty), some movements require months of lengthy meetings involving numerous people (or even committees) to make uncomplicated decisions.

Finally, the movements found another way to add to their organizational confusion. They implemented very poorly. This assured the stifling of leadership. While both concepts, binding consultation and collective leadership, are also highly cherished in our new movement, we do have a substantially different understanding of how they should be implemented.

Our approach will include working to inspire and empower individuals to become civic leaders and real stakeholders in the advancement of God's cause and the well-being of the society at large, rather than having them function merely as leaders or activists solely within our community.

We believe that participatory consultation/counseling is a right and a duty of every member of the community and that all should take part in the decision-making process. In our translation of the prophetic leadership model, there should be solid mechanisms for the people to elect their leaders and counsel them prior to their decisions; and when leaders make mistakes, there should be mechanisms for the community to hold the leaders accountable, veto bad decisions, and even discharge leaders when necessary. However, within in such a context, we believe in an empowered leadership that makes final decisions. Otherwise, leadership becomes unnecessary and meaningless. Why should we need to select a leader merely to commence and conclude meetings and possibly count votes?

Ultimately, the Islamic movements' leadership model became a jumble of binding *shura* and collective leadership, disfigured democracy, and crippling bureaucracy. Its dysfunction combined with intellectual and strategic ambiguities to unreasonably delay decision making. When and if decisions were eventually made, they were generally vague and rarely implemented. The movements consequently became so consumed in managing their organizations and ongoing activities that they were no longer driven by the divine mission or guided by any clear vision.

Moreover, in spite of all their elaborate and often impressive bylaws, behind the scenes, the movements were plagued, especially during elections, with cynical power struggles, which were mostly "tribal" and/or personal and sometimes became quite spiteful. On the surface (particularly during the era of strict secrecy), most movements managed to preserve a puritan image by keeping all of these negative affairs hidden within the leadership (or at least within the ranks) and by rationalizing them with convenient and ready-made explanations. The bottom line, however, is that neither a true leadership nor a significant internal reform could have been tolerated.

Leadership in the Muslim American community

As stated previously, if true leadership requires a clear and coherent vision for the future and a definitive roadmap for getting there, there is no true leadership in our community. What we do have is a leadership void and a leadership mess. There is no mission that requires leadership, and leadership is neither cherished by the prevailing culture of our community nor tolerated by the prevailing structure of our organizations. Both the culture and these organizational systems tend to foster power struggles among the few individuals who want to lead (and often don't mind using any available means to secure a position of power and control). Meanwhile, most people in the community are alienated and are disinterested in either leading or following.

We also have plenty of facilities, service-providing organizations, and activities that only require management and activists to run them, as well as conferences and other events that need speakers. Our community's managers, scholars, speakers, and activists are presently filling our leadership void, and so they are often mistakenly viewed as leaders.

Managers: These are people who are managing Islamic centers and organizations that offer services and programs to the community. They need neither a well-developed vision for the future nor great leadership skills. They only need management and administration skills, which some do have, but, in fact, many do not. The unqualified are able to hold their positions because of their membership in a particular "clan" or through financial or political maneuvering. Some of these individuals effectively own the centers or organizations, or they have been there too long to be removed. In other cases, people find themselves in management and/or leadership positions simply because nobody else wants the job.

Most managers and activists are bogged down in their struggle to keep things going and to keep their positions. At the national level, they are consumed with bureaucracy, with organizing conferences and banquets, and with communications. Most of these activities are designed to impress the members and donors and to make up for the leaders' lack of vision and real accomplishments. Some groups are actually becoming virtual/e-mail organizations that exist only in cyberspace with limited impact (if any) on the ground. At the local level, community efforts consist of managing their bureaucracies, coordinating activities and programs, and overseeing the expansion or remodeling of their facilities.

For all the above reasons, national and local managers and activists spend most of their time and effort on fund-raising activities and internal politics to sustain their organizations and secure and boost their own positions. Many national and local organizations reached a plateau in their development a long time ago, and now they are, essentially, just spinning their wheels.

These statements are not meant to question leaders' intentions, as most are sincere, dedicated, and hardworking people. However, they are human beings; and for many, these positions represent an essential part of their lives, personalities, and status. For some, their position is their career and source of livelihood. Many are experienced enough to know that, in the prevailing culture and structure, it is politics rather than vision, skills, or accomplishments that guarantees their standing and influence.

Because most managers and activists have hardly had any training (before or after assuming their positions), it should come as no surprise that only a few of them are efficient in the performance of their duties. Therefore, only a few centers and organizations are well managed.

Additionally, because of the limited number of available positions within these largely stagnant institutions, chronic power struggles often take place for the few positions that do exist. When these struggles, which are often "tribal" and/or personal, are finally settled, it is usually after they have caused further fragmentation and alienation of the community. Under these circumstances and in the absence of vision, strategy, and skills, it is only natural that community activism has very limited relevance, impact, creativity, or inspiration.

Imams, scholars, and speakers: This is the second category of people who are filling the leadership void in our community and are mistaken for leaders. These people possess knowledge and a talent for public speaking that may enable them to educate and inspire others, but that does not necessarily mean they are able to lead. Some Imams have actually established their own "private" centers or leveraged control over the centers that hired them.

These categories constitute a tiny segment of the small sector of our community that regularly frequents Islamic centers and/or supports Muslim organizations. They are usually surrounded by a small group of helping hands, while the majority of the *masjid* congregation is passive, and most of the community is largely left behind. In the absence of true leadership, again, that comes as no surprise.

Although most community members respect these scholars and imams and expect them to lead, the truth of the matter is that they are only able to teach and deliver motivational speeches. While this is a crucial role that needs to be filled, their inadequate and/or inappropriate attempts to lead are unfair and disempowering to them and to the community. With few exceptions, most of the speakers are average and uninspiring preachers who usually simply reiterate what they read without much processing. Their sermons often fall short of "relevant," and there is no take-home message that would otherwise provide a much-needed sense of direction.

There are some gifted speakers who are reasonably motivational. Still, their content is often superficial or, worse yet, deceiving, confusing, or depressing. The superficial speeches are more like entertainment. Their short-lived effect is like an energy drink. Other times, speakers charge people up, but with a conflicting message that sometimes causes more harm than good—or suggests that everything is fine or, to the contrary, everything is hopeless. Many speakers tend to be out-of-touch and/or unduly angry.

Generally, speeches are lacking in compassion. They also lack civic and humane tones, and they fail to offer viable solutions to the pertinent problems that our community and our society face. Plus, they are often brimming with "us-versus-them" dichotomies and/or "yes-but" constructs. It is no wonder that most speeches are inconsequential.

Again, our critique is directed toward the prevailing culture and systems of our community in order to chart out a brighter future for our community. This is not intended as an attack on individuals who are basically caught up in a stagnant, obsolete system. Many of those folks are very well-intentioned, self-sacrificing, and dedicated people. One can only salute those individuals for what they do and respect the organizations (especially Islamic centers and schools) for the invaluable services they provide to their members and congregations. We are, in no way, trying to discredit individuals or belittle their great effort and accomplishments. Our focus is on the present condition and future direction of the community, not on the sincerity/intention and dedication of individuals. Our concern is merely that our community was built in an improvised manner and based on an inadequate model; and so it became "stuck" at a certain level and is desperately in need of being rebuilt utilizing the prophetic model. That is the only way the community can fulfill the divine mission and become a relevant, widely respected, and impactful component of our society at large.

Given the difficult background of our community, one should not be surprised by our leadership void/mess—or by the fact that our institutions struggle to manage the status quo. Nor should we be shocked by a small elite group that wrestles for positions and control or amazed that most Muslim Americans are disengaged and alienated. This scenario represents the situation in most of the Muslim countries and Islamic movements from which our community originated.

Again, most Muslim Americans have hardly any tradition or experience in community organizing and civic engagement. Most have never experienced leadership by consent and have never participated in a fair and free election of candidates who campaigned and were elected on the merit of their vision, credentials, and past performance. Many immigrant Muslim Americans come from systems and cultures that stifle and shun true leadership. They have never seen leaders who actually earned—rather than inheriting or seizing—their positions of leadership, and they have no experience with leaders who are held accountable for their actions and performance. In many of those aspects too, the situation of our African American Muslim community is not significantly different from the situation of the immigrant community.

Our people tend to link the concept of leadership with the holding of official positions. Therefore, they think that leadership can only be exercised within the context of an institution. That's why they tend to be preoccupied with management and bureaucracy and pay little attention to mission, vision, and strategy. These fundamental items are typically thought of later on, perhaps when developing a Web site or publishing a brochure; and what the organization actually does usually has very little to do with mission, vision, or strategy. So people rush to incorporate, and then they fight for the limited positions available and scramble to decide on the organization's identity and direction. Most Muslim organizations get stuck at that lose-lose juncture and ultimately end up stagnated with a bunch of activists alienated from the very community they profess to serve and represent.

Two factors made the leadership model of the Muslim American community even more dysfunctional than the inefficient model that was imported from the Islamic movements. First, as discussed at length, our community and its organizations were designed for a limited time and purpose. Yet we adopted a model devised by movements that were preparing themselves to change their regime and govern their state. This explains why the maintenance of the cumbersome organizational structure preoccupies so many activists and demands so much effort. And because our scope was so narrow, our organizations and the positions within these organizations are few in number. There is little prospect for growth. Many organizations have reached a plateau long ago, and now they are just spinning their wheels. This is compounded by the fact that many administrators are micromanagers (or more precisely, control freaks), so they tend to establish organizational structures that are very centralized.

A second factor, which worsens the dysfunction of our leadership model, is our attempt to blend the inappropriate imported brand of leadership with leadership styles in use in the secular world of American corporations and nonprofit organizations. When Muslim Americans discovered the corporate and nonprofit leadership models, they added some of those provisions to their imported model, which was already a hodgepodge. They tried in vain to mix some elements of the prophetic model with the structures and mechanisms of democracy. That's why, in most centers and organizations, you find several governing bodies with no clear assignment of responsibility, authority, or chain of command. Instead, there are (1) a *shura* council, which is an attempt to blend the idea of a board of trustees or board of directors with the concept of the legislative body of a state; (2) an executive committee; (3) an executive director and/or imam; (4) a general assembly; and sometimes, (5) an advisory board. However, behind all of this bureaucratic window dressing, most organizations amount to a one-man show, or a one-clan show, as the de facto model. These resemble the one-man or one-party show of most Muslim states, which also have elaborate and impressive systems. Ironically, this notoriously dysfunctional model is usually defended in the name of binding *shura* (consultation), collective leadership, democracy, and/or accountability (checks and balances).

Whereas the prophetic leadership model makes everyone a leader and everyone responsible and assigns more responsibility to the leader commensurate with his authority, the prevailing leadership model in our community combines the worst of both worlds: disputed authority and disavowed responsibility. It is no wonder that it has been a recipe for stagnation, power struggle, and our community's endless fragmentation and alienation. Moreover, it has largely failed our community because the ceiling of such a model is the preservation of the status quo and the management of a community that is isolated, disengaged, and complacent. This places us on a slow boat to nowhere!

The governance model of Muslim countries is being deserted by most of the countries that previously applied it. Those countries are now becoming true states governed by the law and by functional institutions. Furthermore, the leadership/governance model of the Islamic movement that stifles leadership and initiative in the name of collective leadership and precludes initiative and blocks decision making in the name of the binding *shura* is unheard of. Such a strange concept certainly has nothing to do with the original prophetic leadership model.

Our movement strongly believes in the democratic system as a plausible translation of the original Medina concept of a constitutionally governed and citizenship-based state. The democratic system, at its best, is a good encapsulation of most of the Islamic guidelines of governance. We also strongly believe in the prophetic model of community building and governance. However, we believe that the governance models that are currently in use, in the Islamic movements and the Muslim community, are bad emulations of the prophetic model, just as the governance models in most Muslim countries are bad emulations of the democratic system. In both cases, any resemblance to good governance or to the original prophetic model is an optical illusion.

Our new movement is a serious attempt, not only to "translate" divine guidance and the divine mission into a way of life and a societal reform project but also to emulate the prophetic model of community building and governance.

Our community needs to be rebuilt. That will require our commitment to the divine mission, the resolution of our identity crisis (including commitment to America as a homeland), and the restoration of the prophetic leadership/governance model with its simplicity and incredible effectiveness.

4—A MUTILATED RELIGION: OUR CRISIS OF UNDERSTANDING ISLAM

We now come to the "mother of all" root causes of the Muslim American crisis—our deficiencies in understanding and implementing Islam and our weak commitment to the divine mission, which is also our defining mission.

Indeed, it is our frozen and mutilated Islamic construct that led us to abandon our mission. The construct also significantly contributed to our identity crisis and resulted in our leadership void. Through our misunderstanding and confusion, we lost our religious incentive for self-development, social outreach, and civic engagement. Our high aspirations faded, and there was no longer any need or appreciation for true leadership and unity.

Moreover, our inadequate, incoherent, and imbalanced Islamic construct not only engendered our identity crisis but also combined with our lack of sense of mission to deny us the drive and the ability to confront our overall, community-wide crisis. Mixed with a foreign and largely unhealthy culture and a heavy dose of anti-American political views, this amorphous Islamic construct has prevented us (including Muslim Americans who were born and raised here) from committing to America as a homeland and from effectively engaging with our sociopolitical environment. We failed to reconcile (let alone to fuse) the two components of our identity (the Muslim and the American), and we ended up torn between two or possibly even three different worlds: America, our country of origin, and the enclave that we refer to as our Muslim community.

As we did with the root causes of our crisis, let us discuss the main deficiencies in our prevailing understanding and implementation of Islam. Let's also consider why and how we ended up with such a frozen and mutilated Islamic construct. This will hopefully make the case for (1) a major and complete paradigm shift and (2) the most critical tenet of our project—the rediscovery, revival, and renewal of Islam, and the development of an original and inspiring, authentic American Islamic construct that will enable our transformation. No amount of modification or repair will give our existing construct the functionality our community needs. If we are to become a positive force in America and relevant to societal reform, we urgently need a new American Islamic construct.

The Islamic paradigm

As discussed in detail in part 2, Islam is a mission that is centered on uplifting individuals and inspiring and empowering them to realize their full potential as they strive to become the best embodiments and instruments of God's will. It transforms individuals and turns them into agents of change in their environments. It fuses their hearts, minds, and efforts together, thus generating a vibrant, relevant, and impactful societal reform movement, with outreach and impact that don't stop growing.

Because Islam was initially able to accomplish this under the most unfavorable conditions with the most unlikely candidates, we know it is capable of producing these same results at any time and in any society, including ours. Correctly understood and appropriately applied, Islam succeeds because of the qualities of universality and timelessness, a compelling sense of mission, and its incredibly effective leadership model. Also, Islam eliminates all the sources of waste and conflict, both in the individual and in communal life. It sets the bar of aspirations very high, and it removes any barriers that hold people back and prevent them from aspiring to achieve their full potential.

> For he (the Prophet) commands them what is just and forbids them what is evil; he allows them as lawful what is good (and pure) and prohibits them from what is bad (and impure); He releases them from their heavy burdens and from the yokes that are upon them. So it is those who believe in him, honor him, help him, and follow the light which is sent down with him,- it is they who will prosper [Qur'an 7:157].

Whenever we see waste and conflict in ourselves or in our community, as is the case nowadays, and whenever we fall short in our aspirations and achievement, we must seriously question and revisit our understanding, implementation, and promotion of Islam. We must also champion its revival and renewal.

A proper and healthy construct of Islam ensures an enduring unity of purpose and leadership, and it guarantees relevance and mobilization within any context. However, a proper and healthy construct of Islam cannot be achieved unless Muslims develop an original and indigenous Islamic construct by translating the divine guidance, the divine mission, and the prophetic model into a viable way of life, functionally appropriate for the current historical, geographical, and sociopolitical context. That revised model must produce individual and collective role models and provide answers to people's questions and solutions to their problems. A proper and healthy construct also needs to have a relevant and rallying cause and a platform for renaissance and reform.

The goal of this challenging exercise should be to ensure that Islam becomes an indigenous/mainstream, rooted, relevant, and inspiring religion, without compromising authenticity and without compromising the essentials (*thawabit*) of Islam. And because things in life are always changing, this is not just a onetime exercise; therefore, our duty doesn't stop there. We must also see to it that Islam continuously evolves. Through our constant intellectual and spiritual renewal and effective engagement of our environments, we can ensure that Islam remains fresh, relevant, and inspiring.

It is not the Muslims' duty to preserve Islam. God already promised to do so. Rather, it is our duty to preserve its freshness, relevance, and capacity to inspire and empower individuals, guide life, and reform/regenerate societies. When we set as our goal the preservation of Islam itself, we miss the point; and we basically end up trying to reinvent the wheel. Oftentimes, such efforts backfire, as was the case when Muslims called for "closing the door of *ijtihad*," in an attempt to protect Islam from deviation. The result has been that Islam has become frozen and outdated, which led people to desert it and to search for alternative sources to answer their questions, solve their problems, and guide their lives.

Because the sources of Islam are constant, but life is constantly changing and presenting people with new challenges and opportunities, the best (if not the only) way to "preserve" Islam is through constant intellectual renewal and effective civic engagement. These efforts establish a desperately needed two-way synergism between Islam and life; whereby Islam constantly infuses guidance and empowerment into individuals, communities, and societies, and the changes in society inspire the continuing evolution and relevance of Islam.

Life's challenges demand that we constantly "dig" in search of Islam's infinite treasures. The primary goal of our mission is to produce an authentic, original, American Islamic experience; and that will include successfully meeting the ongoing challenge of constantly entrenching Islam in our time and our society. Our Islam must be indigenous, relevant, and inspiring— without compromising any of its principles. This exercise must start with a fresh understanding of the texts of Islam in our context. Then our search for Islam's infinite treasures must continue indefinitely. This is a process of constant renewal, revival, and engagement; and it is both an individual and a collective duty. Essentially, this process of intellectual and spiritual renewal will serve the same purpose that God's messengers served throughout the history of humanity—the delivery of a fresh, customized Islamic revelation. In our case, that means a new construct. When God sealed the prophethood with the last prophet, Muhammad, He promised to preserve His final, universal, and timeless guidance. However, He assigned to the believers the task of "translating" it and keeping it relevant through an ever-evolving understanding and implementation. Indeed, the community of followers of Muhammad stands at the interface between the perfect and timeless divine guidance (which consists mostly of general guidelines and methodologies) and the ever-changing reality that continually confronts us with new challenges, issues, and settings. Consequently, we must constantly refresh our understanding and implementation of Islam, and we also have to constantly explore and tap our inexhaustible source of guidance. We must pursue wisdom wherever it might be, and we should apply it appropriately in light of our reality.

So to ensure and maintain the relevance of Islam and our own relevance as well, we must stay abreast of our reality. We must remain cognizant of how our society works, and this requires us to be consistently informed and engaged. This is really the only way we may fulfill the mission of Islam. Islam is essentially about change and reform. It requires a proper understanding of our reality. It also demands a relevant understanding and "translation" of the divine guidance. We are the connection for the continuous back-and-forth interaction between the divine guidance and our ever-changing world.

This continuous interaction with the divine guidance and with our reality to ensure an ever-fresh and relevant Islamic construct constitutes the cornerstone of our project. That's why we will make a concerted effort to intellectually engage Muslims and invite them to embark on serious and in-depth reflections, discussions, and research about our faith and our reality. In doing so, we should rely predominantly on the original texts/sources of Islam. These must be understood in light of our reality. Additionally, we should look selectively and creatively toward Islamic and human history and heritage. Our main focus should be on ensuring the relevance of our faith and the betterment of our society and our world and ourselves.

Although it may appear easier and safer to try to avoid this often tedious and painstaking exercise by clinging to the work of a different era and circumstances, in actuality, doing that is the surest way to guarantee stagnation, irrelevance, and intellectual shallowness.

It was the proper bridging between divine guidance and "facts-on-the-ground" reality that facilitated the astonishing success of the AK (Justice and Development) Party in Turkey. As mentioned before, this bridging approach was also behind the successful initiation of several Islamic movements. On the other hand, the stalling of this process is the main reason behind the decline of several Islamic movements. They ended up intellectually frozen and out of touch with their reality. Their leaders' attempts to make up for this with increased activism, victimization, organizational discipline, bureaucracy, and expanded membership all failed.

The specific outcomes to be achieved through this ongoing renewal, made possible by the communication between divine guidance and our reality, consist of

– the development of a relevant civic platform that addresses the issues facing our country at all levels (local, state, national) and in all pertinent areas (social, political, economic, environmental, etc.). This platform will serve as our ticket to civic engagement, and it will determine who our allies and opponents will be. It will be promoted through relevant civic discourse, and constantly reviewed, adjusted, and prioritized.

– the development of relevant religious literature and discourse in a common language that resonates with the American people: "We sent not an apostle except (to teach) in the language of his (own) people, in order to make (things) clear to them" [Qur'an 4:14].

– the development of exemplary individuals, families, and communities to serve as models of engaged, impactful difference-makers within our society.

How and why the Islamic paradigm stalled

As God's final message, Islam is meant to be a universal and timeless religion and way of life. It has plenty of built-in flexibility that makes it valid for all times and compatible with every culture.

Moreover, Islam is timeless not only in its relevance but also in its ability/capacity to evolve and to inspire renaissance and reform movements. However, all of this hinges on Muslims' proper understanding and practice of Islam. In other words, while Islam is timelessly relevant, inspiring, and empowering, Muslims' understanding and implementation of Islam may or may not be. In this regard, Islamic history is a mixed record, and at times, we see cyclic recurrences of alternating renaissance, stagnation, and decline. At our own point in history, the curve is definitely not going upward for Muslims. Indeed, Muslims' grossly inadequate understanding and implementation of Islam, half-hearted commitment to it, and ineffective methods are cementing their irrelevance and petrifying their dismal situations. Muslim Americans are not an exception, but we aim to change that.

While, as Muslim Americans, we appear to be in better shape than most Muslims globally, we are actually a mere microcosm of the Muslim world. Our prevalent version of Islam is devoid of any sense of mission, and our vague construct is deficient in its humane and civic dimensions. Islam in America today is encumbered by significantly unhealthy cultural baggage. It has engendered a severe identity crisis that is largely to blame for our ambivalence toward America and our isolation, stagnation, and fragmentation.

Every successful renaissance movement throughout Islamic history has been enthused by a call to go directly to the original and pure sources of our religion (the divine guidance) and has rallied the people behind an Islam-inspired compelling cause. Together, these two factors help remove the mental and psychological barriers that individuals often face, consequently unlocking their potential and energy and raising their aspirations.

Indeed, every Islamic renaissance movement (starting with Muhammad's movement itself) began by creating a mental and psychological shift in society. Our movement is no exception. Making Islam relevant and empowering again is a fundamental goal that we are determined to achieve. Not only do we want to create a shift in our people's mind-set toward Islam and America, but we also want to boost their individual and collective aspirations and sense of responsibility.

The essence of being a Muslim is to completely submit to God and to wholeheartedly strive to fulfill His purpose. This requires the proper understanding and implementation of both the divine guidance and the prophetic model. It also requires the effective execution of the divine mission. Here's what it takes: Muslims, individually and collectively, must ensure the continuous relevance, freshness, and appeal of the divine guidance. We must ensure that the divine mission is translated and fulfilled effectively. Finally, we must ensure that the movement is relevant, impactful, and constantly consolidating and expanding.

This community-wide effort should include individual efforts and collective cooperation. We must all work to become the best embodiments and the most effective instruments of Allah's will. We are talking about a lifelong journey of self-development, social outreach, and civic engagement. And because the message is universal, and the mission is expansive, Muslims should constantly strive, individually and collectively, to move to the next level and engage an ever-wider circle in their environments. They should strive to rise to the occasion and meet the demands of the mission. America today offers many challenges to be met and opportunities to be seized.

As outlined above, because the divine guidance is fixed and permanent but consists mostly of general guidelines and because the divine mission was defined in general terms, the main duty of Muslims is to "translate" the divine guidance and mission into a currently relevant platform and movement aimed at fulfilling God's purpose and seeking His pleasure. This process of translation was the thrust in the prophetic model and in the life of Muhammad and his community. That community was the perfect embodiment of the divine guidance, and it carried out perfect execution of the divine mission. Both individually and collectively, Muhammad and his companions spared nothing to become the best embodiments and instruments of God's will.

The Prophet and his movement focused on the paramount issue of *Tawheed* and on rooting in society the proper concept of God and belief in Him. That was the foundation of a great platform and a great movement of revival, renaissance, and reform that changed the course of history and the face of earth within one generation. It turned the poor and illiterate Bedouins into leaders of the world and champions of a great civilization. In his farewell pilgrimage and sermon, Muhammad was clearly hinting that the revelation was about to end but that he was transferring the responsibility for his mission and movement to his companions, and through them to his followers till the end of time.

This whole paradigm was shaken badly by the assassination of Uthman (about twenty-five years after Muhammad's death), by the subsequent civil wars, and by the transition to dynasty rule (discussed in detail in chapter 2). However, even though there were numerous ups and downs and twists and turns, Muslims reasonably upheld the divine guidance and the prophetic model and continued to champion the divine mission for centuries. To be sure, some elements of the prophetic paradigm were gradually fading; and periodically, the community had to cope with notorious rulers and with rebellious and/or deviant groups. However, the foundations laid down by the Prophet were incredibly resilient. As a result, for centuries, Muslims continued to resist and fight back against religious, social, and political epidemics. They were able to recover from occasional regressions. Notably, Islamic scholarship and intellectualism remained largely autonomous and vibrant throughout this period.

Two factors, though, would coalesce to gradually freeze Islamic thought and confine it to the domain of personal matters: (1) The dynasties grew less and less tolerant of dissent and of the "interference" of scholars in public affairs. With few exceptions, the scholars, who feared chaos, responded by choosing societal order and stability at the expense of freedom. Moreover, there was rarely any open defiance of the Islamic essentials by the rulers. Thus, gradually, a sort of division of labor between the rulers and the scholars took hold, with the scholars avoiding public affairs and focusing on personal religious matters. Ironically, personal matters tend to be the most constant part of Islam, the area that least requires intellectual reflection and creativity. (2) Quite absurdly, the scholars and the masses chose to "freeze Islam" to protect it from deviations that kept popping up. This solution was not only ill conceived and shortsighted but was also futile because it affected the relevance of Islam without actually deterring deviant groups who did not need anyone's permission. In fact, their task was certainly facilitated by the freeze.

As a result of the freeze, Islam was not only stripped of its sense of mission but was also gradually detached from life, particularly public affairs. The confinement of scholarship to personal matters greatly reduced the need and incentive for *ijtihad* (scholarly interpretation of Islamic law), and the freeze made Islam irrelevant, uninspiring, and out of touch.

In recent history, with the exception of the Islamic movements' founding phases, there has hardly been any serious attempt to refresh the Islamic paradigm. For a number of reasons discussed in part 2, the Muslim American community has never tried. In fact, we have never recognized the need to develop an original American Islamic construct. Instead, we imported a frozen, foreign, and inadequate construct. This paradigm had already stagnated and lost its relevance, effectiveness, and inspirational capacity, even in the countries of origin. As the malfunctioning of the prevailing construct in the Muslim world became more and more obvious, and as the Muslim American community began to be weaned from the "myth of return," the deficiencies of the imported construct became clear and undeniable. Moreover, as has been true overseas, our construct became frozen in time and in space. Although the community direly needed to embark on the "translation" exercise to develop an original, unique Islamic construct and although the community needed to be rebuilt accordingly, it did not have real leadership or the intellectual critical mass to do so. The few serious attempts that were undertaken were aborted. Consequently, we have settled for superficial adjustments to our imported paradigm; none of which have yielded any significant improvements in terms of growth, unity, mobilization, relevance, impact, or integration.

In the rest of this section, we will discuss our community's main deficiencies in its understanding and practice of Islam.

Main deficiencies in our Islamic construct

Lack/fading of the sense of mission: This is by far the most serious deficiency, and it is the cause of several others. Islam is essentially a life mission. It is the sense of mission that drives several critical tenets of the Islamic paradigm, such as self-development, social outreach, civic engagement, leadership, unity, and scriptural study and interpretation (*ijtihad*). Accordingly, when our sense of mission begins to fade, our entire Islamic paradigm begins to collapse, leading to the disengagement, isolation, stagnation, and fragmentation of Muslim societies and communities.

As indicated earlier, Muslims' sense of mission began to fade long ago, starting with the era of dynasties. After some successful rebounds, Muslims largely abandoned their defining mission, and that set off a chain reaction that brought them to their current dismal situation. That actually sums up the history of a community/nation that was engendered by Islam and its compelling sense of mission but then lost its way.

The contemporary Islamic movements did have, no doubt, some great success in reviving Islam and reconciling it with modernity; and they paved the way for a very large number of people to rediscover and commit to Islam as a religion or as a way of life. However, these movements in the Muslim world did not succeed in restoring the Muslims' compelling sense of mission. With the exception of the few Islamic movements, which are also resistance movements (fighting occupation, not just opposing government to seek power), being mission driven, and living for a cause are still alien concepts in the Muslim world, even among activists.

In the Muslim community and in the Muslim world in general, there is a very short supply not only of true leadership (as indicated earlier) but also of mission-driven individuals. Being mission driven means fully committing to do what needs to be done to fulfill God's purpose. A mission-driven Muslim is someone who always strives and challenges himself/herself to become the best embodiment and instrument of the will of Allah. It's a wholehearted commitment to a cause and to a vision, and it means owning the responsibility for both. This commitment raises the bar of aspirations, engenders a lot of passion and determination, unlocks people's potential, and unleashes tremendous energies. The best example was the great transformation of the companions of the Prophet upon embracing Islam as their life mission.

The majority of Muslims are nonpracticing, though a sizable minority observe—more or less regularly—the rituals of Islam, and many even abide by its teaching in their lives. There are also activists, but they comprise a very small minority of Muslims. Whether they are freelancers or part of a group/organization, these activists not only espouse Islam as a way of life but also dedicate some of their time and money to Islamic activities (e.g., educational, social, political, etc.). Such activism, whether consistent or erratic, is rarely driven by a cause or by results and should not be mistaken for a mission. Also, we should not misinterpret opposition to government by any Islamic movements or political parties as a divine mission. This is just a struggle for political power.

Most Muslims, including activists, basically live for themselves, in their own worlds, and with limited life aspirations. This is very much the situation in the Muslim American community, which is essentially a microcosm of the Muslim world.

In the absence of a compelling mission, most Muslims (including activists) do not consider themselves to be responsible for anyone but themselves and their family or, at best, for the members of their organization or congregation. Compare that limited sense of responsibility to the great responsibility that God assigned to all Muslims as part of the divine mission. In the words of one companion: "God sent us to save humanity!"

As the sense of mission faded, so did the incentive for self-development, the need for a movement and leadership, the force that unifies the community, and the drive that propels us to be socially and civically engaged as individuals and as a community. Without a compelling mission, people cannot be motivated to improve and push themselves. Any efforts at self-development, without a compelling mission, will be ineffective. Also, in order to fulfill a mission, people must join forces, establish a movement, and establish appropriate leadership. For these same reasons, people normally do feel motivated to reach out to others and to be civically engaged.

If we were to consider Islam as a building, the divine mission would be its foundation. If Islam were a vehicle, the mission would be its engine. And if Islam were a human body, the mission would be its heart. When Islam loses its compelling mission, it loses much of its relevance and its ability to inspire and empower. The result is a version that has little to do with the Islam preached by Muhammad. The Prophet's Islam was essentially a mission and a movement for change.

The fading of the sense of mission causes (and reflects) tremendous damage to the Islamic paradigm, and that is very sufficient reason to call for the development of a new Islamic construct. That will involve major deconstruction and reconstruction. The key to our renaissance is to inspire Muslims to rediscover and commit to Islam, not just as a religion and way of life but as a life mission—and to become not just practicing or even active Muslims but mission-driven Muslims!

Confusion between the constant essentials and the variables; between the clear-cut and the disputable; and even between religion and culture

The main duty of Muslims, as heirs of God's final and universal message, is to properly translate the divine guidance and the divine mission within their contemporary historical, geographical, and sociopolitical contexts and to ensure the constant evolution of the divine guidance and divine mission. In that way, we practice an Islam that has perpetual relevance and renewal. This translation must be done all over again whenever Islam is introduced into a new society and whenever Muslims become stuck in a particular construct for too long. As indicated earlier, for quite some time now, Islam has been largely frozen and confined to personal matters. Consequently, a large number of Muslims have become hostage to past literature and past accomplishments. For centuries, most Islamic publications have been merely reproductions of past works—lacking in intellectual value and creativity.

Our total reliance on our past heritage has not only precluded us from leveraging the inexhaustible sources of divine guidance, the Qur'an and Sunna, but also has created considerable confusion between what is purely divine guidance and what is human interpretation. Plus, it has crippled our minds—using them for rote memorization and consumption rather than as tools for creative thinking, contemplation, and production.

A proper understanding of Islam mandates that we rely on the Qur'an and authentic Sunna as our starting points, ultimate references, and as our only binding sources of guidance. Our methods should stem predominantly from these original texts. Our Islamic literature, heritages, cultures, and historical experiences should be used very selectively as sources of lessons and inspiration and as supporting documents, but only after they have passed the tests of authenticity and relevance. The body of Islamic knowledge should be purged of any materials that are of questionable authenticity or relevance. In that way, Muslims can be freed from the shackles of unhealthy culture and heritage.

This process of constant revival and renewal is of utmost importance because, while Islam itself is infallible, its understanding and implementation by humans can go very wrong. And even when the divine guidance and mission are successfully translated within a particular context, this translation should not be allowed to freeze. A paradigm that is functional in one place and time is generally not transferable from one era to another or from one place to another.

In a verse that God repeated three times in chapter 54 of the Qur'an (surat al-Qamar), we are asked,

> And We have indeed made the Qur'an easy to understand and remember: then is there any that will receive admonition? [Qur'an 54:40].

In another verse, we read,

> He has chosen you, and has imposed no difficulties on you in religion [Qur'an 22:78].

There should be no difficulties, then, in understanding, practicing, and promoting Islam. Yet some believe the average Muslim cannot understand Islam, and that they, therefore, may as well not try. Our excessive reliance on Islamic literature of the past and on Muslim scholars, instead of studying the original sources firsthand, is an unhealthy trend. It has stifled our intellectual development and creativity, and it has precluded the evolution, freshness, and relevance of our understanding. Ultimately, it has prevented us from properly implementing and effectively promoting true Islam. Muslims' reliance on literature and ideas that do not fit their own situation is one of the main reasons for the stagnation and irrelevance of the Muslim world, as well as for the Muslim Americans' identity crisis and unwillingness and/or inability to effectively engage their real-world environment. The damage caused by reliance on Islamic literature of the past has been particularly harmful to our Muslim American community because most of that literature was produced in completely different historical and sociopolitical contexts. Moreover, it is read indiscriminately.

For all these reasons, we are calling on Muslim Americans to embark (individually and collectively) on a direct study of the boundless treasures of the Qur'an and Sunna in order to produce a relevant, authentic Islamic understanding and implementation of these divine sources, as well as a relevant discourse and platform. Our scholars and literature can always be consulted, but they should not be followed blindly or taken as a substitute for our own efforts. By creating this shift toward our original texts, our movement aims to inspire an intellectual dynamism and creativity geared toward Islamic revival and renewal. We also hope to eventually achieve self-sufficiency in terms of scholars and original (and refurbished) Islamic literature within our own community.

However, while we are strongly encouraging Muslims to seek guidance through personal reflection and contemplation of the original sources, we firmly believe that issuing *fatwas* (religious rulings) should be limited to those qualified scholars who have firsthand knowledge and understanding of the American context. *Fatwas* should not be issued in a vacuum, and their applicability varies with the context.

Moreover, not only must we distinguish between the original, authentic, sacred, and infallible sources of guidance (the Qur'an and Sunna) and everything else that is human and fallible, but we also must clearly decide what is constant and clear-cut on the one hand, and variable and disputable on the other. Indeed, there is significant confusion in this regard.

Although there is no doubt about the authenticity of the entire Qur'an, and although a good part of the Sunna also remains undisputed, most of this authenticated material has been subjected to multiple interpretations. Moreover, this has been taking place ever since the time of the companions. Muhammad's death ended our direct connection with heaven, and so it also ended earthly authority in rendering the final word on disputed matters. As a result, there have been a lot of differences—big and small—first among the companions and then among the scholars of Islam throughout history. There have been disagreements about the interpretation of many verses and Hadiths and about *fiqh* (jurisprudence) matters. Those differences endured, and there has been no real push to resolve them.

Interestingly, Muhammad himself did not see a need to resolve some of these differences, and he went so far as to approve different opinions on the same issue.[37]

All of this confirms and demonstrates the great flexibility of Islam, particularly in public affairs. Such flexibility is very natural for a religion that was meant to be universal, comprehensive, and timeless. Although Islamic teachings do provide some strict guidelines, they also offer enormous elasticity. It is the duty of all Muslims, during all time periods, to revive, renew, and customize Islam's guidance to ensure that it is relevant, indigenous, and inspiring. However, we Muslims must be careful. We must make sure that our customization of the guidance is in absolute compliance with the indisputable precepts.

At one point in history, Muslims who were concerned about the potential corruption of Islam decided to put an end to scholarly interpretation and analysis of Islamic law. They were determined to "close the door of *ijtihad*." This largely stifled the flexibility, the agility, the creativity, and the evolution of Islam. After that decision, Muslim scholars became largely dependent on the material produced earlier on, limiting themselves to studying it and reproducing it. Ever since then, Muslims have been relying on those scholars and their reproduced materials.

Moreover, many devoted Muslims confined themselves to the work of one particular scholar or school of thought. Rather than trying to make Islam relevant, they found it easier and safer to go for extra stringency to protect themselves from deviation and protect Islam from corruption. This tendency runs contrary to the prophetic approach. Muhammad always chose the easiest of the available lawful options, and he always tried his best to make Islam appealing to people.

Ultimately, by following inappropriate or obsolete literature instead of the timeless original teaching, Islam became too rigid and even frozen. As a result, its followers and scholars became out of touch and irrelevant, and they failed to keep up with the progress of life.

Not only are we calling upon Muslims to rely predominantly on the original authentic sources of guidance and to free themselves from the

---

37 Once, the Prophet instructed an expedition not to pray Asr (afternoon prayer) until they reached their city of destination; but he later approved of those who skipped that prayer as well as those who tried to reach the city before the time for Asr prayer. Also, in an expedition that took place during Ramadan, the Prophet approved of both those who fasted and those who did not, based on the permission for travelers to break their fast.

shackles of unhealthy culture and heritage, but we are also trying to stimulate widespread intellectual dynamism and creativity among Muslims in the interpretation of those original and authentic texts. This process should not undermine the undisputed matters and should be done within the strict guidelines of Islam. Within these guidelines, we encourage Muslims to reflect upon and contemplate the sources of guidance to dig out more of their inexhaustible treasures. We should seek the most relevant—yet authentic—interpretations.

Obviously, the more knowledge a person has, the more contribution he/she should make to this intellectual revival and renewal movement. However, everybody is encouraged to raise issues, in addition to contemplating the sacred texts.

In all of this, we need to be limited only by the essentials of Islam and its guidelines, not by the intellectual product of people in different parts of the world or from different times in history.

Neglect of maqasid (overarching goals of Islam), masalih (public interest and common good), and context

Islam has six overarching goals (*maqasid*), which correspond to the preservation of six vital items: faith, life, reason/intellect, wealth/property, honor, and lineage. All of the Islamic precepts aim to ensure the well-being of humanity in this life and in the hereafter. Neglect of those *maqasid* (goals) is a very serious mistake that results in a literalist, superficial, noncoherent, and irrelevant understanding of Islam. This leads to misguided implementation in terms of methods, priorities, and activism.

The establishment and maintenance of justice is one of the most important objectives of divine revelation:

> We sent aforetime our apostles with Clear Signs and sent down with them the Book and the Balance (of Right and Wrong), that men may stand forth in justice; and We sent down iron, in which is (material for) mighty war, as well as many benefits for mankind, that God may test who it is that will help, Unseen, Him and His apostles: For God is Full of Strength, Exalted in Might (and able to enforce His will) [Qur'an 57:25].

We believe that in our understanding and implementation of Islam, serious consideration must be given to the *maqasid* (six overarching goals), the *masalih* (common good), the context, and the social norms (*urf*). Upholding the *maqasid* of Islam, serving the *masalih* of people, taking the context into consideration, and conforming to the letters of the texts are all very delicate and critical. Indeed, Islam's constant evolution and freshness and its timeless and universal relevance are primarily due to its guiding *maqasid* and to the emphasis Islam places on the *masalih*, the *urf*, and the context. On the other hand, any abuse of the *maqasid* and *masalih* may undermine the essentials of Islam and dilute its essential teachings (*thawabit*). Likewise, neglect of the *maqasid* and *masalih* stifles the vitality and flexibility of Islam and therefore hampers its timeless and universal relevance. The balance between *thawabit, maqasid*, and *masalih* has never been easy to strike, but a disregard of the *maqasid* and *masalih* (and also, of context) is so detrimental that it must be challenged. This is one of the main factors behind Muslims' marginalization and irrelevance and behind the alienation of many people (including Muslims) from the prevalent rigid and out-of-touch version of Islam that is unable to provide sound answers and viable solutions to today's issues and concerns.[38]

The most striking examples of rulings driven primarily by a concern for the *maqasid* (overarching goals) and *masalih* (common good) occurred very shortly after Muhammad's death. It should come as no surprise that these examples involved the Prophet's closest companions, men whose diligence in adhering to the scriptural sources was unquestionable. Both Abu Bakr and Omar knew very well, not only the letter but also the spirit of the original texts. Moreover, they were not confined by any Islamic heritage or literature.

Abu Bakr's first major decision as *khalifa* was to repress the mutiny of those who refused to pay *zakat* (regular charity) after Muhammad's death. The decision was based largely on *masalih* and *maqasid*, and it was met with the objection of most of the companions who had a stronger textual argument. However, Abu Bakr was serving a higher purpose. He was protecting Islam from cherry-picking modification and protecting the state from disintegration that would have seriously threatened the very existence of Islam and the community. Also, he encountered similar objections when he and Omar decided to collect the different parts of the Qur'an and combine them into

---

38   Tariq Ramadan. (2009). *Radical Reform: Islamic Ethics and Liberation* [Book].

a single written document. The companions argued that it was something that Muhammad hadn't done. Abu Bakr and Omar, however, insisted on proceeding on the basis of *masalih* (common good and public interest), not on scriptural evidence. They said the move was needed to preserve the Qur'an after the death of many *hafiz* (memorizers of Qur'an) during the wars of regression (*al-ridda'*). Up to that point, the Qur'an had been preserved primarily through memorization and unbound sheets.

Omar's rulings were even more striking because they dealt with clear-cut Qur'anic verses and rulings of Muhammad. Omar decided to suspend the penalty of theft during a famine that struck Medina. Omar reasoned that the penalty for theft had been justly instituted by God to punish and deter criminals and that it was not designed to harm hungry people for whom the state had failed to provide jobs or even food. Also, Omar modified the Qur'anic specifications for the distribution of charity by excluding one category of recipients (*Al-Mu'allafatu Qulūbuhum*[39]). He reasoned that their prior inclusion was meant to neutralize potential opponents—a concern that was no longer necessary. He also altered the manner of distributing the spoils of war, and he made several other decisions based on *maqasid* and *masalih*.

Abu Bakr and Omar, each, took a different approach to arranging for the transition in leadership that was to follow them. Both of their approaches to transition differed from the course taken by Muhammad. Islamic guidelines require consultation with and the consent of the community, but they do not prescribe a specific mechanism. Although Muhammad did not explicitly appoint a *khalifa*, Abu Bakr himself explicitly appointed Omar; and Omar chose six companions to select his successor from among themselves.

These were critical decisions with immense repercussions. Yet they were based more on the *maqasid* and *masalih* than on a literal understanding and implementation of the scriptural texts. These momentous decisions were made by scholars and leaders, men whose strict adherence to the text did not prevent them from taking into consideration the *maqasid*, the *masalih*, and the context of their situation. In making the decisions, they applied their deep knowledge of the spirit of Islam as well as the letter of Islam.

In order to make Islam relevant and viable again so that it can fulfill its function of uplifting people and reforming society, we must be wise and brave enough to not only consider *all* possible and credible interpretations of the

---

39 *Al-Mu'allafatu Qulūbuhum*: Ones who convert or are inclined to Islam. Literally those whose hearts are softened/reconciled.

original texts but also to seek out the best interpretation given the context in which we live. This is what Dr. Tariq Ramadan refers to as the reformist approach.[40] That's how we will achieve the goal of this project: to make Islam an indigenous, appealing, and inspiring religion—and also a viable way of life and an impactful movement of change—without compromising on essentials.

While it is true that the Qur'an and Sunna, taken as a whole, comprise valid sources of guidance for all times and circumstances, it is precisely because of their universality and timelessness that not every verse or Hadith is equally relevant at all times and in all places. This is particularly true of those verses that deal with social issues (*muamalaat*) and public affairs. The variable applicability is even more poignant when we are considering what our Islamic heritage means and does not mean in a new place and time. Consequently, as we explore the Qur'anic verses, the Hadith and the authenticated literature, let us focus most intently on what is most relevant to our context.

In particular, two elements of context should be taken into consideration: (1) the prevalence of sound customs (*urf*) within society and (2) particular circumstances that may exist or arise. Scholars agree that *urf* is one of the sources of jurisprudence, and the Maliki and Hanafi schools of thought (*mathaahib*) seriously consider it in their methodology for understanding and applying the scriptural sources within a particular context. Also, Imam al-Shafi, one of the greatest scholars of Islamic history, actually changed some of his rulings (*fatwas*) after he moved from Iraq to Egypt due to his consideration of the new context. Moreover, some students of the founders of important schools of thought modified some of the rulings of their teachers.

---

40 Dr. Tariq Ramadan challenges those who argue defensively that reform is a dangerous and foreign deviation, and a betrayal of the faith. Authentic reform, he says, has always been grounded in Islam's textual sources, spiritual objectives, and intellectual traditions. But the reformist movements that are based on renewed reading of textual sources while using traditional methodologies and categories have achieved only adaptive responses to the crisis facing a globalizing world. Such readings, Ramadan argues, have reached the limits of their usefulness. Ramadan calls for a radical reform that goes beyond adaptation to envision bold and creative solutions to transform the present and the future of our societies. This new approach interrogates the historically established sources, categories, higher objectives, tools, and methodologies of Islamic law and jurisprudence, and the authority this traditional geography of knowledge has granted to textual scholars. Tariq Ramadan. (2009). *Radical Reform: Islamic Ethics and Liberation* [Book].

This sometimes took place even when no significant difference in time and circumstance had occurred. For example, Abu Zaid al-Qayrawani, one of the most prominent scholars of the Maliki School, kept a dog within in his remote residence. When asked about this act, which ran contrary to the teachings of Imam Malik, he said, "If Imam Malik lived in our time and circumstances, he would have a lion, not just a dog, for protection."

Our movement project does require that, in developing a proper and relevant understanding and implementation of Islam, we rely on the scriptural sources as the *only* binding sources. However, this project also requires that we learn to distinguish between Islamic essentials and variables as we apply the divine guidance to the context in which we live. We must keep our eyes on the *maqasid* (six overarching goals) and *masalih* (common good).

One final note for this section: the Qur'anic verses and Hadiths pertaining to belief and worship do apply everywhere and always. They are invariable.

Neglect of knowledge

Both the Qur'an and Sunna (as well as Muslims during the golden days of Islam) heavily emphasize the importance of acquiring knowledge without making an undue distinction between religious and nonreligious topics. Knowledge itself is an essential requirement for reinforcing our faith and fulfilling the divine mission. Indeed, the more knowledgeable a person is, the greater the likelihood that he/she will properly understand and implement the divine guidance, fulfill the divine mission, and engage in the sociopolitical environment. On the other hand, incorrect and inadequate knowledge can severely hamper people's contributions to God's cause or may even undermine it.

Our community has a serious and complicated problem when it comes to seeking knowledge. First of all, we tend to neglect knowledge altogether. Few people consistently read and study despite the fact that the first verses of the Qur'an to be revealed started with "Iqra (read)" and included the words "pen" and "teaching." Second, we have erected an artificial and detrimental separation and disconnect between religious knowledge and mundane (nonreligious) knowledge. As a result, most of the Muslims who do study focus almost exclusively on religious materials that often lack diversity and depth. Third, there is confusion between knowledge and information. Therefore, some people think they are learning, while, in reality, they are haphazardly collecting shallow and noncoherent information with questionable relevance and utility. Other people, rather than acquiring practical knowledge that offers solutions to today's problems, busy themselves instead with theoretical and/or hypothetical matters—or with issues that exist in different parts of the world and/or existed during different times in history.

To address this deficiency, our movement aims to

- restore a thirst for knowledge and wisdom—and also reestablish the tradition of lifelong learning—by linking the pursuit of knowledge to the fulfillment of the divine mission;
- improve the community's concept of what knowledge is (as opposed to mere information) and raise awareness that the pursuit of knowledge is essential to keep our minds sharp and tone our intellectual "muscles" so that our brains are not simply storing vast amounts of basically worthless information;
- eliminate the artificial separation between religious and nonreligious knowledge by emphasizing the importance of knowing God and knowing how this world was shaped and how it functions; and
- stimulate and maintain an intellectual momentum that translates into an in-depth and meaningful debate about our faith, our country, our situation, and our future.

Knowledge is essential if we hope to uplift ourselves and others and better our world—the main tenets of our mission. Any useful knowledge is Islamic knowledge. This is because from the Islamic perspective, the purpose of knowledge is to enable us to discover and leverage the laws that God embedded in this universe to govern the physical part of it and the human part of it. As Muslims, we must learn to benefit from both revelation and reason, which never contradict one another. While the Qur'an is not explicitly a book of the exact or social sciences, it is our exclusive source of information about God and the unseen. By knowing God and by knowing how the world was created and how it functions, we can establish and nurture a strong relationship with Him; and we can fulfill His purpose for creation by properly conducting our lives and effectively fulfilling our mission. Moreover, divine guidance is essential in precluding mankind's application of scientific discoveries in a destructive manner.

Fading/neglect of the spiritual, humane, civic, and aesthetic dimensions of Islam

One of the main reasons religions lose their appeal and power to inspire is that they lose balance and coherence when some aspects are blown out of proportion while others are neglected. This often involves an overemphasis on legalistic matters, rituals, and formalities. Unfortunately, that is what has happened to Islam. Even though the contemporary Islamic movement has revived several important aspects of Islam, its attempt to appease some Islamic groups and its failure to evolve have caused it to neglect some other aspects of Islam, which are critically important.

Indeed, the prevalent version of Islam today is dominated by literalism, legalism, ritualism, and formalism. In an excessive reaction to some Sufi deviations, spirituality has been neglected or relegated to occasional formal activities. On the other hand, groups that emphasize spirituality often do it at the expense of other important aspects and in violation of clear-cut Islamic precepts. Plus, the emphasis on spirituality is sometimes used as a justification for isolation and disengagement. Simultaneously, other groups have gone to the other extreme with regard to spirituality, and they have instead focused either on acquiring knowledge (that has questionable depth, coherence, or utility) or on promoting activism (with questionable relevance or impact).

This unilateral focus of most Islamic groups strips Islam of its balance, coherence, appeal, and inspiring power. It is no wonder that many group members lack both depth and balance in their personalities, and that they usually fail to impress or inspire even people around them. The neglect of the human and civic dimensions has turned some Muslim communities into virtual Bedouin cults lacking in civility. Ironically, while in its early days, Islam turned the Arab Bedouins into champions of a great civilization; nowadays, many converts in modern societies have adopted something resembling a Bedouin lifestyle.

Such disregard for these fundamental elements of the divine mission has engendered a binary perspective that classifies people into Muslims and non-Muslims, or practicing and nonpracticing Muslims—with a thick barrier separating devoted Muslims from all the rest. These separations have prevented the integration of activists from both African American and immigrant Muslim segments into their larger communities and have caused the alienation of devoted Muslims even in predominantly Muslim societies.

Many practicing Muslims tend to be rather nonsociable and aloof—except for their shallow interaction with other like-minded people.

The overall neglect of the divine mission and of these vital dimensions largely accounts for the insulation and civic disengagement of our Muslim American community, as Islam has become a religion to preserve and not a mission to fulfill. We regard people around us as non-Muslims to avoid—not as fellow human beings and citizens with whom we have a lot of commonalities and common concerns and with whom we must cooperate for the sake of the common good.

Moreover, even in Muslim countries, many devoted Muslims also find it difficult to interact, even with nonpracticing Muslims. They find it hard to commit to a country that is ruled by a secular government, especially if the majority of citizens don't adhere to the teachings of Islam. This explains why most Muslim activists are neither mission driven nor truly patriotic. Nonetheless, it is the mission-driven patriot Muslim, the one who is focused on societal reform, who will be the key to any successful Muslim renaissance.

Fusing the divine mission together with American patriotism is our movement's "secret recipe" for the revival/renewal of Islam and the renaissance of our community. This is the key to our contribution to the reform of our society. Up until now, our lack of a sense of mission and our perception of an incompatibility between religious devotion and patriotism have been the main causes of our severe disengagement, isolation, complacency, and stagnation. Being apart from society, instead of a part of society, has fostered an identity crisis that is blocking our integration and development. Consequently, once we experience a paradigm shift, we will be freed from the heavy burdens that have held us back for decades.

Another fundamental dimension of Islam that we aspire to revive is character. The importance of nobility and robustness of character cannot be overemphasized as reflected by Muhammad's summary of his mission by saying, "I was sent but to perfect good manners." And Muslim scholars quote the statement, "Religion is about our proper interaction with others." This is repeated so often that many people think it is a Hadith. And when told about a person's outstanding character, Omar ibn al-Khattab asked, "Did you travel with him? Did you deal with him with money?" This indicates that only when tested may the character of a person be accurately and reliably appraised. And when the answer was negative, Omar said, "So you probably praised him because you were impressed by his worship." Indeed, being a devoted (or active) Muslim does not guarantee an exemplary and robust character. Many people who have dealt closely with members of Islamic groups, or have come close enough to those groups to know what was really going on inside, haven't been impressed by the character of some members of those groups. Lack of character distinctiveness and lack of inspiring vision largely explain those groups' failure to significantly impact their communities (beyond offering needed programs and services) and failure to evolve into mass movements. Moreover, a neglect of Islam's aesthetic and emotional dimensions, along with the shallow spirituality of many Muslims, has made Islam appear to be dull and dormant. It has also made many Muslims seem rude.

With all that is presently missing in our community's understanding and implementation of Islam, one might well ask, "What is left of Islam?" Unfortunately, it has been so distorted that its prevalent version has little to do with the pure, simple, balanced, and empowering version that inspired Muhammad's great movement of change. Muhammad's Islam gave birth to a great civilization, and it did that within a short period of time despite very unfavorable conditions. That potential is available to us today, but we need to change. Rather than finding excuses and scapegoats, we must find it within ourselves to accept full responsibility for abandoning our divine mission, neglecting some of Islam's critical aspects, and failing to ensure its balance, relevance, and ability to inspire.

Reviving all these neglected aspects is key to the revival and restoration of Islam as an appealing, inspiring, balanced way of life—and also as a message, mission, and a model and movement for change, which in turn constitutes the cornerstone of our renaissance and reform movement.

We aspire to revive those neglected aspects so that devotion to Islam will be associated with higher and more robust moral standards, increased civility, increased patriotism, increased compassion toward others, and increased spiritual, emotional, and social vibrancy.

Presumption of haram ("forbidden, per Islamic Law") and the resulting tendency toward extreme rigidity or extreme laxity

These are two extreme trends that resulted from the above-mentioned deficiencies, and there is a clear tendency toward one of two extremes when it comes to our community's compliance with the divine guidance and fulfillment of the divine mission. While the majority of Muslims largely neglected our mission, some individuals made a misguided commitment to it.

Moreover, some Muslims mistake rigidity for piety. They think Islam is better served and preserved through stringency. They find it easier and safer to err on the side of prohibition—not realizing that prohibiting something that is lawful is as bad as permitting something that is unlawful. This attitude has alienated them not only from non-Muslims but also from the vast majority of Muslims who cannot relate to an Islam that is too rigid, too conservative, too complicated, and too impractical and out of touch. Moreover, reacting to undue stringency often takes people to the other extreme, and they may consider some things to be permissible even when they are not really sure what Islamic guidelines indicate.

Our movement's approach calls for restoring the presumption of lawfulness, which is a well-established Islamic ruling that puts the burden of proof on the one who is prohibiting something. However, at the same time, we urge Muslims to refrain from second-guessing about religious matters. Consequently, in our efforts to educate ourselves and others about Islam, we will follow Islamic methodology, which always sets clear baselines while inviting people to compete for goodness and righteousness in a race that knows no limits.

This is the tradition of Muhammad who always taught by his example that we should choose the easiest, lawful option, but that we should strive relentlessly to perfect our worship and performance of good deeds. We should always help people find the easiest permissible solution for their problems while simultaneously challenging them (and ourselves) to push harder. Sufyan al-Thawri, one of the greatest scholars of the generation of Muslims to come after the companions, said, "(True) *fiqh* (jurisprudence) is the permission you gain from a trustworthy scholar. But everyone could be good at stringency/prohibition."

We will go a long way in making Islam an appealing, relevant, and inspiring force in our community and our society by restoring Islam's sense of mission; returning to the pure, simple, original Islam and its sources; taking into account the context in which we live and the *maqasid* (six overarching goals) and *masalih* (common good); reviving fundamental but neglected aspects of Islam; and focusing on the acquisition of useful knowledge that eases people's lives and solves their problems. This will all be done without compromising on Islamic essentials (*thawabit*). These are the principles that guide our movement's understanding of Islam, and they also guide our efforts to properly and effectively implement Islam within the context of the twenty-first century in the United States of America.

PART IV:

MAIN TENETS OF OUR PROJECT, VISION, STRATEGY, APPROACH, AND PLATFORM

CHAPTER ONE: WHAT ARE WE CALLING FOR?

Given our roots, our founding, our evolution, our current state, and our daunting challenges, and notwithstanding our great potential and the great cause that God has called upon us to undertake, we strongly believe that nothing short of remaking our community will suffice. That cannot be accomplished by working through existing Muslim institutions. These organizations are good for their original purpose, and while many are reasonably fulfilling the objectives they were established to meet, most of the organizations were developed for a limited objective. The model that they were designed upon and their founding charters will not allow them to perform beyond their present limits, unless they genuinely commit to the cause and to the country, reinvent themselves accordingly, and streamline their efforts in that new direction.

The foremost challenges our community faces are (1) charting a new course toward real empowerment, integration, and relevance and (2) determining how to effect the necessary (and sensitive) changes in as smooth a manner as possible. This must be done with maximal preservation of previous accomplishments and minimal disruption of ongoing operations. This will require a committed group of trailblazers who possess an extraordinary ability to confront brutal reality, to articulate a compelling message calling for change, and to model that change without attacking any entity or individual in the community.

Bridging the gap between where we are and where we could and should be requires a sweeping change in our community that spans our identity, thought process, mission, Islamic construct, culture, approach, discourse, priorities, and structure. This change represents a major mental shift that must start with rediscovering our religion and then resolving fundamental issues, which we have ignored for far too long. We must do this together so that we can transform our inward and overseas-focused, isolated, activity-oriented community into a fully integrated, mission-driven, and impactful community that is focused on America. For individuals, this will be the equivalent of a "born-again" experience similar to that of the companions when they wholeheartedly embraced the original, pure version of Islam as their life mission. For the Muslim American community, it will be a white revolution—a renaissance (through far-reaching reforms) aimed at rallying our community around the clear cause of contributing to the needed societal reform.

We hope the previous sections of this book—in which we confronted our brutal reality and made the case for urgent and fundamental change—have reinforced (or, at least, didn't shake) the resolve and commitment of our readers to effect this direly needed change. This change must begin, first within ourselves individually and then among those in our immediate environments.

In parts 2 and 3, we discussed in detail the ideological foundations of Islam and Muslims' neglect of the divine mission and deviation from the prophetic model. Based on those foundations and our appraisal of the state of our community and in order to address the daunting challenges our community faces, we now introduce the following defining components of our proposed movement:

1. Islam is a life mission of actively striving to fulfill God's purpose in order to seek His pleasure

That's our understanding of Islam, and this is the first connection and distinction that we want to establish in this project. We are calling for actively striving to seek God's pleasure through fulfilling His purpose, not just passively worshipping Him, abiding by His commandments, and performing good deeds. This understanding is what prompted our renaissance movement, and it will always drive, guide, and sustain it.

An essential part of the change that we seek is to reintroduce Islam as a life mission for the individual and a rallying cause for the community. We hope this effort will produce phenomenal results that are similar to the ones witnessed at the dawn of Islam. Indeed, Muhammad and his companions were not just passive or even active Muslims. They were able to transform the world and champion a great civilization because they espoused Islam as their life mission, and they dedicated their lives to comprehending and fulfilling God's purpose. They were constantly striving and challenging themselves to become the best possible embodiments and instruments of God's will.

Had Muhammad proclaimed the brand of Islam, which is widely practiced today, he wouldn't have needed to build a movement; and the "establishment" of his time wouldn't have fought him. However, the impact of his message would have been minimal.

With the compelling life mission of Islam, the Prophet transformed those individuals and turned them into agents of change in their respective environments. And through an incredibly effective leadership model and mentorship process, he cemented them and fused their hearts and minds and hands into an incredibly effective and impactful movement. That's the prophetic legacy that we are determined to revive and experience, and that's the prophetic model that we are determined to restore.

The Islamic paradigm is built on the divine mission, and all its components are meant to be mission driven and are woven together by the divine mission. When the sense of mission fades, the whole paradigm crumbles and its components become obsolete. When that happens, Islam has limited impact on the individual, let alone on his/her entourage or on the society at large. Because this movement is an attempt to restore the original and authentic Islamic paradigm, the first thing that we are calling for is for Muslims to rediscover their religion and recommit to it as a life mission.

Islam is usually defined as submission to God and as a way of life. Some people/groups add to that some sort of activism. These definitions are not wrong, but they are not sufficient, and they can be misinterpreted. Submission to God can carry a passive connotation. When espoused as a way of life, Islam, oftentimes, becomes a private/personal religion. And the activism that is added is usually a routine, convenient, erratic exercise with very questionable relevance or impact on society.

We are not calling on members of our community to become practicing, or even active, Muslims. Rather, we are calling on all Muslims, regardless of their level of devotion or activism, to become mission driven, to espouse Islam as a mission, and to conduct a mission-driven life. Rather than repeatedly calling on people to participate in activities or to attend or to be passively served, we want to commit people to the divine mission. We want to inspire, empower, and organize Muslims to fulfill that divine mission, each in his/her own circle and together in the society at large. That's what will make our life and our worship more meaningful and our activism more relevant, purposeful, and impactful.

This transformation that we hope to initiate is essentially to stop living for ourselves and start living for God and His cause. Rather than being comfortable that we are practicing Islam conveniently and possibly doing something for God, we want to constantly challenge ourselves to determine what needs to be done (God's purpose) and do it regardless of the amount of sacrifice or change that is required. Indeed, Islam is neither a hobby nor a pastime. Nor is it something that we engage in to feel good about ourselves or to find some sort of fulfillment.

The beauty of Islam is that, while it calls on us to completely dedicate our lives to God and His cause, we reap all of the benefits, in this life and in the hereafter, because God is free of all needs. When we live for God, there is no need to choose between focusing on this life and the hereafter, or between individual and communal interests. We are on a path that leads to a meaningful and pleasant life in this world and to salvation and bliss in the hereafter. This is what God wants for all people.

2. The divine mission is about serving the greater good, uplifting people, and reforming society

This is the second fundamental connection in the Islamic paradigm that our movement aims to restore. A proper understanding and functioning of the Islamic paradigm requires a realization that the mission of Islam, although divine in its origin and ultimate goal, is essentially humane, civic, and social in nature. Comprehending this is essential to our new Islamic paradigm. Unfortunately, the vast majority of contemporary Muslims, including those who are devout and active, fail to make the connection between the divine origins of Islam and its humane, civic, and social mission.

Muhammad profoundly encapsulated the interrelatedness between all of Islam's aspects when he said, "The most beloved to God are those people that are the most beneficial to others."[41]

Islam emphasizes doing good, calling to that which is good and enjoining that which is good.

> O ye who believe! bow down, prostrate yourselves, and adore your Lord; and do good; that ye may prosper [Qur'an 22:77].

> Let there arise out of you a band of people inviting to all that is good, enjoining what is right, and forbidding what is wrong: They are the ones to attain felicity [Qur'an 3:104].

The scholars agree that Islam came to us just to ensure the well-being of people in this life and in the hereafter.

Islam's compelling sense of mission engenders great passion and sustained motivation, and therefore precludes stagnation and complacency. Islam's strong humane, civic, and social dimensions channel our passion toward constructive action, thus precluding both the confinement and the derailment of that passion. Consequently, when Islam's sense of mission has faded, it becomes dormant and incapable of inspiring community renaissance and societal reform. And when the humane, civic, or social dimensions are weakened, the religious passion may cause more harm than good.

Seeking God's pleasure is the ultimate goal of all Muslims, but working on that goal requires striving to do God's will; and doing God's will entails working for the greater good. An Islam that lacks either of these vital connections is a brand of Islam that falls short of the goal; and that leads to a passive, disengaged, and isolated community. It also significantly limits people's aspirations and development, and it diminishes the impact of individuals and the community on society. Without commitment to do God's will and serve the greater good, individuals wouldn't have the incentive to reach out and be engaged beyond the members of their group/cult. All "others" would be seen either as disbelievers, deviant believers, or simply second-class believers who only need to be avoided, converted, indoctrinated/recruited, taught, or (in the minds of some extremists and all terrorists) perhaps eliminated. The weaknesses of the humane, civic,

---

41   Hadith reported in the books of Daraqutni and Hasan.

and social dimensions of many prevalent Islamic constructs cause many ripple effects on individuals' mind-sets and behaviors and on community dynamics. Chief among the damaging effects are social insulation and civic disengagement and the inability to deal with the "other," which includes everyone who is not Muslim, not devout, or does not belong to one's own group or cult.

Our call to Muslims is this: To seek Allah's pleasure, you must dedicate yourself and your life to Allah and to His cause and strive to fulfill Allah's purpose which consists of the uplifting of your people, the improvement of your society, and the service of the greater good.

There are three primary ways that we can contribute to the uplifting of our society, all of which are emphasized in Islam:

- Serving people through our charitable work
- Providing guidance to people by educating them about what is beneficial to them
- Improving the conditions in which people live (societal reform)

Islam strongly and frequently upholds the values of fairness, kindness (*ihsan*), and benevolence (*albirr*) toward all people—regardless of their racial, ethnic, national, or religious affiliation. These are universal/humane concepts, but Islam gives them a higher purpose; and it reinforces them by purifying the intentions, enhancing the motivation for kindness, and reining in any tendency toward bias/unfairness, even when one is able to deceive people and circumvent the law.

Moreover, Islam instructs us that when it comes to kindness, those who are closest around you and those who have the greatest need for your help should take priority. People's religious affiliation is not mentioned as a factor in the verses and Hadiths that command kindness and fairness. The requirements for kindness call for kindness to parents, cousins, neighbors, and everyone.

> Serve Allah, and join not any partners with Him; and do good-to parents, kinsfolk, orphans, those in need, neighbors who are near, neighbors who are strangers, the companion by your side, the wayfarer (ye meet), and what your right hands possess: For Allah loveth not the arrogant, the vainglorious [Qur'an 4:36].

For instance, kindness to our parents—which is often mentioned in the

Qur'an immediately after reference to belief in and worship of God—does not diminish in importance, even when they are trying hard to get us to abandon Islam.

> And We have enjoined on man (to be good) to his parents: in travail upon travail did his mother bear him, and in years twain was his weaning: (hear the command), "Show gratitude to Me and to thy parents: to Me is (thy final) Goal" [Qur'an 31:14].

> But if they strive to make thee join in worship with Me things of which thou hast no knowledge, obey them not; yet bear them company in this life with justice (and consideration), and follow the way of those who turn to me (in love): in the end the return of you all is to Me, and I will tell you the truth (and meaning) of all that ye did. [Qur'an 31:14–15].

On the other hand, the Qur'an warns us against bias in any circumstances; and it commands us to exhibit fairness with all people in all contexts, including people who are close to us, as well as those who have transgressed against us.

> Allah doth command you to render back your Trusts to those to whom they are due; And when ye judge between man and man, that ye judge with justice: Verily how excellent is the teaching which He giveth you! For Allah is He Who heareth and seeth all things [Qur'an 4:58].

> O ye who believe! stand out firmly for justice, as witnesses to Allah, even as against yourselves, or your parents, or your kin, and whether it be (against) rich or poor: for Allah can best protect both. Follow not the lusts (of your hearts), lest ye swerve, and if ye distort (justice) or decline to do justice, verily Allah is well-acquainted with all that ye do [Qur'an 4:135].

> And let not the hatred of some people in (once) shutting you out of the Sacred Mosque lead you to transgression [Qur'an 5:2].

> O ye who believe! stand out firmly for Allah, as witnesses to

fair dealing, and let not the hatred of others to you make you swerve to wrong and depart from justice. Be just: that is next to piety: and fear Allah. For Allah is well-acquainted with all that ye do [Qur'an 5:8].

It was the strength of these humane, civic, and social dimensions and these indiscriminate acts of fairness and kindness that enabled Islam to engender—and enabled Muslims to champion—a great world civilization.

By instilling a compelling sense of mission and by boosting the humane, civic, and social dimensions of our Islamic construct, we hope to inspire and empower Muslims to become socially connected with people around them, irrespective of the faith of those people. We hope to encourage and empower Muslims to become civically engaged on issues affecting the whole country, not just the issues affecting Muslims here or abroad.

Our movement intends to work toward building a ready image of Muslim Americans as caring and compassionate humans that are civically aware and engaged citizens. Then, when we proudly credit Islam for our behavior, people will respect our faith, as well as us as individuals. Unfortunately, the alternative approach does not work. When we invest our energies in projecting our distinct religious affiliation, it creates barriers that often preclude meaningful interaction.

Islam constitutes an extra incentive for caring about society and interacting with people. We should freely reach out and connect with people around us, bound only by the limits of Islam. If and when we are drawn to a situation that Islam prohibits, we can simply decline in a polite manner and not hesitate to mention our reason. Our observance of Islamic obligations and limits does not have to interfere with our social interaction. Restoring the balance between the religious, humane, civic, and social dimensions of Islam will pave the way for our civic engagement and integration within American society. This will take us a long way toward resolving our identity crisis and fusing our Islamic devotion with American patriotism.

3. Commitment to America as a homeland and to Americans as our people

In simple terms, patriotism means putting the interest of one's country before any other interests (including personal, business, or community interests) and being willing to sacrifice anything (including one's life) for your country.[42] Our movement is calling on fellow citizens (including and especially Muslim Americans) not just to be good or even active citizens but also to be staunch patriots. Genuine Islam only reinforces genuine patriotism.

There can be no significant change in our community without the unequivocal resolution of the identity issue and without putting an end to any ambivalence that is preventing our people's full commitment to America and their effective integration in—and engagement with—American society.

The reasons behind the first generation's identity crisis and ambivalence toward America are clearly understandable, given the roots and background of the immigrants and African Americans. However, this fundamental issue has been ducked or addressed superficially for far too long. It is long overdue that we confront it head on, get to the bottom of it, and ensure that it is not passed on to future generations who should not have to deal with it. It is essential, if we are to survive (let alone thrive) in America, that we develop a genuine and coherent Muslim American identity and become genuinely and openly loyal to this nation and proud of our American citizenship. This should translate into faithful and engaged citizenship by Muslim Americans who are raising their children to be loyal and proud American citizens. At the very least, we should stop interfering with our young people's identity, a process that has sadly produced stateless generations who belong nowhere.

Indeed, an essential part of the change that we seek is to commit our people to America. This requires the unequivocal resolution of the identity issue. We are seeking to inspire Muslim Americans—and indeed all Americans—to become die-hard patriots and to act as role models in loving and defending this country and in generously sacrificing for its security and prosperity. Our movement is seeking to inspire Muslim Americans to be at the forefront of preaching love, kindness, compassion, brotherhood, and cooperation between all American citizens, irrespective of their religions. We want Muslims to think and behave as Americans who have chosen Islam, not as Muslims who just happen to live in America (whether naturalized or not). At the very least, as stated above, we should stop interfering with the integration of others, including our children, into American society.

---

42 We emphasize here that placing (and defending) American interests before all else should never be at the expense of our Islamic principles, or universal values, or international law, or the welfare of humanity.

We are seeking to shift the focus of our community away from defending our civil rights and toward working for the well-being of our country and for the well-being of all American citizens. In politics, this will mean that we are no longer obsessed with the goal of electing Muslim public officials. Instead, we should try to make sure that public offices are held by the best available candidates. When a Muslim, or anyone else, runs for an office, his/her faith should never be an issue. If anything, being a Muslim should help, not hurt, a candidate's reputation and public image; but our own advocacy for a candidate should not be based on a person's religion. When we succeed in meeting our objectives, Muslim Americans will no longer think or behave like a marginal, victimized minority.

Commitment to America and focus on America will be the natural outcome of embracing a genuine American identity and a commitment to the divine mission. That's exactly what the contemporary Islamic movement did in its early days: They blended faith and patriotism. The result was people who spared nothing in serving and defending their country and their fellow citizens. As discussed before, eventually, a number of factors combined to weaken both the patriotic and civic dimensions among Islamists (and Muslims in general). When these deficiencies were brought to America, they had a negative effect on our community, especially in relation to the identity crisis and the shunning of civic engagement. In America, things were further complicated by the "myth of return" (the idea that immigrants would go back to their countries of origin) and by the difficult background of both branches of our community, immigrant Muslims and African American Muslims. The result was a community whose focus was inward and overseas, with little or no attention to America, the big space in between—where we live!

Consequently, a vital part of the change we are seeking is to focus both Muslim and non-Muslim Americans' attention and efforts on what is happening in our society at large and on what can and should be done to make things better and shape the American future.

Our relevance and contribution to the well-being of our country should be the main indicators of our performance. Our community will be just one segment of the society for which our renaissance project is designed. Those who respond to our call, Muslims and non-Muslims, constitute the base from which (and through which) we will advocate our societal vision in cooperation with those who are ready to work with us. This is a huge departure from the current situation in which our talk and work are exclusively focused on our community (more specifically the *masjid* community) and overseas (mainly discussing issues and responding to crises).

We realize that this tenet of our project will be problematic for many Muslim Americans who are struggling to reconcile Islam with American citizenship, let alone with American patriotism. It will also be somewhat awkward for many non-Muslim fellow citizens who are not patriotic or who confuse patriotism with good citizenship. This is because for many, America is perceived more as a corporation than a homeland. It is the American Constitution, rather than a strong attachment to their homeland (or even to their fellow citizens), that serves to bind the American people together. When President Bush established the Department of Homeland Security, some people found the word "homeland" strange and were not very comfortable with it.

Many of our fellow citizens may object to the concept of patriotism. Others may have been taking it for granted and may have confounded it with some superficial manifestations of good citizenship. The truth of the matter, though, is that excessive individualism, materialism, and capitalism significantly contributed to the fading of American patriotism. It might be that America's great diversity and prevalence in the world have reinforced the humane and civic dimensions in the American psyche, but at the expense of traditional patriotism. It might also be that the vastness, the stability, and the security of the United States – and its geographic distance from most of the world – have had the effect of dampening, rather than igniting, American patriotism.

When individuals, states, corporations, communities/minorities, and parties selfishly compete, that competition may stimulate progress and growth; but when such competition exceeds acceptable limits and ethics are abandoned, a toll may be taken on everyone's interests, including the country's interests. That's where the harms outweigh the benefits. We believe that all those entities should put the interests of the country first, even as they continue to compete and reap the fruits of their hard work. In other words, we all should compete and cooperate in the interest of the greater good.

Although turning Muslim Americans, who suffer from a serious identity crisis and whose loyalty to America is questionable, into role models for American patriotism may seem farfetched, we believe it will be easier than one might guess. Many Muslim Americans came from societies where the people are staunch patriots and are attached to their homelands—in spite of government corruption and oppression and the globalization of individualism and materialism. Those people demonstrated a great ability to rise up to meet the challenge of a national cause. That's what has always been manifested in the zeal with which people support their national sports teams and in the recent revolutions that swept across the Middle East. Consequently, our potential to inspire a commitment to America as a homeland and to instill a deeper sense of patriotism on the part of all Americans may be one of the most plausible (and significant) contributions that we can make.

What is holding Muslim Americans back, though, is our identity crisis. That stems primarily from the Islamic construct prevalent in our community—a construct that is intertwined with a foreign culture, infused with a strong dose of anti-American political views, devoid of any sense of mission, and weak in terms of humane, civic, and social dimensions. It appears that the prevalent political Islam is both "too religious and too political" to allow for the fulfillment of our needs in America and in this life in general.

In contrast, the new American Islamic construct our movement is proposing is bound only by the original divine sources of guidance. It is decoupled from culture and heritage. It is driven by our divine mission, and it has a staunch humane, civic, and social dimension. Our construct reinforces the virtues of compassion toward all other human beings and patriotism toward one's country. Indeed, our construct assigns a higher purpose to compassion and patriotism. If we first "sell" Muslims on this construct, their commitment to America as a homeland and to Americans as their people will be much easier than some might think. If this project is successful, and with God's help it will be, we will facilitate and witness the transformation of Muslim Americans into role models for patriotism and compassion.

Islam is a divine mission that is about the uplifting of our people, the betterment of our society, and the service of the greater good. So in addition to our common natural attachment to the country, let us not forget that America is a part of God's land. It is where He placed us and assigned to us the task of fulfilling the divine mission. The American people are our partners in fulfilling that mission, even though our sources of inspiration and motivation may differ. Moreover, the humane, civic, and social dimensions of our mission require that we actively strive to uplift all people, starting with those who are closest to us in kinship, affinity, and proximity. This mission is about people, and Muhammad linked the pursuit of God's pleasure and the uplifting of one's people.

The commitment to America as a homeland and the attachment to Americans as our people will enable us to go a long way toward resolving our identity crisis, as well as many other related issues. Some "issues" are a little absurd. Consider the question of whether Muslim Americans should join the military. Indeed, they should feel encouraged to do so because joining the military is the clearest indication and manifestation of one's patriotism. That is because it means being ready to serve and willing to give one's life, if necessary, for the country.

Like other countries, America has been and may in the future be engaged in wars that are ill conceived and/or ill conducted. And like other American citizens, Muslim American soldiers may refuse to participate in such wars. In most countries in the world, serving in the military, law enforcement, security forces, and all the agencies that protect the homeland (including intelligence) was—and in some cases continues to be—considered a noble act that makes an individual and the whole family proud. It has been the deviation of these institutions from their proper missions that has caused people of conscience (including patriots) to become reluctant to serve in them. Entirely deserting something that was initially noble and has noble aspects, however, may stem from flawed logic, selfishness, and/or cowardice. It is like refusing to participate in politics and public affairs because the political process has become corrupted. This will only make matters worse. Imagine if everyone adopted the attitude behind desertion!

On the other hand, if people of conscience participate in any intrinsically noble endeavor and pay the price of bravely sticking to their principles, they will render a great service to their country and the people. Their actions will be no less worthy than putting their lives on the line to defend their country and its citizens. Muhammad said, "The best (*jihad*) is (to speak) a word of justice to an oppressive ruler;"[43] and "The leader among martyrs is Hamza,[44] and a man who stands up to a tyrant ruler and gives him advice, and so the ruler kills him."[45]

A compelling divine mission geared toward the uplifting of people and the betterment of society, mixed with a strong dose of compassion and patriotism, will take us a long way toward the renaissance of our community. This will

---

43 Hadith reported in Sunan of Abu Dawood.

44 Hamza was an uncle of Muhammad. Hamza was killed during the battle of Uhud.

45 Hadith reported in Musnad of Imam Ahmad.

ultimately enable us to substantially contribute to the generation of a more just, prosperous, and sound society.

For a variety of religious, political, and psychological reasons, many Muslims find this logic difficult to fathom. However, it is the natural outgrowth of a proper understanding of Islam, and it will lead to our being able to chart a better future for our community and our country. Again, if such a transformation proves too difficult for some members of the community, we urge them to relocate to another country where they can commit to the land and people. Or, at least, they should stand out of the way of those born and raised here in America who know no other country.

Two additional points must be made before we proceed to the next essential component of our movement. First, we must unequivocally stress that our platform of advancing and defending American interests before all else should, nonetheless, never be implemented at the expense of our Islamic principles or of universal values and international law. Nothing we do or advocate should involve the abuse of others. In no way, shape, form, or fashion are we suggesting that the ends ever justify illegitimate means.

To advocate destructive means to achieve currently desired ends would be indisputably shortsighted and wrong. It would only backfire down the road—the lesson America learned from Vietnam and the lesson Russia learned from Afghanistan. It's also what we should know from our past patronage of notorious regimes that have served to earn us the hatred of the populace in those countries and have made us deal with more complex problems. Iran is a case in point.

There must always be limits—even to those things that are healthy and positive. Without reasonable restrictions, patriotism may very well degenerate into ultranationalism and chauvinism that leads not only to aggression against other people but also to the destruction of those who are its proponents. Hitler served as a case in point for that catastrophic reality.

The second point we wish to make is that, although our call for patriotism stems from conviction and is not merely a reaction to our current circumstances, it may well help to indirectly solve two of the major challenges we face: our image problem and our questionable loyalty.

Unfortunately, in invoking the historical experiences of other American minorities (such as African Americans, Jews, and Catholics) in their painstaking process of integration, many Muslims emphasize the successful outcomes of their struggles more than the strategies these people adopted, the price they paid, and the sacrifices they made. For instance, after Pearl Harbor and during the subsequent internment of many Japanese Americans, although their loyalty was questioned (similar to the questioning of ours after 9/11), Japanese Americans did not wither, pull into a shell, or disengage from America. Interestingly, rather than adopting an attitude of victimization and employing a civil rights strategy, Japanese Americans accepted that the burden of proof was on them. So Japanese Americans responded with superpatriotism and actually flocked into the military.

During one of the most famous speeches in U.S. history, then presidential candidate John Kennedy noted, "I am not the Catholic candidate for president; I am the Democratic Party's candidate for president who happens also to be a Catholic." Thus, he asked Americans to judge his candidacy on the issues that really mattered—not on his status as a religious minority. Considering the historically momentous African American experience, one reason that the civil rights movement triumphed was that it was a mainstream movement that avoided the mentality of victimization and anti-American rhetoric. More recently, one of the main reasons why Barack Obama became the first African American president was that he did not run as an African American candidate.

So in conclusion, we firmly believe that the combination of a divinely inspired, compelling mission with strong humane, civic, and social dimensions, along with staunch patriotism and extraordinary compassion, will constitute powerful engines that propel this movement and its champions—the mission-driven and compassionate patriots.

To date, those engines have been either dysfunctional or out of sync. That explains our isolation, disengagement, stagnation, and complacency. It also explains why all the religious rhetoric does not motivate most American Muslims to do much beyond routine rituals and activities. Moreover, when the rhetoric does motivate people, it only creates internal tension within the individual or results in destructive acts.

Our goal is to synchronize and fire up those engines to sustain the motivation of our members and enable them to realize their full potential and full impact.

Only for God or for the country or for their people are individuals willing to sacrifice consistently and generously. This is because, unlike activists who may be willing to give or do something, individuals who are driven by a compelling (divine) mission, by patriotism, and/or by compassion, often commit to giving and doing what needs to be done (including putting their lives on the line). In Qur'anic terms, they are willing "to strive for God as is His due."

4. The divine mission requires a commitment to a lifelong journey of self-development, social outreach, and civic engagement

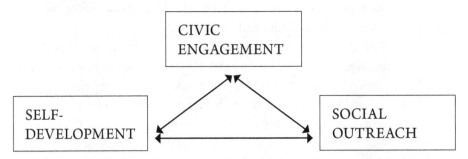

This synergetic cycle/triangle reveals the relationship between the three defining activities of our movement. This constitutes the support structure for our life mission that is centered on the uplifting of people and the betterment of society.

Our commitment to these three complementary activities is the natural, practical fruition of the three previously discussed commitments to the divine mission, to the homeland, and to fellow citizens. The life of mission-driven and compassionate patriots should be centered on these three fronts, which converge to form a synergetic, self-sustaining cycle. As a result of their commitment to these activities, individuals dedicate their lives to promoting that which is good and forbidding that which is evil—the thrust of the divine mission of Islam—and they strive to live with God and for God and to be the best embodiments and instruments of God's will.

Striving on these three fronts is the true meaning of *jihad* and is very consistent with understanding Islam as a life mission that is centered on the uplifting of people and the betterment of society. Many people (Muslims and non-Muslims) confuse the concept of *jihad* with *qitaal* (*fighting*) or, worse yet, terrorism. This gross misconception is totally due to a lack of understanding of the context under which certain Qur'anic verses were revealed and/or the context in which Muhammad took certain courses of action. Muslims may fall prey to such misunderstandings when they fail to consistently ask the fundamental question, "What would Muhammad have done during our time and under these circumstances?"

A study of history indicates that all the wars and battles fought by Muhammad were in self-defense or to secure basic freedoms—rights that are guaranteed by the American Constitution. This is all the more reason that we Muslim Americans should uphold and defend the Constitution to the best of our ability and that we should become civically engaged to ensure the betterment of society. The uplifting of people can only happen through self-development and through civic and social interaction. These activities will work together to help us advocate necessary social reform, and that will help society achieve and maintain sound policies and norms. Social interaction is essential for social cohesion and cooperation for the common good, and that is critical for the health and strength of the society.

The diagram pictured above depicts a self-repeating pattern among these three activities. The more successful we are in self-development, the more effective we are in positively impacting the people and the conditions around us. Likewise, the more socially connected and civically engaged we are, the greater our incentives and opportunities for self-development. Also, the more we interact with one another, the stronger the society, and the more likely we will all cooperate for the common good. Moreover, any positive policy reform that we may effect through civic engagement will have a substantial positive impact on the people and their lives.

A detailed guide on self-development, social outreach, and civic engagement is beyond the scope of this book, but the following benefits are some of the main outcomes that can be expected from a commitment to this lifelong journey:

- Vibrant spirituality
- Extraordinary and robust manners
- A deep, broad, and coherent knowledge and contextual understanding of the letter and spirit of our religion, of life, and of how our world was shaped and how it functions
- Physical and psychological wellness
- Financial stability/independence
- Steadily expanding skill sets
- Increased organization and effectiveness
- Increased passion for the cause, patriotism, and compassion toward people
- Increased family cohesion and empowerment

- – A constantly expanding, solidified, and integrated social network
- – Increasingly effective civic engagement with more prominent "players" on a growing number of issues

The purpose of a lifelong journey focused on these endeavors is continuous, comprehensive, and balanced self-improvement. Our ultimate aim is the realization of our full potential, including a steadily increasing ability to positively impact our environments and expand our spheres of influence. Our success at positively affecting our environment may be viewed as a performance indicator—a measure of our success in participation in the project.

In this section, thus far, we have outlined four commitments: to divine mission; to service of the greater good; to support for America and Americans; and to improving our effectiveness through civic engagement, social outreach, and self-development. These commitments, added together, will help to create (and continually replicate) the mission-driven compassionate patriots who will become powerful agents of change in their respective environments. These individuals will constitute the keys to the success of our movement, and one of our main goals is to have as many of them as possible.

One might ask, "What role does *dawa* play in all of this? Is it not an essential part of the mission of Islam?" The answer is yes. *Dawa* is an essential part of the divine mission, and it is a salient but integral part of the proposed paradigm. However, *dawa* is not about converting people to Islam. Rather, it is about inviting people to that which is best for them in this life and in the hereafter. Indeed, a quick look at destructive behaviors and societal illnesses indicates that Islam prohibits them all.

Dawa is also about educating people regarding God's final and universal message to humanity. There is no more effective *dawa* than to turn the divine guidance into viable models and solutions (through self-development) and to promote the models through social outreach and to infuse the resulting solutions into society through civic engagement. In other words, the most effective *dawa* is accomplished by example, interaction/exposure (*mu'amalaat*), healthy relationships, and contribution to the greater good.

On the contrary, in-your-face methods that propagate the teachings of Islam to strangers may provide a sense of fulfillment to the propagators, but these tactics are usually ineffective and may actually cause more harm than good.

This concludes the individual track of our project. The rest of this chapter will focus on the need for a concerted collective effort to build our movement. Indeed, as we know from Muhammad's model, vital as they are, scattered efforts by individuals in their respective environments cannot generate either the societal reform or the community renaissance, which constitute the ultimate objectives of this project.

Both the prophetic model and practical considerations point to the necessity of establishing a movement to achieve the goals of this revival/renewal, renaissance, and reform project. This collective track, which is built on the individual track, is meant to crown, integrate, and synergize individual efforts—not to substitute for them or displace them. Our goal is to combine, improve, and focus individual efforts so that they can make a profound difference in American society.

Consequently, we are calling on those who buy into our mission to fulfill it in their respective environments and to join their hearts, minds, and efforts together in a movement that fulfills the divine mission in the society at large. At this early stage, we are also calling on the pioneers to join with us now in establishing our renaissance movement.

5. The obligation to establish a movement

An essential component of this project is the firm belief that establishing a movement to fulfill the divine mission and effect needed change is an individual and collective obligation, as well as a practical necessity. If such a movement already existed, Muslims would be obligated to join it. Since it does not exist, working to establish it becomes imperative for every Muslim. Again, in the words of Omar ibn-Khattab, "There can be no Islam without a movement."

Specifically, we are talking about a movement that is built according to the prophetic model to rally people in general and Muslims in particular to fulfill the divine purpose. We are not talking about organizations that provide services and organize activities.

With all due respect to the dedication and hard work of the members of our Muslim American organizations and with full appreciation for the invaluable services/programs they offer, we believe that although such organizations can serve as arms or parts of a movement, they cannot act effectively as stand-alone entities. They definitely do not constitute an alternative to the movement—either when taken separately or even combined, especially in the absence of any effective coordination.

By establishing such organizations before establishing an actual movement, our community put the cart before the horse. We forsook an obligation (*fardh*) for a supererogatory (extra, nonobligatory, "beyond the call of duty") deed (*nafila*). Taken separately or combined, our organizations have been mistaken by many Muslims for an actual movement in the same way that their activism has been mistaken for a mission, and their management has been mistaken for true leadership. For quite some time in our community, "doing something" has replaced the need for doing what needs to be done as prescribed by the divine guidance. Our prevailing paradigm is a deceptive simulation of the prophetic model, and the resemblance is only in appearance—like fake jewelry is a simulation of authentic jewelry. For many people, the imitations seemed to eliminate the need for the real stuff.

Although this is our assessment of the current state of affairs in our community, we have no intention of interfering or competing with existing organizations and their operations. In fact, we are calling on all the pioneers in our community to buy into our movement and join us. We must all strive together to effectively resolve the crisis that faces us. We can move to the next level by rallying all of our individual members and organizations behind the biggest and worthiest cause possible—the fulfillment of the divine purpose. That will transform us into a mission-driven, mainstream, and inclusive community, or simply a movement.

Some of the main characteristics that distinguish this movement include the following:

- It is a mission-driven movement built around and driven by the divine mission. It includes an expansive vision, a solid intellectual foundation, and a clear strategy. It is not focused on bylaws, facilities, or activities. Contrary to what many activists think, Muhammad did not start by building a *masjid* (mosque). Rather, he built his movement in Mecca around the divine mission. His *masjid* in Medina was both a house of worship and the headquarters for the movement.
- It is a mainstream societal movement—not a community project.
- It is an inclusive mass movement—not an exclusive, elitist fraternity or club.
- This movement focuses on inspiring and empowering people, not on service and control.
- Ours is a renaissance project and movement built and guided according

to the prophetic leadership model: respected, empowered, and consultative leadership by consent. This ensures swift decisiveness, cohesion, and discipline; and it precludes dictatorship, bureaucracy, disavowed responsibility, disputed authority (power struggle), and paralysis.

6. Restoring the prophetic model and reviving the prophetic experience

One of the main ideas that sparked our movement is the firm belief that the life of Muhammad was meant to serve as both an individual and a communal model that is replicable in all contexts. Like the divine guidance (the Qur'an), the model revealed through Muhammad's life has a timeless and universal replicability. However, our success in applying the model today hinges on our in-depth and proper understanding of its letter and spirit— knowing not only what Muhammad (as an individual and as the leader of his model community) actually did during his lifetime but also knowing what he and his successors would do if they lived in the context in which we now live. The fundamental question we should consistently ask is: "What would Muhammad do?" The prophetic model is a model of how individuals should understand and practice Islam and fulfill its mission and how the community of believers should be built and led in different contexts.

At the heart of this transformational model is a compelling mission that individuals espouse and a unified leadership that individuals elect, counsel, help, and follow. The result of this unity of purpose and leadership is an unprecedented and sustained sense of responsibility, mobilization, cohesion, decisiveness, and discipline. This allows for the movement's continuous growth and increased impact, as well as smooth transition from one level of development to another. Because that model has worked incredibly well in extremely unfavorable contexts, we believe it should produce similar results in any context, whenever it is properly simulated.

In this project, we want to reconstruct the prophetic model and retrace the prophetic steps, keeping in mind that while our context is different from Muhammad's in many ways but also similar in many ways, our situation is, overall, definitely much more favorable.

Again, our work is guided by the fundamental question: "What would the Prophet have done in our time and circumstances?" We may also ask, "How would the companions and the community that survived Muhammad and inherited his mission have proceeded?"

This is because we believe that the proper replication of the prophetic model is both mandatory and possible and that our community has been unable and/or unwilling to take a serious shot at this simulation. The few attempts that took place fell way too short, either because they were too superficial or too literalist, or because they were lacking in essential components. Additionally, the attempts did not start on the right footing. What was needed then and what we undertake today is commitment to the divine mission properly translated in the American context.

By advocating the mandate for the restoration of the prophetic model and by asserting that it is both feasible and necessary, we hope to generate some serious and in-depth reflections and discussions about this model and about how we could best simulate it to rebuild our community. We believe that such an exercise will clearly reveal to all of us how far off we are—individually and collectively—from the prophetic model in terms of our understanding and implementation of Islam, our aspirations, our commitment, the effectiveness of our operations, and our impact and relevance. Something has gone seriously wrong, and there is an urgent need for fundamental change, or better yet for a new beginning. Our call to our community and its members is to let us rediscover and emulate the prophetic model in our context.

7. Great emphasis on true leadership, mentorship, and brotherhood

Our movement seeks to inspire every Muslim (and every American) to not only have a leader but also serve as a leader—and to have a mentor and serve as a mentor. This is an essential aspect of Muhammad's model of leadership. Indeed, Muhammad successfully transformed most of his companions into leaders, including many who had very unfavorable backgrounds. Throughout his life, he never hesitated to appoint many of his companions to lead challenging tasks that were commensurate with their skills.

We also want to establish a warm environment of true brotherhood, affection, respect, trust, and decency. These are the Islamic mechanisms we need in order to blend mission-driven and compassionate patriots into a cohesive and impactful societal reform movement. This will take place without reducing people's individual responsibility and without suppressing their individual traits. Indeed, the movement is not meant to do the job for individuals and is not meant to stifle individual initiative, creativity, or independent and critical thinking. Originality is welcome, and we have no desire to make the movement's members copy one another in terms of their thinking, conduct, focus, or skills.

True leadership is about having a strong sense of calling and responsibility. It involves being able to exert a positive influence on one's environment. It is not just about occupying positions. With this understanding, we are challenging members of our community to become, not just community activists but civic leaders whose sense of mission and responsibility encompasses the whole nation. We need people who strive to impact their whole environment, not just the Muslim portion of it. We are calling on our fellow Muslims to develop needed skills to compete in the big league (i.e., on the local, state, regional, and national level)—not just at the Islamic center and within the Muslim community. Our youth should get involved in their student governments and other campus organizations, not just their MSAs.

In getting involved, community members don't need to go through a Muslim organization. Rather, they need to chart this new course of direct and mainstream civic engagement. Then they can pull Muslim individuals and organizations around them into the big league and into the mainstream. That's our understanding of collective leadership: everyone could and should be a leader and should have a compelling sense of mission and a sense of responsibility for the cause, the country, and the community. This is an essential part of the prophetic model of leadership.

The other side of the prophetic model has to do with how the community of believers (the movement) should organize itself, make decisions, and manage its affairs. In this regard, the prophetic model, which calls on all Muslims to become leaders, urges leaders in every context to have a higher leader from among their ranks. The model assigns clear roles, and it prescribes extensive consultation and a sound and effective decision-making process. That's what the companions did during the time of the Prophet and after his death. As discussed in part 3, the leadership model did not change significantly after Muhammad's death because he did not lead based on revelation or infallibility. Indeed, some of the Prophet's decisions were not sanctioned by the Qur'an, and some decisions were not successful. Otherwise, his model would not be replicable by average human beings; and that would have defeated the whole purpose of sending a final and universal messenger with a timeless and universal model.

In this project, we cherish both sides of the prophetic model of leadership, and that's why we call it a leader-of-leaders model. Therefore, we want to create a culture that encourages community and civic leadership across the board and where all members of the community fulfill their roles of selecting their leaders and then counseling and helping those leaders make the best decisions. We are all responsible to ensure the successful execution of those decisions, irrespective of any prior opinions. We must all undertake this as an act of worship and also as a right and a duty.

A compelling mission with unified and effective leadership will ensure the sustained mobilization and cohesion of the movement. Thus, these factors will largely determine the movement's decisiveness and effectiveness. However, another mechanism is needed to ensure the inculcation of the mission and leadership and therefore the spread and continuity of the movement. That mechanism is mentorship. Mentorship should drive and guide the process of self-development. Mentorship and self-development, together, ensure the development of the "leader within you"[46] and "the leaders around you."[47] The Qur'anic term for mentorship is *tazkiya*, which means both purification and realization of full potential. And the Qur'an uses the term for both meanings: self-development (*tazakka, zakkaha*) and mentorship (*yuzakkihum*).

> But those will prosper who purify themselves [Qur'an 87:14].

> Truly he succeeds that purifies it, And he fails that corrupts it [Qur'an 91:9–10].

> Allah did confer a great favor on the believers when He sent among them an apostle from among themselves, rehearsing unto them the Signs of Allah, sanctifying them, and instructing them in Scripture and Wisdom, while, before that, they had been in manifest error [Qur'an 3:164].

This last verse, which was mentioned with slight variations three times in the Qur'an, delineates the "job description" of the Prophet: teaching

---

46 John Maxwell. (1993). *Developing the Leader within You* [Book].

47 John Maxwell. (1995). *Developing the Leader around You* [Book].

people the scripture and wisdom and mentoring them. Through this process, individuals are better able to understand and effectively engage their world in order to realize their full potential and impact.

Given a compelling mission, great compassion, staunch patriotism, a unified leadership, an effective leadership model, and a good mentorship process, how can we lose? No elaborate organizational structure and intensive activities could match our performance or probability of success. With our approach, we can achieve a much better simulation of the prophetic model, and we will thus have a much better guarantee of sustained motivation, cohesion, growth, and impact on the community.

We are asking people to commit to the mission and the homeland, to the three tracks (self-development, social outreach, and civic engagement), and to an effective leadership model and active mentorship process. We believe that will not only galvanize and unify the community but will also engender a meaningful social life, which will include true brotherhood. This movement will be built on mutual understanding, respect, trust, and commitment to a common cause; and it will be characterized by vibrant spirituality, impeccable and robust manners, and mature personalities.

8. The development of a new and relevant (yet authentic) Islamic construct bound only by the original texts and the essentials of Islam

None of the above is possible without this vital component, because Islam is what engendered our community, and because Islam—or more accurately our understanding of Islam—is the code that runs all aspects of our individual and communal life.

And when Islam does not produce the expected results that it promises, we should question our understanding and implementation of Islam and even our commitment to Islam. Rather than remaining in denial or trying to rationalize or even patch the situation, we should challenge ourselves and hold ourselves accountable. We should revisit our source code: our Islamic construct. Next, let's consider some of the guidelines in developing a new Islamic construct.

Relying on the root sources of guidance: The Qur'an and Sunna

One of our main limiting factors is that many community members, leaders, and groups/organizations are strictly attached to some Islamic literature and interpretations that were developed in different contexts. Interpretations, literature, and practices from other times and places will not necessarily fit in twenty-first-century America. It is like putting wagon wheels on a new car! Using obsolete or inappropriate materials and concepts limits the growth, evolution, inclusiveness, integration, and openness of the community.

There is considerable confusion between what is timeless and constant and what is variable and subject to change. The fact that our prevailing versions of Islam are infused with alien cultures leaves us in a situation that is preventing Islam and Muslims from being relevant and from effectively engaging with—or impacting on—American society. Indeed, Islam remains largely a foreign religion in America, and our community remains largely a foreign community. Even converts and those who are born and raised in America subscribe to this imported mix of Islam and culture; and rather than help in mainstreaming Islam, they become foreigners in their own country.

The Islamic education being provided to Muslim Americans and the Islamic knowledge sought have only a questionable usefulness and relevance. As a result, the way we understand, practice, and promote Islam is largely irrelevant and leads automatically to isolation and disengagement.

Islam is not just a theory, nor is it implemented in a vacuum. It is meant to uplift life at all levels (personal, family, social, global), at all times and in all contexts. And other than a few things that Islam requires and specifies in detail, Islam consists essentially of guidelines for our lives. There is considerable built-in flexibility, and that makes it timelessly relevant. Authentic Islam has the capacity to effectively engage and uplift any society. This is only true, however, if we are talking about the original, pure, and culturally unbiased Islam taken from the timeless and infallible sources of guidance. It is that Islam that could and should be translated and understood in the light of our present reality or any other reality. That Islam works anywhere and at any time. This original and pure version of Islam will always shape up differently from one era to another and from one society to another. And the effective interaction between the guidance of Islam and any particular reality not only produces a unique brand of Islam but also helps us to dig up more of the infinite gems of Islam. One of the most knowledgeable companions, Ibn Abbas, said, "Qur'an is explained by the progress of time."

Indeed, the way Islam is understood, implemented, promoted, and advocated in any particular context is not transferable to a different context in another time or place. An effective and relevant version of Islam must be derived or "translated" from the original infallible sources of guidance. It must be homegrown and must constantly evolve in time to keep up with changes and maintain the capacity to guide people. If Muslims in a particular place have failed to evolve or if they move to a different setting, the exercise of rediscovering Islam from its sources and the processes of understanding, implementing, promoting, and advocating Islam must all be done in the light of the new reality. All other literature and experiences may only be useful as sources of inspiration and lessons, but not as sources of specific guidance. In her book *Muhammad: A Prophet for Our Time*, Karen Armstrong said, "Paradoxically, Muhammad became a timeless personality because he was so rooted in his own period."

Making Islam and Muslims relevant in America requires us to develop a genuine and relevant American Muslim identity, lifestyle, discourse, and platform. This could not be accomplished unless we change our approach to knowledge, both in terms of sources and objectives. We need to focus on the direct study of the Qur'an, the Hadiths, and the *Seera* of the Prophet. Our purpose in this study should be to understand the text in light of our reality, and we should seek the best ways to implement its guidance in our lives. We must also promote the divine guidance and advocate it in society in a relevant way. So again, our study of the Qur'an, the Hadiths, and the Seera should aim at finding answers to the pressing questions of our time and our society and solutions to the problems we face today. Thus, our focus should be on useful and relevant knowledge, and we should rely primarily on the timeless sources of guidance. All other literature should be used just as helpful tools to understand those original sources, not as sources of guidance themselves. Indeed, we are now relying too much on Islamic heritage at the expense of the study of the timeless sources.

It is true that only scholars who are well versed in the different branches of Islamic knowledge are in a position to issue a ruling (*fatwa*). However, as sources of guidance, the Qur'an and Sunna are much more accessible to ordinary Muslims. All of us should make a concerted effort to study these sources to improve our understanding and practice of Islam. Studying the original sources will help us apply their values and solutions to our private lives as well as to our engagement with society.

Moreover, our search for useful knowledge should not be limited to Islamic literature. Rather, we should do as the Prophet recommended: we should seek wisdom and claim it wherever it may be. All knowledge that helps us understand life or how this world functions or how we can effectively engage it and shape it may be regarded as Islamic knowledge. That is true because this knowledge helps us to discover God's rules (*sunan*) that govern the universe: both the physical and the human part of it. Indeed, one of the reasons behind the isolation and disengagement of our community is that our community leaders and activists are not only largely disengaged but are also narrowly focused in their reading and study. Those who do read usually limit themselves to Islamic literature and, oftentimes, to a narrow subcategory of Islamic literature. However, Islamic or non-Islamic, any human effort is not infallible, and therefore literature should be read critically, not blindly.

Getting people to rely on the timeless sources of guidance to seek useful and relevant knowledge, but to also broaden their knowledge by diversifying their reading, is an essential part of our strategy to make Islam and Muslims rooted in America and relevant here and now. That's how we may improve our lives and the lives of others, and it will help us succeed in making a significant and lasting contribution to the well-being of America through the infusion of the timeless, universal, and culturally neutral guidance of Islam. On the other hand, continuing to rely on Islamic heritage at the expense of the sources of guidance, importing Islamic models rather than developing our own, and shunning the human (and American) heritage will only prolong our isolation and irrelevance. Rediscovery of Islam from the sources and reassessing the prevalent Islamic construct is certainly a challenging task, but it is unavoidable, even though the findings and indications may not be easy to admit or implement.

Given that divine guidance is fixed and forever, but that life is different from one place to another and at different times, the only way Islam could remain valid at all times and in all circumstances is if Muslims continuously strive to make it relevant and root it in their own time and context. The only way to accomplish this is through

- the present-day contextual understanding of the original texts to produce an original Islamic experience and an indigenous, relevant, viable, mainstream, and inspiring Islamic construct—all without compromising the authenticity and the essentials of Islam;

- constant revival and renewal by way of *ijtihad* (individual, independent analysis and interpretation), through intellectual reflections and discussions, and also via effective social interaction and civic engagement.

This is the way to ensure both the authenticity of our Islamic construct and the constant evolution and relevance of our paradigm. This is, then, the way to prevent Islam from freezing, detaching from life, or lagging behind it.

At all times and in all places, Muslims must perform this exercise and redo it if they move to a different place or if circumstances change in ways that require another paradigm shift. This is the first critical step in building or rebuilding a community.

In the case of our community, it is a "no-brainer" to notice that Islam hasn't produced the results or outcome that it promises. Just compare our community to the prophetic community, which was meant to be a model; and compare the state of our community to the Qur'anic descriptions of the community of believers in terms of characteristics and roles.

By confronting brutal reality and engaging in deep and extensive reflections, discussions, research, and study, we concluded that our community has largely abandoned the divine mission and has failed to simulate the prophetic model. The prevalent Islamic construct is largely irrelevant in America. The pillars of Islam notwithstanding, beyond some beliefs, rituals, and appearances, the prevalent Islamic construct has little to do with the original Islamic construct. That original construct was meant to be contextually translated and constantly renewed. The reason we have fallen short is obvious: we Muslim Americans have never developed our own, original, American Islamic construct. That largely explains why we find ourselves stuck and stagnant; and that's why our community needs to be rebuilt and needs a new beginning.

We brought with us foreign Islamic constructs and used them to build our communities. That is, in and of itself, a big problem; but two factors have compounded the problem. First, although some of the imported constructs were developed by contemporary reformers and reform movements with a reasonable—and at times remarkable—success, those constructs did not evolve significantly after their initial development. Stalled Islamic constructs help to explain why those Islamic movements have been scrambling for relevance and why their reform projects have stalled. The problem lies at their intellectual foundation.

Second, because Muslims in general and movement activists in particular have remained more or less engaged in their own societies in the Muslim world, their prevalent Islamic constructs did evolve somewhat, though at a very slow pace. On the other hand, because the Muslim American community has been largely insulated and disengaged and because we had very few scholars who were able and willing to exercise *ijtihad,* our imported Islamic constructs have been essentially frozen despite our residence in a dynamic and changing American society. Our constructs did not even keep up with the very slow-paced evolution that was taking place elsewhere in the Muslim world! That explains why the Muslim American community (particularly the segment comprising activists and those who are most involved in Islamic centers and Muslim organizations) is much more conservative than their Muslim world counterparts. For instance, it took Muslim women in America quite some time before they started adopting some of the new Islamic fashions that became common in the Muslim world; and many are still clinging to the cultural dress they brought with them. Moreover, the Muslim American groups and communities are lagging behind their "mother" movements/groups in terms of gender desegregation and participation by women, especially in leadership positions and governing bodies. Ironically, some *fatwas* that were produced to solve some pressing problems facing the Muslim American community had to come from abroad and were met with an uproar in many circles within our community. At the same time, the intellectual and organizational attachment to some Muslim scholars and groups in the Muslim world has been causing the community untold amounts of damage. So in a way, we are getting the worst of both worlds.

For all those ideological and practical reasons and because the prevalent, worn-out Islamic construct is neither sustainable nor patchable, we have a dire need to rediscover Islam from the original sources and to apply it to the present American context. This will require tremendous efforts at deconstruction and reconstruction. We will begin by decoupling Islam from foreign culture and heritage. We will wed it, instead, to American culture. That is how we can produce an original/unique and relevant Muslim American construct.

Islam is compatible with every culture. It has always been good at sanctioning what is beneficial and at eliminating excesses and filling in voids. Islam has also always been good at rejuvenating itself by leveraging everything good in every culture. The Prophet indicated that wisdom is the stray of the believer, who has the better right to it wherever it may be found.

Muslim scholars agree on a golden and time-tested rule that links God's commandments with the greater good. Because the renewal of Islam is an essential and delicate component of our project, some clarifications may be needed.

First, in developing a new construct, our focus is not on matters of creed (*aqidah*) or individual/personal jurisprudence (*fiqh*), particularly as they relate to acts of worship. After all, these areas have been the most worked out and are the least affected by change. Also, there are some scholars and councils who are doing a reasonable job of addressing the issues related to the *fiqh* for Muslims in general, including western Muslims. This does not relieve the Muslim American community from the duty of producing its own critical mass of homegrown scholars. We will need their expertise and effort in order to take advantage of the great flexibility of Islamic jurisprudence and to develop a relevant yet authentic body of *fiqh* to support our new paradigm. In developing a new Islamic construct, our focus is on translating the divine guidance into viable models and solutions and relevant discourse, simulating the prophetic model and movement. In this way, we can fulfill the divine mission after translating it into a relevant and exciting platform.

Second, this development of a fresh Islamic construct is an obligation and a dire need, not an attempt to make Islam convenient. On the contrary, our approach seeks both relevance and authenticity, so ours is the middle course and the hardest one. In fact, in addition to the severe deficiencies in our community's foundation and guiding paradigm, the main reasons we have remained stuck include the community's intellectual stagnation and shallowness. Indeed, most of us, including our leaders and activists, opted for a convenient and simplistic Islamic construct that is not driven by mission, relevance, results, or impact. Such a construct hardly triggers any intellectual efforts or creativity. Most of us have limited ourselves to inherited and imported constructs, models, and literature that are largely irrelevant and ineffective here in America.

And rather than upgrading or replacing the "brain" (the Islamic construct), the bulk of our effort has been geared toward inflating the "body" with more activities and facilities.

And even though members of our community differ tremendously in their level of devotion (or activism) and in their ideological orientation, most of us subscribe to some sort of convenient and simplistic Islamic construct that is largely uninspiring and nonevolving. Such constructs are conducive to complacency and low aspirations. They make people satisfied with their situation and with their work, irrespective of the relevance of their efforts to the divine mission or the impact of their efforts on society or the challenges facing them or the available resources and opportunities.

Moreover, there is a general feeling that what we have is "the true Islam" and that any renewal efforts are unnecessary, impossible, or risky. In other words, we have the idea that things should not be different or could not be better. It is no wonder that the ceiling of our community is the management of the status quo and, whenever possible, some lateral expansion (bigger and more facilities and activities). Our resistance to change is fierce. This "blind" clinging to what we have inherited, the rationalization of the status quo, and our fierce resistance to change are reminiscent of the typical response that the prophets received when they initiated their reform movements.

> Nay! they say "We found our fathers following a certain religion, and we do guide ourselves by their footsteps." Just in the same way, whenever We sent a Warner before thee to any people, the wealthy ones among them said: "We found our fathers following a certain religion, and we will certainly follow in their footsteps." He said: "What! Even if I brought you better guidance than that which ye found your fathers following?" They said: "For us, we deny that ye (prophets) are sent (on a mission at all)" [Qur'an 43:22–24].

The situation is also similar to the extreme positions that some of the followers of the founders of different schools of thought (*mathaahib*) adopted. They literally stuck to the work of their scholar and rejected everything else, including any Hadith of which their scholar was unaware.

The thrust of the new Islamic construct is to begin with figuring out what needs to be done and doing it (the purpose of Allah) based on the commandments of our *deen* (the letter and the spirit of Islam). What this means to us as an individual or a group, in a particular situation, depends on the dynamics of our reality and, additionally, on our potential, our challenges, and our opportunities. This is a mission-driven and relevance-oriented construct. On the other hand, the prevailing constructs say that just doing something is okay and better than doing nothing. They tell us that we only need to do what we can fit within the existing paradigm and only what is compatible with the existing organizational structure and operations. The difference is important. We will be doing what needs to be done, not just preserving or possibly stretching what is already there. That applies to our thinking as well as our actions.

The following are some of the characteristics of the new Islamic construct that we are advocating as an essential component of this project:

- In developing a new Islamic construct, we are bound only by the original sources, the divine guidance, and the prophetic model as understood in the American context. Any other literature or historical experience, including interpretations of divine guidance and of the prophetic model, may be used selectively, critically, and creatively if they pass the test of authenticity and relevance. But these will not be seen as binding or even as a starting point.

- Our goal is to make Islam relevant and indigenous in America and to inspire and empower its followers to do their best, aspire highly, realize their full potential, and develop themselves into exemplary and impactful citizens and community members. All should take place within the boundaries of the essentials of Islam. Our success in developing the new construct will be evaluated based on those outcomes.

- This construct, like everything else in this project, is mission driven. Indeed, this new construct is meant to drive the renaissance of our community and to turn it into a relevant and mainstream societal reform movement with a significant and sustained impact.

- There will be a strong emphasis on the spiritual and intellectual aspects and on the humane, civic, and societal dimensions of Islam. These aspects constitute the roots and the fruits of Islam, and their neglect—together with the fading of the sense of mission—constitutes an essential cause and manifestation of the mutilation of Islam at the hands of its own followers, albeit oftentimes with the best of intentions.

- Serious consideration will be given to our American context and social norms. This is an essential requirement to ensure the relevance of the new Islamic construct and a critical mechanism to ensure the fusion between the scriptures and our current reality. This is the way to make Islam an indigenous, mainstream, and viable faith, way of life, platform, and discourse. Islam cannot be understood or implemented in a vacuum, and it is not a one-size-fits-all garment. It is a universal, timeless, and remarkably flexible guidance that is always dynamic and entails just a few, but fundamental, essentials. Islam takes the proper shape when it is rooted in current time and blended with the present context, not only at the societal level but also all the way to the local and personal level. That's why scholars don't (or at least should not) issue a *fatwa* before knowing the details of the case at hand, and that's why Imam al-Shafii changed his *fatwas* when he moved from Iraq to Egypt. The evolution of Islam should never stop, and its inexhaustible treasures should be constantly dug out through intellectual exercise and civic engagement.

The universality, timelessness, and eternal vitality of Islam are ensured, not only by its flexibility and compatibility with every culture but also by its capacity to be enriched and rejuvenated every time it mixes with a new culture. Islam endures through intellectual creativity and civic engagement and through the synergetic relations it establishes, not only with different cultures but also with human progress. Indeed, Islam inspires progress, which in turn digs out more of the treasures of divine guidance. In a part of a Hadith, the Prophet said about the Qur'an: "Its wonders are inexhaustible, and scholars will never have enough of it." And Ibn Abbas said, "Qur'an is explained by the progress of time."[48] It is also important to note that sound social norms constitute a source of legislation in some schools of thought (*mathaahib*).

For all these reasons, in developing a fresh and relevant Islamic construct and trying to root Islam in our time and context and in trying to establish this synergetic relationship, it is essential to decouple Islam from the long-ago and far-away heritages, cultures, contextual understandings, and implementations of Islam. Instead, we must adopt all of America's sound social norms and cultural elements that are compatible with Islam.

---

48   Hadith reported in Sunan Al-Tirmithi.

Emphasis on and serious consideration of the maqasid and masalih

This is another essential mechanism that ensures the timelessness, universality, and eternal vitality of Islam. Indeed, the texts of Islam must be understood and implemented, not only in light of current reality but also in light of the spirit and the overarching goals (*maqasid*) of Islam and in light of the people's well-being and public interest (*masalih*). Remember that Islam aims not only to ensure the salvation of people in the hereafter but also to ensure their well-being in this life.

In his renowned work, *Qawa'id al-Ahkam*, 'Izz al-Din 'Abd al-Salâm (d. 660/1262) indicates that "the greatest of all the objectives of the Qur'an is to facilitate benefits (*masalih*) and the means that secure them" and that the realization of benefit also includes the prevention of evil. He added that "all the obligations (*al-takalif*) of the *Shari'ah* were predicated on securing benefits for the people in this world and the next."

Islam is predicated on the benefits of the individual and the community. The laws of Islam are designed to protect these benefits and facilitate the improvement and perfection of the conditions of human life on earth. Islam *is*, in other words, concerned, from the beginning to the end, with benefiting us as God's creatures.

Muhammad and Islam were sent as a mercy to humanity, which means the intention was to make our lives easier, more pleasant, more meaningful, and more successful—not the opposite. Muhammad indicated that the best people are those who are most useful to others. The scholars agree that the greater good (*al maslaha*) is the foundation and the purpose of the divine guidance. The sanctity of life, freedom, justice, human dignity, and human rights are essential principles of Islam.

Technically speaking, the scholars have classified the entire range of *masalih and maqasid* into three categories in a descending order of importance. The first is life's essential *masalih,* or *daruriyyat.* Next in importance come the things that are needed to support the essentials, the complementary benefits, or *hajiyyat.* Third, in order of importance, are the embellishments, or *tahsiniyyat.*

There are five essential interests (*daruriyyat*), and they deserve special attention here: faith, life, lineage, intellect, and property. Some scholars add the protection of honor, which was initially thought to have been covered under lineage. Imam Taher bin Achour considered freedom as an overarching goal of Islam. These are, by definition, essential to normal order in society as well as to the survival and spiritual well-being of individuals. They are so important that destroying or undermining these interests will precipitate chaos and the collapse of normal order in society. The precepts of Islam seek to protect and promote these values and to support measures for their preservation and advancement.

The goal and purpose of the texts should not be neglected in the name of conformity; and rigid conformity to rules, if it runs against the essential purpose and outlook of Islam, is generally considered unacceptable. The general premises and overriding objectives of Islam have a higher order of importance than do specific rules, so rules should be read in the light of their broader premises and objectives. Indeed, Islam should be taken as a unity. The fragmented and atomistic approach fails to tie the relevant parts of the texts together.

In the event of a conflict arising between the various classes of interest, the lesser of these may be sacrificed in order to protect a higher interest. When there is a plurality of conflicting interests, and none appears to be clearly preferable, then prevention of evil takes priority over the realization of benefit.

The *maqasid* (overarching purpose of Islam) equips us with insight and provides us with a framework in which detailed Islamic knowledge can become more interesting, more meaningful, and more relevant. Those overall goals of Islam constitute a great source of inspiration and guidance, not only in understanding and implementing Islam but also in translating its teachings into viable solutions and sound positions on pertinent issues. Without those vital elements, Islam loses its fluidity, vitality, and its timeless and universal relevance and capacity to uplift people and inspire renaissance, reform, and progress.

Another important factor that should be taken into consideration in trying to figure out and fulfill the divine purpose is the end result or consequence (*ma'alat*) of any decision or ruling. In more than one instance, the Prophet did not take what would be considered as the normal course of action because of the adverse consequences that were feared as a result of so doing. That's why he did not restore the *Ka'bah* to its original position: the faith of the people was still fragile, and the move may have induced them into disbelief, as he explained to Aisha. That was also the reason why he did not pursue the hypocrites, even though he was aware of their subversive activities.

In conclusion, in trying to determine and fulfill the divine purpose, conformity to the divine text should be pursued in conjunction with careful consideration about the overriding objectives and special circumstances of the present time and place. Things to consider include social norms and the potential consequences of our actions, keeping in mind that Islam seeks to establish justice, alleviate hardship, and secure benefits for the people in this world and the next.

Presumption of lawfulness/permissibility and easing people's lives

In designing our construct, we also apply this principle. In addition to the primary goals of relevance and serving the greater good, our new construct seeks to ease the lives of people, not to complicate things. One of the greatest scholars of Islam, Sufyan al-Thawry said, "The true *fiqh* is a permission that you get from a trustworthy scholar. But everyone can take stringent positions."

Whenever he was given a choice between two matters, the Prophet would choose the easier one unless it was forbidden. In more than one Hadith, the Prophet abhorred the tendency toward stringency.

People must be given all the options, and those options should not be restricted in the name of being on the safe side. Every individual may choose to shun some of what is permissible out of piety and may (and should be encouraged to) intensify his/her worship. Although people should not be shopping around for easy options, they should be told about all the options and encouraged to seek what is right and what is most pleasant to God, which might be different for different individuals and different communities and in different contexts. Plus, hard doesn't make right. Indeed, Muhammad indicated that God loves people to challenge themselves but also to enjoy His permissions.

Developing a fresh Islamic construct is a collective and individual duty

Obviously, those with more knowledge are expected to make a bigger contribution, but everybody should participate in this process, through reflection, discussion, research, and raising questions. We should challenge the prevailing intellectual shallowness and complacency, and we should bring about an intellectual dynamism in our community.

Developing a relevant yet authentic construct is an obligation, and it is a necessity for the revival and renewal of Islam and for rooting it in society. This is the only way to make Islam an indigenous and inspiring experience, one which can spark the renaissance of the community and facilitate its transformation into a relevant, impactful, mainstream societal reform movement. Our project's main goals are to ensure the community's greatest relevance and its service of the greater good and our fulfillment of the overarching goals of Islam. This construct, which is driven by those objectives, is bound only by the original sources of guidance. It is to be understood in the American context, taking into consideration America's sound customs/norms. Yet it is open to everything useful, both from Islamic heritage and from human heritage.

This construct is built on strong and vibrant spiritual and intellectual foundations, but it is staunchly humane, civic, social, and modern, unlike the prevalent paradigm that overemphasizes politics and activism. That prevalent paradigm tends to be too ritualistic, legalistic, and formalistic; and it falls short in the vital areas of depth, coherence, and inspiration.

Our new construct is proposed as an alternative to that prevalent construct, which is frozen, deficient, limited, and exhausted. Indeed, the ceiling of the prevalent construct is what we see now. It has reached its peak, and so the community is largely stuck, stagnant, and complacent, with leaders who do not aspire for more than managing community affairs and offering basic services, facilities, and activities/programs that cater to a small and largely passive segment of the community.

For individuals, the ceiling has meant being good, practicing Muslims, and possibly active. The limited efforts at outreach and civic engagement by some Muslims, however, are lacking in vision, depth, and consistency. These are mostly erratic and ceremonial individual efforts that are largely guided by individual ambitions and/or a victimized minority mind-set. Most of those activists still think and behave as Muslims who happen to live in America or happen to be American citizens. Very few of them are engaged in a mainstream manner as faithful citizens. And those who are engaged do it on their own, not through Muslim organizations.

We hope that the new construct will produce a new breed of Muslim Americans: mission-driven, compassionate patriots. Religious devotion is a plus, but not a requirement for someone to be accepted and respected in this movement and take part in this project.

9. Confronting brutal facts and tracing and tackling root causes of crises

We are also calling on people to face some tough realities. Our movement is not only driven by our compelling mission and expansive vision but also by a firm belief in the possibility of fundamental change. The need for that change is urgent, partly because both our country and our community are facing severe and compounded crises that were neither thoroughly assessed nor adequately addressed. We are nowhere close to where we should or could be. We believe this is jeopardizing our future and that the situation is neither sustainable nor patchable. It is definitely not acceptable. Neither more of the same nor patchwork will salvage our future. A new beginning is needed, and a new course must be charted.

In launching this renaissance and reform project, we are shedding denial, and we are discontinuing strategies that may have involved dodging, scapegoating, justifying, and/or complaining. We are through with spinning our wheels, and we have stopped seeking egocentric solutions. These have all been futile approaches that, sooner or later, would cost far too much even if the price is deferred or paid incrementally. Unfortunately, most people seem to prefer one or more of these bad alternatives.

We believe that, while crisis is sometimes unavoidable for an individual, a community, or a country, it is not okay to remain in denial, to disavow our responsibilities, or to resort to futile approaches, even if those approaches are convenient and comforting. Therefore, we have dedicated a good part of this book to analyzing our community's (and the country's) crisis and the root causes of the crisis. In our efforts to implement our project and inspire and empower people, we will work at raising the awareness of the people, and we will strive to stir up serious reflections and discussions about our situation and our future. We do this in the hope that people will take charge and become part of the solution.

In the process, we will try to eradicate sources of complacency and despair among people, and we will strive to fuel people's motivation, sense of responsibility, and resolve. We will urge Muslim Americans to focus their energy and thinking on the mission at hand—our divine mission—a mission which requires that we tackle our crisis and effect needed change. In other words, we will try to turn the increased awareness into an increased sense of urgency.

As is true in our approach to developing a new Islamic construct, we believe that inclusiveness openness and transparency must apply in our reflections and discussion about our crisis. These interactions should not be elitist or conducted in closed circles. Rather, this conversation and process should be an open, frank exercise that invites the participation of all Muslim Americans.

10. Upholding the American Constitution, the civic/secular nature of the state, and the pluralistic nature of American society

This item was not emphasized or clarified earlier, not because it is unimportant, but because it is the framework within which all our work will be conducted; and it has more to do with what we are *not* advocating than with what we are advocating.

Indeed, even though we are calling for fundamental and structural change within society, this is a reform movement—*not a revolution*. It is an attempt to push our country "toward a more perfect union," and it is an effort to inspire and empower our community to make a significant and sustained contribution to the needed change and reform in America. Specifically, *we are not aspiring to establish an Islamic state or to Islamize American society.* We respect and treasure the unity and diversity of this country, the fundamental liberties that are guaranteed by the Constitution, and the civic/secular nature of the American state. We should all defend those foundations against any attempt to shake them. Such attempts could only pave the way for disastrous scenarios.

We advocate support for the American Constitution as the foundation of our country. The American Constitution has held our country together and enabled us to achieve something that is very rare in the history of humanity: political unity within a very diverse society, a unity that has been achieved and maintained through guarantees of civil rights and human liberties, rather than through suppression. America has realized this great feat, while many other countries have had to choose between forced unity and social order at the price of liberty on the one hand, versus chronic civil strife or dissolution on the other. Consider the experiences of the Soviet Union, Yugoslavia, China, or Rwanda.

American Muslims constitute a small minority in America, but that is not why our movement is taking this stand in support of a secular state and a pluralistic society. Rather, this is a well-founded position rooted in our belief system and based on the lessons drawn from historical and contemporary experience.

Islam does not sanction theocracy. In fact, it does not even propose a well-defined political system. Rather, as in many other areas of life, when it comes to government, Islam just provides guidelines for good governance, including the upholding of freedom, justice, and equality—and rule by accountable leaders who are supported by popular consultation and consent. The first Islamic state of Medina under Muhammad was a constitutional state based on citizenship; and Imam Al-Banna considered the constitutional democratic system to be closer to Islamic guidelines than any other system. He rejected any alternative, in fact, citing similarities between some aspects of democracy and some of the governance guidelines of Islam, such as sovereignty, national unity, and the accountability of government.

Most Islamic movements advocate the attainment of liberty and democracy as the thrust of their reform efforts. Diverse Islamic countries, such as Iraq and Lebanon, dream of a secular, nonsectarian democracy like ours, while they struggle with their own paralyzed, sectarian systems of government.

Unlike many other secular states, America is not antireligion and does not ban religion in the public square. There is no prohibition against religiously inspired civic engagement. Try comparing America's great tolerance for religious expression with French or even Turkish secularism. The American Constitution offers everything a Muslim citizen could ask for: guaranteed freedom of religious practice and expression, the right to assemble, an elected and accountable government, the rule of the law, a separation of powers between the branches of government, a system of checks and balances, and freedom to organize. It prohibits government interference in religious matters, yet it still allows religious groups to influence government.

We certainly don't want our country to digress toward sectarian politics or to suffer civil strife or breakup. The Constitution not only guarantees our liberties but also guards against such disastrous scenarios. Consequently, we should defend it.

Some Muslim activists may find this position to be shocking or unacceptable because, for some, the raison d'être of an Islamic reform movement is to establish an Islamic state. However, most of these people have forgotten (if they ever knew) that the contemporary Islamic movement started as a societal reform project. Its leaders later clashed with their countries' oppressive regimes and ended up being sucked into a power struggle in order to carry out reform efforts. In fact, most movements have already shifted their focus from establishing an Islamic state into fighting for freedom and democracy. Because we in the United States have neither an oppressive regime nor the need to fight for freedom and democracy, our movement is and will always remain a societal reform project, and we will seek to move all Americans toward "a more perfect union." We will always work for the best possible conditions for our country and encourage the biggest possible contribution from our community.

Muslim Americans, no less than other Americans, have serious reservations about some domestic and foreign policies, and there is certainly a dire need for both political and economic reform. Also, there will always be debates over the interpretation of the Constitution and on the constitutionality of certain laws and policies. However, all our efforts to sustain, repeal, change, or reform those laws and policies must take place within the framework of the Constitution and through efforts to influence public opinion and voting. We will build coalitions and petition government. The Constitution merely delineates the rules of engagement, thereby ensuring fair play on a level playing field.

Our movement will challenge (and work tirelessly to change) policies that are unfair, not in America's best interest, inconsistent with America's founding values, or based on a questionable interpretation of the Constitution. However, while we will always try to win the "game" for America and the American people; we will also always play by the rules and accept the results and the decisions of the referee (which, technically, is the people). Such is the nature of this sport called democracy.

11. Our global perspective

The focus of this movement is predominantly domestic and local. Neither America nor Muslim Americans should feel responsible for solving all the problems in the world. As discussed previously, the overseas focus of immigrant Muslim Americans stemmed from our myth of return and its accompanying illusion: "mission accomplished!" The completed "mission" was limited to establishing a community and facilities as a temporary shelter for return-myth-deluded immigrants who expected to one day go back to their nations of origin. So once we met our primary basic needs and ensured the preservation of our identity, our community's focus and resources shifted to the never-ending crises back home. This resulted in the proliferation of relief organizations and the explosive growth of relief efforts and in the addiction of many immigrants to ethnic TV channels and Web sites.

The goals of this movement are far bigger and more challenging than the limited initial goals of the community, but our goals are, nonetheless, predominantly local and domestic. This is not to say that we are indifferent toward what is happening in the world, particularly in the Muslim world. Such an attitude would be not only unacceptable but also impractical given our religious connection to Muslims everywhere, our longing for global peace and justice, the unique global role of the U.S., the effects of globalization, and the communications revolution. Rather, our domestic focus is driven by perspective and priority. Like most indigenous Islamic movements around the world, we believe that all citizens should be patriotic and should put the well-being of their country before all else.

Islam is a practical religion. It directs people to take care of themselves and those in their immediate environments first. That's our primary responsibility, and where we live is where we can have our biggest impact. However, while our focus should be on local and domestic issues, it is imperative that we have a global perspective. On global and all other issues, our movement will

- adopt one standard, always standing for justice regardless of who is involved;
- advocate American interests within the boundaries of our Islamic principles and within the boundaries of American and international law;
- grant special importance and consideration to issues that involve America and/or Muslims and to those in which we believe America could and should seek to make a difference;
- conduct any overseas activities in a legal and publicly open manner through the U.S. government or through mainstream organizations; and
- conduct our humanitarian efforts on the basis of compassion.

Our political positions will be inspired by our principles and guided by pragmatic considerations. We will stand strong in support of American interests and in advocacy for peace and justice at home and globally.

CHAPTER TWO: THE TENETS OF OUR APPROACH

1- Islam inspired

While it is civic in nature, objectives, and methods, this project is divine in its origin and its ultimate goal. The thrust of this project is to seek the betterment of our country and our people (and the whole world); but we are doing that in response to God's call and in pursuit of His pleasure. Indeed, at the heart of this project is a strong connection between seeking the pleasure of Allah (our ultimate goal) and striving to fulfill His purpose (our mission), which is essentially to uplift ourselves, our people, our country, and our world.

The scholars say, "Islam came to ensure the well-being of people in this life and in the hereafter." They also say, "The divine guidance (*al-sharaa*) includes everything that serves the common good."

So our movement and our vision are inspired by Islam and bound by the essentials of Islam. However, because of the civic nature of this movement, people need not be religious or even Muslims to champion this project. Obviously, as Muslim Americans, we have better access to Muslims, and we are better able to explain to Muslims the reasons they should participate in this project. However, our message is not religious and therefore is directed toward all citizens; and our movement will be open to all citizens who buy into our platform fully or partially, as members and/or partners.

2- Mission driven

This project is built on our commitment to Islam as a life mission. That mission is centered on uplifting people and serving the greater good. This has two fundamental implications. First, we will constantly strive to be not only the best embodiments of the divine guidance but also the best instruments of divine will. Second, our main promotion strategy is to "sell" the mission to people (particularly Muslims), inspire and empower them to undertake the mission, and urge them to then "sell" it in their natural environment. For the champions of this movement, this task of embodying, fulfilling, and "transmitting" the mission should take precedence over any other activity. All our individual and collective plans and actions should be mission driven. Indeed, the key to the successful implementation of our project is the mission-driven Muslim, who is currently in very short supply compared to the numbers of practicing and active Muslims.

Our focus will always be on seeking the most efficient ways to fulfill our mission and advance our cause. We will not be swayed by proposals or opportunities that do not clearly and efficiently serve the mission. If the mission is not served by what we do, expanding membership, increasing activities, raising budgets, and building facilities will be like spinning our wheels. Unless activities serve the mission and make us more efficient, they only keep us busy and give us an illusion of accomplishment.

Our strategy is more in line with the prophetic approach than with the prevailing approach in our community, which currently emphasizes structure and activities that seldom reflect any mission or vision. Indeed, a clear, noble, and compelling mission was one of the two pillars of the prophetic paradigm that galvanized and unified people. The other pillar was a sound leadership model.

3- Country focused (committed to America as our homeland)

This is a fundamental tenet of our project. This is not a community project, but rather a societal reform project. It is inspired by Islam, and it will be built on our commitment to Islam as a life mission and on our commitment to America as our homeland.

The previous two tenets (being Islam inspired and mission driven) are likely to mobilize only devout Muslims; and while that is an important group, it is but a small slice of our Muslim minority in America. It is our commitment to America as our homeland that makes our movement mainstream and inclusive, because it is the country—not the religion or the ideology or the level of commitment to Islam—that most Americans, including most Muslims, share with us. Caring about our country and its people and serving the common good are the concepts that should resonate with the vast majority of citizens (including nearly all Muslim Americans). Indeed, an essential goal and strategy of our societal reform project is to get more and more of our fellow citizens to be civically aware and engaged. We want to enhance everyone's concern for, and contribution to, the common good. In doing so, our goal is to temper the endemic individualism that drives Americans (be they individuals, communities, or corporations) to pursue their own interests without any consideration for (and sometimes at the expense of) the national interest and the common good.

We may differ on policies and priorities, and we may have different sources of inspiration and motivation, but we should not differ on the goal of working to make America (and, in turn, the whole world) a better place. In this context, our differences should be handled in a civil manner so that they do not interfere with our mutual respect and cooperation for the common good.

Caring for our homeland and for our people is not only compatible with the teachings of Islam. These aspects are also fundamental elements of the divine mission, because the divine mission is about stewardship (*istikhlaf*), development (*i'mar*), reform/betterment (*islah*), enjoining and inviting that which is good and forbidding that which is evil, benevolence (*albirr*), and uplifting people (*tazkiya*).

Our movement is an attempt to develop and use a new but authentic Islamic construct to seamlessly mesh together the concepts of service to God, to one's country and people, to one's faith, and to the world. We will be able to blend all that with our individual, personal ambitions. This renaissance movement is an attempt to resolve the numerous artificial dichotomies and incompatibilities that have been tearing apart the Muslim (and the human) personality. A central issue has been our severe identity crisis, and that has hindered our growth, engagement, and integration into society.

Rather than denying, rationalizing, or patching up our identity crisis, we are unequivocally resolving it. We are preventing its passage to future generations and to converts. Our commitment to America as a homeland and the fact that we care for Americans as our people are two of the main reasons our movement calls for a new beginning and for charting a new course. The only other alternative is to dodge or patch up our identity crisis or "resolve" it superficially and tactically, which would set the whole movement project on the course for failure.

Our faith is not only compatible with love for our country and supportive of our compassion toward the American people but also reinforces those natural feelings and gives them a higher and nobler purpose. Consequently, we believe that no deficiency in American history, politics, or society should interfere with anyone's loyalty and commitment or with their pride in being Americans. This is true for everyone, including those who have chosen to make this country their home. Importantly, it is also true for future generations and converts. Commitment to one's homeland and caring for one's people are not conditional. If anything, problems should only enhance our commitment, our involvement, and our service for the greater good.

Our movement not only seeks the best possible conditions for America and all Americans but also seeks to ensure the biggest possible contribution of Muslim Americans toward that end. By unlocking the tremendous but largely untapped potential of our community, we bring a wonderful gift to America. Because of the strong link between seeking the pleasure of God and serving the greater good, our thinking, our planning, and our action should all focus on what's happening in the nation (at all levels) and on what we can do to improve things.

4- Designed for mainstream societal reform with an integrated civic platform

Most Muslim organizations are focusing on serving and protecting the Muslim community and striving to defend its image and rights. Without a doubt, this is a noble cause, if done properly. However, the goal of this project is to develop a mainstream societal reform movement that is directed toward and open to all segments of society. The focus includes all pertinent issues affecting American society. Our movement is not centered on the Muslim community, and its scope is not limited to issues that affect or concern only Muslim Americans. Our goal is not to merely maximize the gains that the community can get from society. Rather, in seeking the well-being of the entire nation, we want to maximize the contribution of Muslim Americans.

Because Muslims are the primary target audience for this book, however, the reader should understand that the prominent Islamic religious content herein is intended to rally Muslim Americans behind our project and its civic platform. At a minimum, we hope that Muslim American readers who are struggling with the issues we raise will, after reading these pages, be inspired to weed out the roots of their identity crisis and of their social isolation and of their civic disengagement. Indeed, Muslims—observant and nonobservant—rise and fall on Islam. When it is properly understood, rooted in their time, and reconciled with human progress, Islam is a great source of inspiration and empowerment. On the other hand, when it is frozen in time and out of touch, Islam may unnecessarily hinder Muslims' growth, progress, and relevance.

Even in our initial focus on Muslim Americans, our goal is to inspire and empower them to be at the forefront of the movement for change in America and to maximize their contribution to the greater good. We are calling on Muslim Americans, driven by their commitment to the divine mission and/or to our American homeland, to increase their civic awareness and become genuinely and consistently engaged as concerned citizens seeking the well-being of the nation. We should all strive to be as involved as possible in all issues affecting the nation (not just the issues affecting our Muslim community and ourselves). Our priorities should be determined by the impact of the issues on the nation. Obviously, the nature and availability of our resources will also help to determine priorities. Our civic engagement should not be "reactionary" (activated only when we come under attack), tactical (designed to improve our image), erratic, or selfish. Neither should our civic engagement be prompted by a minority mind-set or by a sense of victimization. Rather, it should be driven by our faith and by our commitment to good citizenship.

Consequently, in this civic engagement, Muslim Americans do not need to coalesce or lock arms together in some sort of isolated solidarity. Nor do they need to create artificial niches of activism. Rather, they need to be engaged directly in their natural environment and connect with the entire society, including families, friends, neighborhoods, workplaces, professional communities, and civic organizations. We will be constructively engaged at the local, state, and national level.

Like all citizens, Muslim Americans are urged to join and work with existing societal institutions. If there is a need to organize, our organizations should—as much as possible—be mainstream, inclusive, empowering, and nonbureaucratic. We should redefine "Islamic activity" as "an activity that serves a good purpose from the Islamic perspective, without violating the teachings of Islam." Islamic activity should not be defined as "activity by Muslims for Muslims."

Even though this book is stuffed with religious tone, the "product" that our movement advocates is a civic platform that is to be promoted through relevant civic discourse, and whenever possible, through broad coalitions. Our movement's civic platform will reflect our perspective on pertinent societal issues and on what we deem best for America. We will seek to engage, on any particular issue, both those who agree with us and those who disagree. Irrespective of the positions different people take, a key component of our movement is to heighten people's civic awareness, concern, engagement, and contribution to the common good.

While our movement comprises an attempt to apply the teachings of Islam within the American context, Americans of all faiths will be invited to assess what we are doing and to provide feedback on the merits of our platform. In fact, everyone is invited to participate.

5- Aimed at community renaissance

Our project is a mainstream, societal reform movement. It is built on a civic platform that seeks the well-being of the nation, tackles all pertinent issues that affect the country, and seeks to increase the civic awareness, concern, and engagement of all citizens. We want to maximize everyone's contribution to the greater good. Therefore, our movement is directed toward everyone and open to all citizens.

In parallel, we are also calling on all Muslim Americans to open up and directly engage their immediate environments as concerned citizens—without necessarily coalescing as Muslims or going through Muslim organizations. In fact, we plan to spend the bulk of our efforts on charting this new and direct track for Muslim Americans and on streamlining and integrating the efforts of individuals and organizations who take this track.

At the same time, we will seek to pull as many of our community members and organizations in this direction as possible, without becoming bogged down in community politics or in the management of the status quo. Though we would like to see current operations and services continue (in spite of their limitations), our first and foremost commitment is to empower our community so that it will become relevant, impactful, and vibrant. We yearn to move the community to the next level—a level that is commensurate with our great faith, mission, legacy and potential, and challenges and opportunities.

We are powerfully motivated because we are very concerned about the state and the future of our community. The Muslim American community appears to be largely stagnant and stuck, with an acute identity crisis, with no clear role, and with no clear sense of direction.

6- Set to advocate and support revival and renewal

No significant progress by Muslim Americans, either on societal reform or on community renaissance, would be possible without the revival and renewal of Islam first.

Although the prevailing version of Islam is largely free of flagrant deviations in matters of creed, it is mutilated. It is not indigenous, and it is not rooted in our time period. When it comes to enabling community renaissance or societal reform, that's a disqualifier.

The prevailing version of Islam in the United States was imported from a different part of the world, and it had been extrapolated from a different historical era. So people have been practicing an Islam that is largely frozen in time and in space. On top of this intellectual stagnation, the understanding and practice of Islam has suffered a great deal during the last couple of centuries. This has been due to Muslim decline and marginalization.

As a result, Islam became largely a dormant and uninspiring religion. It has become too legalistic, formalistic, ritualistic, and out of touch. The great, timeless, and universal message of revival/renewal, renaissance, and reform has been downgraded and frozen into some routine rituals and a list of "dos and don'ts." And in the process, Islam has lost its capacity to guide and inform life, its ability to inspire and enable people, its resourcefulness in answering people's questions, its ability to solve their problems, and its power to unlock the potential of individuals, groups, and societies.

Frozen in time and out of touch, Islam became good only as a personal and passive religion that, in the best case scenarios, makes people observe (major) acts of worship and leads them to refrain from committing major sins. Oftentimes, the more religious the person becomes, the more isolated, passive, and complacent he/she becomes. Religion and daily life went separate ways to the point that success in life became irreconcilable with religious observance, and people had to choose between the two. People found it necessary to look for alternative ideologies to guide their lives, as Islam began to be perceived as a problem.

It was no accident that the contemporary Islamic movement's motto was

"Islam is the solution," and that the movement was built on the premise that the problem is not to be found in Islam itself, but rather in Muslims' improper understanding and practice of Islam.

The Islamic movement did a remarkable job in reversing this trend and in reviving and renewing Islam, thus reconciling it with science, politics, economics, and life. This made Islam, once again, relevant and inspiring. And in a relatively short period of time, many Muslims began to view Islam, indeed, as the solution; and the most devout Muslims became the most successful people in their education and in their professions. Moreover, the Islamic movements/parties became the largest and most popular political entities, with leaders and participants who expressed people's concerns and advocated their aspirations.

The keys to the Islamic movement's accomplishments have been the decoupling of the original texts of Islam from Islamic heritage and the fostering of an understanding of the texts in light of political and social reality. This has helped to produce a unique, contemporary, national experience. This revival/renewal exercise led to the understanding of Islam as a mission of renaissance and reform. It also caused people to commit to that mission. The revival was supported by a deep understanding of political reality and a solid commitment to the homeland, along with great compassion for fellow citizens. The result was a vibrant, indigenous mass movement that effected a resounding change. However, the movement did not evolve (intellectually) beyond a certain point. That is why this model did not keep up with the changes and challenges of life. It was the product, not the process, that was exported to other Muslim countries with little or no adjustment. Therefore, the initial success of our imported Islam was short lived and of lesser scale. Afterward, the community stumbled, as did the mother movements and for similar reasons.

When the model was taken "as is" to the West in general and to the U.S. in particular, it was only useful in building and managing Islamic centers and schools and in providing some basic services and educational and social programs. The model did not enable the community to transition beyond that point, and the community became stuck in transition. The community's needs, challenges, and aspirations outgrew the model, and the community went into a haphazard lateral expansion. More and bigger centers and schools have often been mistaken for growth.

So we find ourselves back at "square one" with a version of Islam that is neither indigenous nor inspiring. It is mixed with an unhealthy foreign culture and a heavy dose of anti-American political views. Some of the essential aspects of the original Islam have faded, and some minor aspects were blown out of proportion. This has left us with an Islam that has been stripped of its sense of mission and is lacking in spiritual vibrancy. It is also devoid of intellectual vitality, creativity, and depth. It is an Islam that has weak humane and civic dimensions.

Indeed, our faith is in dire need of rediscovery, and our Islamic construct needs a lot of deconstruction and reconstruction in order to become relevant, indigenous, and inspiring. Our new construct must be rooted in a compelling sense of mission, which takes into account our American context without compromising Islam's essential teachings. Islamic heritage is a good resource, but it should be used selectively and creatively. The original texts of Islam must be our starting point and our only binding sources in this process. In studying the texts of Islam, the question that we should be asking is "What does this verse or Hadith mean for us here and now, and how may we best implement it and advocate it in a relevant way?" While the divine guidance and the prophetic model are timeless and valid for all times and places, some of their provisions are neither constant nor equally relevant for all times and all circumstances. We should consider not only "the letter" of Islamic teaching but also the spirit, the context, and Islam's overarching goals (*maqasid*).

Our world is fast paced, interconnected, and changing. We are here, Islam is here, and we have responsibilities. We must ensure the constant evolution of our construct so that our faith, our message, and our lives are able to keep up with the changes and challenges of this sometimes hectic world. In matters of pure worship, to be sure, we should certainly strive to emulate what the Prophet actually did; but in matters of human interactions and in fulfilling our mission and building our movement and in engaging our environment, we should try to figure out what the Prophet would do here and now. In doing so, our goal should be to ensure the relevance of our faith and the betterment of our country and even our world.

This duty is a direct implication of three facts: Muhammad is the seal (last) of the prophets; the Qur'an is God's final, universal, and timeless message; and Muslims are the heirs of Muhammad and his message. It is the original texts of Islam that are perfect, timeless, and universal, not specific human reconstructions of Islam in a particular historical and geographical context. Limiting ourselves to embracing a particular human reconstruction of Islam—one that was developed in a different context—defeats the claim that Islam is a universal and timelessly relevant religion. Our aim is to bring to life in the American context the timeless divine guidance, which is valid for all times and places, and which is therefore compatible with all cultures.

Revival of Islam to ensure its constant evolution and relevance is the most important duty that Muslims have, individually and collectively. This is critical to our success in fulfilling our defining mission; and that divine mission is critical to our relevance and to the impact we can have on human progress and civilization. This project is a humble but serious attempt to do just that. This revival/renewal involves the following:

- Restoring and emphasizing the compelling sense of mission in Islam and rediscovering it, presenting it, and committing to it as a life mission that is centered on uplifting people, societal reform, and service of the greater good.

- Decoupling the original texts of Islam from distant culture and from heritage, and embarking—individually and collectively—on the direct study of the original texts of Islam in the American context to produce an original Muslim American experience. Thus, we can see to it that Islam becomes an indigenous, relevant, and inspiring faith that enables the renaissance of our community and the betterment of American society. This will hopefully engender some intellectual vitality that is critical for the renewal and revival of Islam.

- Activating the process of *ijtihad*. While issuing *fatwas* should be limited to scholars who are knowledgeable about the texts and the context, all Muslims are urged to seek—individually and collectively—the best and most relevant understanding and implementation of the divine guidance and the prophetic model through contemplation, research, and discussion. This process should be continuous, not "one and done."

- Reviving the two endpoints of the Islamic construct: the spiritual dimension (the starting point) and the civic dimension (where the "rubber meets the road"). Indeed, an essential objective of our revival and renewal of Islam is to inspire and empower members of our community toward spiritual vibrancy, civic engagement, and civic leadership. Spiritual vibrancy is at the heart of Islam as a faith, and civic engagement is at the heart of Islam as a mission. The two combine to make us ever more devout worshippers and better instruments of God's will.

- Reversing the prevailing notion that things are prohibited until proven otherwise. We must end the abuse of prohibition in the name of being "on the safe side." Let us restore the fundamental Islamic concept that says that things are permissible until proven otherwise. The burden of proof should be on the one who prohibits.

- Effecting a paradigm shift from an exclusive focus on authenticity (and oftentimes, rigidity) irrespective of relevance, to a focus on relevance and impact within the boundaries of authenticity. We will do this without compromising Islam's essentials.

- Balancing the letter of divine guidance and the prophetic model with their spirit; restoring the fundamental concepts of *urf* (social norm) and al-*masalih al-mursala* (what is beneficial for people). Balancing our practice in this way is essential to the maintenance of Islam's flexibility, universality, and timeless relevance.

- Restoring the humane, social, and aesthetic dimensions of Islam and its great sense of compassion (in addition to the spiritual and civic dimensions mentioned above). This effort should end (or at least temper) the binary attitude, which categorizes people as Muslims or non-Muslims. It should also pave the way for social outreach and charitable work, irrespective of people's religiosity or faith. Indeed, the religious dichotomy largely accounts for our isolation from society and also for the disconnect within our community between observant and nonobservant Muslims. We need to view all people, especially all Americans, as our fellow human beings and fellow citizens. We need to focus on commonalities and shared interests and concerns. We need to exhibit mutual respect and strive for greater cooperation for the common good.

7- Aimed at reform—not a revolution

Even though our movement is about change, for very valid reasons, the change that we are advocating does not challenge or question the American

Constitution (particularly the Bill of Rights) or the fundamental nature of either the state or society. Moreover, this is not a tactical strategy, and it was not adopted because we Muslim Americans constitute only a small minority. Rather, it is a fundamental element of our approach to improving ourselves, improving our society, improving our country, and improving our world. Particularly in the current atmosphere, our reader may misunderstand the heavy religious content in the preceding sections of this book and may gather that our movement is a religious movement set out to Islamize the American government and society. That is not who we are, and it is not what we are doing.

Although our movement is inspired by Islam, our goal is neither to convert Americans to Islam nor to establish an Islamic state. Rather, we seek the betterment of American society within the framework of the U.S. Constitution, and we staunchly stand by and support the civic nature of the state and the pluralistic nature of society. That is what our country was built upon, that is what is keeping it together, and that is what we wish to support and reinforce. As indicated earlier, achieving political unity in a diverse society by guaranteeing liberties, rather than suppressing them, constitutes a very rare accomplishment in human history. It is the dream of most diverse societies, and therefore, it should obviously be preserved.

Moreover, American secularism does not ban religion in the public square, and the Constitution keeps the state's hands off of religion (per the First Amendment). Unlike other nations where reform was possible only through a revolution and the drafting of a new constitution, the United States Constitution provides a sound framework for reform and change, whether we seek improvements in policies and laws or in social norms.

8- Individual/family centered

This movement is about inspiring and empowering people, rather than managing/serving and controlling them. The key to the new movement's success is individuals and their families, not organizations. This is a quasi-reversal of the prevailing approach in our community, which is centered on high-maintenance and bureaucratic organizations that focus on managing and serving people as customers and spectators. Currently, people are told—implicitly or explicitly—that they need only to plug in, attend events, participate in activities, and/or support the organization. That, they are told, will do the job for them.

Existing forums don't give a sense of belonging or a sense of empowerment, and they don't encourage creativity. As a result, our community is loaded with largely untapped talents and resources. We just have to believe in people, reach out to them, and creatively dig up their latent potential by committing them to the mission. We must instill in them a sense of responsibility and ownership and begin treating them as partners and stakeholders.

A considerable portion of our community comes from a background that stifled (or did not encourage) individual initiative, creativity, and self-reliance. Many of our fellow Muslim Americans have no tradition of self-development or self-governance, nor of civic engagement or community organizing. Activists among them have come from Islamic movements with rigid structures and selective membership. Their excessive emphasis on activism and compliance does not foster independent thinking, individual initiative, or creativity. This explains why most of our people, including those who are active, are not growing personally and are not civically engaged in any meaningful way. Despite great potential, they are not self-starters; and they are not inclined to be creative or to take initiative or to take risks.

In the same way that those in the Muslim world rely too much on their governments, we in America rely too much on local and national Muslim organizations to handle our community's affairs. The big difference is that people in the Muslim world are disengaged by force; whereas in our community, people are disengaged by choice or because they feel excluded by those in charge (leaders who ironically complain about the disengagement of the masses). Muslim Americans and their leaders seem to be comfortable with this state of affairs, even as they exchange the blame for it.

This paradigm, which is consistent with our founding paradigm, may have worked somewhat reasonably in the past because we were playing in the minor league. Our goals were limited to "self-sufficiency." We were operating under the myth that we would return to our countries of origin, and we were thinking as a (victimized) minority and focusing on the preservation of our identity. We only wanted protection from society, and we were content as long as the mosques, Islamic schools, and organizations could meet our immediate needs for services, programs, and facilities. Regardless of the merits of this paradigm, it has been exhausted, has reached its limits, has expired, and is unsustainable. It is directly responsible for some of the main dilemmas of our community. It has resulted in a community that is largely stagnant, isolated, and disengaged—a community with a small number of activists struggling just to manage and maintain the status quo, while most Muslim Americans are alienated.

But as we are trying, through this project, to move the community to the big league; and as our focus shifts toward growth, relevance, integration, and impact on the future, the current approach will not serve our purpose and must be changed. In particular, it is not consistent with our project. Our project is mission driven, not activity and bureaucracy oriented. We are country focused, not Muslim American community centered. And we are aimed at results, growth, and impact, not at busyness and spinning-wheel activism. We need to reverse the present trend and start relying more on individual initiatives and less on organizations. A more consistent approach is to encourage individuals and families to espouse and fulfill the mission directly in their respective environments. The function of organizations, then, is to inspire and empower individuals and families and to streamline, integrate, and synergize their efforts.

It is only through inspiring and empowering people and networking that an effective movement can be built. Consequently, we need to virtually switch roles—have individuals do the work while our organizations' primary roles should be (1) the fostering of an environment of personal growth and creativity, and (2) the support of creative, dedicated individuals and their families (throughout their life cycle) by providing them with the tools and the venues they need to fulfill the divine mission and effect change. This will allow those who join the organization to not only lend it a helping hand but also to help it grow and to grow with it. Plus, our ultimate goal should not be just to get people to become active but also to get them to be community organizers and civic leaders in their own environments.

Our approach is a bottom-up and true grassroots approach that "sells" individuals and families on the mission, inspires and empowers them to fulfill it directly in their respective environments, and invites them to establish forums and grassroots organizations in their local communities. These forums and organizations will participate in—and in turn, be supported and networked by—state and national organizations that will crown local efforts.

In our approach, individuals and families are champions of a mission and a movement. They are potential civic leaders, not just minor supporters and helping hands for dysfunctional organizations. We invite and urge everyone to own up to their responsibility for the advancement of the cause, for the well-being of the country and community, and for the betterment of their own future. Initially, this approach may not be well received by some community members who have been "babysat" or "handled" for quite some time. However, our movement is far more in sync with Islam's great emphasis on individual responsibility and with the prophetic model of community building. It is also much more conducive to growth, integration, creativity, and scalability to better fit changing circumstances and needs.

In a way, to use the business analogy, rather than asking people to work for us and do something in the small, nonchallenging, and artificial environment of our community, we are encouraging them to become entrepreneurs and start their own business, to do what needs to be done, and to prove themselves in the real and competitive field—which is to say, in society at large.

Consistent with this inspiring and empowering individual/family-centered approach is our exposé of reality as is and our invitation to people to confront the brutal facts. This message of change and hope is a great departure from the prevailing depressing and/or soothing discourse.

Indeed, because our movement is about serving the mission and the nation and effecting the needed change (not about promoting an organization or impressing people and getting their support), we must tell people what they need to hear, not just what they want to hear.

Our approach dismisses the current protectionism. Instead, we urge more people to join in the mission, raise public awareness and concern, and enhance their own sense of responsibility. This approach will unlock more potential, and it will dig out more energy and creativity, in individuals, families, groups, and society.

Individuals and families who commit to the divine mission and buy into our vision and approach are urged to embark on a lifelong journey of (a) self-development and mentorship (which will naturally lead to family development), (b) social outreach and networking, and (c) civic engagement. These three tracks, which constitute the individual's primary duties and the practical translation of the mission, will be discussed next.

9- Geared to restore self-development and mentorship

Our community is in urgent need of fundamental change to become relevant so that we can make a significant and sustained contribution to the changes needed in society. Ultimately, though, a meaningful change starts within the individual. This requires individuals to embark on a journey of self-development and civic engagement to realize their full potential.

The key to the success of our movement project is the civically aware, concerned, and engaged citizen who cares for this country and its people and who constantly challenges himself/herself to contribute more to the greater good.

For Muslims—especially devout ones—in addition to citizenship, our emphasis is on Islam in general and the divine mission in particular. We define the divine mission as uplifting people and serving the greater good. So the strategies for success among Muslims include "selling" the mission and grooming mission-driven Muslims.

In all cases, when someone buys into the concept of concerned and active citizenship on religious or civic grounds, we want such a person to embark on the three processes of self-development/mentorship, social outreach, and civic engagement. That's how we may uplift ourselves and our people; and thus we can all serve our people and our country, and therefore fulfill the divine purpose. That is also how our project of Islamic revival/renewal, community renaissance, and societal reform can be carried out by Muslim Americans and others in a grassroots empowered manner.

Even though the three tracks run in parallel, the self-development component is the key to the success of the other two. Yet without the other two processes (social outreach and civic engagement), self-development may lose a lot of steam. In that event, self-development could become a futile and inefficient exercise with limited impact or no impact. Indeed, all three processes are very interconnected, and they are closely related to our commitment to the divine mission. Together they constitute the practical manifestation of that commitment, and they provide the tools to fulfill it. The entire construct constitutes the backbone of the Islamic paradigm, which we are trying to reconstruct through this project.

Because our project is individual/family centered, self-development and mentorship are critical to its success, as these uplifting processes will largely determine the fruitfulness of our social interaction and the effectiveness of our civic engagement.

Even though self-development is a universal concept that we will promote to all fellow citizens, we will present the Islamic perspective on self-development. That is simply because this book is primarily geared toward

Muslim Americans. However, most if not all nonreligious aspects of self-development apply equally to everybody.

Self-development is a mission-driven process that stems from the belief that God created us with a tremendous potential, which must be cultivated and realized. He assigned us a humongous mission that we must live up to and fulfill to the best of our abilities. Plus, God gave us divine guidance, and we must strive to fully and wholeheartedly embody that guidance.

Self-development is a comprehensive, continuous, balanced, and integrated process. It involves self-purification, self-improvement, and self-empowerment. Self-development makes a person ever stronger and more distinguished; and it is an individual responsibility. As you embark on this journey, your goals should be to (a) realize your God-given potential (be all you can be); (b) model your message (be the change, turn yourself into a role model); and (c) maximize your impact through social outreach and civic engagement. Indeed, self-development is about striving to become the best embodiment and instrument of God's will.

However, as has been the case with civic engagement, self-development has been functionally reduced in scope and depth to some sporadic, superficial/shallow, and purposeless activities with questionable effects. Some approaches taken toward personal development may have even produced negative effects, such as suppressing creativity, limiting aspirations, and producing an unbalanced and/or noncoherent personality. This defeats the whole purpose of personal development, which is meant to help people. Personal development should help us aspire highly and realize our full potential and prepare us to effectively engage in and impact on society. The fading of the concepts of personal development and civic engagement in our community should come as no surprise, simply because it is the natural and automatic result of the fading of the sense of mission among the vast majority of Muslims who have either abandoned the divine mission or equivocated it with "activism." In spite of the dedication and sacrifices of many activists, Islamic activism remains largely inconsistent and aimless, and its value and impact are limited.

Family development, which is an extension of self-development, simply means creating a conducive and empowering family atmosphere in which family members cooperate to realize the same objectives that personal development promotes: high aspirations, realization of our full potential, and preparation for effective engagement in (and impact on) society. This empowers family members, both individually and collectively (as a harmonious entity). This is the main duty of spouses and the main function of the family.

Mentorship is the forgotten prophetic tradition, even though it was the Prophet's main duty after conveying the message, as indicated in several places in the Qur'an. Mentorship is the extrapolation of the concept of family development to the community level. It is the process by which members of the community uplift one another and the community and help one another fulfill the individual and collective objectives of self-development. Mentorship is also the main duty of every generation toward the next one(s). Like family development, mentorship requires a favorable communal environment. Thus, everyone should strive to establish and maintain a safe, inclusive, and healthy communal environment.

Restoring the tradition of mentorship will help to make our interactions more fruitful and meaningful as learning opportunities, which in turn should help to draw us closer to one another. This will also enhance our relationships, our cohesion, and the quality of our social life.

Restoring the process of self-development, family development, and mentorship is a critical element of our project. As we try to commit people in general to America as a homeland and commit Muslims to Islam as a life mission, we will invite everyone to develop their families, find a mentor, and mentor others.

Self-development, family development, and mentorship feed into one another. Together, these activities constitute a synergetic cycle that turns individuals, families, and communities into role models of the message and the change – and into effective champions of the mission.

Only through this route may our project materialize in a significant and sustained way. Every attempt to short-circuit these processes is doomed to fail or achieve only short-lived success.

Finally, it is crucial to emphasize that while the family should enable the process of self-development, and the community should enable both self-development and family development, self-development is essentially an individual responsibility. Individuals should own up to their responsibility for their own development and for the development of their families. Plus, they should contribute their share to and take an active role in the mentorship process among the people around them.

10-Emphasizing social outreach and networking

After self-development and mentorship, this is the second but parallel track that we urge everyone who commits to Islam as a life mission and/ or to America as a homeland to embark upon. Social outreach/networking is critical both for societal reform and for community renaissance, simply because it ensures social cohesion. That social bonding, in turn, paves the way for citizens' cooperation for the greater good. Indeed, the more cohesive the society is, the healthier and stronger it is. And the more people know each other, the more they respect, support, and positively impact one another.

Social outreach/networking also paves the way for sharing and exchanging information, knowledge, and experiences. It creates opportunities for mutually beneficial cooperation. Moreover, citizens are usually civically engaged at different levels and in different domains. So social interaction will probably enhance the general population's civic awareness, concern, and engagement. This will create opportunities for cooperation in areas of common interest. Furthermore, because people tend to despise that which they don't know, maximizing social interaction is instrumental in combating bigotry and prejudices. This is very important, given the history of America and the great diversity of the American society.

In summary, maximizing social outreach is critical to the success of our project both through its direct positive effect on the society and the country and by enabling the processes of self-development (and family development and mentorship) and civic engagement. The point to remember is that social outreach and civic engagement are definitely among the keys to our success.

Given all these benefits of social outreach/interaction, it is no wonder the Qur'an tells us that God created us from one pair (male and a female) and made us into nations and tribes so that we may know one another.

> O mankind! We created you from a single (pair) of a male and a female, and made you into nations and tribes, that ye may know each other (not that ye may despise (each other). Verily the most honored of you in the sight of Allah is (he who is) the most righteous of you. And Allah has full knowledge and is well acquainted (with all things). [Qur'an 49:13].

The verse says that humanity constitutes one family and that one purpose of human diversity is for people to get to know each other.

The Constitution guarantees Muslims the same rights as everyone else, including the right to proselytize. However, social outreach has nothing to do with proselytizing and trying to convert people. We do not oppose proselytizing, if it is done correctly with relevant discourse; but we do have serious reservations about some of the current in-your-face approaches that tend to turn people off and reinforce public skepticism about Islam. Again, we emphasize, conversion is not the objective of this project, and our approach to social outreach is humane and civic, not religious. We need to reach out to people around us and treat them as dignified human beings and fellow citizens, or as our brothers and sisters in humanity and in citizenship. We are not going to limit our audience and membership to Muslims (never mind to observant Muslims), nor are we going to try to convert non-Muslims.

Our objective is to enhance social cohesion and cooperation for the greater good by enhancing mutual understanding and respect, both in society at large and in our immediate environment (neighborhood, workplace, and pertinent civic communities/groups). We want to connect with people in those circles, and we want to contribute to the bonding of these groups together. We want the champions of this movement to become social magnets.

Active social networking is very important to societal reform, as it helps to reverse the endemic selfishness, individualism, and social disconnection among people. Networking can also undo the rapid decrease we have seen in caring, solidarity, and compassion in our society.

It is true that America became the envy of the world largely because of Americans' rogue individualism and self-reliance. If individualism is paired with consumerism and carried too far, however, things are apt to backfire. That's how you get the "me-first" psychology that we see too often today.

While we realize that each one of us will end up connected to people at different levels of the spectrum of relationships, we want to keep nurturing existing relationships and building new ones to expand and solidify our social network.

In our social interaction, we want to focus on commonalities and areas of common interest. We want to make those relationships and interactions as fruitful and meaningful as possible, and we want to gear them to enhance the quality of our lives. Our social interactions and relationships can and should enhance our civic awareness, concern, and engagement. They should, therefore, facilitate our individual and collective contribution to the greater good.

The question that one may ask is: "So what about *dawa*?" The answer is very simple. If *dawa* means inviting people to that which is good and presenting Islam in the best possible way, rather than being defined as "converting people," then social outreach and networking is *dawa* or at least is the best approach to *dawa*.

Indeed, Islam is intended to serve people's best interests in this life and in the hereafter. So inviting people to Islam means inviting them to take part in what we believe is good for them in this life and in the hereafter. Of course, in this very diverse society, Islam is hardly a commonality; and in fact, faith in general cannot even be viewed as a commonality. Because faith is a sensitive matter in America, we should keep our outreach interactions social and civil. We should focus on our mutual interests and concerns and on contemporary events at all levels and on what we could and should do to make our world a better place.

As part of our mutual understanding, we may want to learn about each other's faith. Beyond that, however, we should avoid talking about faith unless someone shows interest and curiosity. And then we should talk about our faith in the right way: spontaneously, nonintrusively, noncondescendingly, and nonexcessively. We should educate without aiming to convert.

So from our perspective, *dawa* means inviting people to that which is good for them (and for the country) in this life and in the hereafter. Because of the diverse nature of society (especially in the current reality), inviting people to goodness should be through civic (nonreligious) discourse that focuses on mundane issues of common concern and mutual interest.

Some Muslims may elect to preach Islam as a religion through missionary work of a sort. However, the best way to promote Islam is through exemplary conduct, decent and honest social interaction, and significant contribution to the greater good. That's why we focus on the three tracks: self-development, social outreach, and civic engagement. The outcome of this approach should always be good for America and good for Islam. If in the process, someone becomes interested in learning about Islam, we should respond to their curiosity in the right way and in the right dose. This is true irrespective of whether the person is just curious or is considering conversion. If someone decides to convert, we should welcome him or her and integrate them into our community/movement without acculturation and without disconnecting them from their (natural) environment.

Our goal is to uplift ourselves and our people and to better our country. This will automatically make our religion and our community relevant and respected.

11- Committed to spreading and deepening a tradition of civic engagement

Our community needs to become not only much more inclusive to all Muslim Americans but also much more rooted in society. Indeed, with an ambivalent identity and without any sense of common mission, this community has been built on isolation and exclusiveness. We have been unwilling and unable to open up to American society. The isolation has been reinforced by the "myth of return," our traditional lack of civic engagement, our intimidation by isolationist groups—and also by some disturbing misconceptions we have had about Islam and about America.

There have always been some timid outreach efforts and some political participation. Such efforts expanded beginning in the mid-'90s and especially after 9/11. However, our outreach efforts continue to be sporadic, and they lack purpose and substance. They are conducted mostly as a routine activity, or even as a necessary defense mechanism to protect the community and defend its image. So we are still in the same paradigm of protection through isolation, except that the protection of our community after 9/11 required some outreach efforts. It is no wonder that we are doing only as much as necessary, and sometimes only halfheartedly.

Up to this point, the vast majority of people in our community have remained socially isolated and civically disengaged. Efforts to open up and reach out do exist, but they certainly require a lot of upgrading and evolution if they are ever going to take root in most of our people's minds and psyches. There is much to be done if we are to experience genuine, meaningful, and sustained civic engagement. This is the change that we aspire to effect: to root the tradition of civic engagement in our community and make it a spontaneous, passionate, and consistent process that stems from genuine patriotism and/or from a commitment to the divine mission.

Our outreach and civic engagement efforts should be an integral part of our fulfillment of the divine mission and should aim at serving the greater good. Although we do need some institutions to empower people, civic engagement shouldn't be left to institutions—or to the few individuals who are passionate about it. Rather, all members of our community should be encouraged and empowered to reach out to people around them and to volunteer and support good causes. We should also engage our local governments and communicate with the media and religious institutions and participate in civic society.

Because our community's isolation has been reinforced for so long, a considerable degree of work is needed to effect a paradigm shift. We need to move (1) from protective isolationism to empowered integration and civic engagement, and (2) from the concept of outreach as a controversial religious matter or a necessary burden for the few toward a new realization that civic engagement is a religious and civic duty for everyone and the thrust of the divine mission.

Self-development is the best translation of *tazkiya*. Social outreach/ networking is the best translation of *dawa*. And civic engagement is the best translation of the concept of enjoining that which is good and forbidding that which is evil, a concept that encapsulates the defining mission and characteristic of the community of believers. Combined, the three processes should constitute the fulcrum of the life of the mission-driven and compassionate patriot. Through these three processes, we better ourselves, our people, and our country. Thus, we fulfill the divine purpose, and that is the way to seek God's pleasure and rewards. There is hardly anything that has more (direct) effect on society and hardly anything that is a better indicator of societal health than the level of civic awareness, concern, and engagement of a nation's citizenry. The same thing could be said about the community. That's why enhancing the civic awareness, concern, and engagement of citizens (including Muslims) is a cardinal objective of our project, both in the short run (when we may focus more on Muslims) and in the long run (when we will reach out to all citizens).

Our approach to civic engagement calls for direct, genuine, mainstream, and consistent engagement with our sociopolitical environment so that we can uphold the best interests of our country at all levels (local, state, national). This civic engagement is divided into two main branches: (1) charitable work to help the victims of unfair and/or unsound policies and also to help the victims of both natural and man-made disasters and (2) advocacy work to reform unfair and/or unsound policies and to hold public officials accountable.

The first type of engagement, charitable work to help victims of natural or man-made disasters, is a manifestation of the great emphasis that Islam places on charity, and it allows us to put our concern and compassion for others to work. A culture of giving (time, money, and expertise) toward the greater good must be instituted within our community. To be sure, such a culture already exists in our community, but it is neither widespread nor consistent. Plus, our charity efforts are either confined to our own community (mosques, schools, Muslim organizations) or overseas (relief work). That's why we believe that our charity efforts need a lot of reinforcement and tweaking to focus on the well-being of the society at large, including our community.

The second type of civic engagement, advocacy work to improve policies and hold officials accountable, will have a great bearing on the political climate of our society. By advocacy, we mean making connections with different components of our environment and society at large (politics, media, religious/civic groups) to positively influence policies, social norms, and public opinion. Indeed, the more active our citizens are, the more responsive and responsible the political arena will be. In turn, a more positive political climate encourages more participation from citizens. The opposite is also true and is, unfortunately, indicative of the current state of our society. Here is the good news: what has spiraled downward can now spiral upward.

For all those reasons, civic engagement constitutes the main thrust of the paradigm that we are trying to restore. It is the reflection and translation of our commitment to Islam as a reform mission and to America as a homeland, and it is where the two commitments converge. The more genuine and solid our commitments are, the more passionate, intensive, and consistent our civic engagement will be.

Indeed, our civic engagement rests on rock-solid religious and civic bases that are fused together, compelling us religiously and patriotically to faithfully serve our country and our people, day in and day out. The central idea backing it must be a firm belief that the more we contribute to a better America, the more pleased God will be with us and the better will be our present and future—both as individuals and as a community.

Driven by an inspiring faith and a genuine citizenship, the civic engagement that we advocate has very little in common with the type of outreach and civic engagement currently preached in our community. The current brand of activism is largely driven by a minority mind-set and a sense of victimization. That's why the "outreach" to date has been largely reactionary, defensive, erratic, superficial, inconsistent, and inconsequential; and it is why the prevalent self-centered rhetorical approach and discourse constantly swing between expressions of anger and apologetics.

Our brand of revitalized civic engagement involves the implementation of the concepts of *tadaafu'* (which literally means engagement) and enjoining that which is good and forbidding that which is evil. All Qur'anic verses and Hadiths that implicitly or explicitly call for the fulfillment of those duties, and/or warn against a failure to do so, combine together to mandate our civic engagement. They also warn against civic disengagement.

Because civic engagement is one of the noble Islamic concepts, but one that has become distorted or diluted through superficial imitations, it is important to clearly define our perspective on it. We need to know what civic engagement is and what it is not. Following are some of the main characteristics of the civic engagement that we are advocating:

- **Genuine**: It must be driven by a genuine concern for the well-being of our country and our people. It must not be a mere tactical maneuver. The civic engagement we advocate requires putting national interests first, and it involves serving our country and the American people (insofar as those interests are moral, legitimate, and not at the expense of other people or future generations). It calls upon us to serve honorably and energetically, even when no one gives us credit for our efforts and even when our sincerity and loyalty are questioned.

- **Mainstream:** It must be an engagement within mainstream America. That means (1) we are engaged as citizens, not as a victimized minority; (2) we are engaged within the framework of the Constitution, in the context of the secular state, in association with pluralistic society, and, of course, in accordance with the rule of law; (3) we are concerned about and involved in all issues that affect the nation (not just our community); and (4) we direct our discourse to all citizens, and so our message must be relevant to and comprehensible by all segments of society.

- **Direct:** Because our civic engagement is about society at large (not just the Muslim American community), we don't need to operate as a minority block or to go through a Muslim organization. Therefore, as faithful citizens, we should be directly engaged with mainstream civic institutions that work on behalf of all citizens, not just with Muslim institutions that work only on behalf of Muslims. Currently, only a few members of our community are civically engaged, and most of those few understand civic engagement to comprise nothing more than joining or supporting a Muslim public affairs organization, and possibly answering its action alerts. The whole paradigm, up until now, has been driven by a minority and victimization mind-set.

- *About giving not gaining:* Our civic engagement will focus on what we can contribute to society, not what we can get from it.

- *Proactive, systematic, and consistent:* Our efforts must not be reactionary or seasonal.

- *Islam inspired and principled, but also civic and pragmatic*: Our platform and our positions will be informed by our faith and principles, but they will be expressed using purely civic language. We will seek what is possible, not what is desired but untenable. For instance, our movement desires to see our nation freed of many detrimental behaviors. Our faith prohibits them, and they are indisputably harmful for those who indulge in them and for the society at large. We will not hesitate to express our own position to educate the public about the potential harms of such behaviors or to advocate against them. However, we will only demand what is possible, and we will do that through civic discourse, not by promulgating religious dogma. Some of those harmful behaviors are private on one level, but they become a matter of public concern on another level. We will focus on eliminating (or at least limiting) detrimental social effects without interfering with individuals' liberty and privacy.

- *Supportive of liberty and justice for all*: We will uphold the constitutional guarantee of liberty and justice for all. This is a potentially sensitive matter that deserves special attention. While we will seek to positively influence people's choices, social norms, and government policies through our civic engagement, we will never infringe on individual freedom and privacy. We should also resist any attempt by government to infringe on those rights except when the exercise of such freedom is irresponsible or illegal or when the exercise of such freedom inflicts harm on others or on society at large.

Islam commands that there should be no compulsion in religion; therefore, no behaviors should be forced upon people. We will strive to establish justice for everyone in America and to help level the playing field in all domains (social, economic, political). In particular, we will advocate for a living wage for all workers and a dignified life—with all basic human needs being met for all citizens. Justice in Islam is defined as giving everyone his/her due. Because justice encompasses most other virtues, it is considered to be the master virtue. The establishment of justice is so fundamental in Islam that God sent messengers with revelations for that purpose. Moreover, He instructs believers to stand out firmly for justice for all people in all circumstances. That is God's command and purpose, and thus it is our mission. It is unfitting for Muslims to seek justice only for themselves or to adhere to double standards in the matter.

- **Results Driven:** Our civic engagement will be results driven—not ceremonial or aimed at showcasing ourselves. In contrast to the prevalent attitude among Muslim activists and organizations that disavow responsibility for obtaining positive results, we will take full responsibility, hold ourselves accountable, and urge others to hold us accountable for results. We will not be in denial, nor will we look for excuses or scapegoats (such as conspiracy theories or the frequently abused Islamic concept of divine destiny) to justify our failures. We will not whine, and we will not feel victimized. Our resolve will not be shaken by our setbacks; we will just learn whatever lesson we are to learn, pick ourselves up, dust off, and move on. We are definitely not "in it for a photo-op," and we will not be "happy just to be there." Indeed, we are in it to win it—to do our best to ensure that the things we believe will benefit our country do prevail and that those things that are harmful are eliminated, even as we always play by the rules and accept the outcome. And while we may not win the Super Bowl or the World Series, we're not going to settle for just playing—or even being in the playoffs. We want to make progress, even if it is only partial progress or is delimited as a result of some compromising.

- **Coalition based:** Because of the nature of American society and the U.S. political system, few agendas or campaigns come to fruition without a reasonably broad coalition backing them. Therefore, in our civic engagement, we will actively seek to join and build coalitions in order to advocate our positions.

- **Country focused and issue oriented:** In our civic engagement, our focus will be on what is best for America and its future. In pursuing the best interests of America, we will be bound only by our values, by the law (American and international), and by our concern for human welfare. In other words, we want the greatest possible accomplishments for America, but they should not be achieved through illegitimate or immoral or illegal means, and they should not come at the expense of future generations. This will put us—every now and then—at odds with some Muslim countries or groups and will always put us at odds with any and all Muslim groups that aim to destroy America. At home here in America, we should expect that various Muslim citizens and groups may well be on different sides of a given issue, and we may be supporting different propositions, parties, or candidates. This is simply because we have different perspectives on what is best for America, or because some of us are community centered, not country focused. Plus, there will always be differences in how to best understand and implement and translate our faith and how to best serve our country. That's perfectly okay.

    Being country-focused will automatically make us issue oriented. Advocating issues is not about supporting or opposing people or parties or groups. Indeed, in deciding whom to support, whom to oppose, or whom to work with, our focus will be on what is best for America. We will not be driven by emotions. For instance, we will not support a Muslim or even a Muslim-friendly candidate against another candidate who is more competent and/or has a better agenda for America. On the other hand, we will not hesitate to work on a particular issue with individuals and groups whom we may not "like" and/or with whom we are at odds concerning some other issues. By getting people of differing opinions to link arms on issues of common concern, coalitions are able to make positive change.

- **Focused on local and pertinent issues:** Currently, most Muslim Americans are well informed about international issues. They spend quite a lot of time following and talking about those issues without doing much about them, except for making occasional contributions to relief efforts and/or participating in protest activities. Only a very few Muslim Americans are interested, much less involved, in domestic, state, or local issues—especially when those issues don't directly affect our community.

We want to reverse this paradigm because "all politics are local." All of us should focus the bulk of our efforts on engaging the system and the players (public officials, media, political parties, civic/religious groups) in our districts, cities, states, and nation. The bottom-up approach is not just the natural way, but it is also the only way to effect significant and sustained (short-term and long-term) impact.

- *Focused on what is hot while building momentum for what is important:* We are not a special-interest group. Therefore, in our civic engagement, we should encourage people to do their best to be informed about all issues while becoming involved (as they see fit) in those issues that are of high priority. In addition to giving precedence to local issues, we should try to be in sync with national concerns and aware of public opinion. And while we should always give priority to issues that have the greatest impact on the nation's well-being and future, it is critical that we maintain a balance between short-term and long-term interests and between what is chronically important and what is urgently pressing. This is partly because the effectiveness of our efforts depends on our ability to influence public opinion, a task that is usually much easier when people are attentive.

12-Focused on developing human and financial resources and on inspiring and empowering

Because our movement is individual and family centered, it is only natural that our focus will be on developing human resources rather than on developing facilities and programs (as has been done). We will concentrate on inspiring and empowering our fellow community members and citizens to do the job, rather than on supporting our organizations and/or a few activists to do it for them. Instead of treating people as passive spectators, consumers, or supporters, our approach is designed to inspire and empower individuals and communities. To that end, we will also build the needed empowering institutions (including financial institutions).

Financial development is needed not only to empower individuals and communities financially but also to build the necessary institutions to inspire and empower individuals to fulfill the mission and champion this renaissance project. This is the only way to break through our current stalemate. Our situation right now is due not only to lack of vision and leadership but also due to the fact that the current firefighting mode of operations has alienated most Muslim Americans who might otherwise have shared their talent and resources to benefit the greater good. We have also inefficiently utilized the limited resources that have been available. As a result, this mode of operations has "run its course" and has reached its ceiling, both in terms of its goals and means. It is no wonder that we are largely stagnant and spinning our wheels.

Among the keys to the success of our movement is the individual/family. Thus, a good deal of our efforts and resources should be spent on inspiring and empowering the individual/family throughout all the stages of the life cycle. Everything else, including organizations, buildings, and so forth, should be pursued and developed as needed but should be regarded as supporting tools and avenues, not as substitutes for the individual/family or as ends in and of themselves. This approach, however, does require the establishment of several institutions to inspire and empower people and communities.

Financial development to empower individuals and families to fulfill our mission is critical for the success of our movement. Our individuals, families, and communities can't do but so much if they are struggling financially. Also, in order to be effective, institutions require adequate and stable financial resources. Moving our community from its current maintenance of the status quo into real growth and impact necessitates a shift. We need to move from the firefighting mode toward a more systematic and planned approach. That will require direct and indirect assistance from strong financial institutions.

By "financial development," we mean building financial institutions that will directly and indirectly help communities and individuals. Our efforts will include coaching people regarding existing opportunities and resources so they can achieve financial stability and independence. Thus, these financial institutions will encourage and empower communities and individuals to grow constantly.

Human and financial resource development will be important for the community's successful growth and integration. We should establish institutions that focus on building and networking the talents that are needed. We will also work to motivate young people and give them incentives to specialize in the needed fields at the best universities.

13-Designed to confront our crisis and effect the urgent and fundamental change

This project is mission driven and country focused, not just crisis driven or community centered. Nevertheless, it is built on a thorough diagnosis that led us to the conclusion that our community and our country are both in a serious crisis that calls for urgent and structural change.

Our approach calls for confronting the crisis and tracing and tackling its root causes. Moreover, we believe that the crisis is of our own doing because of what we did and what we failed to do. Therefore, we should own up to our responsibility for the crisis and also to our responsibility for fixing it and effecting the needed change. This is a major departure from the prevailing attitude that is characterized by denial, patching, scapegoating, victimization, excuses, and conspiracy theory. These denial tactics constitute one of the main reasons why we are largely stagnant and why we continue to do the same thing, irrespective of the results.

As we reject this self-deceiving attitude, we equally reject any depressing approach. We just believe in the simple medical logic that says proper diagnosis leads to effective treatment, and the sooner the better. Likewise, confronting and diagnosing our crisis, tackling its root causes, and owning up to our responsibility are absolutely required actions if we want to get out of the crisis. Another reason we are not afraid to confront our crisis is that we have conditioned ourselves so that the depth and complexity of our crisis will only fuel our hope, our resolve, and our sense of urgency. Our confidence and determination are based on two matters of faith. First, we are relying on God and are just aspiring to be instruments of His will. Second, we have an unshakable belief in the potential and future of our country and our community. That was the attitude that the companions adopted at the most difficult junctures in the early years of Islam. It worked then, and it will work now.

14-Focused on youth and on the future

Acknowledging that our community is in a crisis because of our own doing should inevitably steer us away from trying to patch and fix our current state of affairs, and it should direct us instead toward planting the seeds for a better future. Of course, our future is synonymous with our youth; so while this movement will devote considerable effort to human resource development in general, priority will be given to the younger generations.

We are now reaping the fruits of what we have sown in the past. If we want to experience real change and shape a better future, we must start planting the "right" seeds now. This involves inspiring and empowering young people to assume as much responsibility and leadership as they are willing to take—so that the next generation can tackle our strategic and intellectual issues. Our community institutions must focus on motivating young people and providing training opportunities and incentives that encourage them to specialize in the needed fields and at the best universities. At this stage of our journey, we should be eager to pass the torch on to these people who embody our future.

Because our crisis is so deep and complex, with so many interconnected facets and roots, and because we missed the train and did not keep up with changes, we are left with only one option: We must chart a new course and a new beginning for our future and our youth, even as we try to maintain the ongoing operations and sort out our experience. The prevailing paradigm is simply too entrenched and too overstretched to allow for any change or growth, much less a renaissance. We concur with President Obama's 2008 campaign statements[49] expressing the belief that our country needs to undergo a process of remaking, and we believe that also applies, and quite obviously, to our community. Whether we are talking about remaking the country or the community, though, such a process should not be expected to be easy or smooth. Times have changed, and the opportunities for easy transition have passed. However, by confronting the brutal facts and planning appropriately for the future, we will be able to make the right and tough decisions, and to do so in a timely way. That is how we can begin to keep up with change.

In pursuing the renaissance of our community, we must make sure that

---

49   President Barack Obama. February 5, 2008. [Speech]. "Change will not come if we wait for some other person or some other time. We are the ones we've been waiting for. We are the change that we seek."

it is done with minimum possible disruption and maximum gains preserved and carried over. We are calling on our community to cooperate to make the transition as smooth as possible as we embark on two parallel tracks: (1) charting a new course and (2) maintaining ongoing operations. This is because both tracks are required, and they need to overlap during the transition. The best possible outcome is in the best interest of everybody. A selfless cooperation that puts the interests of the country and the community above any individual or organizational consideration is what God commands and expects from us.

On the other hand, if we slide into mutual attack and sabotage, we all lose, both in this life and in the hereafter. Human nature and history in general and our history and culture in particular do not give us any reason to be very optimistic about avoiding mission-ending conflict among ourselves. We can only hope, pray, and do everything we can in an effort to avoid such a slide. We cannot afford to be in a position to choose between stagnation and confrontation (self-destruction).

Our movement project is a humble but serious attempt to develop a vision for the future and smoothly transition to it and to sort out our experience and legacy to pass on to future generations. We want to offer future generations maximum gains and lessons learned, but minimum baggage and liability (and hurdles and shackles). This involves inspiring and empowering young people to take charge; and again, we should be eager to pass on to them as much responsibility and leadership as they are willing to take.

In addition to shifting the focus of our community from futile activities to mission, from shallow education to empowering inspiration, and from inward insularity and overseas obsession to a new American patriotism, we also want to shift the attention of our community from the past and the present to the future. Currently, people are hostage to their past and are consumed by managing the status quo and "putting out fires." At the top of the chain of command, there are managers who come and go and who believe their job is essentially to maintain the status quo. Many of these people are already exhausted and burnt out. There is hardly any attempt at strategic thinking or strategic planning, and our community is largely led by managers and speakers who are not equipped to develop the vision and the message. Our community needs to produce people who are able to effectively tackle our intellectual and strategic issues. We need to upgrade the skills of our managers and speakers. We must also establish a solid two-way connection between those who deal with the future and those who handle the day-today operations. That's how master plans are developed, implemented, and constantly adjusted with a reasonable level of continuity.

We aspire to get our community and its institutions to be driven by the divine mission, committed to—and focused on—America, and guided by an expansive and integrated vision for the future of our country. This naturally includes a vision for the future of our Muslim American community.

We should transition away from the "status quo-maintenance" mode of operations that relies on activities, meetings, and crisis management. We must move, instead, toward a mode of operations that focuses on the development, implementation, and adjustment of a vision with a clear timeline and performance indicators. If this new approach includes close monitoring of the environment and frequent scenario analysis, it will help in dealing with issues proactively and preventing them from turning into crises that derail our progress and squander our resources. Moreover, proactively or not, our approach should aim at dealing with root causes and resolving issues, not just containing and suppressing them. Currently, we are doing almost the opposite. We duck issues until they blow up in our faces; and when they do blow up, we rush to contain them instead of resolving them. The minutes and reports of our local and national organizations speak volumes about our mode of operation, and these documents confirm the need for fundamental change in our approach.

15-Emphasizes the spiritual, intellectual, strategic, and civic dimensions

One reason our community is largely stuck is that we have fallen into the activity trap, and we mistakenly consider activities to be actual accomplishments. Plus, we have confined our activism to our community—or more precisely to a small segment of our community—which constitutes a small and noncompetitive "market."

So irrespective of relevance or impact, activism has become an objective in and of itself; and most activists and organizations have a low ceiling and limited aspirations. They are struggling to keep things going; and some are vying for a bigger share in that small market or to be the big fish in that small pond. When the status quo becomes our highest calling, we should be very concerned about our future.

This "routine maintenance activism" is disconnected from both sides of the spectrum. On one hand, it is not mission driven and does not rest on strong spiritual, intellectual, or strategic foundations. On the other hand, it is not results driven and does not lead to any civic empowerment or leadership. No wonder it is neither purposeful nor impactful. It is largely activism for the sake of activism. It is so addictive and confining that the most activists hope for is to organize more activities, bigger activities, or better activities – irrespective of relevance or impact. All of this lacks a clear sense of direction, and it is devoid of clear vision and strategy. There are no clear performance indicators. Plus, it is all happening within a paradigm that long ago became exhausted and reached its low ceiling. It is long overdue that we admit that our spiritual, intellectual, and strategic weaknesses could not be fixed by any overdose of activism. We must begin to clearly distinguish between activities and accomplishments and to evaluate activities based on relevance, growth, advancement of the cause and service of the greater good.

We should realize by now that more elaborate bylaws, more frequent meetings, and/or more activities will not remedy our lack of a shared vision, our shortage of intellectual and interpersonal harmony, nor the community's deficiencies in trust and character.

For all these reasons, we built our movement project on a very strong spiritual, intellectual, and strategic foundation, and we are focusing our efforts on civic empowerment/leadership in order to better serve our cause and our country.

We will only contemplate and implement those actions that fit naturally into this paradigm. Our approach is purposeful, relevant, and impactful. We will always be on the lookout for new and creative ways to advance our cause. We will constantly revisit and scrutinize our programs and methodologies, and we will keep only what is working. The rest need to be fixed, upgraded, or simply discarded. Means are not meant to be constant, and they should not become hindrances. And means should never be mistaken for goals.

In our project, only the essentials of our faith and our guiding principles are permanently fixed. Everything else will remain a living document, always open to crystallization, modification, and upgrading.

Rather than resorting to elaborate and cumbersome structures to ensure discipline and control operations, a strategy that has proved futile elsewhere, we will focus on instilling and nurturing a clear and shared vision and on creating and maintaining an atmosphere that is spiritually vibrant, morally sound, and socially warm. We will employ a simple and flexible but effective organizational structure as needed. Our clear, swift, and participatory decision-making process will ensure decisiveness and discipline.

In this context, we will be very inclusive; and our operations will be very flexible without compromising clarity, agility, decisiveness, discipline, or the tenets and advancement of our project. It is the centralization of our vision and strategy that must be maintained—not the management of an organization.

In brief, our movement will rely more on people than on paperwork. We will focus on the foundations (spiritual, intellectual, strategic), and we will be aware of our goals and committed to them: mission, impact, and relevance. We are very flexible about the means of achieving our goals, as long as they are legal, ethical, mission directed, and in line with our foundations.

16- Determined to support faithful citizenship—not to embody victimized minority status

In carrying out this project, we will think, talk, plan, and work as faithful citizens, not as a victimized minority. Our focus will, first and foremost, be on what is best for the nation and on what we can contribute to its betterment, not on what is best for our community and ourselves and what we can gain from society. By so doing, we will automatically serve the best interests of our community in this life and in the hereafter. This is because what is good for the nation as a whole is good for all of its parts. The opposite is not always true. It is also because the betterment of our society is our divinely assigned mission.

This shift of attitude may require some extra effort with, and on the part of, the older generations (both immigrants and African Americans) for reasons discussed elsewhere in this book. Some are so ambivalent about America that they still doubt whether we can be civically engaged/involved in this country and even whether we should wish for (never mind work for) the well-being of America. As a matter of fact, a good chunk of the younger generation, and converts too, may also need some rehabilitation. Regardless of age group and regardless of how we came to Islam, it is clear that self-definition as members of a victimized minority, or even as Muslims who just happen to live in America, is a "no-win" proposition. One main goal and requirement of this project is to phase out the victimized minority mind-set. Our future generations and converts should define themselves, not as victims, but instead as Americans who chose Islam as their faith and source of inspiration. This is the only way we can remain true to the bases and goals of our project: commitment to Islam as a life mission of reform and to America as our homeland. We may still be counted as members of a minority, but for us, this is our homeland, and all American citizens are our people. And when it comes to loyalty and contribution to our country and caring for our people, we don't concede to anybody, and second place is not an option. We are not concerned about being treated as first-class or second-class citizens. Our focus is on constantly pushing and challenging ourselves to make the biggest possible contribution to the greater good.

17- Geared to encourage direct and expansive engagement of our natural environment

Even though this aspect was discussed under civic engagement, it is included here because it applies to the whole project as well. First, let us be clear about what we mean by "natural environment." Each citizen belongs to a variety of natural, sociopolitical groups. All Americans have relationships in different contexts and settings: their families, neighborhoods, workplaces, professional communities, religious communities, friends, civic organizations, cities, counties, states, and the country at large. We belong in all these circles, and therefore we need to engage them all, and we need to do that as frequently and as robustly as possible. That's why in our project, rather than snatching people from their own natural environments and creating artificial enclaves for them, we will inspire and empower them to directly engage their natural environment. In that way, people can effect positive changes in the various settings in which they live and work. Direct engagement, here, means straightforward interaction through existing societal institutions. We choose this path primarily because we don't think of ourselves as a minority worrying about its rights, and therefore our civic engagement is not dependent upon facilitation by some extra layer of minority-based organizations. Other than organizations to meet the specific religious needs of Muslims, we should avoid establishing exclusive Muslim organizations, especially if the goal is to engage the entire society.

Because we have lagged behind in transitioning to a mission-driven, country-focused community, we may have to build some Muslim organizations to help Muslims catch up in terms of integration and to inspire and empower them. Making the shift from self-perceived "victimized minority status" to one of being faithful American citizens could, indeed, be facilitated if Muslim Americans had access to organizations that were better designed for the task. The more effective such organizations become, however, the less needed they will be. Eventually, then, they should either be phased out or, better yet, they should evolve to become mainstream and inclusive institutions that constitute Muslim American contributions to our overall society.

Even the charters of our existing Islamic centers and schools should be changed. While continuing to fulfill their fundamental religious function and serve their congregations, they should become springboards for engagement and change, as opposed to enclaves of isolation for our protection from society. They should concentrate on inspiring and empowering people to be exemplary and to engage their fellow citizens in their natural environment. Moreover, Islamic centers should, as institutions, strive to engage their own sociopolitical environment, and they should uphold contribution to the greater good as a guiding priority.

It is partly in order to pull Muslim institutions in this direction and get them on board for societal engagement that we will engage our local Muslim communities. The American Muslim institution (mosque, school, etc.) is one of the important components of our environment, and its isolation has been detrimental for everyone. We do this, of course, in parallel with our direct engagement of other societal components.

18-Focused on relevance and results-driven efforts and measured by impact

In contrast to the prevalent attitude among Muslim activists and organizations that disavow responsibility for results, our efforts are results driven. We take full responsibility, hold ourselves accountable, and urge other people to hold us accountable for results. We will look neither for excuses nor for scapegoats to justify failure. We will never be in denial, nor do we blame anyone but ourselves. That is what Islam teaches us. And that is also what the prophetic community learned the hard way.

We will not resort to the true but widely abused Islamic concepts of divine destiny (*qadr*) and trial and tribulation (*ibtilaa*) to justify failure. We will never resort to conspiracy theory or blame our opponents for doing their homework.

Those attitudes that we are rejecting account, to a great extent, for the widespread complacency, low aspirations, and lack of resolve in our community. By denying our own responsibility for our shortcomings and failures, we guarantee that our crisis is neither acknowledged nor confronted, and that our future is up in the air. That is not surprising because the community is led by activists, many of whom don't have what it takes to lead, have low aspirations, disavow responsibility for results, are struggling to keep the status quo, and are always ready to justify any failure. Following leadership like that has brought us exactly where we are.

Through this movement project, we will strive to make everything we do relevant; and we will evaluate our work, not by how many activities and meetings we have, nor by the impact we have within our movement or even our community, but by the movement's impact on society at large.

Even in our understanding and implementation of Islam, we will always seek relevance without compromising authenticity and the essentials. This distinguishes us from some Muslim groups who are very adamant about authenticity of the texts but who make no effort to understand or implement them in a relevant way.

19-Designed as a movement—not an organization

Ever since Islam came to America, our community and its leaders have been mostly thinking in terms of organizations, activities, and buildings. Traditionally, in our community, whenever we've gotten together, it has been to establish an Islamic center or school, organize some type of activity, and/ or incorporate an organization. In the absence of a compelling mission and expansive vision, those tools have become ends in and of themselves; and activists' utmost dreams have been to maintain—or possibly improve and expand—their organization, activities, or facility. So the schools and centers struggle financially and organizationally to keep things going. Oftentimes, the organizational bylaws, many of which are gridlocked, become quasi-sacred—the most important and talked about matters, as if the only things bringing people together were the creation, interpretation, amendment, and enforcement of bylaws. Indeed, the leadership of many organizations conduct themselves as a supreme court whose job is to ensure compliance with the bylaws irrespective of anything else.

This state of affairs is very disturbing because bylaws are meant to facilitate, not hinder, the operation of the organization. An organization should be nothing more than a tool to serve the mission. Another disturbing issue with the current mode of operations is the nature of our organizations' membership, which tends to be either exclusive or meaningless. This should not come as a surprise because most existing organizations are service providers; and oftentimes their "owners" are obsessed with control. They provide services to a largely passive audience that pays for the services through dues and donations.

This model has contributed a good deal to the alienation and stagnation within our community, and we are determined to reverse it. This is why our project is mission driven not activity oriented. Ours is also a country-focused societal reform project; and therefore, it is not Muslim-community centered, much less organization centered.

We are not promoting an organization that recruits members to participate in activities. Rather, we are working to build our movement by rallying individuals, mosques, and organizations around our divine mission, which we want them to support and fulfill by directly engaging with their sociopolitical environment. There is nothing to control, so there is no control to worry about. Plus, we are not asking anyone for anything. We are aiming to reach out to a maximum number of people and instill within them a sense of mission and responsibility. We want to unlock their potential, raise the bar of their aspirations, and inspire and empower them to fulfill the mission and effect change. We invite them to do that through existing mainstream institutions and/or by establishing their own mainstream and inclusive organizations or forums. It is the number of such people and their impact and contribution to the greater good that will measure the success of our movement. Any institution that we build is designed to support and empower those individuals to do the job in their environments.

Currently, in the absence of a rallying cause and clear expansive vision, members of our community are clustered around their Islamic centers and Muslim and/or ethnic organizations. This largely explains our fragmentation and, to some extent, our stagnation.

We hope that our community will be receptive to our approach, even though it may wake them up from a nice dream and put them in charge and therefore may cause them some discomfort. However, there is no other way to chart a course for a better future. Plus, we are in this business to do what needs to be done, not to impress people, much less to deceive them.

Undeniably, this project has its designers and owners who will seek to steer it in the right direction, but this will be done through leadership, mentorship and dissemination of the vision, not through tight control, rigid organizations, exclusive membership, or organizational gimmicks.

Ultimately, our movement will take the shape of a broad-based coalition/ network of individuals, affiliate organizations, and partners. It will be loose in structure but clear and firm in its vision and message.

Muhammad built a movement—not an organization—and we believe that our approach is much closer to the prophetic model than is the prevailing approach. That prevailing approach has resulted in a largely stagnant and very fragmented community, has alienated most Muslim Americans, and has disconnected organizations and groups.

Moreover, our approach offers a practical pathway and mechanism to achieve a meaningful unity, which is a highly cherished concept in Islam and in our community. Ironically, unity is something that people keep talking about and cherishing, even as the community becomes more and more fragmented.

20-Based on inclusiveness

In order to fulfill our gigantic mission and boundless vision, in order to build a movement (not another owner-controlled, noninclusive organization), and in order to meet the needs of our great and diverse community and nation, we can only be inclusive. Ultimately, we seek participation and involvement from all American citizens. Our diversity is marvelously multidimensional along the lines of gender, age, ethnicity, faith, schools of thought, levels of religious devotion, and political affiliation. As was the case with the prophetic movement, the role that anyone may take in this movement depends on his or her commitment, contribution, and skills or expertise.

The only reason for groups to resort to exclusiveness is that they are comprised of control freaks or have something to hide or are driven by a narrow agenda and/or rigid ideology. None of this applies to our project.

As long as people are respectful and honest and we agree on the issues at hand, their private lives and their sources of inspiration will not deter us from working with them. We will only avoid individual people or groups if our association with them is embarrassing. Even those who are in legal or moral trouble should not be abandoned, as long as they are not persisting in their misconduct.

Many existing Muslim groups are exclusive to so great an extent that some might refer to them as cults. These groups tend to have many strict requirements and very few options for people and organizations to join or work with them. Theirs is oftentimes a zero-sum approach: "You are either with us or against us." In contrast, our relationships with individuals and organizations will span a continuum and a wide spectrum of compatibility; and we seek participation by people who differ from us and from one another in many ways, socially, politically, and personally.

Our inclusiveness is multidimensional (gender, faith, ethnicity, age, schools of thought, level of religious devotion/commitment, etc.). We are aiming to be a forum where everyone feels welcome, appreciated, and empowered as human beings and as citizens, irrespective of any other considerations, as long as they are serious about uplifting themselves and/or serving the greater good.

Inclusiveness goes hand in hand with the other tenets of our movement, and it is our remedy for one of the biggest dilemmas of both our community and our society: compounded exclusiveness and fragmentation.

It is not by coincidence that the vast majority of American Muslims are not associated with any Islamic center or Muslim organization. These are good people with plenty of potential. Their inclusion in the community could be beneficial for them and good for the cause, but our community and its institutions are not inclusive. There is no significant effort to reach out to the left-behind majority. Moreover, there is also no real effort to welcome those who do come on their own unless they fit our particular and exclusive profile (ethnic, ideological, gender, age). With the exception of Eid and Friday prayers, the community and its institutions have failed to reach out to Muslim Americans in any meaningful or effective way.

Those who do stick around against all odds have no sense of belonging and no sense of responsibility. They feel like aliens. Meanwhile, the overstretched (and few) activists complain about the disengagement of the majority. Again, both sides are complaining: One side feels alienated, and the other feels overloaded and possibly frustrated by their own inability to mobilize and organize the masses. Yet each side seems to get what they need the most, control for one and services for the other. That's why there is hardly any effort to challenge or change the status quo, especially after many failed attempts. This gridlocked situation is one of the main limiting factors of the growth and evolution of our community. Therefore, an essential part of the change that we seek is to redefine the community to include all Muslim Americans, devise creative ways to reach out to all of them, and create inclusive forums to accommodate them all. Moreover, the focus should not be on lecturing and providing services to passive people but instead on inspiring, empowering, and organizing people to effect change in their own lives and their own environments. When it comes to community affairs, people should be treated as stakeholders and partners, not as guests, customers, or spectators. People should not be taken for granted; and our leadership and institutions should focus on instilling in people a sense of mission and responsibility, and empowering them with tools and venues to be effective both in their personal development and in their civic engagement.

21- Dedicated to adopting and maintaining an effective leadership model

Together with an effective mentorship process, an effective leadership model is a key requirement for transforming mission-driven individuals into a movement, especially in light of the great inclusiveness and organizational flexibility that we are advocating.

Because it is about inspiring and empowering individuals and building a movement, our project will rise or fall on leadership and mentorship, which also constituted the pillars of the model that the Prophet used to build his movement and fulfill his mission. That model, which has worked in very unfavorable conditions, will always work. It is also noteworthy that, in terms of fragmentation and the lack of a sense of mission and direction and the lack of high aspirations, the Prophet found himself in a tribal community that looks, in some ways, very much like ours.

Of course, the Prophet's message was essentially a message of *Tawheed*, but he was not only a preacher. Rather, he was the founder and leader of the greatest movement in the history of humanity—a movement which championed the divine mission and effected a colossal and lasting change in record time. The way the Prophet accomplished all of that was by offering people a compelling mission and unified leadership, by mentoring them, and by instilling in them a strong sense of mission and a culture of leadership and mentorship. That's how he inspired and empowered them, and it's how he streamlined their efforts.

Indeed, the two main secrets of the incredible success of the prophetic model are the compelling mission and the incredibly effective and simple leadership model. Both the mission and the model were deeply rooted in faith.

Muhammad succeeded in doing something that humanity, throughout its history, has rarely—if ever—been able to do: nurturing people who are great leaders and great soldiers at the same time. Moreover, he did it without any elaborate organizational structures and without any real power over people.

He was able to fuse the hearts and minds of his companions to generate a very cohesive and compact community without tempering the companions' rogue individualism, their freedom, or their creativity. He combined some success factors that are considered incompatible (mutually exclusive), such as

- an undisputed leadership by consent with clearly assigned roles and responsibilities;
- extensive and meaningful consultation that everybody (including the leader) views as a duty and a right;
- a remarkable swiftness in making decisions; and
- incredible compliance and discipline in executing decisions.

Under this divine leadership model, individual leadership did not become a dictatorship, nor did extensive consultation lead to paralytic indecision. All options and perspectives were considered, and expertise was leveraged. Extensive consultation was maintained, and its purpose was achieved without indecision or power struggle. Compliance and discipline did not turn into blind obedience.

22-Clear/transparent, cohesive, decisive, disciplined

These are vital characteristics if our project is aiming for effective engagement and sustained growth and impact; and therefore they are essential characteristics for the success of the movement. The very same characteristics had a lot to do with the incredible success of the prophetic model.

Our project is somewhat unique when compared with other contemporary efforts relating to Islam. Unlike many past and present experiences here and abroad, wherein people have chosen to "shoot first" (establish organizations and begin working) and ask questions later (contemplate mission and vision), we are putting mission and vision first. This project is built—from the outset—on a crystal clear, yet limitless, idea. We believe this will help us avoid the dilemma of many Islamic projects that have been built on a vague and/or limited idea. Because of that design flaw, many projects have quickly stumbled and struggled between clarity and growth, oftentimes achieving neither. As a result of such shortcomings, Islamic groups usually attract an assorted membership who—in spite of their sincerity and hard work—are lacking in ambition, resolve, discipline, and sophistication.

All those factors combine to deny the groups the drive and/or the ability to move forward, and they get caught in a vicious cycle. Any progress or growth creates tension, and the groups quickly hit the low ceiling permitted by their limited vision, inappropriate structure, and/or by their marginal skill set. The result is usually a retreat, which restores harmony but leads to stagnation. As the cycle goes on repeating itself, with every round, some sort of split occurs. Usually those who have pushed for reform and progress end up leaving. In between cycles and sometimes even during the tense ascent and the harmonious descent, members of the organization usually settle for the lowest common denominator, as their energy and efforts are being consumed by struggling to manage the status quo.

Our movement will always be guided by clarity of mission. In order to avoid the pitfalls of vagueness, indecisiveness, and lack of discipline from which our community has formerly suffered and to maximize our chances for sustained growth and effective engagement with our environment, we are insisting on launching our movement with unequivocal clarity. This means transparent clarity in all of the movement's fundamental intellectual and strategic aspects. Our decision-making process is thus clear, transparent, and streamlined. We believe this will spare us from being forced, at some point, to choose between cohesion on one hand and clarity, decisiveness, and discipline on the other. If we ever find ourselves in such a situation, we are determined that we will not sacrifice the latter (clarity and decisiveness) for the former (cohesion). Tolerating vagueness, indecisiveness, and lack of discipline is shortsighted and futile. While it may keep people together in a deceiving and crippling unity, it also hinders progress and kills the project. Deferred problems eventually become chronic, and chronic problems suck up a lot of energy and resources just to manage and contain the problems. Plus, chronic problems typically metamorphose into crises that blow up in the faces of the leaders and members.

Indeed, for the success of our project, we are relying, after God's help, on the clarity of our vision, on the soundness of our strategy, and on the excellent functionality of our model. Our community has had enough disappointments from lousy and limited experiences that have quickly hit a low ceiling and either gotten stuck or dissolved.

In general, a movement's success depends on two main factors: (1) prelaunch determinants such as the clarity, soundness, and strength of the mission and vision—and the quality of the leadership and its core group; and (2) postlaunch factors such as effective engagement of the sociopolitical environment and the timely tackling of the challenges and changes encountered in order to achieve maximum results with minimum costs. Both factors require assembling people (especially the core group) based on a crystal-clear vision and strategy and also designing the movement to ensure swift and disciplined decision-making and execution.

We have adopted our "well-begun-is-half-done" approach, not only based on so many experiences that have failed or stagnated because of their false start, but also because we are in this business to do what needs to be done. We are not an organization that survives on dues and donations and finds itself forced, therefore, to be colorless in order to attract and cater to different constituencies. Instead, our approach to building a mass movement relies on our clear and expansive vision and on our flexible implementation strategy, both of which are individual centered, not organization centered. Plus in our humongous and inclusive project, there is already a place for everyone. Therefore, we do not need to resort to vagueness and doublespeak to be everything for everybody.

Indeed, we believe that only people with clear and shared vision should be in the same organization. Those who differ on some fundamental issues should build or join different organizations and then establish relationships or mechanisms of coordination to cooperate with other groups when their agendas overlap.

For all of the reasons we have discussed herein, when we began to introduce our project, we resisted every temptation to implement our movement through an existing entity, which would have meant dilution of our purpose and twisting our methods. Likewise, we have refused to hastily move in any of the traditional directions: establishing bureaucracy, organizing activities, or acquiring buildings.

23-Stressing sophistication and specialization

Even though they lacked adequate training in community organizing and development, the leaders and managers of our Muslim community in America lived up to their roles and did a remarkable job, especially in the founding phase of our community. This was possible partly because of their dedication and partly because of the community's limited charter and needs. Once the community began to settle and expand, however, its needs and challenges expanded and diversified. The challenges could no longer be met by simple dedication and hard work, and the skill gap in our community has been steadily widening.

Indeed, our community is in desperate need, not only of the efforts of large numbers of Muslim Americans and others but also of the specific contributions of an expanded pool of activists who are proficient in many fields. Sophisticated expertise in a number of fields is vital for our growth, empowerment, and integration. Some of those fields include youth and family counseling, social sciences in general, political science, media, public policy, grant-writing, law, and management of nonprofit organizations. Unfortunately, there is currently no significant effort, nor even any plan, to close the skill gap and tackle the severe shortage of specialists. There is not even a plan or organized effort to leverage existing talents.

An essential part of the change that we aspire to bring about is the revival of the Islamic traditions of excellence and perfection (ihsan and itkan). Thereby, when we undertake a task, we should strive to perfect it; and when we choose to work in a field, we should strive to gain expertise and sharpen our skills. It is not enough to simply be involved and active, nor even to do an "okay" job. We must strive toward proficiency and excellence. As individuals, we must work to deepen and broaden our knowledge. We also need to diversify our experience through reading, participating in various training opportunities, and engaging our civic environment. We require the involvement of specialists in a number of fields, as their expertise is needed to uplift our community. Again, the role of our leaders and institutions is to inspire people and open up doors for them. Hopefully, one day, we will have one or more institutions dedicated to personal development to help our people realize their potential and thus empower our community with the needed talents.

CHAPTER THREE: MAIN CHARACTERISTICS OF OUR PLATFORM

Someone once said that the most serious threat to democracy is the notion that it has already been achieved. In examining the extent to which democracy exists in a system, one must question whether all individuals are equal in the eyes of the law, and whether all individuals have equal access to the mechanisms of government.

As a societal reform movement, our project holds—as a key objective—the inspiration and empowerment of our fellow citizens. We want to help everyone become better informed and more engaged. That's how we hope to strengthen and perfect our democracy. Toward that goal, we are presenting the following list of foundational principles to be used to encourage and guide both platform development and civic engagement. This is by no means a detailed platform or a complete set of policy proposals. Rather, it is a list of guiding policy principles and a template that serves as the basis for platform development and civic engagement. The principles we uphold and commitments we make, then, should include the following:

- **Rule of law:** Upholding the Constitution of the United States, especially the First Amendment and other guarantees of "liberty and justice for all," as this protects and encourages the civic nature of our government and the pluralistic nature of our society.

- **Universal rights and equality:** Stressing the universality of rights to "life, liberty, and the pursuit of happiness," as outlined in the Declaration of Independence—and insisting that justice, human dignity, security, and prosperity are essential for every American and are not to be pursued for one group at the expense of others.

- **Informed national security:** Enhancing the security of the United States in the face of increased domestic and global threats by calling attention to the often-ignored root causes of threats and by advocating a more integrated security strategy that involves and attends to the concerns of all stakeholders.

- **Government "by the people":** Promoting a strengthened democracy, one which is more accessible and responsive to the public. This can be achieved through enhanced civic awareness, through encouragement of citizen involvement, and by working to reign in the influence of money and special interests on policymaking and politics.

- **Economic stability and society-wide prosperity:** Strengthening the economy and employment by promoting manufacturing and business strategies designed to create real society-wide wealth (not bubbles), wealth that is beneficial to the entire country and all Americans. Stability and prosperity also require the reining in of public and private debt and the promotion of increased financial responsibility, not only by institutions in the government and corporate worlds but also by individuals. Individuals can enhance economic wellness through thriftiness, saving, investment, production, and even export—and by encouraging others to buy American and buy local.

- **Strong middle class:** Generally promoting the importance of the middle class as the backbone of American society and our economy.

- **Expanded, need-cognizant "justice":** Promoting a concept of justice, which includes social, economic, political, and environmental justice for everyone in society. Social and economic justice involves reduction of the wealth gap and maintenance of a social safety net to ensure basic necessities and dignified living for all. This means not only working to address poverty and its ramifications of hunger and homelessness but also working to create pathways for the unemployed and the disabled so they can become productive and support themselves. It also includes advocacy for high-quality accessible education and healthcare for everyone. Environmental justice includes protecting the environment and discouraging shortsighted activities, which may create wealth and jobs today, but may destroy people's health and lifeline in the future. Of course, political justice includes equality before the law for each and every person.

– **Ethics and faith:** Strengthening American society and improving our quality of life by encouraging and endorsing spirituality, morality, social cohesion, compassion, solidarity, philanthropy, volunteerism, healthier lifestyles, mutual understanding and respect, and cooperation for the common good. This also involves tempering individualism, materialism, and consumerism. At the political level, it means promoting legislation and social norms that encourage virtues and discourage vices. The goal is to limit the negative effects of vices on society, but to do so without interfering with individual liberties and private lives.

– **Strong families:** Strengthening, protecting, and empowering the institution of the family to fulfill its vital role as the building block of society and the incubator and first school of future generations.

– **Corporate good citizenship:** Encouraging corporations to be more socially responsible and less prone to seeking only profit-for-profit's sake. This means encouraging a system that is more humane, more just, and more democratic—and thus a system that is more geared toward people's happiness and less geared toward preeminence of corporate profit. High levels of production and consumption do not necessarily result in a healthier and happier society.

– **Healthy competition:** Promoting legislation and social norms that enhance the overall public good by preventing special, elite-status treatment for individuals, partisans, corporate interests, communities, or states. All of these entities should compete fairly, but they should also cooperate for the common good as they pursue their respective ambitions and interests. Competition breeds excellence, but only if it is fair; and cooperation breeds excellence as well.

- **Institutional transparency:** Promoting honesty, transparency, and accountability in politics and in business and fighting greed, corruption, bigotry, irresponsible behavior, and political expediency.

- **Ageless, timeless respect for others:** Balancing short-term gains with long-term considerations and fighting any tendency or temptation to export problems to future generations or abroad.

- **Informed public:** Raising awareness of social problems, such as crime, drugs, gambling, teen pregnancies, and pornography; and also raising awareness of challenges and opportunities in the promotion of an ethical and just civil society at home and abroad.

- **Global justice:** Promoting freedom, human rights, democracy, and good governance across the entire world; and advocating just causes and supporting the global fight against poverty, crime, illiteracy, diseases, corruption, and oppression. Advocating policies that promote American interests without violating American (founding) values (e.g., "liberty and justice for all"). Promoting honest diplomacy and bi/multilateral approaches to addressing and solving international problems/issues.

- **Global prosperity:** Encouraging the development of underdeveloped countries and opposing any and all kinds of abuse of individuals, groups, or nations; promoting free and fair trade.

Our American democracy is based on liberty as well as equality. Abraham Lincoln said, "Those who deny freedom to others deserve it not for themselves." Lincoln believed in government "by the people," but if people are to play a meaningful role in their own, complex government, they must be very well informed.

> I know of no safe repository of the ultimate power of society but the people. And if we think them not enlightened enough, the remedy is not to take power from them, but to inform them by education.
>
> —Thomas Jefferson

Domestically and abroad, we will pursue the advancement and interests of our country and the well-being of our people. However, this will always be done according to U.S. and international law, and always within the boundaries of our principles and values. Among other things, that means that, in pursuing our goals, we will not recklessly abuse the rights and interests of other people or future generations. Ends do not always justify the means. Within those boundaries, in every position we take, the benefits must outweigh the harm.

CHAPTER FOUR: WHY CHANGE IS POSSIBLE— OUR BASES OF HOPE

Despite the formidability of the project, the severity of the crisis, and the expected obstacles and fierce resistance to change, we are neither intimidated nor discouraged.[50] In spite of the very challenging state of our country and our community and in spite of some discouraging signs from the history of both, we are more optimistic about the prospect of change than some may expect. Moreover, if our analysis of our reality and our history is well founded, so also is our optimism.

Every reform movement, be it religious or civic, has faced resistance and opposition. This will always be true because many people do not want to confront their reality, particularly if they have established a "comfort zone" to escape an unpleasant reality. If there is no "fire," no immediate threat to their status quo, they ask, "Why rock the boat?" Due to circumstances in the world, in the country, and in our community—in our case, there are even additional reasons for resistance and obstacles that increase the odds against change. Nevertheless, be assured, we will beat those odds.

Ironically, both the impediments we stand to face in our attempt to effect change and the basis for our hope converge on the fundamental issues of

---

50   Jeffery D. Sachs. (2011). *The Price of Civilization: Reawakening American Virtue and Prosperity* [Book]. Page 8: Jeffery D. Sachs states, "Successful reforms are almost always initially greeted with a broad chorus of skepticism. 'That is politically impossible.' 'The public will never agree.' 'Consensus is beyond reach.' These are the jeremiads we hear today whenever deep and real reforms are proposed. During my quarter century of work around the world, I've heard them time and time again, only to find that deep reforms were not only possible but eventually came to be viewed as inevitable."

identity and mission. Indeed, the seeming lack of a rallying cause and the serious identity issues are behind most of our difficulties. Yet ironically, it is also our identity and our great cause that are the main bases of the hope for change. Indeed, with our great faith, our great country, and our great cause, it would be much easier and more natural to make history than to justify failure. So unless one doubts the legitimacy of any of these sources of greatness, they'd have to conclude that success would be a natural outcome of our circumstances. Neither sociopolitical paralysis nor failure is our destiny. We simply must be true to our great identity, and we must champion our great cause. That's why the key to effecting change and to launching and inspiring a genuine and relevant American Islamic movement is to lead and inspire the commitment of our community's members and institutions to embrace Islam as a life mission and America as a homeland.

ELEMENTS OF OUR STRENGTH AND HOPE

1- Our Faith

While the greatness and potential of our country and community offer tremendous hope, our biggest source of hope and inspiration is Islam. Indeed, from a small number of mostly poor, illiterate, pagan Bedouins belonging to feuding tribes, Islam gave birth to a great movement that transformed the world in the span of one generation—despite harsh religious persecution and conspiracies to uproot it that lasted for nearly twenty years. That was definitely a much more hostile environment than ours, and the conditions must have appeared much more unfavorable. Yet success was inevitable.

Such an extraordinary phenomenon was not a onetime event. Rather, throughout its history and under all kinds of circumstances, Islam has repeatedly inspired movements of revival and reform that have effected meaningful change. Is it too much to hope, in the twenty-first century and with all the advantages we are privy to, that Islam can transform our Muslim American community into a movement for change?

Our hope for the possibility of change for the better—indeed, for our community and for all of America—is based on our firm belief that Islam is a timeless and universal source of guidance, and our belief that Muhammad's legacy provides a timeless, universal model for understanding, practicing, and promoting Islam, and for building an effective Muslim community. However, as Karen Armstrong indicates in her book *Muhammad: A Prophet for Our Time*, the key element to the success of the prophetic movement was that it was rooted in its time.

Similarly, the key to our success is to develop a genuinely American (not just "Americanized") Islam and a genuine and coherent Muslim American identity. Doing that will mean a relevant and viable Muslim American lifestyle, individual, and communal models, a meaningful platform, and pertinent discourse.

We have made Islam and ourselves irrelevant by holding tight to our foreign and ambivalent identity and by sticking to our foreign, out-of-date version of Islam. We have imported and clung to an Islam that was distorted, frozen, and blended with some decadent aspects of foreign culture.

Indeed, the root causes of our unwillingness and/or inability to integrate and therefore become relevant are (1) our reluctance to unequivocally resolve the issue of identity and other fundamental issues, and (2) our fear of going all the way to the timeless sources of guidance to understand and implement them in a way that is relevant to our American reality. Instead of blending the original version of Islam with American culture, we have transplanted the products of blending exercises, which were performed by other cultures, in other times and places. These products are not transferable in time or in space, with or without customization, simply because they were developed to deal with a unique setting.

This is especially true because rooting Islam in time and space was not always successful. That means that when we rely on what people have done in another era or another culture, we may end up transplanting an experience that failed or did not evolve, even in its own birthplace. Plus, in this global village, the products of civilization are transferred downward from the more advanced to the less advanced, not the opposite. That is further indication that it is futile for us to try to transplant to America a model from any other part of the world.

We need to note that continuous change is a defining characteristic of our world, and the communication and digital revolutions have remarkably accelerated the pace of change. However, while these advances may have made our world smaller, they have not eliminated the distinguishing features of regions and people. Therefore, it is only natural that understanding and living Islam and fulfilling its mission will happen differently in different times and places. Importantly, the prime responsibility of Muslims, at all times and in all places, is to root their faith and themselves in their times and in the societies in which they live.

In fact, the exercise of rediscovering original and pure Islam and making it relevant is needed, not only in America but also across the world. If the litmus test for a proper and relevant understanding and practice of Islam is whether or not a community is relevantly and effectively engaged within their society, it is apparent that—even in the Muslim world—Islam has not been successfully revived/renewed for a long time now. If our faith is one of our bases for hope, and it certainly is, then Muslims have some work to do. As Muslims (and particularly as Muslim Americans), this is the challenge that we face, and this is the challenge that we must undertake.

2- Our Country and Community

Indeed, in spite of some troubling past and present events, trends, phenomena, and policies, America continues to be a great and unique country. This is due, largely, to our Constitution and founding values, the essential elements of American democracy, which guarantee fundamental rights and liberties. Through the Constitution, America offers us a level playing field and fair rules for civic engagement. With its deeply entrenched pluralism, America continues to be unique in granting its citizens the opportunity to live out their dreams and in offering its communities the opportunity to organize and make a difference. It is a dynamic and vibrant society where the systems, the norms, and the policies are amenable to reform by committed and well-organized people. Motivated and organized Americans can make a difference, no matter how short they may be in resources.

However, as American citizens, we should be loyal to America not only because of its greatness, uniqueness, and what it can do for us, but also primarily, simply because it is our country. Everything else is an add-on or a supplement. Yet the add-ons are also vital to our success. America's uniqueness and greatness should help Muslim Americans develop a genuine and coherent Muslim American identity and facilitate our successful integration within the larger society—in spite of the issues that have contributed to our previous ambivalence toward America and our chronic isolation from society.

Indeed, compared to any other country, America offers considerable advantages to its citizens, including its religious and ethnic minorities. The details of those general advantages and elaboration on those advantages that are specific to Muslims are beyond the scope of this book. However, one can safely assert that there is hardly a better place in the world for Muslims to thrive and significantly impact, not only America but also the whole world, particularly the Muslim world. We, like all Americans, are fortunate to be here.

The great potential that lies in our community, although largely untapped and dormant at the present time, is another huge basis for hope. In many aspects (including level of education and income), the average Muslim American fares significantly better than the average American. Moreover, our community has repeatedly demonstrated a remarkable ability and willingness to mobilize behind important causes. That has often been the case from the founding phase with the swift proliferation of Islamic centers and schools, all the way to our impressive response to 9/11. All along, the Muslim American community has also responded impressively to crises and disasters in the Muslim world. However, the problem that leaves us with potential energy instead of kinetic energy has always been our community's lack of adequate leadership. We need leaders with an expansive and integrated vision. Given our needs and goals and potential, we need a leadership that can sustain mobilization and growth. We require leaders who can help us integrate efforts to produce the needed synergy, momentum, and enthusiasm and who can do that regardless of any emergencies. That is not what we have had; and when that limitation is resolved by our mission and movement, the positive impact of Muslim Americans on society in this country (and the world) will be breathtaking!

Another factor in our favor is uniquely represented by President Obama's 2008 election campaign. At least on the domestic front, his campaign for office was transformed into a movement for change. The slogan was "Yes, we can!" That sense of optimistic urgency resonated with an American public that understands in its heart that change is needed. Yes, we can! The success of numerous groups in America, in advancing their causes and achieving relevance, should also serve as a source of inspiration for us—particularly since many of these groups do not exceed either the size or potential of Muslim Americans as a group. America is still the land of opportunity; and yes, indeed, we Muslim Americans can!

However, let us not fool ourselves. American society is a highly competitive society. While many opportunities exist, success and relevance are hard earned. Individuals and communities have to prove themselves, and must be, not only serious and dedicated, but also persistent and sophisticated.

Our community suffered a major blow to its image, prospects, and progress with 9/11. However, the community was steered in the right direction by leaders and prominent organizations that assessed the situation properly and acted swiftly and decisively. The immediate goal was to weather the storm, and that goal was achieved with reasonable success. This has paved the way to take the community to the next level of development. That means enhanced integration into society, and it must be facilitated by the introduction of some long-overdue reforms. Our community's collective response to the "shock therapy" of 9/11 was great; and within a few years, the community was significantly transformed. Unfortunately, once the storm appeared to be over, the whole process was stalled by those who were passively resisting change. They never believed in the reforms. They didn't understand America, nor did they commit to it. They did not even appreciate that our community and its standing will not and should not go back to the pre-9/11 conditions. Once again, our community missed a great opportunity and was let down by some incompetent and shortsighted leadership. However, some of the residual gains were significant nonetheless, and the community today is much more receptive to fundamental reforms. Leaders and organizations that are unable or unwilling to evolve will make themselves irrelevant and will miss the train of change and reform.

3- Our Cause

We have our faith as a great source of inspiration and empowerment, our community as a fount of great potential, and our country as a great place in which to thrive. Likewise, our cause is a winning cause due to its divine nature and noble purpose. Indeed, we are answering the call of both God and country—seeking only His pleasure and the well-being of our country, our people, and humanity at large. How could a cause be nobler or more deserving?

Indeed, God's work will be done, and His purpose will be fulfilled. So those who aspire and strive to become true, faithful embodiments and effective instruments of the divine will cannot fail.

The divine purpose calls on members of the human family to strive to be exemplary and engaged citizens, to aspire highly, to realize their full potential, and to cooperate for the greater good. Compared to the situation of Muslims almost everywhere else in the world, Muslim Americans are privileged because fulfilling the divine purpose meshes seamlessly with upholding the American Constitution. In particular, justice and peace at all levels constitute the top objectives of the divine message and the Constitution, both of which uphold the equality of all people as unequivocal.

Muhammad linked his success with the rule of law and the prevalence of peace when he said, "When my mission is accomplished, a person will be able to travel from Sana'a to Hadramout fearing none but God and worrying only about a wolf attacking his sheep."[51] We may take this for granted, but that was a powerful and profound characterization of the prevalence of freedom, peace, and the rule of law – benefits that Islam promises but which the people of Muhammad's Arabia could hardly envision. Also recall that, in a famous incident when the second Caliph was reprimanding a prominent governor in reference to a Christian citizen living under Muslim rule, Omar ibn al-Khattab made it clear that liberty is a self-evident truth and an unalienable right endowed by the Creator.[52]

There will always be mistakes and setbacks, and generous sacrifices will always be needed. That is part of the growing pain and the price of relevance in this life and the price of heaven in the hereafter. Even at the time of the Prophet and his great companions, engaging with the sociopolitical environment was not flawless, risk free, or without sacrifices and setbacks. However, the companions were very effective in achieving repeated successes and accomplishments, containing damage, and quickly recovering from setbacks. That's how they were able to surmount obstacles and break through ceilings.

Finally, but most importantly, our hope rests exclusively on God's guidance and help, which He promised for those who strive in His way and champion His cause. Indeed, from an Islamic perspective, success comes only from God, and it is granted for those who advocate His cause and effectively use His rules, regardless of their faith and intention. Moreover, God promised that the advocates of His cause will not be overcome.

However, God's support is neither unconditional nor exclusively for Muslims, and therefore should not be taken for granted and should not be

---

51   Hadith narrated by Khabab bin Al-A'rt and reported in Sahih Al-Bukhari.

52   Which resonates with the Declaration of Independence: "We hold these truths to be self-evident, that all men are created equal, that they are endowed by their Creator with certain unalienable Rights, that among these are Life, Liberty and the pursuit of Happiness."

used as an excuse for unfounded hopes, inadequate planning, or sloppy, half-finished work, nor for an unwillingness to make sacrifices. As discussed at length in part 3, a number of requirements have to be met for Muslims to qualify for God's "extra" help (which falls outside of the ordinary fruits earned from effectively leveraging His universal laws).

In a nutshell, those requirements entail the fulfillment of the divine mission with pure intention and utmost passion and sophistication. Indeed, Islam states, and history confirms, that only when Muslims meet these requirements do they become united, empowered, and relevant, and thus qualify for God's guidance and help. Interestingly, that was the case even during the life of the Prophet, and Muslims learned this lesson in different ways in the battles of Badr, Uhud, al-Ahzab, and Hunayn.

4- The Recent Inspiring Movements for Change Sweeping the Muslim World

Until January 14, 2011, most of the Muslim world was in a bind with no exit in sight. With very few exceptions, notoriously corrupt and ruthlessly oppressive oligarchies reigned everywhere, and all of the major stakeholders (including the acquiescent masses) appeared to be content with their "stability in exchange for freedom" deal.

Embraced neither by the ruling elite nor by the opposition to the regimes, the young generations held aspirations that were "too high." They were unwilling to continue settling for stability at any price. They rejected their governments' shallow attempts at modernization, which amounted to window-dressing reforms that did not include freedom or justice or meaningful political reform. And as we have witnessed, these young people were becoming too sophisticated, ambitious, confident, and angry to be further subdued by the aging and out-of-touch autocratic regimes.

On the outside, there was no indication that the people in Tunisia, Egypt, Libya, Yemen, Jordan, Syria, Algeria, Bahrain, Morocco, and Oman were ready to rise up and demand change anytime soon. Someone—either an individual or a group with an accurate assessment of reality, clear vision, and a sound plan—has to lead a movement for change, and the leadership void in the Muslim world is a chronic problem.

Indeed, ever since they achieved independence from their colonial oppressors, the Muslim elite have repeatedly let their people down because of their serious lack of integrity and/or competence. After several failed attempts of opposition groups to effect change, the masses gave up on those groups and took charge themselves. They discovered a simple but effective recipe for change (at least in the first phase of their movements): they used information technology to promote their cause and coordinate their efforts.

Once they broke through the barriers of fear, they were able to corner their regimes and strip them of their two main instruments of control: fear and control of information. That rendered the regimes helpless, and thus the chronic stalemate between government and opposition was broken.

These rousing movements of change have also inadvertently put the Muslim American community to the test and presented it with a golden opportunity to move into the big league. Now that the brave, resolute, and creative youth in the Muslim world have made history by precipitating considerable change in far more unfavorable conditions, how will our community respond?

The first thing we need to do is learn from these inspiring movements: Yes, even in the most dire circumstances with limited resources, major change is possible if people truly want it and are willing to pay the price for it. Our situation can and should be far better. We must find a way to effect the needed change and shape a better future.

The equation for change is always the same: when people change themselves (their mind-set, attitudes, willpower, aspirations), God will change their conditions. When people firmly believe in and fully commit to a just cause, God will support them.

> Verily, never will Allah change the condition of a people until they change it themselves [Qur'an 13:11].

> O, ye who believe! If ye will aid (the cause of) Allah, He will aid you and plant your feet firmly [Qur'an 47:7].

The renowned Tunisian poet, al-Chebbi, translated this equation into a poem that inspired the Tunisian people throughout their struggle against occupation and dictatorship: "If the people want (dignified) life, God answers their call."

The people in the Muslim world are not the same today as they were before the revolutions. They first changed themselves, and now their situation is changing rapidly. What previous generations dreamed of and struggled for is now being realized in just a few short days. These movements for change were initiated when the masses took charge, breaking free from all their mental, cultural, and psychological shackles—and stopped waiting for the elite/establishment to lead the change. It all started by rejecting the status quo and all the arguments used to justify it, including "We are not responsible for the results," "Things are better off than they were before," and "There is no better alternative." People decided to create the alternative.

Change, as they have demonstrated, can only be implemented by the masses. Counting on leaders and elites to rally and inspire the people toward change leads to recurring letdowns. Now that the Muslim masses have dismissed the status quo in their respective countries, they must continue to pray that their movement for change will give birth to new leadership.

A similar phenomenon is emerging within the Muslim American community. There are brilliant and ambitious young people who are not impressed with existing entities; and they are pursuing all opportunities to bring about change. This trend, which started a while ago, is promising—and optimism is enhanced with the boost of the winds of change from the Muslim world. Indeed, our youth, compared with those changing the Muslim world, are in a much better position to change our community and contribute to the needed change in America.

The recent events abroad are acting to remove one of the major hurdles facing our community in general and our youth in particular. That hurdle is our public image, a problem that is largely associated with all the dark aspects, which are rather slanderously advertised regarding the Muslim world. Until recently, the image of the Muslim world, especially in the West, has been associated with corruption, oppression, and decadence. That stigma has put us on the defensive and has forced us to become apologists and de facto defense attorneys for Islam and Muslims. Our public image has also not been helped by the fact that we American Muslims have not yet succeeded in developing viable models and solutions or in making a significant contribution to society. Is it surprising that we are misunderstood? In 2011, however, much changed. Indeed, the creative and brave youth of the Muslim world amazed the entire world with their inspiring model of change.

Can young Muslim Americans divorce themselves from disengagement, complacency, routine activism, and the community's minor-league mind-set? Will they dare break through the low ceiling of aspiration in our community to chart a new path of relevance and greatness, as their counterparts in the Muslim world have done?

Our country and community are in a severe crisis and are in urgent need of fundamental change. However, our conditions are conducive to change. We all need to engage in serious reflection and discussions about our crisis, our mission, and our future. We need to commit ourselves to what needs to be done—not do only what is convenient. We must not limit ourselves to managing or even polishing that which we've inherited—not under any name.

God did not command us to do just something, but to do what needs to be done. We are assigned and designated to be the best people and the leading community sent to humanity. That's our religious and civic calling. Our mission, our formidable external and internal challenges, our great opportunities, and our future, all call upon us to scrap the excuses, break the shackles, aspire highly, and to be difference-makers and game-changers. It's okay to be in crisis, but it's not okay to remain in denial and to continue business as usual. Compared to the people in the Muslim world, our task is much less complex, and our conditions are much more favorable.

INDEX

A

Abbas, Ibn, 262, 270
Abduh, Shaykh Muhammad, 90
Abel, 46
Abraham, 55, 60–61, 63, 76, 332, 355
Abu Bakr, 69, 199, 228–29, 357
Adam, 25, 41
Afghani, Sayyid Jamal al-Din al-, 90
African American Muslim community, 34,
    36, 124, 135, 148–50, 210
Ahkam, Qawa'id al-, 271
Ahmad, Imam, 48–49, 80, 173
Al-Fudul Pact, 179
Ali, 85
alignment, purposeful, 57
Allah, 24–25, 37, 50
    rebellion against, 40
America, 3, 186
    as not antireligion, 277
    capitalism of, 14
    current state of, 6, 9
    history of, 14
    image of, 8
    legacy of, 36
    world prominence of, 15
American Revolution, 179
Armstrong, Karen, 263, 337
    Muhammad, 263, 337

B

baby-boomers, 7
Bakr, Abu, 69, 228–29
Banna, Al-, 92–94, 101, 277
Bedouin tribes, 31, 354
bin Basheer, Al-Numan, 47
bin Basheer, Numan Al-, 47
Bukhari, Sahih Al-, 47–49, 175, 341
Bush, George W., 12, 247
    administration of, 12, 162

C

Cain, 46
Caliph, 31, 68–69, 84–85, 199–200, 341,
    357
capitalism, 14. *See also under* America
change, advocacy for, 1
Chebbi, al-, 343
Cheney, Dick, 11
choice consequences, 54
civic engagement, 160–61, 164–65, 176,
    182–83, 192, 217–18, 252–54, 270,
    285, 290, 295–97, 299, 301–9, 317,
    329
Civil Rights Act of 1964, 135
Clear Signs, 82, 227
Collins, Jim, 170
colonialism, 88

GLOSSARY

Al-Ahzab
The battle in which Quraish and their confederates marched toward Medina attacking the Muslims.

Ansar
God's helpers.

Aqidah
The Islamic creed, or the six articles of faith, which consist of the belief in God, angels, messengers and prophets, scriptures, the Day of Judgment, and destiny.

Badr
The battle that comprised the first Muslim victory over the Meccan army near a well called Badr near the Red Sea coast.

Da'wah or Dawa
The call to Islam, preaching, sharing the message of Islam.

Fardh
A religious duty, or an obligatory action.

Fatwa
Juristic legal opinion of a scholar.

Fiqh
Jurisprudence, refers to understanding the Islamic laws.

Hadith
The term "Hadīth" is used to denote a saying or an act ascribed to Prophet Mohammad.

Hafiz
Memorizers of the Qur'an.

Hilf al-Fudul
Alliance of the Virtuous; it is a seventh-century alliance created by various Meccans, including the Prophet Muhammad, to establish fair commercial dealing. Because of Muhammad's role in its formation, the alliance plays a significant role in Islamic ethics.

Hunayn or Hunain
The battle between the Bedouin tribes Hawazin and Thaqif and the Muslim army (Mohammad and his followers).

Ibadah
Worshiping God.

Ibtilaa
Trial and tribulation.

Ijtihad
A term meaning the effort by a jurist to formulate a specific legal opinion; also scholarly interpretation of Islamic law. The opposite of *ijtihad* is *taqlid*, Arabic for "imitation."

Islah
Reform.

Jihad
Struggle. Any earnest striving in the way of God, including personal struggles, physical struggles, struggles for righteousness, and struggles

against wrongdoing. *Qitaal* (fighting) may sometimes be a *jihad* activity, but it constitutes only one of many kinds of struggle which are referred to as *jihad*.

Jumaah or Jumu'ah
Friday prayer.

Ka'bah
A black stone surrounded by a shrine, the "Ka'bah" is located near the center of the Great Mosque in Mecca. This is Islam's most sacred spot on Earth. Making a pilgrimage to this place constitutes the fifth pillar of Islam. Each year, at the time of the pilgrimage (the *Hajj*), over two million Muslims come to make their required seven-circle, counter clockwise walk around the Ka'bah. The *Hajj* ritual of pilgrimage to Mecca dates back thousands of years to the time of Abraham (Ibrahim), the prophet who built the first Ka'bah and established the ritual of the *Hajj*.

Kawwamina lillah
Standing for God.

Khalifa
Literally successor. Within the Islamic federal system, this also means the leader – the successor to Muhammad as political leader of Muslims, in a succession that began with the rightly guided Caliphs.

Khilafa
A transliteration of the Arabic word which is also translated as "caliphate." The caliphates are the succession of regimes governing Muslims which began (after Muhammad) with the four rightly guided Caliphs. Muhammad was the last of the prophets, but the rightly guided Caliphs succeeded him as political leader of the Muslim *umma*. The most recent version of this type of government was the the Ottoman Empire, which collapsed in 1924.

Ma'alat
The end result or consequence (of any decision or ruling).

Maqasid
Goals or purposes, such as the purposes of Islamic law. Islam has six overarching goals (*maqasid*) related to preservation of faith, life, reason/ intellect, wealth/property, lineage, and honor.

Masalih or Masaleh (Al-masalih al-mursala)
Public interest and common good. That which is beneficial for people. The concept of "the greater good" (*al maslaha*) is at the foundation of the divine guidance, and it is also vital in every kind of human decision making. Scholars have classified the entire range of *masalih and maqasid* into three categories. The most important is life's essentials (*daruriyyat*). Next in importance are the things humans need to support the essentials, the complementary benefits (*hajiyyat*). Third, in order of importance, are the embellishments (*tahsiniyyat*).

Masjid
A place of worship for Muslims, known in English as a mosque.

Mathaahib or Math'hab
School of religious jurisprudence, school of thought.

Medina
"City." The City of the Prophet.

Al-muallafati qulubuhum
Those whose hearts to be reconciled.

Mu`amalaat
Rulings which deal with man's interaction with creation in general.

Nafila (or Nafilah)
A supererogatory (extra, nonobligatory, or "beyond the call of duty") deed or act of worship.

PBUH
An acronym that stands for "Peace Be Upon Him," a blessing which is affixed to Prophet Muhammad's name.

Qadr
Divine destiny.

Qitaal
Fighting.

Rashidun
Arabic for "rightly guided."

Rightly guided Khalifa
The title of the first four caliphs (*khalifas*) who were successors (in a line of successors) to Prophet Muhammad as the political leader of all Muslims. The rightly guided Khalifas are believed by most Muslims to be most righteous rulers in history. They were Abu Bakr, 'Umar, 'Uthman, and Ali.

Sabr
Patience, endurance, self-restraint.

Shariah or *Shari'ah*
Laws defining rights and obligations.

Shura
Consultation. The Qur'an and Muhammad urge Muslims to make decisions based on consultation with those who will be affected by the decisions.

Seera or Sirah
Life or biography of the Prophet Muhammad; his moral example as presented in the Hadith and the Sunna.

Sunan
Laws or rules; and also laws that govern the universe (e.g., the law of gravity).

Sunna
The path of the Prophet Muhammad, i.e., what the Prophet did or said or agreed to during his life. He is considered by Muslims to be the best human moral example to follow.

SWT
An acronym placed after the name of God. Often, the letters are lowercase (swt). It stands for the Arabic *"subhana wa ta'ala,"* which means "Glorious and exalted is He."

Ta'beed
Calling or inviting people to worship God.

Tadaafu'
Arabic word meaning "engagement," which, in the context of Islamic practice involves counterbalancing some people's deeds by other people.

Tanzeem
Literally organization.

Tarbiya
Indoctrination process.

Tawakkul
Trust in God, reliance on God.

Tawheed
Doctrine of the "Oneness of God."

Tawteen
Patriotism; also integration into society.

Tazakka
Got purified. Self-development.

Tazkiyah, Tazkiyyah or Tazkiya
Purification of the soul; spiritual self-purification; self-development which includes mentorship (helping others to improve).

Thabat
Perseverance and steadfastness.

Thawabit
The essentials or constants of Islam.

Ubudiyah
Worship.

Uhud
The battle at the mountain (Uhud) in Medina where the Meccans defeated the Muslims (Mohammad and his followers).

Umma
The worldwide community of believers.

Urf
Customs or social norms of a given society.

Usul
Principles, origins.

Usul al-Fiqh
The study of the origins and practice of Islamic jurisprudence (*fiqh*).

Yuzakkihum
Mentorship to purify others.

Zakat
Charity on a regular basis. This literally means purification alms, a charitable donation, a religious and social obligation. It is the third pillar of Islam.

Zakkaha
The purification of oneself. Self-development.

This timely work is a "must read" for anyone who is concerned about the future of American Muslims. For activists, this is a "game changer."

The modern American Islamic movement has suffered from the dysfunctional separation between Muslim intellectuals and the activists. We resemble a body without neurological connections between the brain and the muscles. Dr. Ghannouchi has bridged the gap with this book. He is able to do that because he is not only a scholar and a well versed intellectual – he is also an activist who has not confined himself to an ivory tower. In fact, one may say that he has gotten his hands wet and even scalded in his efforts to help other Muslims and other people in general.

In the intricacies of this organized work, Dr. Ghannouchi analyzes the current situation for American Muslims. In Chapter 3, he details "the manifestations of our community crisis," defining eight characteristic problems – all of which are right on the mark. What gives this work unique value, though, is the combination of that timely and appropriate analysis with guidance toward a fresh start for American Muslims and a better future for all Americans.

I highly recommend this work as a genuinely essential book which has been urgently needed for a long time, and never more than right now.

– Dr. Maher Hathout
Senior Advisor
Muslim Public Affairs Council

This is an important book. It constitutes the gateway to a new life for Muslim Americans. Within the pages of this volume, American Muslims and other readers will find a path that will lead us all beyond our current concerns about day-to-day existence and security, guiding us toward higher aspirations involving achievement and growth. With out-of-step leadership that is lacking in vision, it is not surprising if Islamic efforts in America often lack relevance.

– Imam Mohammad Hilali
Director
Islamic Society of Wichita, Kansas